SAGE was founded in 1965 by Sara Miller McCune to support the dissemination of usable knowledge by publishing innovative and high-quality research and teaching content. Today, we publish more than 750 journals, including those of more than 300 learned societies, more than 800 new books per year, and a growing range of library products including archives, data, case studies, reports, conference highlights, and video. SAGE remains majority-owned by our founder, and on her passing will become owned by a charitable trust that secures our continued independence.

Los Angeles | London | Washington DC | New Delhi | Singapore

New Frontiers in Asia–Latin America Integration

Thank you for choosing a SAGE product! If you have any comment, observation or feedback, I would like to personally hear from you. Please write to me at contactceo@sagepub.in

—Vivek Mehra, Managing Director and CEO,
SAGE Publications India Pvt Ltd, New Delhi

Bulk Sales

SAGE India offers special discounts for purchase of books in bulk. We also make available special imprints and excerpts from our books on demand.

For orders and enquiries, write to us at

Marketing Department
SAGE Publications India Pvt Ltd
B1/I-1, Mohan Cooperative Industrial Area
Mathura Road, Post Bag 7
New Delhi 110044, India
E-mail us at marketing@sagepub.in

Get to know more about SAGE, be invited to SAGE events, get on our mailing list. Write today to marketing@sagepub.in

This book is also available as an e-book.

New Frontiers in Asia–Latin America Integration

TRADE FACILITATION,
PRODUCTION NETWORKS,
AND FTAs

Edited by

Antoni Estevadeordal
Masahiro Kawai
Ganeshan Wignaraja

www.sagepublications.com
Los Angeles • London • New Delhi • Singapore • Washington DC

Copyright © Asian Development Bank Institute, 2015

All rights reserved. No part of this book may be reproduced or utilized in any form or by any means, electronic or mechanical, including photocopying, recording or by any information storage or retrieval system, without permission in writing from the publisher.

First published in 2015 by

SAGE Publications India Pvt Ltd
B1/I-1 Mohan Cooperative Industrial Area
Mathura Road, New Delhi 110 044, India
www.sagepub.in

SAGE Publications Inc
2455 Teller Road
Thousand Oaks, California 91320, USA

SAGE Publications Ltd
1 Oliver's Yard, 55 City Road
London EC1Y 1SP, United Kingdom

SAGE Publications Asia-Pacific Pte Ltd
3 Church Street
#10-04 Samsung Hub
Singapore 049483

Asian Development Bank Institute
Kasumigaseki Building 8F
3-2-5 Kasumigaseki, Chiyoda-ku
Tokyo 100-6008, Japan

Inter-American Development Bank
1300 New York Avenue,
NW Washington, D.C. 20577, USA

Published by Vivek Mehra for SAGE Publications India Pvt Ltd, typeset in 10.5/13 Berkeley by RECTO Graphics, Delhi and printed at Chaman Enterprises, New Delhi.

Library of Congress Cataloging-in-Publication Data

New frontiers in Asia-Latin America integration : trade facilitation, production networks, and FTAs / edited by Antoni Estevadeordal, Masahiro Kawai, and Ganeshan Wignaraja.
  pages cm
 Includes bibliographical references and index.
 1. Asia—Foreign economic relations—Latin America. 2. Latin America—Foreign economic relations—Asia. 3. Asia—Commerce—Latin America. 4. Latin America—Commerce—Asia. 5. Asia—Economic integration. 6. Latin America—Economic integration. 7. Free trade—Asia. 8. Free trade—Latin America. I. Estevadeordal, Antoni. II. Kawai, Masahiro, 1947- III. Wignaraja, Ganeshan, 1962-
  HF1583.Z4L295   382'.91—dc23   2015   2014035033

ISBN: 978-81-321-0976-1(HB)

The SAGE Team: Shambhu Sahu, Sandhya Gola, Anju Saxena, and Rajinder Kaur

Contents

List of Tables	vii
List of Figures	ix
List of Abbreviations	xi
Preface	xiii

1. Introduction   1
   *Antoni Estevadeordal, Masahiro Kawai,
   and Ganeshan Wignaraja*

Part I
Trade Facilitation

2. Origin and Beyond: Trade Facilitation Disaster or Trade Facilitation Opportunity?   23
   Brian Rankin Staples and Jeremy Harris
3. Accelerating Regional Integration: Issues at the Border   40
   Douglas H. Brooks and Susan F. Stone
4. Trade Logistics and Regional Integration in Latin America and the Caribbean   73
   Pablo Guerrero, Krista Lucenti, and Sebastián Galarza

Part II
Supply Chains

5. Supply Chain Dynamics in Asia   111
   Ruth Banomyong
6. The Internationalization of SMEs in Regional and Global Value Chains   140
   Hank Lim and Fukunari Kimura

7. Regional Integration Behind the Border:
   Applying a Value Chain Approach   170
   Grant Aldonas

Part III
Asia–LAC Relations

8. PRC's Outward FDI to Latin America: Trends and Motivations   193
   Gloria O. Pasadilla
9. Asia–Latin America FTAs: An Instrument for Interregional
   Liberalization and Integration?   210
   Ganeshan Wignaraja, Dorothea Ramizo, and Luca Burmeister
10. Prospects for Regional Cooperation between Latin America and
    Caribbean and Asia and Pacific: Perspective from East Asia   260
    Erlinda M. Medalla and Jenny D. Balboa

About the Editors and Contributors   300
Index   303

List of Tables

3.1	Trade Growth in Asia's 10 Leading Exporters, 1987–2007	43
3.2	Trade in Asian Subregions and Other World Regions, 1990–2007	44
3.3	Costs of Exporting, by Region, 2006–2007	53
3.4	Commodity Aggregation	59
3.5	Time Costs of Exports in APEC Asia	61
3.6	Impacts of Trade Cost Reduction of 25%	62
3.7	Changes in Bilateral Exports	65
4.1	Trade Agreements in Latin America and the Caribbean, North–South Agreements	80
4.2	Trade Agreements in Latin America and the Caribbean, South–South Agreements	82
4.3	IIRSA Project Status and Financing Structure	98
4.4	Comparison of Average Inventory Levels, Losses to Markets, and Logistics Costs in Latin America and OECD, 2004	100
5.1	Players in the Security Supply Chain	119
5.2	Routing Alternatives between Thailand and Viet Nam	124
5.3	Comparison of Cost Components for One Leather Seat Cover (Mexico vs. Thailand)	135
7.1	Cost and Delay for Processing Foreign Trade at Border	185
8.1	M&A in the PRC's OFDI (US$ million)	198
8.2	Greenfield Investments of Top Company Investors in Latin America and the Caribbean	202
9.1	Shares of Latin American Countries' Trade and Investment with Asia and Number of FTAs, 1990–2012	221
9.2	Shares of Asian Economies' Trade and Investment with Latin America and Number of FTAs, 1990–2012	222

10.1	Analytical Framework for Regional Cooperation	265
10.2	Asia-Pacific Intra-Regional Trade by Geographic Grouping (percentage of the region's total trade)	266
10.3	Inward Foreign Direct Investment	267
10.4	Growth in International Trade	268
10.5	Population	277
10.6	GDP	278
10.7	Merchandise Trade, 2012 (US$ billion)	279
10.8	Services, 2012 (US$ billion)	279
10.9	Tariff Trade Restrictiveness Index (TTRI)	280
10.10	Latin America and the Caribbean: Ranking of the PRC, Japan, and the Republic of Korea in Each Country's Trade, 2000 and 2007	281
10.11	Latin America and the Caribbean Exports by Major Exports Region, 2007	283
10.12	Latin America and Asia-Pacific: Trade by Regions and Products by Technology Intensity, 2006	285
10.13	Grubel Lloyd Indices for Some Latin America and Caribbean Countries with Asia-Pacific, 2006	287
10.14	Logistics Performance Indicator, 2012	290
10.15	ISO Certifications in 2012, by Standard	291
10.16	Some Research and Development Indicators	294
10.17	PISA Rankings and Scores, 2006	296

List of Figures

3.1	Growth in Output and Trade	46
3.2	International Logistics Performance Index (LPI)	54
3.3	Ranking for Trade Facilitation Measures	57
3.4	Changes in Exports by Sector	64
4.1	Manufactured Exports by Regions (% of merchandise exports)	75
4.2	Intra-Regional Exports of Major Trading Blocs (% of merchandise exports, 1990–2012)	76
4.3	Index of Intra-Industry Trade by Region	86
4.4	Total Import Freight Expenditures as a Share of Imports, 2006 (%)	88
4.5	Return of Investment in Transport Infrastructure Hardware	90
4.6	Heavy Vehicles Average Ages—Central America and Selected Countries 2010–2012	90
4.7	Average Distance Traveled (km truck/year)—Central America and Selected Countries	91
4.8	Central America Trucking: Percentage of Empty Backhauls	92
4.9	Tariffs (US$/km/year) and Trucks Average Age—Central America and United States	92
4.10	Logistics Costs as Percentage of Product Value for Selected Economies (2004)	94
4.11	IIRSA Corridors	96
4.12	IIRSA Project Portfolio by Sector	97
4.13	IIRSA Project Portfolio by Countries	98
4.14	Mesoamerican Project Corridors	101
5.1	Role Played by Logistics Service Provider in Global Supply Chain	123
5.2	Supply Chain Routing Alternatives between Thailand and Viet Nam	124
5.3	Pipeline of Weekly Shipments between Thailand and the United States	134
6.1	Intra-Regional Trade (export and import ration in percent)	141
6.2	Trade Share of East Asia with Partner (%)	142

6.3	Trade Pattern inside East Asia (%)	142
6.4	Production/Distribution Networks (geographical fragmentation)	144
6.5	The Theory of Fragmentation	145
6.6	Fragmentation in a Two-Dimensional Space	146
6.7	Roles and Characteristics of SMEs	152
6.8	How SMEs Fit into Global Value Chains	155
7.1	Agro-Exports Supply Chain—Upstream	182
7.2	Peru Agro-Export Supply Chain—Downstream	187
8.1	Chinese Stock of OFDI	195
8.2	Chinese OFDI Stock in Latin America and the Caribbean, 2010	200
8.3	Distribution of Projects by Sector	204
8.4	Distribution of Number of Projects by Business Activity	205
8.5	Chinese OFDI to Latin America and the Caribbean	206
8.6	Chinese OFDI to Latin America and the Caribbean by Sector	206
8.7	Latin America and the Caribbean Exports to the PRC of Ores and Metals	207
8.8	Latin America and the Caribbean Exports to the PRC of Mineral Fuels, Lubricants, and Related Items	208
9.1	Trade Flows between Asia and Latin America, 1990–2012 (US$ billion)	213
9.2	Trade Flows from Asia and PRC to Latin America, 1990–2012 (US$ billion)	215
9.3	Top Asian Traders with Latin America, 1990–2012 (% of total trade)	216
9.4	Top Latin American Traders with Asia, 1990–2012 (% of total trade)	217
9.5	FDI Flows between Asia and Latin America, 2003–2012 (US$ billion)	218
9.6	Growth of Asia–Latin America FTAs, 2004–2020	220
9.7	Asia's FTA Trade Coverage with Latin American Countries, 2004–2012	223
9.8	Latin America's FTA Trade Coverage with Asian Economies, 2004–2012	224
9.9	Distribution of Approaches to Tariff Liberalization, Services Coverage, and New Issues	228
10.1	FTAs in East Asia, 2000 and 2012	272

List of Abbreviations

ABF	Asian Bond Fund
ABMI	Asian Bond Markets Initiative
ACD	Asia-Cooperation Dialogue
ACFTA	ASEAN–PRC FTA
ADB	Asian Development Bank
AEC	ASEAN Economic Community
AFAS	ASEAN Framework Agreement on Services
AFTA	ASEAN Free Trade Area
AIA	ASEAN Investment Area
APEC	Asia-Pacific Economic Cooperation
ASA	ASEAN Swap Arrangement
ASCM	Agreement on Subsidies and Countervailing Measures
ASEAN	Association of Southeast Asian Nations
BSAs	Bilateral Swap Arrangements
CLMV	Cambodia, Lao People's Democratic Republic (Lao PDR), Myanmar, and Viet Nam
CMI	Chiang Mai Initiative
EAS	East Asian Summit
ECOTECH	Economic and Technical Cooperation
EDI	Electronic Data Interchange
EMEAP	Executives' Meeting of East Asia and Pacific Central Banks
EPA	Economic Partnership Agreement
EPZs	Export Processing Zones
ERPD	Economic Review and Policy Dialogue
EU	European Union
FDI	Foreign Direct Investment
FEALAC	Forum for East Asia–Latin America Cooperation
FTAA	Free Trade Area of the Americas
FTAAP	Free Trade Area of the Asia-Pacific
FTAs	Free Trade Agreements
GATS	General Agreement on Trade and Services

GATT	General Agreement on Trade and Tariffs
GDP	Gross Domestic Product
GLI	Grubel Lloyd Index
GPA	Government Procurement Agreement
GVCs	Global Value Chains
ICT	Information Communication Technology
IDB	Inter-American Development Bank
IET	International Entrepreneurship Theory
IMF	International Monetary Fund
IPR	Intellectual Property Rights
JETRO	Japan External Trade Organization
JIT	Just In Time
LDCs	Least Developed Countries
LEs	Large Enterprises
MFN	Most Favored Nation
NAFTA	North American Free Trade Agreement
NIEs	Newly Industrialized Economies
NTBs	Nontariff Barriers
OEM	Original Equipment Manufacturer
PISA	Programme for International Student Assessment
RCEP	Regional Comprehensive Economic Partnership
ROO	Rules of Origin
RTAs	Regional Trade Agreements
SENASA	*Servicio Nacional de Saneamiento Ambiental* (National Agricultural Sanitary and Phytosanitary Service)
SMEs	Small and Medium Enterprises
SPS	Sanitary and Phytosanitary Measures
TILF	Trade and Investment Liberalization and Facilitation
TPP or P4	Trans-Pacific Strategic Economic Partnership Agreement or Pacific 4
TRIMS	Trade-Related Investment Measures
TRIPS	Trade-Related Aspects of Intellectual Property Rights
UNECLAC	United Nations Economic Commission for Latin America and the Caribbean

Preface

Amid a fragile present-day world economy beset by multiple economic and geopolitical risks, economic ties between Asia and Latin America are expanding, but many challenges remain. This book examines a critical policy question: How can Asia and Latin America increase economic integration between them in the future?

The interregional comparative chapters in this book examine key issues in reducing trade costs and boosting intra- and interregional cooperation. The focus of the chapters is a critical examination of specific modalities to reduce trade costs and to deepen integration between Asia and Latin America. Three key modalities are covered: trade facilitation, logistics, and infrastructure; production networks, supply chains, and small and medium-sized enterprises; and free trade agreements (FTAs). Studying these modalities has proved fruitful as they constitute new frontiers in research and policy analysis in the field of Asia–Latin America integration.

The time seems ripe to consider what the next stage of the Asia–Latin America trade relationship might look like. The chapters in this book point to several important policy implications. First, the relationship should be diversified and steps taken to ensure that the benefits are not concentrated in a small number of sectors located in a handful of countries. Second, increased investment in transport infrastructure, port management, trade facilitation, and logistics is critical to reduce trade costs. Third, implementing second-generation structural reforms at the national level can improve policy transparency and help attract production networks and supply chains led by multinational corporations. Fourth, harmonizing provisions in the extensive, overlapping trade architecture that has developed between Asia and Latin America would help avoid the transactions costs that arise when firms trade under multiple FTA regimes.

This book is the outcome of a long-standing knowledge partnership between the Inter-American Development Bank and the Asian Development Bank Institute. We are most grateful to several individuals who contributed to the preparation of this book. Jenny Balboa provided research and coordination assistance. Robert Davis, Kae Sugawara, and Grant Stillman organized the publication of the book.

The opinions expressed in this book are those of the authors and do not represent the views of the Inter-American Development Bank or the Asian Development Bank Institute.

Antoni Estevadeordal, Masahiro Kawai,
and Ganeshan Wignaraja

1

Introduction

Antoni Estevadeordal, Masahiro Kawai, and Ganeshan Wignaraja

Context and Aim of the Book

Globalization and liberalization over several decades are associated with a shift in the world's economic center of gravity toward new players from the developing economies (see Jorgenson and Minh Vu 2013). Early signs suggest that this shift in the global economy has been hastened since the global financial crisis. As a part of this trend, Asia and the Pacific, and Latin America and the Caribbean[1] are increasingly expanding their roles in the world economy. Less known perhaps is that the two regions are also increasing economic integration between them, notably through the growth of interregional trade since the early 2000s.

At first glance, the trend toward closer integration between Asia and Latin America may seem surprising due to some unfavorable initial conditions. The two regions are separated by a vast geographical distance, and interregional trade is constrained by large interregional trade costs (e.g., freight costs, logistics, customs, as well as import tariffs and nontariff measures). Other barriers to interregional trade and business activity may arise from differences in language, culture, and business practices, but it is difficult to quantify their importance. However, focusing on such unfavorable initial conditions can be deceptive and masks progress in interregional integration.

---

[1] Hereafter in this introduction, Asia and the Pacific will be referred to as Asia, and Latin America and the Caribbean as Latin America.

Differences in factor endowments between the two regions, coupled with falling transport and logistics costs in international trade, have laid the foundations for growing interregional trade. With the sluggish economic recovery worldwide from the global financial crisis and ongoing debt problems in the eurozone economies, Asia and Latin America have attempted to sustain their own robust growth with sound macroeconomic policies and continued structural reform. Greater "South–South" interregional trade and investment has followed better national policy management, a business environment conducive to the private sector, and factor endowments. In spite of these encouraging developments, there is little doubt that relatively high trade costs remain a major barrier to closer integration between Asia and Latin America.

The past decade has seen the spread of several bilateral free trade agreements (FTAs) seeking to reduce trade costs and link the two regions. Interest in this emerging trans-Pacific architecture has increased with the announcement of negotiations for an ambitious plurilateral trade bloc in the form of a Trans-Pacific Partnership (TPP) in 2011. If successfully concluded and backed by structural reforms at the national level, the TPP has the potential to transform the future scope and depth of integration in Asia and the Pacific.

Amid a fragile present-day world economy beset by multiple economic and geopolitical risks, it is critical that Asia–Latin America economic ties are increased and strengthened in the future. This book examines a critical policy question: How can Asia and Latin America increase economic integration between them? The interregional comparative chapters in this volume examine key issues and challenges in reducing trade costs and boosting intra- and interregional cooperation. The focus of the chapters is a critical examination of specific modalities to reduce trade costs and to deepen integration between Asia and Latin America.

The specific modalities covered in the volume are:

- cross-border trade facilitation, logistics, and infrastructure that facilitate imports, exports, investment, and business activity;
- global production networks and supply chains that locate manufacturing stages across geographical space, thereby fostering processing of commodities and labor-intensive industrialization including the development of small and medium-sized enterprises (SMEs); and
- the emerging trans-Pacific architecture based on FTAs that reduce trade, investment, and behind-the-border regulatory barriers between members of agreements.

These modalities are a fruitful area of study as they constitute new frontiers in research and policy analysis in the field of Asia–Latin America integration. As Asia–Latin America integration is a relatively new development, the topic has received little attention in the growing literature on regional economic integration. Additionally, the economic implications of these specific modalities and their interrelationships have been understudied within the scant literature on Asia–Latin America integration.[2]

To set the stage for subsequent chapters on specific modalities, the remainder of this introduction provides overviews of Latin American and Asian integration, phases of Asia–Latin America integration, and an outline of the chapters in this volume.

Overview of Latin America Integration

Latin America has a long tradition of regional integration projects, dating back to at least the middle of the 20th century. The scope, content, and ideological underpinnings of these initiatives have, not surprisingly, evolved considerably with the shifting winds of economic policy making in the region. The initial integration initiatives in the 1960s and 1970s sought to create a regional market protected from the global economy in order to accelerate the development of domestic industries. As countries in the region embraced economic liberalism in the 1980s and 1990s, new regional blocs emerged with the goal of reducing barriers to trade in goods and also liberalizing services and capital flows, encouraging foreign direct investment (FDI), and promoting broader cooperation in areas such as regional infrastructure, trade facilitation, and monetary policy.

The ambitious goals of the so-called "new regionalism" were not always met, however, the momentum behind greater trade liberalization stalled in some Latin American countries by the early 2000s. Over the past decade, as a result, regional integration projects in Latin America have become more diverse. While many countries continue to move in the direction of deep integration—mainly via bilateral and plurilateral agreements that increasingly include industrialized country partners—a subset of countries have pursued different visions of regional integration, focusing on overcoming market failures rather than trade barriers per se and in some cases taking steps to restrict trade and investment flows altogether.

---

[2] Recent studies include: Krasniqi et al. (2011) and Gonzales-Vigil and Shimizu (2012).

Origins of Integration: 1960s and 1970s

The main thrust of the region's postwar integration projects was to create the conditions for the continuation of import-substitution industrialization (ISI) projects that were in vogue in the region at the time.

These policies, which in broad terms sought to develop domestic industries through a combination of high external tariffs and a heavy dose of public investment and state planning, managed to achieve fast growth and a degree of industrialization, especially during the 1940s and 1950s. However, this model began to lose momentum in the following decade, first in the smaller economies and later in the larger ones. Rather than questioning the fundamental precepts of ISI, governments in the region blamed small domestic market size for its disappointing performance. An integrated Latin American market, the reasoning went, would allow industries to realize efficiency and productivity gains through economies of scale.

Regional integration in this era, thus, emerged as a strategy to breathe new life into a flagging state-led development model. As such, the so-called "old regionalism" envisioned the following policy levers: eliminating barriers to trade and investment among participating countries; maintaining or increasing (already-high) protection against third parties; implementing state planning and public investment at the regional level; and regulating FDI to support the development of domestic industry.

Three regional integration projects from this era epitomize the "old regionalism" framework: the Latin America Free Trade Area (LAFTA), which sought to establish a free trade area among six South American nations and Mexico; the Central American Common Market; and the Andean Group (1969)—the latter two utilizing a common market approach.

These initiatives generally failed to obtain the outcomes that policy makers in the region hoped for. For one, tariff liberalization was limited, and as a result increased intra-regional trade and investment flows did not materialize, although the Central American Common Market stands as a partial exception. The aspiration of lowering tariffs ran up against the tenacity of protectionist mentalities at the national level, undermining the regional project from the start. Negotiations to remove barriers proceeded at a snail's pace, tied down by the use of positive lists to determine tariff reductions (Devlin and Giordano 2004).

In addition, uneven trade balances among partners created serious political tensions surrounding the likely distribution of costs and benefits from integration. Sparse regional infrastructure represented a further obstacle to realizing economies of scale at the regional level, inhibiting regional trade throughout this period. Finally, more ambitious plans to replicate sectoral planning at the regional level never got off the ground.

Debt Crisis and Paralysis

The debt crisis, which beset most of the region in the early 1980s and led to a decade of stagnant growth, initially put a halt to regional integration as policy makers scrambled to stabilize national economies. However, the debt crisis also provided the impetus for long-postponed structural reform in many economies. The standard reform package included trade liberalization, as lower tariffs came to be seen as an important pillar of price stabilization.

As a result of these reforms, average tariffs in the region dropped from over 40% in the mid-1980s to around 12% by the mid-1990s. Many countries in the region also participated in the Uruguay Round of multilateral trade negotiations, adopting its comprehensive provisions. In addition to the unilateral and multilateral paths, governments in the region undertook a new round of regional integration initiatives beginning in the early 1990s, as seen in the emergence (or reemergence) of intra-regional blocs such as Mercosur, the Andean Community, the Caribbean Community (CARICOM), and the Central American Common Market, as well as an uptick in bilateral FTAs, driven by Chile and Mexico.

These initiatives ranged from free trade areas to customs unions with ambitions of becoming common markets. In a stark contrast to the first vintage of regional integration projects, this "new regionalism" developed in a policy framework that privileged open, competitive market economies driven by private enterprise. In many ways, the new regionalism represented a natural extension of the structural reform process initiated in the 1980s, serving to "lock in" commitments to macroeconomic stability, open capital accounts, and fiscal consolidation. In addition to consolidating structural reforms, the new regionalism sought to facilitate economic transformation by encouraging intra-regional trade, which has a considerably higher share of higher value-added manufactures than extra-regional trade. Regional markets serve as an outlet for an important array of products in which Latin America has a comparative advantage—such as textiles, dairy goods, meat, and food processing—but which face high levels of international protection. In this way, regional integration has been viewed as a means to advance longer-term strategic objectives in the face of imperfect and incomplete markets at home and abroad (IDB 2002).

The 1990s also witnessed for the first time an interest in "North–South" agreements aiming to integrate countries in the region with industrialized economies, something that would have been politically inconceivable in Latin America in prior decades. The implementation of the North American Free Trade Agreement linking Mexico with the United States and Canada represented a landmark agreement in this sense, opening up the possibility of preferential access to the world's largest market for countries in the region. The Free Trade Area of the Americas (FTAA), first floated in 1994, captures the gestalt of this period with its enthusiastic vision of seamless integration from Canada through the tip of South America.

Deep Integration and Divergence: 2005 Onward

Similar to the earlier round of regional integration projects, the new regionalism did not achieve all of its aims. The FTAA, the emblematic initiative of the era, never came to fruition, and other initiatives such as Mercosur and the Andean Community saw their progress toward greater integration peter out amid economic and political crises. More generally, the package of deep structural reforms undertaken throughout the region failed to meet policy makers' hopes for fast growth, export gains, and job creation.

In response, governments in the region began to rethink their economic strategies in the early 2000s, including on trade policy and regional integration. The result has been the emergence of competing visions of regional integration in Latin America. Some countries have remained committed to market-driven integration and economic openness, embarking on a new round of bilateral and regional FTAs. At the other end of the spectrum, a group of countries convened under the banner of the Bolivarian Alliance for Peoples of Our America (ALBA). Other countries sought to reorient the regional project to balance trade liberalization with a renewed focus on functional cooperation; this approach can be seen in the creation of the Union of South American Nations (UNASUR), led by Brazil (Estevadeordal, Giordano, and Ramos forthcoming).

For the countries that have embraced deeper integration, the strategy of choice in the current phase of integration has been bilateral FTAs, with a focus on extra-regional partners in North America and Asia. In total, a full 36 FTAs involving Latin American countries have been signed since 2006 alone. Agreements with Asian countries have increased from none in 2004 to 24 by the end of 2013. The preference for bilateral deals reflects both the lack of progress on the multilateral front, with the Doha Development Round of World Trade Organization (WTO) negotiations stalled, as well as competitive pressure to secure preferential access to advanced economies' markets. In this context, the Pacific Alliance (AP, in Spanish) among Chile, Colombia, Mexico, and Peru has emerged as a new model of integration, trying to achieve convergence among pre-existing agreements in addition to other integration commitments in financial and labor markets. The alliance is characterized by a high degree of pragmatism and results-based initiative (Estevadeordal, Giordano, and Ramos forthcoming).

Another salient feature of the current phase of integration is participation by some countries in plurilateral agreements such as the TPP, a highly ambitious integration initiative spanning countries in North America, Asia, and Latin America, which will be described in more detail.

While the proliferation of new agreements is a positive trend, the upshot of all this activity is a regional trade architecture that is fragmented, complex, and overlapping. For countries that have aggressively pursued multiple integration strategies, the challenge will be to work toward greater harmonization of existing agreements in order to reap the maximum possible benefits.

Overview of Asian Integration

Emergence of the Global Factory in Asia

Asia's experience of regional integration is different to that of Latin America. It has largely been a market-driven process emphasizing the spread of global production networks and supply chains throughout Asia over several decades. With a handful of relatively recent formal regional cooperation institutions (e.g., Association of Southeast Asian Nations or ASEAN, South Asian Association for Regional Cooperation or SAARC, Bay of Bengal Initiative for Multi-Sectoral Technical and Economic Cooperation or BIMSTEC, and Shanghai Cooperation Organisation or SCO), the regional integration process in Asia has been described as "institution light" (ADB 2010). Moreover, deep or policy-led integration through bilateral or plurilateral FTAs is also a new post-millennium phenomenon in Asia.

In the 1960s, Asia was characterized as a region with little prospect of economic development. The region lacked natural resources, had high levels of poverty, and some economies were mired in wars and internal conflicts. Pessimism about Asia's future development, however, has turned out to be mistaken. Asia's rise over a 50-year period from a poor and underdeveloped agricultural backwater to becoming a center of global manufacturing production is recognized today as an impressive economic achievement. Structural transformation in Asia has been underpinned by a close connection between first globalization and then regionalization. This connection has manifested itself in the rapid spread of sophisticated global production networks and supply chains throughout the region, aptly referred to as "factory Asia" (Baldwin 2008).

Several factors are influential in the creation of factory Asia. Developing Asian economies had ample supplies of low-cost highly productive labor. These developing economies were also geographically close to an already developed and expanding high-income Japan. Efficient Japanese multinational corporations were actively seeking to relocate manufacturing activities across geographical space to less costly locations in Asia. Falling trade barriers and logistics costs, technological progress (e.g., new information and communication technologies, automation, and miniaturization), and rising costs in other production locations spurred the decentralization of manufacturing activities to the most cost-effective locations in Asia. Using strategies of innovation and learning, Asian enterprises acquired the requisite technological capabilities to become suppliers to various multinational corporations in global production networks or trade internationally.

A strong market-driven regional integration dimension is visible in factory Asia (ADB 2008). Final assembly of goods took place in certain low-cost locations linked by a dense network of parts and components trade. Trade within Asia—led by trade in industrial parts and components—increased from 37% of total trade in 1980 to 54% by 2011. Initially, factory Asia involved Japan and ASEAN economies but has since increasingly centered on the People's Republic of China (PRC). There are also some signs that factory Asia has spread to India.

Asian multilateralism—supported through the WTO framework and its predecessor, the General Agreement on Tariffs and Trade (GATT)—and open regionalism—supported by unilateral liberalization by individual economies with intellectual support from the Asia-Pacific Economic Cooperation (APEC) trade group—underpinned much of Asia's approach to international trade policy for several decades. This approach resulted in historically low average

Asian most favored nation (MFN) tariffs of 10.8% by 2000—and these tariffs fell further to 7.4% by 2010.

At the individual-economy level, international trade policy was anchored by the creation of strong infrastructure, outward-oriented development strategies, high domestic savings rates, and major investments in human capital (World Bank 1993). A booming world economy hungry for low-cost labor-intensive imports, falling tariffs in developed markets, inflows of trade-related FDI, and generous inflows of foreign aid also favored outward-oriented growth in Asia.

Rising Asian economic prosperity followed the development of factory Asia. Asia's share of world gross domestic product based on purchasing power parity (PPP) more than doubled from 16% in 1980 to 33% by 2011. Five of the world's richest economies—in terms of PPP per-capita income—are now in Asia: Hong Kong, China; Japan; Singapore; Republic of Korea; and Taipei,China.

Regionalism Led by Free Trade Agreements

Nearing the close of the 20th century, the Asian story of export success and outward orientation was altered by a growth in FTAs which changed the nature of Asia's international trade policies. FTAs, as trade-policy instruments in the region, were largely absent until the 1990s. Today, Asia is a world leader with over 70 FTAs in effect in 2013 (up from 3 in 2000) and more are under development. The region's largest economies (the PRC, India, and Japan) and ASEAN's more-developed economies (e.g., Singapore and Thailand) have become key players in FTA activity. Smaller neighboring economies are now also actively involved in such efforts. Reflecting the growth of FTAs, their importance to trade at the economy level has also increased.

The increase in FTAs in Asia is attributed to factors including the need to remove impediments to broadening the market-led integration of production networks and supply chains, the intensification of FTA activity in Europe and the Americas, and slow progress in the long-running WTO Doha Development Round trade talks (Kawai and Wignaraja 2013).

Well-designed FTAs provide many benefits to member economies in Asia, including greater market access for goods and services trade and reductions in behind-the-border regulatory barriers (including rules governing investment, government procurement, and competition). However, concerns over such agreements have increased as FTAs have spread across Asia. These include the risk of an Asian noodle bowl problem of increased transactions costs for firms from multiple standards and rules of origin (ROOs) in overlapping FTAs; insufficient coverage of behind-the-border regulatory barriers in some older FTAs; and low use of FTA preferences (for a review of recent evidence, see Kawai and Wignaraja forthcoming).

The WTO's ability to make trade rules is coming under question with continuing uncertainties in the future of the Doha Round trade talks. FTA-led regionalism seems here to stay in Asia and will shape the future of trade and investment rules in the region. Measures are needed to deal with concerns about Asian FTAs, including strengthening national support systems for business; rationalizing ROOs in FTAs and improving their administration; forging more comprehensive, deep-integration FTAs that liberalize regulatory barriers; and consolidating bilateral FTAs into large Asia-wide agreements.

New Frontiers in Asia–Latin America Integration

Formal integration between Asia and Latin America is a relatively recent phenomenon. This is not altogether surprising if we consider that most of Latin America and some economies in Asia remained relatively closed off to world trade until the 1980s. Since then, however, far-reaching liberalization processes in both regions have created the conditions for a rapid rise in interregional trade. In reality, this integration has led in turn to the emergence of formal institutions for integration between Asia and Latin America. The two phases of Asia–Latin America integration and key frontier issues are described next.

The Rise of Market-Led Integration

Trade between the two regions only began in earnest after World War II, when Japan's economic take-off spurred demand for natural resources from Latin America. At the same time, the state-led industrialization strategies pursued in Latin America required an inflow of capital and intermediate goods, of which Japan became an important supplier. The rapid growth in the 1970s and 1980s of a new wave of Asian "tigers"—the Republic of Korea; Taipei,China; Hong Kong, China; and Singapore—provided a further boost to Asia–Latin America trade, as these fast-growing economies, such as Japan, had to import large quantities of natural resources. Still, by 1992, trade with Asia accounted for only 8.8% of Latin America's total trade, while Latin America's share of Asia's trade was a mere 2.7% (ADB, ADBI, and IDB 2012).

That would change decisively—at least on the Latin American side—in the first decade of the 21st century. The catalyst was the emergence of the PRC and, to a lesser extent, India as major forces in global trade, spurred by the accession of the PRC to the WTO in 2001. The demand of these economies for raw materials, coupled with the consolidation of trade liberalization in many Latin American economies, brought about an unprecedented boom in interregional trade. From a starting point of around US$59 billion in 2000, total trade reached nearly US$459 billion in 2012; for Latin America, trade with Asia accounted for 22% of its total in that year, surpassing all trade partners other than the United States. On the other hand, Latin America continues to be a relatively minor trade partner for Asia, with 4.8% of its total, although Latin American countries such as Brazil, Chile, and Peru have become key suppliers of strategic natural resources to fast-growing Asian economies.

One of the visible challenges in Asia–Latin America integration is the concentration of trade patterns on a relatively few players from Asia and Latin America. Clearly, Asia is not only the PRC, India, and Japan, and Latin America is not only Brazil, Mexico, and Argentina. The scope and geography of trade between the two regions needs to be broadened considerably to cover ASEAN economies and the rest of South Asia on the Asian side, and smaller Latin American countries and Central America on the Latin American side. Newly-emergent middle classes in both regions represent fertile potential markets for competitive Asian and Latin American exporters.

Accordingly, "better connectivity" is an important frontier issue explored in this book. Better connectivity links goods and services markets, and the foundation for economies of scale—not simply the "hard," physical infrastructure, but also including "softer" components of overall logistics and trade facilitation such as streamlining customs and other procedures, doing what is needed to reduce trade costs and boost greater Asia–Latin America trade. Latin American economies—both firms and governments—need to invest in world-class infrastructure and logistics to reduce trade costs for trading with Asia (see Chapter 4 in this volume). Emphasizing trade facilitation, modernizing customs, and dealing with challenges arising from ROOs in FTAs are also important (see Chapter 2 in this volume).

Furthermore, Asian FDI in natural resources and surrounding sectors—such as related services, transportation infrastructure, and port management—could play an important role, offering opportunities to upgrade the economic relationship on both sides (see Chapter 8 in this volume).

Another frontier issue is "the integration of production networks and supply chains across the Pacific," which will also be examined in this book. The rationale stems from the pattern of trade which has resulted in some trade tensions. The very distinct pattern of trade between the regions, in which Latin American economies exchange commodities for Asian manufactures, has aroused familiar concerns about deindustrialization in some Latin American countries. Meanwhile, the large trade deficits with Asia that characterize most Latin American economies have at times soured the politics of the relationship, leading to tit-for-tat protectionist measures in several cases.

Within the context of the overall pattern of trade, opportunities can arise for Latin American economies to capture more value by incorporating technologically advanced processes in their natural resource sectors and also to improve the competitiveness of manufactures. In this vein, an important avenue is plugging Latin American firms into sophisticated global production networks and supply chains led by Asian firms.

Given the requirements for speed and flexibility in supply chain trade, linking Asia and Latin America more deeply presents a considerable challenge. Success in this endeavor will demand upgrades to physical infrastructure on the Latin American side, as well as further liberalization of transport services, in order to enhance connectivity between the two regions' economies. Tariff and nontariff measures between Asia and Latin America remain high and, in some case, regulations governing FDI remain opaque. Hence, further liberalization of trade and investment regimes is crucial. Promotion of SMEs, which are the backbone of economic activity in both regions will foster a deep base of industrial suppliers and foster more inclusive growth (see Chapter 6 in this volume).

Emergence of a Trans-Pacific Trade Architecture

Yet another frontier issue examined in the book is "the spread and depth of interregional FTAs." The trade surge between Asia and Latin America beginning in the early 2000s was primarily a market-driven phenomenon. Governments in both regions have since followed the lead of the private sector. Over the past decade, a formal trade architecture linking the two regions has emerged. The first interregional FTA, between the Republic of Korea and Chile, entered into force in 2004 and trade negotiators have since inked 23 additional Asia–Latin America FTAs as of the end of 2013. As with trade, a few economies on each side account for the bulk of this activity; in Latin America, Chile (7 agreements) and Peru (5) have been the main protagonists, while on the Asian side Taipei,China has entered into the most agreements (4), although these have all been signed with Central American countries. The PRC, Japan, and the Republic of Korea each have three agreements with Latin American countries.

Concerns have been expressed about the rapid spread of interregional FTAs, particularly the depth of such agreements. The depth of FTAs—in terms of goods, services, and new trade policy issues relating to domestic regulations—defines the potential for interregional liberalization, which is a major influence on interregional integration. Asia–Latin America FTAs seem to display distinct characteristics. By and large, such agreements are notable for the extent of tariff liberalization they envision and their inclusion of "deep integration" disciplines that go beyond trade in goods. The inclusion of provisions for services liberalization; investment and intellectual property protections; and regulatory convergence in areas such as government procurement, competition, and health and safety standards is another feature of some interregional FTAs (ADB, ADBI, and IDB 2012; also Chapter 9 in this volume).

One emerging feature of the evolving interregional trade architecture is the potential role of plurilateral trade blocs such as the TPP. This agreement, which is still being negotiated, brings together 12 countries including 3 in Latin America and 7 in the Asia-Pacific region (including Australia and New Zealand). The TPP represents a highly ambitious, state-of-the-art agreement, envisioning wide-ranging tariff reductions, including sensitive sectors such as agriculture that have often eluded the reach of trade negotiators. The deal also entails robust rules on next-generation issues such as intellectual property, government procurement, investment protection, and competition, which are crucial for achieving deep integration.

The TPP thus holds out the prospect of providing a mechanism to both rationalize the overlapping existing Asia–Latin America agreements (thus avoiding the noodle bowl effect) and expand the geographic reach of the interregional trade architecture to include more economies. The agreement leaves open the possibility of expanding to include new members, although any prospective party would naturally have to agree to the extensive and deep integration commitments entailed in the deal. Development assistance to facilitate domestic adjustment of sensitive sectors such as agriculture and state-owned enterprises would also be needed to expand membership to developing countries in Asia and Latin America.

Plan of the Book

The chapters in this book deal with these frontier issues in Asia–Latin America integration. The chapters are arranged under three headings.

Part I, which presents key issues on trade facilitation and connectivity, is composed of three chapters. Chapter 2 by Brian Rankin Staples and Jeremy Harris suggests that for the past decades, both East Asia and Latin America embarked on development strategies based on opening markets, promoting exports, and attracting foreign investment. As economies in the regions joined the GATT/WTO and used FTAs to further openness, the authors argue that issues on trade facilitation have become even more important as these significantly affected trade liberalization and regional economic integration. Cumbersome trade facilitation—both in its traditional sense of complying with customs procedures at borders and also in the context of managing and administering compliance with behind-the-border requirements—were considered to have become more significant than tariffs in impeding free trade in the past years. The authors identify issues surrounding ROOs as one of the most challenging issues in trade facilitation. Such rules are necessary to determine the country of origin of goods based on a set of technical criteria to determine eligibility for tariff preferences of goods entering an FTA member country. ROOs are complex rules that could be difficult to administer. Staples and Harris recommend strategies by which ROO compliance can be improved, which would also help in making international supply chains more efficient. Among the key recommendations in improving administration of ROOs is to allow co-equal ROOs, which would permit countries to identify a set of rules that can be considered of equal value in terms of establishing origin. They also recommend extension of cumulation, which involves permitting materials that qualify as originating in one country that benefits from preferences in a second country to be used in production of a subsequent good in a third country that benefits from the same preferences. Moreover, the authors argue that ROOs are indispensable tools to also promote consumer and environmental safety. As such, they also recommend using ROOs as a mechanism to create integrated information systems for consumer and environmental protection.

In Chapter 3, Douglas Brooks and Susan Stone emphasize the need for Asia to continue improving trade facilitation measures to sustain economic growth and regional integration. In the context of increasing division of labor and international production fragmentation, they state that efficiency of production does not solely rely on the strength of one economy, but also on the competitiveness of other countries that are part of the production networks and the trade links between these networks. In this regard, the authors argue that trade facilitation measures should be included in bilateral and regional trade agreement negotiations as they have a tremendous impact in improving competitiveness of economies and strengthening trade links, which are necessary to promote regional production efficiency. The authors stress the importance of sequencing and complementarity of reforms in cross-border trade facilitation. The first stage in the sequence would involve building and improving physical transport infrastructure which is critical for strengthening cross-border trade. This should then be reinforced by complementary soft or information and communication technology infrastructure. The final process in the reform sequence involves improvements in trade facilitation that will address problems in trade logistics, information asymmetries, and institutional bottlenecks. Additionally, Brooks and Stone discuss how individual economies could benefit from improving trade facilitation measures. The empirical analysis in their chapter shows that even a modest reduction in trade costs results in a notable gain in gross domestic product and allows countries to diversify trade and move into higher value-added sectors.

In Chapter 4, Pablo Guerrero, Krista Lucenti, and Sebastián Galarza argue that Latin America's inadequate infrastructure and logistics explain why the region continues to lag behind developed countries and many developing regions in reaping the benefits from increased trade liberalization and deeper regional integration. The authors suggest that the region has in the past suffered from chronic underinvestment in infrastructure, weak institutional capacity, and poor project implementation of infrastructure projects. The chapter highlights the need for Latin America to improve global competitiveness by investing in improving freight logistics, trade facilitation, improvement of physical infrastructure, as well as improvement of the logistics corridors and multimodal transport services and regulatory frameworks to simplify international trade procedures. To respond to these problems, the region has broadened its trade facilitation agenda to incorporate physical integration projects and transport and logistics infrastructure that will enhance regional and interregional trade. Deepening trade facilitation measures had become increasingly important in Latin America's regional integration agenda. Given this regional goal, the challenge for Latin American countries is how to reform the current institutional climate such that these reforms will be integrated in domestic policies and the national development framework. Guerrero, Lucenti, and Galarza acknowledge the importance of political will to allow these reforms to be implemented.

Part II examines production networks and supply chains in Asia and Latin America and comprises three chapters. In Chapter 5, Ruth Banomyong emphasizes that the key role of supply chains is to assist in the production, consumption, and distribution of goods and services. A good supply chain system is critical for economic cooperation and development of the region. However, this would require an integrated and seamless logistics system. The author states that lack of adequate transport infrastructure and high logistics costs in some Asian countries impedes the potential to develop an efficient and seamless regional supply chain. Hence, the chapter argues that an integrated transport service would allow supply chains to operate in a reliable and predictable manner. In addition, this should be accompanied by trade facilitation measures that would reduce barriers to trade and unlock institutional bottlenecks. It also needs a transparent and simplified legal regime that would effectively implement integrated logistics operations. Improvement of cross-border infrastructure, coupled with expanded cross-border cooperation among Asian countries, will accelerate the process of integrating the Asian supply chain with the rest of the world and the global market. Furthermore, Banomyong stresses the important role of human resource capacity and the cost of labor as key drivers of supply chains. Citing the results of a case study on automobile assembly operations, the author stresses that labor advantage, either in skills or wages, may offset high transportation costs. Investing in improving human resource skills and capacity was also identified as an important aspect of creating strong supply chains.

In Chapter 6, Hank Lim and Fukunari Kimura focus on the need to strengthen SMEs. According to the authors, SMEs play a pivotal role in the functioning of international and regional production networks and in the provision of critical industrial linkages to set off a chain reaction of broad-based and sustainable development. SMEs are the backbone of Southeast Asia's economy, accounting for more than 90% of all private sector firms. SMEs are also the biggest source of employment in the region, providing 40%–90% of jobs. Better participation of SMEs in global value chains could substantially create more jobs, strengthen the domestic economies, and facilitate regional development. SME participation as subcontractors and suppliers of intermediate inputs to multinational and large domestic firms adds to a sustainable increase in domestic value-added, employment, productivity, and industrial linkages. SMEs' participation also adds to economic resilience against external economic fluctuations and serves as a mechanism for local capacity building. Lim and Kimura state that the crucial issue in improving SMEs is how to transform local firms and SMEs into viable and competitive firms that can be linked to the multinational enterprises. The authors emphasize that successful cases of SME development have adopted long-term comprehensive, coordinated, and consistent policies. They also stress that effective collaboration between the government, trade associations, and education and training institutions is important in reducing the cost for human resource development and capacity building.

In Chapter 7, Grant Aldonas argues that regional integration should include strategies that will help member countries access global markets. Policy makers should consciously provide an environment that would enable local firms to link up with global supply chains. Ultimately, policy makers may have to adopt strategic tools similar to the ones used by private firms in linking with the global supply chains. According to the author, the tool most commonly used by global businesses in making strategic decisions about sourcing is a value chain map. Aldonas suggests that the same tool can be used by policy makers in identifying problems that hinder their countries from effectively becoming part of the global value chains. To this end, he designs a value chain map to identify steps in the production and how costs can be reduced in each stage. The map could also help identify the barriers within the country and at the regional level and explain how these challenges can be overcome. Finally, econometric measures are used to help quantify the effect of barriers imposed on exports by transit cost and distance. Using the value chain map, he proceeds to analyze the Peruvian value chain for perishable agricultural products. Based on the framework developed, gaps in transportation linkages were revealed, as well as costs and benefits of specific improvements in infrastructure. Aldonas states that these tools can help policy makers determine solutions on the impediments that industries face in effectively participating in global production networks.

Part III discusses Asia–Latin America relations. In Chapter 8, Gloria Pasadilla examines the motivation and patterns of the PRC's FDI to Latin America. She argues that Latin America will remain an attractive destination of the PRC's FDI due to the country's high surplus savings and its need to secure food, energy, and other raw materials. Moreover, Latin America's growing domestic market has become attractive for market-seeking firms from the PRC, such as automotive and consumer goods. She shows that PRC investments were heavily concentrated in the Southern Cone (i.e., Argentina, Brazil, Chile, and Peru). These investments seek secure access to the supply of natural resources either by investing directly in mines or agricultural land or by developing the infrastructure around them. In terms of sector distribution, PRC investments in Latin America were heavily concentrated on energy and metals (copper and steel), which altogether accounted for almost 60% of the total value of investments. Transport, particularly railway construction in Argentina and Venezuela, was also significant with a 16% share. Agriculture and hydropower accounted for 7% of investments in Latin America, while investment in real estate was at 5%.

In Chapter 9, Ganeshan Wignaraja, Dorothea Ramizo, and Luca Burmeister chart trends in Asia–Latin America FTAs, using new criteria to painstakingly assess liberalization and depth of such FTAs. The results show that Asia–Latin America FTAs are notable for the extent of tariff liberalization sought and their inclusion of deep integration provisions that go beyond trade in goods. However, it was also revealed that some FTAs adopt a somewhat cautious approach to liberalization of sensitive regulatory barriers in areas such as investment, competition, and government procurement. The authors project that the numbers of Asia–Latin America FTAs will rise by 2020 and stress that future Asia–Latin America FTAs need to improve on commitments on regulatory barriers and provisions on intellectual property rights. Apart from improving the depth of future FTAs, the chapter highlights the need for business support to increase the use of FTA preferences, for forming a large and comprehensive plurilateral FTA, and for enhancing structural reforms. Enhancing FTA-led cooperation between the two regions also calls for stronger partnerships between government, business, and regional institutions to sustain the momentum of interregional cooperation.

In Chapter 10, Erlinda Medalla and Jenny Balboa explore the potential for deeper regional cooperation between Asia and Latin America from the perspective of East Asia. The authors identify significant gaps in trade and investment links between the regions that impede deeper and mutually beneficial interregional partnerships. The two regions are characterized by stark structural differences, and export capacities are very different. Biregional economic links remain weak and have shown little diversification as inter-industry trade still accounts for most of the trade flows, with Asia exporting manufactures to Latin America, and Latin America exporting primary commodities to Asia. Medalla and Balboa highlight the need for Latin America to move up the value chain and strengthen trade capacity to increase trade complementarity with Asia. In particular, there is a need for Latin America to work more on increasing product diversification and to integrate itself in Asian supply chain networks. FTAs can help address some of these issues by breaking down tariff and nontariff barriers between the two regions. Improvements in trade facilitation measures between the regions should also be included in these FTAs. Moreover, it is important to improve physical connectivity between the two regions, specifically air and maritime transportation, to help bring down costs of transporting goods.

References

Asian Development Bank (ADB). 2008. *Emerging Asian Regionalism: A Partnership for Shared Prosperity*. Manila: ADB.

Asian Development Bank (ADB). 2010. *Institutions for Regional Integration: Toward an Asian Economic Community*. Manila: ADB.

Asian Development Bank (ADB), Asian Development Bank Institute (ADBI), and Inter-American Development Bank (IDB). 2012. *Shaping the Future of the Asia–Latin America and the Caribbean Relationship*. Manila, Tokyo, and Washington, DC: ADB, ADBI, and IDB.

Baldwin, R. 2008. Managing the Noodle Bowl: The Fragility of East Asian Regionalism. *Singapore Economic Review*. 53 (3). pp. 449–478.

Devlin, R., and P. Giordano. 2004. The Old and New Regionalism: Benefits, Costs, and Implications for the FTAA. In A. Estevadeordal, D. Rodrik, A.M. Taylor, and A. Velasco, eds. *Integrating the Americas: FTAA and Beyond*. Cambridge, MA: Harvard University Press.

Estevadeordal, A., P. Giordano, and B. Ramos. Forthcoming. Trade and Economic Integration, In J.I. Domínguez and A. Covarrubias, eds. *Routledge Handbook of Latin America and the World*. London: Routledge.

Gonzales-Vigil, F., and T. Shimizu. 2012. The Japan–Peru FTA: Antecedents, Significance and Main Features. IDE Discussion Paper No.335. Chiba: Institute of Developing Economies.

Inter-American Development Bank (IDB). 2002. *Beyond Borders: The New Regionalism in Latin America*. Economic and Social Progress Report in Latin America. Baltimore, MD: Johns Hopkins University Press.

Jorgenson, D., and K. Minh Vu. 2013. The Emergence of the New Economic Order: Growth in the G7 and the G20. *Journal of Policy Modeling*. 35 (3). pp. 389–399.

Kawai, M., and G. Wignaraja. 2013. Patterns of Free Trade Areas in Asia. *East West Center Policy Studies* No. 60. Honolulu: East–West Center. http://www.adbi.org/book/2013/03/04/5531.patterns.free.trade.areas.asia/

Kawai, M., and G. Wignaraja. Forthcoming. Policy Challenges Posed by Asian FTAs: A Review of the Evidence. In R. Baldwin, M. Kawai, and G. Wignaraja, eds. *A WTO for the 21st Century: The Asian Century*. Cheltenham, UK: Edward Elgar.

Krasniqi, V.B., A. Bouet, C. Estrades, and D. Laborde. 2011. Trade and Investment in Latin America and Asia: Lessons from the Past and Potential Perspectives from Further Integration. IFPR Discussion Paper 01060. Washington, DC: International Food Policy Research Institute.

World Bank. 1993. *The East Asian Miracle: Economic Growth and Public Policy*. Oxford: Oxford University Press.

PART I

Trade Facilitation

2

Origin and Beyond: Trade Facilitation Disaster or Trade Facilitation Opportunity?

Brian Rankin Staples and Jeremy Harris

Introduction

Over the last three decades, the countries of Latin America and the Caribbean (LAC) and East Asia have nearly all, to varying degrees, embraced development strategies based on opening markets, promoting exports, and attracting foreign investment. Intra-regional, cross-regional, and extra-regional trade has grown in importance. Trade between Latin America and Asia exceeded US$450 billion in 2012, a sign of the growing importance of this interregional economic relationship.

In the early years of pursuing and supporting these strategies, the primary policy-based obstacles to commerce that had to be addressed were high tariffs. But as these countries have joined the General Agreement on Tariffs and Trade/World Trade Organization (GATT/WTO) and negotiated an ever-increasing number of regional trade agreements (RTAs), tariffs per se are not the trade barrier that they once were. These steps have brought about considerable growth in trade, and have helped the countries of these regions to take greater advantage of the evolving global trading system.

As the importance of tariffs as primary trade barriers has receded, these successes have revealed, and in some cases caused, a new set of obstacles. The important policy obstacles to address now revolve around the concept of trade facilitation, both in its traditional sense as relates to customs procedures at borders, but also in the context of managing and administering compliance with at-border and behind-the-border requirements on the part of importers, exporters, producers, and even reaching back to their suppliers.

Baldwin (2006) has described the nature of the global trading system that has evolved over the past several decades, highlighting the causes and consequences of proliferating RTAs. In this framework, these agreements serve as a useful mechanism for promoting further trade liberalization by signatory countries. But they also leave in their wake an uncoordinated tangle of inconsistent, difficult to decipher, and at times contradictory regulations and restrictions on international trade. This mess, then, calls out for tidying up at the multilateral (WTO) level, thus promoting a "multilateralization" of the regionally established tariff reductions.

Because RTAs have been negotiated in different contexts at different times, they inevitably stipulate different rules for application of the tariff preferences that they establish, as well as divergent standards and other requirements for selling different products on different national markets. In order for exporting firms to benefit from the negotiated tariff preferences in multiple foreign markets, they must be able to manage these diverse rules and regulations.

The information required in order to process an international sale and movement of goods, taking advantage of the preferential tariffs that are negotiated, and complying with the vast array of environmental, security, and consumer safety requirements, is becoming quite significant. This amounts to a before-the-border "thickening." Even where all of the needed information is readily available, the administrative costs of organizing and communicating this information to customs and other border agencies constitute an implicit barrier to trade.

One of the most important of such issues is the rules of origin (ROO) of the rapidly expanding network of RTAs. ROO are the criteria established in preferential trading arrangements for determining and limiting the degree to which materials from countries that are not party to an agreement may be used in the production of goods within a member country, without those goods being considered ineligible for tariff preferences. These ROO can be quite complex to understand and administer, even for sophisticated multinational firms, to say nothing of small and medium sized enterprises (SMEs). The situation can become even more difficult when these rules vary across the different markets that the firms wish to serve.

In addition to ROO, countries are applying a growing set of regulations geared toward promoting consumer and environmental safety, among other issues, which although they apply equally to imports and domestic products, add an additional layer of complexity to international trade transactions, and complexity is cost. Many of these measures, despite their obvious merit in principle, are going up in reaction to high profile, politically charged events, and their implementation is being mandated faster than common sense would seem to indicate. As a consequence, a wide array of costly testing and certification is required where there is little capacity to do so, and in many cases no logical purpose, as the goods in question are swept up in well-intentioned but overly broad regulations.

As we seek mechanisms to ameliorate these problems, we see that "Trade Facilitation" (TF) must be included, but is larger than, the traditional issues of Articles V, VIII and X of the GATT. While these are important, advances on these issues alone would be insufficient to the needs of modern international trade. To be of practical use, TF measures must be designed and implemented with a private sector perspective in mind. The practical issues of certificate formats, value content calculation methods, supplier information requirements, and administrative peculiarities present a wide array of obstacles that go beyond the traditional TF issues.

The remainder of this chapter is structured as follows: the next section addresses the determination and governance of ROO in the global trading system, as well as the implications of this lack of organization and some possible approaches that might better order and facilitate trade. The section titled, "Beyond Origin" looks beyond ROO to other forms of regulation that impose on trade the same type of information requirements as origin, and that must be considered in any origin-related trade facilitation endeavor. The conclusion offers some recommendations of policies that could lead to better facilitation of trade on origin-related matters.

Governance of ROO in a Spaghetti World

The world map of the ROO "spaghetti bowl" is, at this point, well documented.[1] As of mid-2013, the WTO had received a total of 575 notifications of RTAs, of which 379 were fully in force.[2] This averages out to more than two per WTO member, though in fact some countries are more prolific in their trade negotiations than others. The LAC and East Asia regions in particular have come

---

[1] For example, Estevadeordal, Harris, and Suominen (2007).
[2] According to the WTO website at http://www.wto.org/english/tratop_e/region_e/region_e.htm.

to have rather dense networks of overlapping RTAs. For LAC, this is rapidly reaching a saturation point, with nearly all of the important bilateral relationships (in terms of trade value) covered by such agreements. East Asia is not yet at such a point, but is signing and implementing agreements at a rapid clip, such that already these issues are on the horizon.

This is also not just a question of the number of agreements, but of their size and quality. In both regions countries have signed and are implementing agreements with major trading partners (People's Republic of China [PRC], US, India, Republic of Korea [Korea], EU), in addition to a growing array of smaller partners. As a consequence, significant fractions of these countries' trade are regulated by the dispositions of these growing networks of agreements.

At the global level, the effect of these overlapping networks of RTAs is that we find duty free treatment has potentially been established, in principle, for a significant majority of world trade. However, this duty-free treatment is subject to the ROO of each particular RTA. As the rules differ across agreements, and even where rules are the same the eligible suppliers differ, we see that compliance starts to be a significant concern for traders.

We say "potentially" because the rules of the agreement apply only to those goods for which preferential treatment is requested. If the costs of complying, and demonstrating compliance, with the prerequisites for preferential treatment exceed the value of the preferences, then the obligation to comply with these requirements regarding the ROO and the certification thereof disappears as the goods enter and pay the Most Favored Nation (MFN) tariff. While this reality imposes a helpful upper limit on the distortionary potential of RTAs, it also limits the degree to which the tariff reductions can boost trade.

The evolving literature on "multilateralizing regionalism" referenced earlier is based on the expectation that agreeing and applying better central governance of RTAs from the multilateral system under the WTO can lead to smoother operation of trade on a global basis. It is worth asking the question, however, whether we are equally likely to achieve some sort of "regionalization of multilateralism," wherein the growing influence of regional trading institutions may slow the adoption of global standards and such regional blocs cater more to their perceived interests that to global efficiency. In this scenario, it will be the responsibility of the regional institutions to work both individually and collectively, under the auspices of the WTO or otherwise, to reduce the costs of trading both within their spheres of influence, and across blocs.

The WTO is still the forum of choice for efforts to harmonize global standards on this and other issues. It is unlikely that any bloc or blocs will carry enough economic weight to displace the global institution, but it is also likely that regional arrangements will have increasing influence over the agenda. The ability of regional blocs to establish the rules that apply to important segments of international trade will translate into stronger voices in multilateral discussions. It is thus important that these arrangements find efficient solutions to the more pressing problems facing operators in the world today.

This scenario is applicable equally to investment and intellectual property issues, for example, as it is to ROO, though it is the latter on which we focus here. As we discuss below, whatever the mechanics by which it is achieved, if trade costs are to be further reduced, procedural simplification and administrative costs as pertaining to ROO must be a priority.

Implications of ROO Anarchy

While it is true that in some minority of simple cases, where an exporter produces only one product for all customers over time, and with most materials sourced domestically, the costs of the complications from origin inconsistency may not be so bad. But for the majority—producers with dynamic, flexible, fast supply chains—the complexities and constraints of the tangle of overlapping rules can impose costs that exceed the value of the tariff preferences that compliance confers, especially if the margin of preference is low. In such situations, the value of the agreement (or agreements) is lost.

Note that this applies not just to corporate affiliates in one country or region, but within whole multinationals (i.e., from a centralized global perspective). The complexity of origin compliance has in some cases led to the centralization of origin management within corporate structures, especially where supply chains are global. As such, the decisions to claim preferences (or not) can be made not on a case by case basis, but as global corporate policy, and thus affect global preference utilization.

Even where the tariff preferences are substantial enough to merit the compliance efforts, the cost can be significant for large multinational firms that manage fragmented production networks across multiple countries. To the extent that these costs reduce competitiveness, they serve as a brake on international trade and investment.

These costs are present both across subsidiaries of a single company and between companies and their unaffiliated suppliers. Indeed, when suppliers are not wholly-owned subsidiaries of the final producer, the costs are even greater, because it is less likely that efficient channels exist for transmission of the suppliers' origin information. In order for final producers to accurately evaluate their own origin compliance, they require complete information on the origin of their materials, both those they produce themselves and those purchased from unaffiliated suppliers.

Making compliance determinations then involves crawling back up the supply chain, identifying materials used and their suppliers, as well as the originating status of each material sourced from each supplier. At this point, pricing and sourcing confidentiality and sensitivity issues can arise. In fact, it cannot always be taken as given that it is in the interest of suppliers to provide complete information to their clients, as this information could in some cases jeopardize their relationship, for example by identifying subcontractors that the producers could then contact directly, cutting the supplier out of future transactions.

At present, there is no end in sight for the increasing complexities of the global origin spaghetti bowl. The topic, at least, is beginning to generate discussion, both in chambers of commerce and among policy makers. But such discussions are just beginning, and there is no emerging consensus on practical solutions.

One sort of solution that has been put forth deals with the definition of cumulation in RTA ROO. Because RTAs are most frequently negotiated bilaterally, the preferences apply only to goods that are originating in one or the other partner to the agreement. However, once a group of countries comes to have all or most of their constituent bilateral relationships covered by bilateral agreements, situations arise where materials exported from one country to another can enter duty free, but if they are subject to further processing in a second country within the group before being sold to the same final destination, the final good in question may not meet the applicable origin requirements, even though each of its constituent parts, if exported directly from their respective countries of production, would have entered duty free. In this case, the problem lays not so much in the definition of the specific origin criteria in any one of the RTAs involved, but rather in the absence of provision for cumulation of origin among countries within this tangle of agreements.

Solutions that have been put forward[3] involve finding mechanisms for implementing such cumulation provisions. This can take the form of replacing

---

[3] See Cornejo and Harris (2007) and Harris (2008) for similar but different approaches to this problem.

collection of agreements with a single agreement covering all countries, or other more piecemeal arrangements that can produce similar effects with less extensive negotiations, but less reduction in overall complexity. However these problems are to be addressed, the issue of implementation and administration at the border remain.

Origin Administration

Administration of ROO involves both private actors and the public sector. It includes all of the documentation and record keeping requirements established by an agreement and its regulations, all of the customs procedures associated with proving origin, and all of the procedures and potential sanctions deriving from the process of ex post verification of origin. In practice, this is in addition to the design of supply chains that contemplate sourcing from within a given cumulation zone in order to comply with rule requirements. It is one thing to comply with the requirements. It is another thing to substantiate this compliance in such a way as to be able to prove it to the necessary government agencies. Apart from the differing rules and inconsistent cumulation zones across overlapping RTAs, there is also much divergence in methods and procedures for administration of origin. At the global level, other than a few guidelines in the Revised Kyoto Convention (RKC), there is significant multiplicity of administration procedures without multilateral disciplines. Not only do procedures and protocols differ across countries, but they can differ in a single country depending on the agreement under which goods are imported. This generates costs for customs in terms of time and resources, and consequently uncertainty for business.

It is worth pointing out that this is a problem for both preferential ROO, which has been the focus of our discussion in this chapter, and also non-preferential ROO, which are vital for administration of CVDs and antidumping measures. Firms trading in goods subject to such measures in any of their export markets, even if the measures are not aimed at goods from the firms' countries, must be able to adequately document and substantiate that the goods exported do not originate from countries subject to the compensatory duties. Chaos in the definition of the non-preferential rules across countries, as well as uncertainty regarding the application and/or interpretation of the rules in different countries leads to the same difficulties as seen in the case of preferential ROO.

Unilateral Solutions to a Two-Dimensional Problem

Given the tremendous variation in rules, cumulation zones, and administrative procedures relating to compliance and administration of ROO within the two regions, and globally, it is reasonable for business to face significant uncertainty. This uncertainty relates both to compliance, where rules are unclear or interpretations are inconsistent, and to administration, where procedures are unclear, customs officials lack capacity, or legal provisions are incomplete.

This sort of uncertainty is an important barrier to trade. If even a perfectly designed supply chain, which sources only from eligible countries and ensures compliance with processing requirements, can still result in payment of tariffs due to misinterpretations or misapplications of rules by customs, then the additional costs of designing the supply chain represent a failed investment. Where this risk is large or where the potential tariff savings are significant, if investors cannot ensure proper application of the rules by the public sector then the investments may not occur, or the preference may not be pursued. This is a loss both for the investors themselves, and for the countries that could have attracted such investment. And uncertainty due to customs application of the rules is not the only, or even the most important source of uncertainty.

International trade transactions that are not between subsidiaries of the same corporation face the central origin dilemma: balancing the rights and obligations of the producer/exporter and the importer. The only entity that has sufficient information regarding a product's compliance with origin requirements is the producer, but in almost all cases the person responsible for payment of tariffs is the importer. The producer's interest is to obtain the best price for his goods, and thus has to represent them as eligible for duty-free treatment whether or not this is actually the case. The importer, facing some likelihood of verification by officials of the importing country, therefore must take into account the potential tariff obligation and penalties in the event that verification cannot be satisfied.

For the importer, then, the preparation of entry documents involves much more than determining the transaction value (visible on the importer's general ledger) or determining the proper tariff classification (just look at the product), because origin relies heavily on exporter information, which may be faulty, either through fraud or negligence. Whatever the particular underlying circumstances, the issue of origin liability for importers is real.

Furthermore, most agreements allow for post-entry verification of origin up to five years after goods are imported. Verification actions rarely concentrate on a single transaction, but rather will usually cover a series of importations over a longer time frame. The combined tariffs, interest, and penalties for which an importer can be liable based on multiple years of faulty origin information can quickly reach into millions of dollars.

In this context, the public sector has a role to play in designing origin procedures, with a view to ensuring proper collection of revenue. There are two primary factors to consider when designing policies and procedures for mitigating the risks implicit in these situations. The first revolves around origin certification methods, and the second focuses on standards for importer–exporter contracts. Again, there is no single global trend toward an emerging consensus, but rather an ongoing series of experiments with different methods in different countries.

In some sense, importer liability has been exacerbated by origin self-certification methods as they have been implemented by a number of countries, most significantly the US. Under these systems, in most cases a certificate of origin may be issued by the producer, the exporter, or the importer, but only the last of these can be required to sign such a certificate or face the loss of tariff preferences, as well as become liable for additional penalties. Furthermore, the agent who issues the origin certificate is required to maintain the necessary documentation that substantiates the certificate of origin. But still, having either the exporter or, optimally, the producer issue the certificate is still not a shield from liability for the importer, who is in all cases responsible for the duties.

This arrangement does solve problems that can arise in other certification systems, as it is difficult for customs agencies to pursue agents outside the country of import to collect duties and penalties, whereas the importer is generally resident in the country of import. But by concentrating responsibility in the importer, the resulting imbalance of rights and responsibilities can serve as a disincentive to the utilization of preferences, and thus to a reduction in the potential benefits of the agreement.

In addition to the United States, the EU is in the process of moving from reliance on origin-certifying entities to self-certification at least in the context of least developed countries (LDC) regimes. This is happening precisely due to a lot of problems with certificates of origin issued by certifying entities in countries that benefit from EU tariff preferences. Existing EU law regarding importer reliance on entity-issued certifications holds that the importer is not liable if the certificate proves to be false, based on the argument that importers have a reasonable expectation that such certifications are accurate.

When in several recent high-profile cases involving LDC exports such certifications have been shown to be highly inaccurate, importers have used this defense in order to be liable for duties only, and not for penalties, and with more limited retroactive application. As a result of the success of these legal arguments, the EU seems to be moving toward a system of self-certification by registered economic operators.

Beyond reforms of this sort, one solution to the uncertainty for importers is to include a clause in the sales contract to explicitly give the importer the right to recover any tariffs or fines incurred due to faulty origin-related information provided by the exporter. Such contract clauses have witnessed a significant proliferation in recent years. As origin can be reviewed by customs up to 5 years later, there is ongoing contingent liability for the exporter. This solution works relatively well for importers who are large multinational corporations, as these firms have the capacity to pursue enforcement of such contracts in the country of export. For smaller importers, this is more of a challenge, and as such not necessarily a complete solution.

Despite these ad hoc solutions by individual importers, the general result of the uncertainty generated by the variation in rules and administrative capacities is preference liability paranoia for firms and traders. This can be especially hard on the SMEs, for whom the capacity constraints are the most severe. What can be done?

A first step might be the adoption of the previously mentioned origin liability contract clauses in the model contracts of the International Chamber of Commerce. These model contracts are used widely in international trade transactions, and identification of best practices in assignation of origin-related liability and application of such best practices in these model contracts will not only help the contracting parties, but will also serve as an educational tool for courts that will eventually face such contract enforcement cases in the event of discrepancies.

A second idea would be to legally link origin certificates issued by exporters to export declarations for purposes of fraud liability. The goal of this approach is to create a legal mechanism under which exporters may be sanctioned for negligent or fraudulent certification of origin, as such a certificate would form part of a legal document in the exporting country, specifically the export declaration. Indeed, most of the relevant data for origin purposes should be present on the export declaration as well, and so these documents, taken together, would provide a legal foundation for holding exporters liable for erroneous origin certifications.

A number of further short-term and long-term measures merit consideration. First, developed countries should initiate origin administration standardization under the duty-free, quota free process for LDCs. This is a moral duty as much as a practical economic consideration. Furthermore, the volumes of trade that can be associated with the LDCs is sufficiently small, even with significant facilitation, so as to present marginal potential for politically difficult dislocation in domestic markets. Indeed, this may be the perfect context for a proof of concept in broad international coordination of administrative procedures, as the relatively small volume of trade in question lowers both the political and the economic costs of such an endeavor.

Additionally, both governments and private organizations should support e-origin solutions. These include stand-alone systems such as the Inter-American Development Bank's (IADB) Understanding and Using ROO system,[4] as well as the advance of e-commerce origin determination systems including supplier communications programs developed by private sector business software firms. To the degree that these technologies could be integrated into electronic single windows[5] and electronic origin certification systems, their utility would be even greater, especially for SMEs. On a related note, because certainty regarding the proper classification of both products and materials is vital to correct application of origin rules, Harmonized System artificial intelligence systems, wherein linguistic and taxonomy software facilitates identification of the correct tariff classification, should form part of this agenda.

Beyond Origin

Origin, from the private sector perspective, is essentially about supplier management. In order for a product to comply with origin requirements, suppliers must be located in eligible countries, and use materials sourced such that the components they produce count as originating materials when used in subsequent production for preferential markets. Strategically then, what firms need to look for are not just low cost suppliers, but low cost suppliers that are properly located and are origin literate, so that they can provide the necessary compliance information regarding the materials that they supply.

---

[4] www.origincaftaidb.org for the DR-CAFTA version. The IDB has also created modules for Peruvian and Colombian agreements, and is working to expand coverage further.

[5] "Electronic single windows" are essentially web sites that bring together all the information necessary for importers and exporters to comply with trade procedures, obtain certifications and licenses, and file documents, thus eliminating the need to visit multiple government offices for each purpose.

Multiplier Benefits of ROO

There is more to supplier management than just origin, and these other elements can be linked into origin management systems. For example, supplier credit risk was an important issue for firms during the 2008–2009 financial crisis. The sudden and unexpected implosion of a major supplier can have significant adverse effects on a business, so monitoring and ensuring the capacity of suppliers to maintain access to credit must be an element of the firm's strategy.

And there is more. The objective is ROO management, but in the end the method for accomplishing this is complete process- and input-visibility. The issue is fundamentally one of information, and once systems are put into place to manage this information, it becomes relatively straightforward to include additional elements in the dataset. This is important and useful for issues relating to supply chain security, consumer safety, and environmental protection.

The Province of Provenance

Many modern consumer protection and environmental regulations are requiring ever greater amounts of information regarding the place, method, and materials used in the production of goods. This "traceability," and the related supporting documentation, can pose a major challenge to international trade. SMEs will also have to confront these challenges, whether they are exporting directly, or are part of a larger supply chain for products that must demonstrate compliance with these standards. Firms will have to keep informed about the requirements which are constantly changing and evolving, and be able to demonstrate and certify compliance.

There are many examples of this. In the EU, the regulations for chemical products known as REACH (for Registration, Evaluation, and Authorization of Chemical products) came into force in 2006. This requires that all chemical products undergo extensive analysis before being authorized for sale in the European marketplace, with the burden of proof on the producer to show that the product does not pose a health or environmental hazard. These requirements apply not only to industrial chemicals, but to cosmetics, cleansers, and a large number of other consumer products. Having products tested by authorized laboratories and obtaining the required certifications in order to demonstrate REACH compliance can be a significant investment, and once made it is important that this information and certification be available, whether in connection with a final product or materials to be used as ingredients in other products.

Other examples include:

- Traceability of fish and fish products exported to the EU. Requirements have been put in place that will obligate importers to demonstrate that the method of fishing did not involve illegal harvests or otherwise present dangers to protected species. Maintaining documentation of the fishing process is no different, conceptually, from maintaining documentation of other production processes that are germane to origin compliance.
- Product standards (e.g., US wood and other consumer standards). In the US, important requirements have been legislated[6] for wood products in order to protect endangered timber species and biodiversity. Under this law, imported wood and wood products, such as furniture and paper, must declare the source of the wood used, and certify that it was harvested legally and is not an endangered species. This again is supply-chain management, and the identification of the source of materials, especially for wood products where the manufacturer is unlikely to be the harvester of the timber in question, is unlikely to have easy access to the necessary information. Including such information with origin compliance information makes sense.
- Country of origin markings and other MFN applications. Further product information that is origin-related, but distinct from origin, includes country of origin marking rules. These are the criteria that regulate the "Made in" tags and labels on products. Note that there is not a necessary relationship between preferential origin rules and the applicable marking rules. A good may comply with the ROO for a preferential agreement and enter duty free, but not be eligible to carry a "Made in" marking for the country that exported it. Conversely, a product may be marked "Made in" without meeting the origin criteria to qualify for the preferential tariff rate.
- Geographic designations of origin. These matter for products such as Tennessee whisky, Peruvian or Chilean Pisco, Mexican Tequila, Parma ham, and Champagne. To properly carry such designations, these goods must have been produced in their respective geographical areas. In case

---

[6] Legislation known as the Lacey Act.

of a verification or enforcement action, importers/distributors must be able to document and prove that this is the case.
- "Buy America" and "buy China" regimes. In the context of public procurement programs, there are often restrictions on the nationality of goods eligible for procurement. This is the case of the "buy America" restrictions on some elements of the 2009 federal stimulus package in the US, and similar programs around the world. These programs tend to specify their own criteria for what constitutes "national" products eligible for public procurement, but the evaluation and documentation procedures are substantially identical.

As a further illustration of the interrelation of these issues, it is interesting to note that, in the Vietnamese government, ROO administration and product quality and safety policy are managed by a single trade ministry department. While this might seem to be combining unrelated fields of expertise, in reality it is recognition of the fact these issues share a fundamental information management issue. In order to make claims in the international marketplace regarding quality or safety, exporters must be able to document their supply chains, identifying suppliers of key materials used.

This is no different from documenting compliance with ROO for preferential tariff treatment. As better systems and procedures are developed for management and presentation of origin-related information, it will only be sensible to include these other certifications and qualifications in the same systems. All will be necessary, and there are cost-savings to be had by streamlining the information management and communication procedures and technologies.

Conclusions and Recommendations: From "Ugly Duckling" to "Swiss Army Knife"

ROO are something of the "ugly duckling" of the international trading system. They tend to be technically complex, difficult for non-specialists to understand, and suspected (not always unfairly) of being a mechanism for maintaining protective measures in a hidden corner of RTAs. Origin compliance can be costly, and the complexity can serve as a disincentive for the development of sophisticated and efficient international supply chains.

But in the evolving international trading system, the traceability of goods and materials is becoming indispensable, not just for purposes of preferential origin, but for environmental protection, consumer safety, and security purposes as well. Indeed preferential origin may become incidental in the development of traceability systems, a by-product of tracking protocols developed for other purposes.

But that would seem to be putting the cart before the horse. Documentation and administration of preferential origin is an immediate concern, and systems are already in place or being developed that allow firms to manage origin, and the logical sequence would be to turn the ugly duckling into a management tool that incorporates more aspects of the traceability agenda, becoming the all-purpose "Swiss army knife" of international trade traceability.

Information management tools designed for tracking and analyzing suppliers, supply chains, and rules, can readily incorporate non-origin-specific information that must be maintained regarding these suppliers and supply chains for non-origin purposes, such as certification of wood products for export to the US, REACH certification for export to the EU, or carbon footprint in any future imposition of carbon taxes on international trade. The key is to recognize that traceability for these other purposes is an extension of the same origin-related information management challenges firms already face.

With this key similarity in mind, we identify three areas in which action is desired:

Extension of Cumulation: This involves permitting materials that qualify as originating in one country that benefits from preferences in a second country to be used in production of a subsequent good in a third country that benefits from the same preferences, with those materials being considered as originating in the third country. A first context in which this should be applied is in generalized system of preferences programs, allowing cumulation among beneficiaries and subsequently allowing cumulation across preference programs, both unilateral and reciprocal.

Reform of Origin Administration: Standardize origin administration and better defined origin liability. These two issues are related. First, firms need predictability and transparency in the administrative aspects of origin compliance and documentation. As discussed earlier, this allows for lower costs for firms, reducing the origin-related barriers to trade. Second, in cases where these administrative processes identify noncompliance, it is necessary to clearly and predictably assign liability for duties, as well as any penalties. If importers act in good faith on fraudulent origin information provided by exporters, they should not be liable for penalties. The absence of well-defined rights and responsibilities in claims of preferential market access lead to fears of onerous origin liability, and this uncertainty can serve as a disincentive to international trade and investment. Because importers and exporters generally reside in different international jurisdictions, coordination among governments, for the application of penalties for fraudulent claims by exporters as well as for the enforcement of contracts that do clearly define rights and obligations regarding ROO, is of vital necessity.

Embrace E-origin Traceability: Develop and promote integrated information systems. Because ROO, as well as the myriad environmental, security, and consumer safety certifications that have arisen in recent years, are all essentially information management issues involving the identification and tracing of materials and suppliers, the solution must lie in better integrated electronic information systems. While it is not necessarily the role of governments to develop such systems, governments, through customs administrations, should be prepared to encourage their development by others. This encouragement could take the form of a disposition to work with developers of systems in evaluating the sufficiency and reliability of information provided for purposes of compliance with customs requirements. Governments could even facilitate integration of private systems with public systems to allow the rapid transmission of information between them, thus giving greater certainty to international transactions and faster customs clearance times.

Trade facilitation as regards origin and other similar certifications of production processes is fundamentally an issue of information, and of defining which parties are responsible, and liable, for which elements of that information. The objective of policy makers and RTA administrators should be to develop and integrate systems for managing this information in a way that promotes efficient production, allowing sourcing of materials from the broadest possible set of suppliers at the least administrative cost, thus promoting the economic success of firms and the safety and satisfaction of global consumers.

References

Baldwin, R. 2006. Multilateralising Regionalism: Spaghetti Bowls as Building Blocs on the Path to Global Free Trade. Center for Economic Policy Research (CEPR) Discussion Paper 5775. Washington, DC: CEPR.

Cornejo, R., and J. Harris. 2007. Convergence in the Rules of Origin Spaghetti Bowl: A Methodological Proposal. IDB/Institute for the Integration of Latin America and the Caribbean (INTAL) Working Paper 34.

Estevadeordal, A., J.T. Harris, and K. Suominen. 2007. Harmonizing Preferential Origin Regimes around the World. In R. Baldwin and P. Low, eds. *Multilateralizing Regionalism: Challenges for the Global Trading System.* Cambridge: Cambridge University Press.

Harris, J.T. 2008. Rule of Origin for Development: From GSP to Global Free Trade. INT Working Paper 03. Washington, DC: IDB.

3

Accelerating Regional Integration: Issues at the Border

Douglas H. Brooks and Susan F. Stone

Introduction

While the impact of the global economic slowdown on trade was clear, its impact on progress in trade facilitation is less so. On the one hand, the decline in trade volume and value contributed to lower transportation costs and reduced waiting times at border crossings, lessening the pressure for improvements in facilitating trade flows. On the other, the urgency of boosting remaining trade flows to support recovery makes improvements in trade facilitation that much more pressing. The recent drop in world trade was tied to many problems, not the least of which has been access to trade financing. Thus, in times of economic distress, trade facilitation is more important than ever. Among the hardest hit by the slowdown were Asian small and medium-sized enterprises (SMEs) that export or are trying to gain initial access to international markets.

Trade facilitation holds great potential for helping Asia to increase trade and experience more of the benefits of globalization as the global economy recovers. Francois and Wignaraja (2008) show that linking the three largest East Asian economies of the People's Republic of China (PRC), Japan, and the Republic of Korea to the 10 nations of the Association of Southeast Asian Nations (ASEAN) in a free trade area will bring significant benefits to the participants, ranging from a 2.6% increase in national income to over 12%. Including the South Asian economies in a broader regional agreement increases these gains for both East Asia and South Asia. A pan-Asian regional agreement to link the different subregions is shown in the authors' analysis to cover enough countries and incorporate sufficient diversity in production and incomes to allow for regional gains (US$264 billion by 2017)[1] without substantive losses (about US$3 billion) to third parties. However, achieving the full potential of such an agreement would require considerable political will to avoid protectionist tendencies manifested through stringent rules of origin, nontariff barriers, and exclusionary lists of sensitive sectors. Thus while the potential is large, realizing it will necessitate substantial enhancement of trade facilitation to capitalize on potential complementarities. Barriers to trade go beyond tariffs to include factors like high freight costs, delays in customs clearance, unofficial payments, slow port landing and handling, and poor governance. Institutional bottlenecks (e.g., administrative, legal, financial, regulatory, and other logistics infrastructure), information asymmetries, and discretionary powers that give rise to rent seeking activities by government officials at various steps of trade transactions also impose costs. These costs can be lowered through cooperation that facilitates trade logistics for merchandise and services in both inbound and outbound shipments.

There is also room for domestic policy reform to achieve broader benefits (the equivalent of unilateral trade liberalization) in areas such as transparency, competition policy, harmonization, and standardization. An export processing zone or similar sort of industrial enclave—with good infrastructure and policy support for trade facilitation allowing profitability to determine industrial restructuring and the balance between agglomeration and dispersion influences—can make a significant difference in a country with otherwise poor infrastructure or cumbersome procedures.

Broadly defined, trade facilitation includes measures taken by both public and private sectors, including reductions in nontariff barriers and improvements in physical facilities, to smooth the movement of goods and services by reducing time or transaction costs in transit. Thus, trade facilitation may encompass both hard and soft infrastructure that facilitates trade. Measures to facilitate trade are likely to have the greatest positive effects in expanding trade from developing countries, where such measures may increase the trade impacts of lowering remaining border barriers by a factor of two or more (Hoekman and Nicita 2008).

Trade transaction costs (TTCs) may be categorized into directly incurred costs and indirect costs. Empirical estimates of TTCs vary substantially, but

---

[1] US$ = United States dollar.

direct and indirect costs have been shown to be between 1% and 15% of the value of traded goods (Walkenhorst and Yasui 2005). Direct costs (including customs fees, port charges, etc.) tend to be relatively clear to traders. Indirect costs, on the other hand, tend to be less clear and may affect traders in terms of the cost of carrying inventory and market depreciation (Minor and Tsigas 2008). In addition, the inconsistency and lack of transparency associated with indirect costs increase perceptions of risk and reduce firms' willingness to participate in these markets. Given these high risks and the information costs involved, it is the indirect costs that often act as a more significant barrier for SMEs to enter new markets.

TTCs vary by trader-type, sector, and economy. Economies with higher per capita incomes tend to have more efficient border processes, though this is not always the case. Conversely, there are instances where relatively poor economies provide a relatively high quality of border services (Walkenhorst and Yasui 2005). The characteristics of traders can also determine the extent of TTCs, with smaller firms tending to conduct fewer international transactions, leading to larger per unit costs. These cost disadvantages may include having a limited customs track record as well as relatively few specialized personnel to deal with trade formalities, and weaker financial reserves to cope with problems, including unforeseen stock delays (Walkenhorst and Yasui 2005).

Trade facilitation involves reducing trade costs, reducing risk or uncertainty in trade, or otherwise improving economic efficiency (perhaps through spillover effects). Trade costs can take the form of monetary costs (including the value of lost or deteriorated merchandise, and insuring against risk or uncertainties) or time costs. Trade costs play a central role in determining the amount of trade. A recent study (Jacks, Meissner, and Novy 2008) found that trade cost declines explain more than half of the (1870–1913) pre-World War I surge in trade and roughly a third of post-World War II trade growth, while a steep rise in trade costs explains the "entire" trade collapse in the interwar period.

Status of Asian Trade

Supported by improvements in trade facilitation, Asia's trade has soared over the past two decades, with the PRC in particular recording explosive growth. The PRC's exports grew at an average of over 20% a year between 1987 and 2007, while the other eight emerging economies among Asia's top 10 exporters

Table 3.1
Trade Growth in Asia's 10 Leading Exporters, 1987–2007

		Exports			Imports		
		US$ billion, 2000 constant prices		Average growth rate	US$ billion, 2000 constant prices		Average growth rate
		1987	2007	1987–2007	1987	2007	1987–2007
1	PRC	33.3	1,464	20.8	37.2	1,109.7	18.5
2	Japan	297.4	739.9	4.7	172.8	898.6	8.6
4	Hong Kong, China	40.9	420	12.3	41.7	429.6	12.4
3	Taipei,China[a]	83.3	361.1	10.3	79.9	262.3	8.3
5	Rep. of Korea[a]	51.6	289.5	10.1	27.9	421.6	16.3
6	Singapore	35.2	272.8	10.8	30.4	283.9	11.8
7	Malaysia	15.1	211.8	14.1	10.9	170.5	14.7
8	Thailand	9.8	184.6	15.8	11.2	166.9	14.5
9	India	10.2	175.4	15.3	14.8	253.8	15.3
10	Indonesia	14.5	137.2	11.9	10.6	86.4	11

PRC = People's Republic of China, US$ = United States dollar.
Source: United Nations COMTRADE database, available at: http://comtrade.un.org/db/.
Note: [a] First year data for Rep. of Korea from 1989, and for Taipei,China from 1992.

notched up export growth of over 10% a year (Table 3.1). The PRC's imports increased by over 18% a year, while seven of the other eight emerging economies in the table also recorded double-digit import growth rates. In just 20 years, India's trade expanded 17 times, while the PRC's increased over 30 times. The PRC has become the largest trader in Asia, far surpassing Japan.

Developing Asia now accounts for a much larger share of world trade, up from roughly 14% in 1990 to 24% in 2007. Asia's share of world trade has risen less significantly, from 22.7% to 29.2%, due to a drop in Japan's share of world trade (Table 3.2). Excluding Japan, East Asia's[2] share of world trade soared by 9.2 percentage points between 1990 and 2007, from 13.0% to 22.2%, with the PRC's share more than quadrupling from 1.9% to 8.8% so that non-Japan East Asia now accounts for the lion's share of Asia's trade. Intraregional trade within non-Japan East Asia grew faster (15.2% a year) than the region's external trade (10.6%).[3]

---

[2] East Asia here comprises 16 economies: Brunei Darussalam; Cambodia; PRC; Hong Kong, China; Indonesia; Republic of Korea; Lao People's Democratic Republic (Lao PDR); Malaysia; Mongolia; Myanmar; Philippines; Singapore; Taipei,China; Thailand; Viet Nam; plus Japan.

[3] Source: Calculated from United Nations Comtrade data (S2, items-total).

Table 3.2
Trade in Asian Subregions and Other World Regions, 1990–2007

	Total exports (US$ billion)					Share of world trade (%)					Share of intraregional exports in total (%)					Annual growth (%) 1990–2007
	1990	1995	2000	2005	2007	1990	1995	2000	2005	2007	1990	1995	2000	2005	2007	
East Asia (15)[a]	417.8	870.4	1,193.90	2,136.60	3,075.30	13	17.9	19.2	21.7	22.2	100	100	100	100	100	12.5
Intra-regional	136.1	344.7	456.4	901.7	1517.7	4.2	7.1	7.3	9.1	11	32.6	39.6	38.2	42.2	49.4	15.2
Extra-regional	281.7	525.7	737.5	1,234.90	1,557.60	8.7	10.8	11.8	12.5	11.3	67.4	60.4	61.8	57.8	50.6	10.6
East Asia (16)[b]	704.7	1313.3	1,673.10	2,731.50	3,789.50	21.9	27.1	26.8	27.7	27.4	100	100	100	100	100	10.4
Intra-regional	284	646.2	797.8	1,389.50	1,853.40	8.8	13.3	12.8	14.1	13.4	40.3	49.2	47.7	50.9	48.9	11.7
Extra-regional	420.7	667.1	875.3	1342	1,936.10	13	13.7	14	13.6	14	59.7	50.8	52.3	49.1	51.1	9.4
Central and West Asia (8)[c,1]	–	5.6	14.9	34.7	62.2	–	0.2	0.3	0.6	0.4	–	100	100	100	100	22.2
Intra-regional	–	1.87	1.2	2.92	3.93	–	0.1	0	0	0	–	33.4	8.1	8.4	6.3	6.4
Extra-regional	–	3.73	13.7	31.78	58.27	–	0.1	0.3	0.5	0.4	–	66.6	91.9	91.6	93.7	25.7
South Asia (7)[d]	27.2	43.7	60.7	125.8	194.4	0.8	0.9	1	1.3	1.4	100	100	100	100	100	12.3
Intra-regional	0.9	2.1	2.9	8.4	12.1	0	0	0	0.1	0.1	3.5	4.7	4.8	6.7	6.2	16.2
Extra-regional	26.3	41.6	57.8	117.4	182.3	0.8	0.9	0.9	1.2	1.3	96.5	95.3	95.2	93.3	93.8	12.1
EU (27)[e]	1,521.60	2,010.80	2,424.30	4,054.30	5,316.80	47.2	41.4	38.9	41.1	38.4	100	100	100	100	100	7.6
Intra-regional	1018.6	1,401.30	1,641.50	2,732.10	3,601.10	31.6	28.9	26.3	27.7	26	65.9	62.1	61.1	59.7	67.7	7.7
Extra-regional	503	609.5	782.8	1,322.20	1,715.70	15.6	12.6	12.6	13.4	12.4	34.1	37.9	38.9	40.3	32.3	7.5
NAFTA (3)[f]	546.1	853.6	1,223.60	1,478.70	1,834.60	16.9	17.6	19.6	15	13.3	100	100	100	100	100	7.4
Intra-regional	225.8	392.9	681.6	824.4	930.8	7	8.1	10.9	8.4	6.7	41.3	46	55.7	55.8	50.7	8.7

Extra-regional	320.4	460.7	542.1	654.3	903.8	9.9	9.5	8.7	6.6	6.5	58.7	54	44.3	44.2	49.3	6.3
MERCOSUR (5)[g]	64.6	89.1	122.5	219.4	324.3	2	1.8	2	2.2	2.3	100	100	100	100	100	10
Intra-regional	4.9	16.8	20	24.2	38.5	0.2	0.3	0.3	0.2	0.3	8.9	20.5	20.9	13.1	11.9	12.9
Extra-regional	59.7	72.3	102.5	195.2	285.8	1.9	1.5	1.6	2	2.1	91.1	79.5	79.1	86.9	88.1	9.6
WORLD EXPORTS	3224.8	4853.9	6233.1	9859	13830	100	100	100	100	100	–	–	–	–	–	8.9
MEMO ITEM																
Japan[h]	286.9	442.9	479.2	594.9	714.2	8.9	9.1	7.7	6	5.2	12.2	14.4	11.7	10.4	8.8	5
PRC[h]	62.1	148.8	249.2	762	1218.1	1.9	3.1	4	7.7	8.8	5.8	6.2	6.9	11	12.2	18.2
United States[h]	392.9	583	780.3	904.3	1162.2	12.2	12	12.5	9.2	8.4	14.8	13.1	11.4	7.7	7.1	5.7
EA (16) to PRC	34.4	110.1	151	383.1	509.8	1.1	2.3	2.4	3.9	3.7	12.1	17	18.9	27.6	27.5	17.2

Source: Calculated from United Nations COMTRADE database (S2, items-total), available at: http://comtrade.un.org/db/; and International Monetary Fund Direction of Trade Statistics 2008, available at http://www2.imfstatistics.org/DOT/.

Notes: [a] East Asia (15): Brunei Darussalam; Cambodia; People's Republic of China (PRC); Hong Kong, China; Indonesia; Republic of Korea; Lao People's Democratic Republic; Malaysia; Mongolia; Myanmar; Philippines; Singapore; Taipei,China; Thailand; Viet Nam.
[b] East Asia (16): East Asia (15) plus Japan.
[c] Central and West Asia (8): Armenia, Azerbaijan, Georgia, Kazakhstan, Kyrgyz Republic, Tajikistan, Turkmenistan, Uzbekistan.
[d] South Asia (7): Afghanistan, Bangladesh, India, Maldives, Nepal, Pakistan, Sri Lanka.
[e] EU (European Union) includes its 27 members: Austria, Belgium, Bulgaria, Cyprus, Czech Republic, Denmark, Estonia, Finland, France, Germany, Greece, Hungary, Ireland, Italy, Latvia, Lithuania, Luxembourg, Malta, Netherlands, Poland, Portugal, Romania, Slovakia, Slovenia, Spain, Sweden, and United Kingdom.
[f] NAFTA (North American Free Trade Agreement) includes its three members: Canada, Mexico, and United States.
[g] MERCOSUR (Mercado Comun del Sur) includes its four members and one prospective member: Argentina, Brazil, Paraguay, Uruguay, Venezuela.
[h] Japan, the PRC, and the United States share of intra-regional exports in total is only intra-regional exports (share of individual country's export to the region in total region exports).
[i] Annual growth of Central and West Asia is for 1995–2005.

East Asia's exports to the PRC now account for 3.7% of world exports. Whereas in 1990, the PRC accounted for 8.8% of East Asia exports, it accounted for over 32% in 2007. The rapid growth of intraregional trade in particular has benefited from trade facilitation while at the same time, spurring demand for greater trade facilitation efforts.

The economic crisis has reduced output and trade both globally and in developing Asia. While Asia's growth may not have been as severely affected as the world average, the impact on the region's trade has been more drastic (Figure 3.1). Note that the declines in exports in this slowdown (as in the 2001 recession) are much sharper than the concurrent output declines, reflecting a combination of income-elastic demand for imports, inventory effects, trade finance constraints, and increased production fragmentation leading to the multiple counting of value added in merchandise trade.

The Changing Nature of Asian Trade

As Asia's trade has grown rapidly, its nature is also changing—and with it the efficiency of international transactions. Asia's trade is becoming lighter, shifting from bulky goods toward lighter, often higher-value goods and weightless

Figure 3.1
Growth in Output and Trade

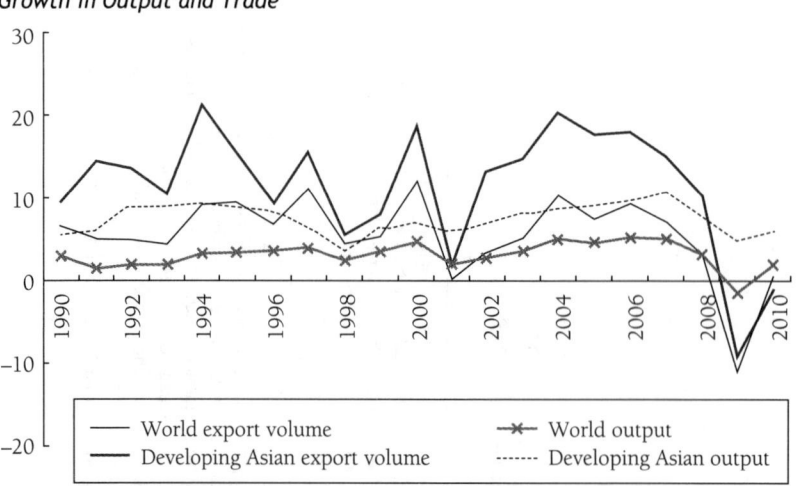

Source: International Monetary Fund, *World Economic Outlook* April 2009.
Note: 2008–2010 data are forecasts.

services. In particular, the information and communication technology (ICT) revolution has generated increased trade in ICT products and outsourced services, as well as greater migration of highly skilled professionals. More generally, the weight-to-value ratio of Asia's trade is declining (Hummels 2009). This has important implications for the choice of transport mode, the distance and destination of trade flows, the location and fragmentation of production processes, harmonization and standardization of customs classifications and inspections, and the demand for supporting infrastructure.

Changes in transport technology, notably improvements in air freight and containerization, have amplified these trends, particularly for time-sensitive goods. Standardized containers facilitate cost savings by allowing goods to be packed once and moved over long distances via a combination of transport modes—for example, truck, rail, ocean liner, rail, then truck again—without being unpacked, reinspected, and repacked. Air cargo shipments have grown rapidly and air cargo involving Asian countries has grown much faster than in the world as a whole, with international flights within Asia experiencing particularly rapid growth. Multimodal shipping and improvements in logistics services have made it possible to trade with more destinations in less time and often at lower cost (Brooks and Hummels 2009). When trade facilitation lowers the marginal cost of trade, exports tend to expand in two ways: new products are exported to new destinations, typically through small shipments from small firms, and existing trade flows deepen.

As these trade patterns have evolved, production networks have fragmented internationally and much of the growth of Asia's trade has been in parts and components for these fragmented global value chains. This trend (particularly in electronics and auto parts sectors) has been an important avenue for Asia's SMEs to benefit from globalization. For all East Asian countries, the share of components in exports and imports within the region has increased much faster than in trade with the rest of the world (Athukorala 2008). In 2005–2006, exports within the region accounted for 60% of total component exports; for component imports, the share was even higher. The increase in component intensity has been particularly noticeable in Southeast Asia's trade with the other developing East Asian economies, most notably the PRC. The Republic of Korea and Taipei,China are also involved in substantial component trade with other economies in the region.

The combination of increased trade in parts and components within Asia and greater long-distance air shipments is generating many more (mostly small) new shipments, which benefits SMEs, while the biggest existing shipments are getting even larger. Thus, in the case of the PRC's exports, the mean shipment is getting bigger, while the median is falling. The pattern in other Asian countries is similar (in some cases, both mean and median are falling, but medians are falling faster) (Hummels 2009).

The diversity of Asian economies, combined with lowering of trade costs, has helped the region to capitalize on global patterns of production fragmentation, expanding intra-regional trade, and expansion of development opportunities. The impacts of new investments in trade-related infrastructure are now being leveraged by coordination across borders in a wide variety of trade facilitating institutional architectures and trade agreements. In this evolving international context, the role of harmonizing and strengthening soft infrastructure stands out as an essential complement for enhanced physical infrastructure. Supported by a conducive policy environment and internalizing regional spillover effects through cooperative arrangements, trade facilitation is reducing trade costs and facilitating trade expansion, regional integration, and economic growth and development.

Wilson, Mann, and Otsuki (2003) found that enhanced port efficiency or reduced regulatory barriers have large and positive effects on trade, and improvements in customs and greater electronic business usage also significantly expands trade, but less than port or regulatory reform. They found that intra-APEC (Asia-Pacific Economic Cooperation) trade could increase by US$254 billion (about 21%) if those APEC members below average in these areas improve their capacity just halfway to the average.

Empirical evidence based on disaggregated trade flows by Martinez–Zarzoso and Marquez–Ramos (2008) indicates that lowering the number of days and documents required to conduct trade increases trade flows to a higher extent in trade of differentiated goods, and that improvements in service infrastructure foster international trade in all sectors. The authors found that, on average, a decrease of US$1 in the cost to export one TEU[4] yields an increase in exports of almost US$11,000 and a one-day reduction in the average number of days required to export a good yields an increase in exports of 0.22%. The facilitating effect on trade flows of a reduction in both the number of days and documents required differs between exports and imports, and across sectors and countries, suggesting that priorities in trade facilitation policy recommendations should take account of different countries' individual industrial and trade structures.

---

[4] TEU stands for twenty-foot equivalent unit, a standard measure of shipping container size.

Improving Access

Congestion has been a growing problem, counteracting advances in trade facilitation. In the case of the PRC, Ma and Zhang (2009) found that in Shanghai, inefficiencies from overloading the physical infrastructure are compounded by a lack of collaboration among stakeholders. Trade facilitation and administrative procedures at customs are unreliable, and the customs transit system needs to be rationalized in order to reduce inspection times and simplify declarations and the documentation process. Shanghai's congestion is reducing its competitiveness in the region, thus endangering its status as a hub and gateway to international markets and suppliers. In recent years, the number of transshipped containers from Shanghai via Hong Kong, China, has accounted for as much as 20% of Shanghai's total container throughput. On the other hand, Suzhou Park in the PRC includes free-trade zones with streamlined customs procedures and dedicated transport routes to ports, and has thereby reduced both costs and waiting times (Hausman, Lee, and Subramanian 2005).

In the case of Indonesia, Patunru, Nurridzki, and Rivayani (2009) found that soft infrastructure plays a vital role in constraining port efficiency, more so than hard infrastructure, although the two are interlinked. Sea port competitiveness may suffer from poor physical infrastructure such as inadequate channel depth, shortage of berths, and limited cargo handling equipment, and storage and transit areas, but it may also suffer from limitations in soft infrastructure, such as labor skills, regulation, bureaucracy, and other institutional factors affecting port capacity utilization. Lack of direct competition between ports controlled by the same government authority is also a critical factor. Yet port performance is crucial to the Indonesian archipelago.[5] Increasing port efficiency enables countries to reap large economies of scale, reducing the average time shipments spend at sea and in ports. Shipping also tends to become more frequent, facilitating timely delivery. In addition, a densely traded route enables an effective use of hub and spoke arrangements, in which small container vessels feed shipments into a hub where containers are aggregated into much larger and faster container ships for longer hauls.

---

[5] In the Indonesian archipelago, where around 90% of external trade (and much of domestic trade) passes through ports, exporters seeking to distribute raw materials tend to follow the "trade follows the ships" principle: they are attracted to ports with shipping routes that best reach the desired markets (Patunru, Nurridzki, and Rivayani 2009). Regions where service-sector exports are more important tend to follow the "ships follow the trade" principle, whereby ships are routed to serve the desired regions.

Indeed, a recent study found that given transport costs constitute roughly 20% ad valorem tax-equivalent on import prices in East Asia, a 10% increase in port capacity has the effect of a 0.3% to 0.5% across the board tariff cut (Abe and Wilson 2009).

Trade growth along a particular shipping route also encourages entry—and where permitted, new competition tends to drive down shipping margins, particularly when complemented by an effective competition policy that constrains monopoly power and removes barriers to entry (Brooks 2005). Hummels, Lugovsky, and Skiba (2007) found that ocean liners charge much higher freight rates for goods whose import demand is relatively inelastic, indicating that shipping firms are most likely exercising market power. In 2006, one in six importer–exporter pairs was served by a single liner service; over half were served by three or fewer.

To raise competitiveness and efficiency, ICT is an increasingly productive complement to physical infrastructure. ICT helps to reduce the costs of finding suppliers, agreeing on contracts, monitoring their implementation, and tracking the location and status of shipments. Fink, Matoo, and Neagu (2002) found that higher telecommunications costs dampen bilateral trade flows, especially for differentiated (rather than homogeneous) products. In particular, as smaller shipments of a wider variety of higher value-added products proliferate, the demand for ICT services rises. The same is true as the growth of trade in services outpaces that in manufactures. Trade in services such as banking and business services, or communications, are highly dependent on well-developed ICT infrastructure in both exporting and importing countries. While the private sector is especially adept in the ICT sector, the need for mutually interfacing logistics services at both ends of a trade route is an area where regional cooperation could help users to share information, learn from best practices, and coordinate capacity building to enhance trade.

To ensure that some areas are not left behind, improved trade facilitation is vital for connecting remote areas and landlocked countries with regional and global markets. Asia's 12 landlocked countries[6]—Afghanistan, Armenia, Azerbaijan, Bhutan, Kazakhstan, Kyrgyz Republic, Lao People's Democratic Republic (Lao PDR), Mongolia, Nepal, Tajikistan, Turkmenistan, and Uzbekistan—are especially disadvantaged. Most are 700–1,000 km from the nearest port; 4 (Kazakhstan, Kyrgyz Republic, Tajikistan, and Uzbekistan) are over 3,000 km from the sea (UNESCAP 2006). These countries strug-

---

[6] Landlocked countries are those that do not have access to an open sea. Some landlocked countries, such as Azerbaijan, Kazakhstan, or Turkmenistan, have access to an inland sea, such as the Caspian.

gle with poor physical infrastructure, small domestic markets that are remote from world markets, and a high vulnerability to external shocks. Unless transported by air at high cost, traded goods from these countries must transit through at least one neighboring state. The impact of customs and transport inefficiencies hamper access to global markets, deter foreign direct investment (FDI), and raise the cost of imports, compounding components of trade cost margins severely for these economies.[7]

In smaller and less-developed economies, such as Cambodia, Lao PDR, Mongolia, and Viet Nam, border procedures are often cumbersome and time consuming. Inland transport is particularly slow and expensive in South Asia where, unsurprisingly, intra-regional trade is low. These costs account for around 88% of total trade transport costs in the subregion (De 2009). Land border crossings are overcrowded and complex requirements expand possibilities for corruption and encourage informal trade. Greater policy attention to efficiency concerns could easily reduce delays and monetary costs. There is therefore a strong case for subregional cooperation to facilitate trade so as to raise exporters' competitiveness in this subregion.

At the international level, cooperation through preferential trade and investment agreements that strengthen structural reforms and increase the attractiveness of a location for foreign investment can leverage domestic policy actions and their impacts on growth, equity, and efficiency, and may help to reduce corruption. Cross-border cooperation in building and maintaining soft infrastructure can therefore lead synergistically to a reduction in trade costs and stimulate further investment in physical infrastructure, trade, production and employment, and growth, facilitating further trade expansion.

While regional integration can help less developed countries and regions to access new markets, suppliers, technologies, and opportunities, and can help to internalize negative spillover effects and capitalize on economies of scale, progress has not been even across subregions. East and Southeast Asia are generally ahead of other Asian subregions in terms of trade and regional integration. It is no coincidence that trade-related infrastructure services are

---

[7] United Nations Conference on Trade and Development (UNCTAD) (2008) suggests that a multidimensional approach is needed to tackle these problems. This involves developing adequate national transport networks and efficient transit systems, promoting regional or subregional economic integration, and encouraging FDI in economic activities that are not distance-sensitive. For example, in 1995, the United Nations General Assembly endorsed the Global Framework for Transit Transport Cooperation between Land-locked and Transit Developing Countries and the Donor Community with a view to enhancing transit systems and enabling Landlocked and Developing Countries to reduce their marginalization from world markets.

generally more available and of higher quality in East and Southeast Asia. In South Asia infrastructure performance and logistics services are lower, and so is intra-regional and interregional trade. Pacific island countries face particular trade challenges for integration, since shipping distances are large and shipments are generally small and of relatively low value added, raising the ad valorem shipping margins. In Central Asia, the transition to independence was accompanied by a need to reorient trade flows to new destinations and originating from new sources, while fiscal difficulties severely limited expenditures for infrastructure maintenance, operation, and expansion.

Trade Facilitation, Soft Infrastructure, and Logistics

The importance of high-quality logistics varies by commodity depending on three factors (Arnold 2009). First is the value of the commodity per shipment unit, for example, per metric ton or TEU. Second is the shelf life of the commodity, reflecting physical deterioration or volatility of demand. The third factor is importers' scheduling requirements; timeliness is particularly important to just-in-time manufacturers—in sectors such as fashion clothing or auto parts—and retailers with coordinated national sales programs. Given its diversity, Asian trade is affected by each of these factors, particularly the supply chain implications. And increasingly, logistics concerns related to higher value-added products are raised.

In addition to the commodity-based aspects of trade facilitation, other forms of soft infrastructure influence international trade. These include availability of adequate credit and foreign exchange at reasonable rates, a reliable system of legal recourse, effective competition policy, and the capacity of existing human capital to process exchanges. Indeed, soft infrastructure may often be more important than physical infrastructure for increasing trade and its profitability.

Inefficient or burdensome institutional structures, bureaucracy and policy may lead to reduced or foregone gains from international trade. During 2006–2007, most developing Asian countries were actively reforming their trade policies, with India being a top reformer. On average, producers in the region require about one month to export whereas exporting takes only 10 days for their Organisation for Economic Co-operation and Development (OECD) counterparts. By subregion, Central and West Asia is still costlier than the rest of Asia (Table 3.3) although some countries such as Armenia are continuously

Table 3.3
Costs of Exporting, by Region, 2006–2007

Region	Documents for export (number)	Time for export (days)	Cost to export (US$ per container)
Developing Asia and the Pacific	8	33	1,202
East Asia (16)[b]	7	23	789
East Asia (15)[a]	7	24	773
Central and West (8)[c]	9	59	2,252
The Pacific	7	25	1,018
South Asia (7)[d]	9	33	1,180
Other developing	7	28	1,325
OECD[e]	5	10	908
World[f]	7	27	1,239

OECD = Organisation for Economic Co-operation and Development, US$ = United States dollar.
Source: World Bank Doing Business Database. http://www.doingbusiness.org (accessed 10 July 2008).
Notes: [a] East Asia (15): Brunei Darussalam; Cambodia; People's Republic of China; Hong Kong, China; Indonesia; Republic of Korea; Lao People's Democratic Republic; Malaysia; Mongolia; Myanmar; Philippines; Singapore; Taipei,China; Thailand; Viet Nam.
[b] East Asia (16): East Asia (15) plus Japan.
[c] Central and West Asia (8): Armenia, Azerbaijan, Georgia, Kazakhstan, Kyrgyz Republic, Tajikistan, Turkmenistan, Uzbekistan.
[d] South Asia (7): Afghanistan, Bangladesh, India, Maldives, Nepal, Pakistan, Sri Lanka.
[e] Czech Republic, Hungary, Mexico, Poland, Slovak Republic, Turkey, and Republic of Korea are not included in OECD average as they are grouped into developing countries. Other 23 OECD economies are included.
[f] The world aggregates were estimated based available data from 179 countries.

reforming to make trading across borders easier. The pattern is similar for importing, with time and cost to import being slightly higher than exporting in the region.

Exploiting complementarity of hard and soft infrastructure raises overall trade and economic performance. This is especially noticeable in the case of networks. Many communication and infrastructure services that are important for economic development and trade expansion exhibit network externalities. Infrastructure networks exhibiting service externalities include telephones, railways, and water supply systems. In the presence of such externalities, the maximum amount that consumers are willing to pay for a good or service depends in part on the number of other consumers who also purchase the item in question. This interrelationship calls for consideration of these network systems' governance in competition policy.

Logistics services are a vital component of Asia's global competitiveness. Supply chains that span the region rely on them, and the location of FDI within the region is shaped by them. Improvements in trade facilitation from raising infrastructure service efficiency can lead to cost savings equivalent to moving production to locations thousands of kilometers closer to trading partners. Economies such as the PRC; Hong Kong, China; Republic of Korea; Malaysia; Singapore; Taipei,China; and Thailand have so far built well-developed logistics systems to facilitate international trade.

An international comparison of logistics performance finds that East Asia performs relatively well compared with other developing regions, notably South Asia, but still lags well behind high-income countries (Figure 3.2).

The challenges of providing efficient logistical support rise as countries move into progressively more complex and higher value manufacturing, and as production processes become increasingly fragmented. Already, there is a premium on timeliness and reliability of delivery, care and security in handling and transporting, and certification and standardization of product quality. Delays have particularly adverse impacts on time-sensitive goods. Goods that are perishable, such as cut flowers and some food products, deteriorate rapidly and tend to face relatively high costs from delays. Fashion and high-technology items may also be vulnerable, with delays also tending to be particularly costly

Figure 3.2
International Logistics Performance Index (LPI)

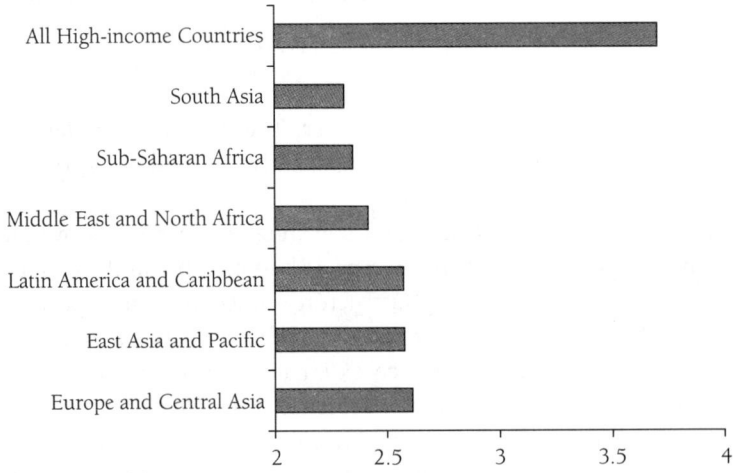

Source: Arvis et al. (2007).
Note: International LPI mainly reflects infrastructure, customs, international shipments, logistics competence, tracking and tracing, domestic logistics costs, timeliness, etc.

for these products (Minor and Tsigas 2008). Furthermore, delays in transit times abroad may have particularly adverse impacts on landlocked countries (Djankov, Freund, and Pham 2008), such as Lao PDR. Both the quantity and quality of logistics services in cross-border trade create competitiveness and value addition. Fortunately, competition among private sector providers of logistics services is continually stimulating efficiency improvements.

Trade Facilitation and Location of Foreign Direct Investment

Amiti and Javorcik (2008) found that access to markets and access to suppliers are the most important factors affecting entry decisions by foreign investors. The influence of market and supplier access on FDI location decisions was four times greater than that of production costs. Trade, investment, and production patterns in production chains are also partly determined by agglomeration and dispersion effects across countries and commodities. Kimura, Takahashi, and Hayakawa (2007) found that geographical distance reduces trade in machinery parts and components much less in East Asia than in Europe. This implies that the service link costs associated with international production fragmentation are substantially lower in East Asia than in Europe, contributing to large differences in the development of international production and distribution networks.

Trade facilitation has an indirect impact on FDI inflows by lowering the cost of spreading production across several countries in order to take advantage of their comparative advantages. Increased FDI, in turn, can further boost regional trade, adding to the direct effect of improvements in trade facilitation across borders. If the advantages of scattering production across economies in a region outweigh those from concentrating it together, trade facilitation makes FDI complementary to trade. For instance, in Southeast Asia's electronics industry, where components are generally small and light (relative to value added) with relatively lower transport costs, cross-border production networks proliferated in the 1990s. This can create a virtuous cycle of trade facilitation, trade, and investment that fosters increased trade and economic growth.

To compete for larger shares of regional supply chains, countries have striven to improve their trade services. In Malaysia, for instance, the government actively promoted infrastructure development in order to strengthen its competitive and comparative advantage. Beginning in the mid-1980s,

Malaysia pursued an FDI-led, export-oriented development strategy, with FDI contributing to the economy's integration in global production networks. Malaysia enhanced its geographical attractiveness to foreign firms as a key link in global supply chains through infrastructure development and the resulting high-quality production and trade services.

Empirical Analysis

The above discussion outlines the necessity of investing in regional infrastructure projects and the importance of trade facilitation in growth. Along with the physical structures that are needed to improve the flow of goods, services, and workers, there is a substantial need for investment in administrative procedures including regulation, customs processes, and practices to facilitate the growth and expansion of regional business opportunities. Given that these costs tend to be a higher percentage of operating costs for SMEs, the investment in trade facilitation is even more important in support of the growth in these enterprises.

Figure 3.3 presents a comparison of competitive measures in trade facilitation across a sample of 134 major and emerging economies (Total), for Asia as a whole (Asia) and finally for APEC Asia.[8] The average rankings are shown for overall infrastructure as well as individual modes of roads, rail, ports, and air facilities. Finally, three measures of administrative costs are given covering the burden of customs procedures (customs), the transparency of government regulation (transp), and the burden of government regulation (regul). As seen in Panel A, APEC Asia performs, on average, better than both the world sample and overall Asia. This superior performance is consistent across all measures and is, in large part, due to the consistently top performance of Singapore and Hong Kong, China.

However, if we look at Panel B, we see that the performance across all of APEC Asia is far from consistent. While in most instances (the exception being regulation), performance is less varied than for Asia as a whole, it is often more disparate than for the entire sample. This is observed for all measures of administrative facilitation, and, as already noted, APEC Asia has the most inconsistent government regulation performance. Thus, while on

---

[8] We define APEC Asia as including Singapore; Malaysia; Indonesia; Hong Kong, China; Taipei,China; Japan; Republic of Korea; Philippines; PRC; Thailand; and Viet Nam.

Figure 3.3
Ranking for Trade Facilitation Measures

Panel A—Average

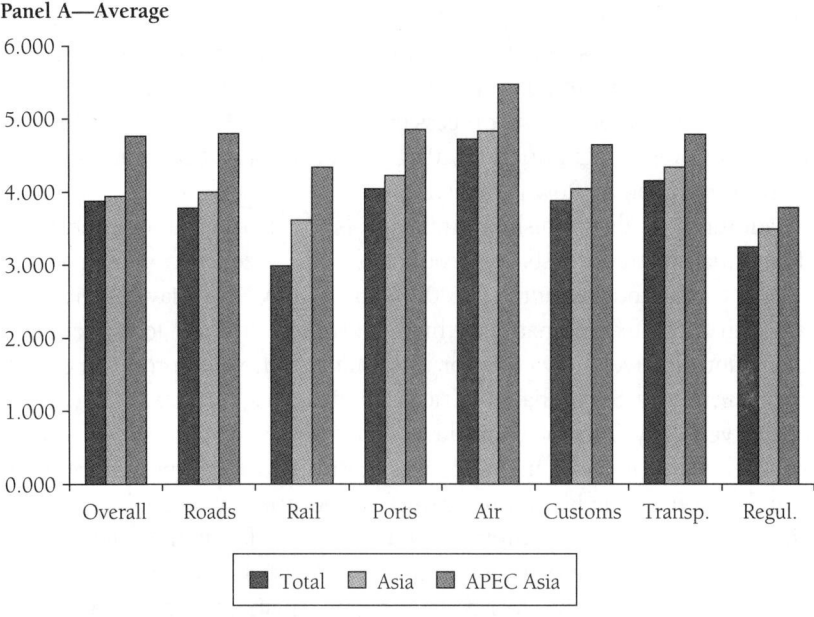

Panel B—Standard Deviation

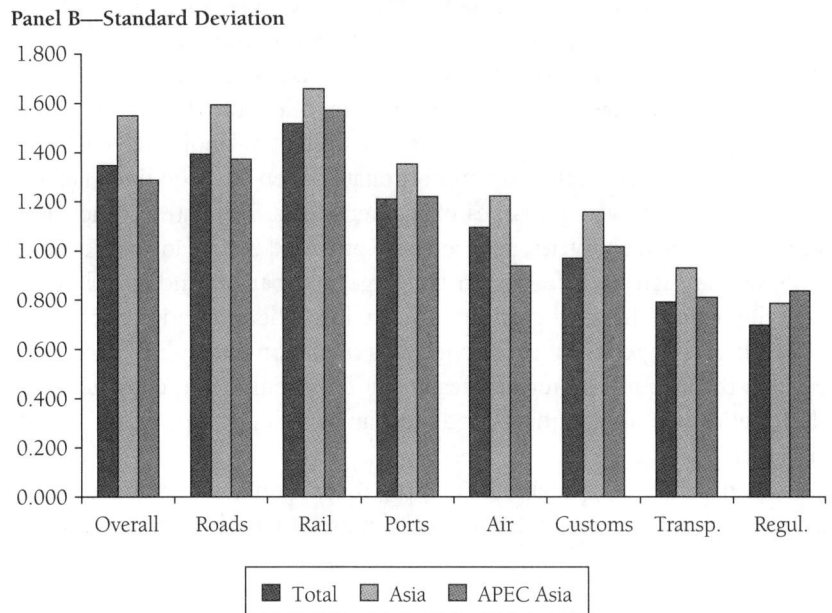

Source: World Economic Forum (2008).

average APEC Asia performs well, it appears there are rather substantial gaps in performance across the region.

To examine trade facilitation at the border, we focus here on how individual pairs of countries interact.[9] The measures presented support what has been suggested by the graphs presented in Figure 3.3; depending on which two countries are involved, the process could be very advanced and efficient, or extremely slow. Thus important insights can be gained by examining the issue from this bilateral flow perspective.

In addition to distinguishing trade costs by partner, the importance of differentiating trade costs by product has also been highlighted in the literature. Christ and Ferrantino (2009) showed how this plays out in Sub-Saharan Africa. The combination of high land transport costs for agricultural products and relatively low costs for metals and high-value products diminishes the ability of Sub-Saharan African countries to participate in exports involving vertically integrated products. They show the diversity of factors influencing transport costs, including weak infrastructure, imperfect information, and of course, the landlocked nature of countries involved.

There is no shortage of empirical work on trade facilitation. The World Bank has been particularly prolific on this subject. If one puts the words "trade facilitation" into the World Bank search engine, it yields over 1,700 citations. The methods most commonly applied are some form of the gravity model and, more recently, a computable general equilibrium (CGE) approach. Francois and Wignaraja (2008) provide a list of CGE papers that measure the impact of free trade agreements (FTAs) in Asia, a few of which apply some sort of trade facilitation scenario. The particular plight of landlocked countries has been of interest given their disproportionate dependence on trade facilitation as well as more general issues of market access. Estimates of increased costs for landlocked countries, such as those provided by Limão and Venables (2001), are as high as 70%. Given the large number of landlocked countries in the region, this is of great importance for trade promotion in Asia. As stated earlier, the growth of production fragmentation and subsequent trade expansion throughout the region means that cooperation and consistency in trade facilities among countries needs to remain a high priority for growth achievement.

As stated earlier, this chapter attempts to expand the existing body of empirical research by examining the role trade cost reductions can play in

---

[9] In all but a few instances, border facilitation involves two countries.

Table 3.4
Commodity Aggregation

Sector modeled	Detailed description
Rice	Paddy and processed rice
Veg/Fruit	Vegetables and fruit
OthCrops	Other crops
Animals	Live animals
Animal Prods	Animal products
Other Foods	Other processed foods
Forestry	Forestry
Fishery	Fisheries
Other Minerals	Coal and other minerals
Textiles	Textiles
Apparel	Wearing apparel
Leather	Leather products
Wood/Paper	Wood and paper products
Electronics	Electronic equipment & machinery
Other Manfcs	Other manufactures
Vehicles	Transportation vehicles

bilateral relationships by sector. We used version 7 of the global trade analysis project (GTAP) database,[10] covering 113 countries or regions and 57 sectors, with a base year of 2004. The GTAP 7 database was aggregated to cover 15 countries and regions, including all APEC Asia countries. The 57 sectors were aggregated to maintain coverage of sectors of key importance to the region, as shown in Table 3.4.

We applied a fairly straightforward experiment on enhancing regional trade facilitation within APEC Asia. We kept the experiment simple in order to examine the details of the outcome at the sectoral and bilateral trade levels. The estimates of trade costs by sector are based on Strutt, Stone, and Minor (2008) and include customs delays, document processing, administration procedures, etc., to determine time costs for trade. Table 3.5 shows the estimates for the time costs of exports from APEC Asia for selected sectors.

In order to determine the impact of these time costs on economic performance, we converted these estimates to tariff equivalents. We assumed that

---

[10] Released August 2008 (see https://www.gtap.agecon.purdue.edu/databases/v7/default.asp). See also Hertel (1997) for a complete description of the GTAP model.

the ad valorem equivalent tariff for time delays in exporting or importing is equal to the per day value (Hummels, Lugovsky, and Skiba 2007), combined with the average time delay for that country (World Bank 2008). The original time costs were applied to a subset of sectors and countries of interest in this chapter.[11] What is most apparent in Table 3.5 is the variation in costs across both sectors and economies.

For example, the costs of transporting fruits and vegetables are high across all economies examined but are even more so for countries in Southeast Asia. This observation is consistent with the literature as noted above. Again, as described above, differences across countries based on products and level of development are observed. For example, the time costs of trade for fruits and vegetables in Viet Nam are more than three times those in Singapore. On the other hand, the costs of forestry products in Indonesia are less than half of those in Singapore. It is clear from Table 3.5 that the impacts of improved trade facilitation will vary a great deal, depending on the sector and economy involved.

We have based our estimated reductions in trade costs on several recent studies of transport enhancements in the Asia and Pacific region (see Stone and Strutt 2009 for a review of these studies.) These studies examined the potential impact of reforms (either in process or already underway) in trade facilitation. For example, full implementation of the Cross Border Transport Agreement in the Greater Mekong Subregion is expected to reduce trade costs by as much as 45% (Banomyong 2008). From this review, we have applied a 25% reduction in the cost of transport across the APEC Asian region. We believe that this gives a reasonable estimate of the types of cost reductions that can be achieved through enhanced trade facilitation in the APEC Asian region.

Results

Table 3.6 presents the macro level results of lowering trade costs within the APEC Asian region by 25%. As expected, GDP expands across the region, as does welfare. Increases in welfare, as measured by equivalent variation income (Hertel 1997), range from US$1.25 billion in the Philippines to US$12.4 billion in the PRC. The PRC gains the most in absolute terms, given

---

[11] The trade cost values determined in Strutt, Stone, and Minor (2008) were mapped to the regional breakdown examined in this chapter. Details of the mapping are available from the authors upon request.

Table 3.5
Time Costs of Exports in APEC Asia

	Singapore	Malaysia	Thailand	Viet Nam	Indonesia	PRC	Japan	Rep. of Korea	HKT	Philippines
Rice	4.3	7.3	7.8	11.6	7.3	6.8	6.8	6.8	8.6	7.3
Veg/Fruit	54.2	180.7	166.6	197.6	180.7	59	88.1	88.1	108.5	180.7
Other Crops	15.5	32.9	3.3	16.1	32.9	14.8	15.7	15.7	31	32.9
Animals	49.7	96.6	47.5	99.7	96.6	74.8	49.6	49.6	99.4	96.6
Animal Prods	5.6	11.3	9.5	24.9	11.3	13.4	13.3	13.3	11.1	11.3
Other Food	88.7	74.2	135.7	119.2	74.2	122.8	141.2	141.2	177.3	74.2
Forestry	14	6.3	53.3	15	6.3	31.8	33.8	33.8	28	6.3
Fisheries	20.4	44.2	23.5	52.5	44.2	80.5	78.6	78.6	40.8	44.2
Other Minerals	47.2	6.7	47.7	51.7	6.7	22.1	37.3	37.3	94.5	6.7
Textiles	66.2	85	107.7	106.4	85	79.9	135.7	135.7	132.4	85
Apparel	66.8	103.9	107.3	163.8	103.9	98.3	107	107	133.6	103.9
Leather	39.6	54.2	54.8	90	54.2	54.9	58.8	58.8	79.2	54.2
Wood/Paper	78.9	128.8	157.1	118.2	128.8	90.7	229.3	229.3	157.7	128.8
Electronic	44.3	77.5	91.4	147.8	77.5	89.5	99.1	99.1	88.6	77.5
Other Manfcs	105.7	138.5	174.7	220.8	138.5	132.5	158.4	158.4	211.5	138.5
Vehicles	85	125	154.5	300.6	125	153	173.9	173.9	169.9	125

HKT = Hong Kong, China and Taipei,China; PRC = People's Republic of China.
Source: Initial estimates taken from Strutt, Stone, and Minor (2008) and recalculated for the regional aggregation shown.

Table 3.6
Impacts of Trade Cost Reduction of 25%

	Change in GDP (US$ million)	Change in GDP (%)	Change in welfare (US$ million)	Change in exports (US$ million)	Change in exports (%)
Singapore	1,301	1.22	1,988	1,388	0.83
Malaysia	2,137	1.86	2,643	1,543	1.00
Thailand	1,629	1.01	3,023	–4,086	–3.37
Viet Nam	1,409	3.27	1,558	–247	–0.76
Indonesia	1,744	0.68	1,889	1,323	1.51
PRC	13,355	0.80	12,394	15,673	2.26
Japan	4,767	0.10	7,374	5,946	0.91
Rep. of Korea	2,652	0.39	4,563	3,421	1.11
HKT	2,951	0.63	3,980	3,243	0.91
Philippines	1,038	1.23	1,249	–134	–0.26

GDP = gross domestic product; HKT = Hong Kong, China and Taipei,China; PRC = People's Republic of China.
Source: Authors' estimates.

the initial size of current trade activity. However, as a percentage of GDP, the biggest winner is Viet Nam. Given that Viet Nam's time costs were consistently among the highest (Table 3.6) it has much to gain from their reduction. Other economies such as Malaysia and the Philippines also experience significant gains.

In terms of welfare gains, incomes across developed APEC Asia (i.e., Japan; Republic of Korea; Hong Kong, China; and Taipei,China) record strong increases, although again the larger dollar values reflect the relatively larger starting points for these economies. Among the developing region, Malaysia and Thailand show substantial welfare gains. The pattern of gains reflects the relative size of trade costs for each economy, but also depends on sectors traded and relevant trade partners. So those economies within APEC Asia with predominantly intra-regional trade flows and high trade cost sectors will gain the most from the reductions applied.

For the majority of economies examined, exports expand, the notable exception being Thailand, and to a lesser extent, Viet Nam and the Philippines. In percentage terms, Thailand's exports decline the most. The details of these changes will be explored below when we examine changes in bilateral trade movements.

Trade Impacts

Examining the change in exports by sector, a general pattern of increases in manufactures and processed goods accompanied by a general trend of decreases in primary goods or more traditional exports, is apparent (Figure 3.4). For example, Viet Nam and Thailand show significant decreases in animal product exports while Viet Nam's exports of electronics increases strongly and Thailand expands its export of vehicles. This pattern of reductions in trade costs leading to new patterns of export growth is consistent with results reported elsewhere. Dennis and Shepherd (2007) suggest that improvements in trade facilitation often lead to a diversification in a country's export base. Indeed, Strutt, Stone, and Minor (2008) found evidence of this effect in the Greater Mekong Subregion. Conversely, in the case of Sub-Saharan Africa, long delays in exporting result in decreased exports of higher value-added manufactures and increased dependence on basic commodities (Minor and Tsigas 2008).

We now turn to an analysis of bilateral trade patterns. Table 3.7 presents three panels identifying the resulting changes in the bilateral exports of three representative sectors. The columns indicate the exporter and the rows show the destination. First is the fruit and vegetable sector. In addition to being an important traded sector for many economies in the region, this sector has high time costs and thus benefits relatively more when these costs are reduced. The second sector represents a traditional manufacturing sector: textiles. Most of the economies in APEC Asia have significant levels of trade in textiles: it thus represents an important sector in their economies. Finally, we examine changes in exports for the electronics sector. This is an important sector in high income economies in the region and a potential growth area for others.

The pattern for fruits and vegetables shows an almost universal regional expansion at the expense of those countries outside APEC Asia. Singapore increases the fruits and vegetables exported to the close economies of Malaysia and Indonesia. Those countries with the highest trade costs—Viet Nam, Indonesia, Malaysia, and Philippines—experience the greatest expansion, especially to the high income economies of the Republic of Korea and Japan, and the fast growing PRC. Japan and the Republic of Korea show significant increases in their exports as well, but these are from a relatively low base. The same pattern is observed in textiles with developing APEC Asia economies increasing their exports of textiles to high-income Asia across the board, with the notable exception of Thailand. Thailand loses market share across all markets, both those within the region and those outside. It is this loss in market share that

Figure 3.4
Changes in Exports by Sector

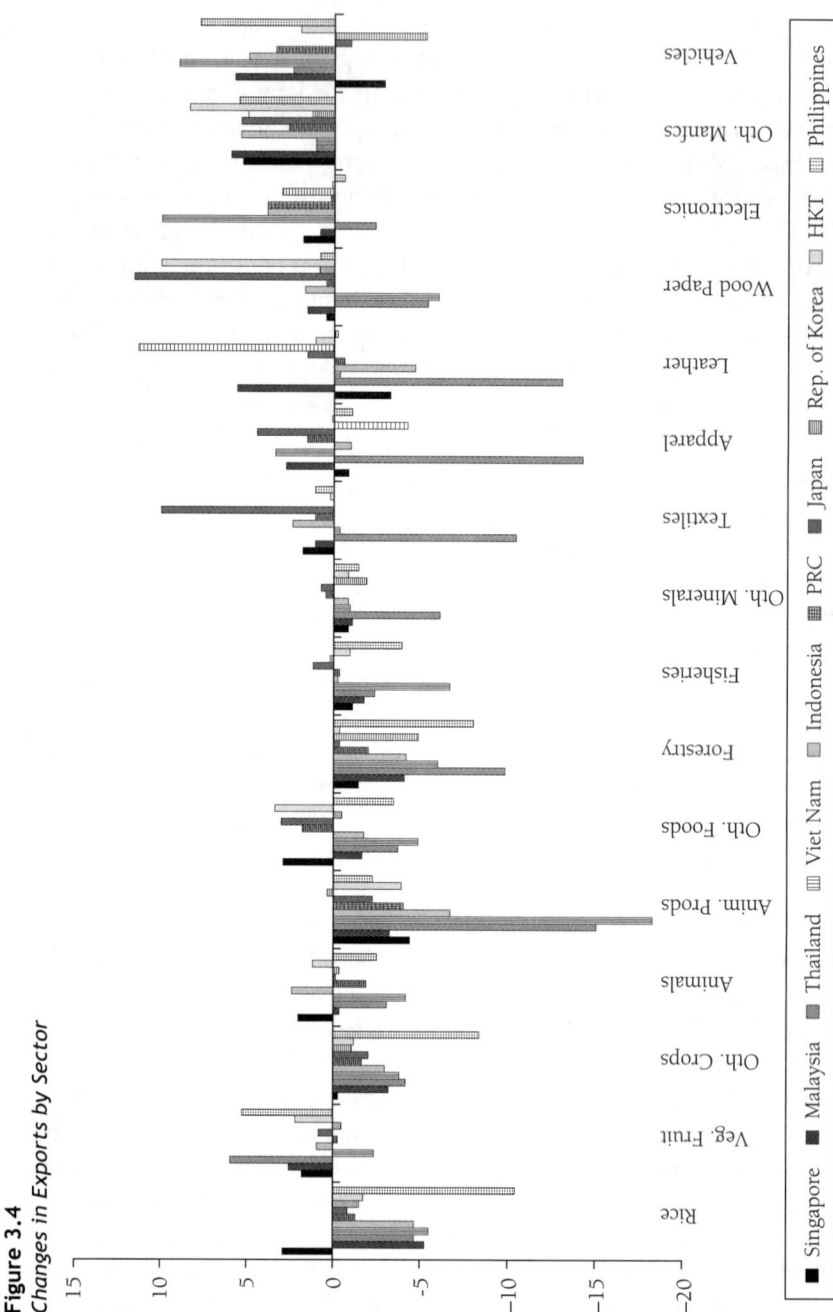

HKT = Hong Kong, China and Taipei,China; PRC = People's Republic of China.

Source: Authors' calculations.

Table 3.7
Changes in Bilateral Exports

Fruits and Vegetables

	Singapore	Malaysia	Thailand	Viet Nam	Indonesia	PRC	Japan	Rep. of Korea	HKT	Philippines
Singapore	0	4	-6.2	-4.3	4.1	-0.3	-1.1	-3.9	-1.6	-0.8
Malaysia	3.9	0	0.3	3.2	2	-0.1	2.7	2.9	3.5	-2.3
Thailand	6.9	3.1	0	-3.2	3.4	2.8	5.4	4.3	6.5	-3
Viet Nam	12.2	-0.6	7.1	0	0.4	2	18.8	12.3	11.6	-4.9
Indonesia	5.6	3.2	1.5	4.6	0	1.4	4.3	4.5	5	-2.4
PRC	-9.8	15.5	18	7.4	16.3	0	-9.1	-10.8	-10.1	10.6
Japan	7.3	15.1	11.8	37.6	16	2.9	0	1.4	6.9	10.8
Rep. of Korea	1.1	8.1	4.8	31.3	10	-2.8	2.3	0	0.8	4.4
HKT	2.7	7.8	-1.7	-1	8.4	3.4	2.9	0.1	2.5	3.2
Philippines	8.9	5.7	4.1	8	6.5	4.7	7.7	7.9	8.5	0
ANZ	-0.9	-4.2	-4.6	-7.2	-3.3	-2.2	-1	-0.6	-1.3	-7.9
RestAPEC	-1.6	-5	-5.6	-7.8	-4.2	-2.9	-1.6	-1.3	-1.9	-8.6
EU15	-1.6	-4.6	-5.2	-7.7	-4.1	-2.9	-1.8	-1.4	-2.2	-8.9
RestAsia	-1.4	-4.5	-6.1	-6.6	-4	-2.6	-1.6	-1.3	-1.9	-9
ROW	-1.6	-4.7	-5.5	-7.4	-3.9	-2.8	-1.8	-1.3	-2.2	-8.6

(Table 3.7 Contd)

(Table 3.7 Contd)

Textiles

	Singapore	Malaysia	Thailand	Viet Nam	Indonesia	PRC	Japan	Rep. of Korea	HKT	Philippines
Singapore	0	5.5	-5.2	9.4	7.1	3.3	8.8	2.3	1.1	5.8
Malaysia	6.8	0	-2.5	-2.8	7.9	4.4	17.4	7.8	4.6	6.6
Thailand	6.6	5.7	0	6.5	7.2	7.8	14.2	4.5	4.4	5.9
Viet Nam	-0.3	-2.1	-6.8	0	-0.6	5.4	11.1	5.5	-2.5	-1.8
Indonesia	6.8	6.3	-2.4	-2.9	0	4.4	17.3	7.7	4.5	6.6
PRC	6.2	3.8	-3.4	-2.1	5.4	0	16.8	9.2	3.9	4.1
Japan	0.3	2.7	-7.1	5.3	4.2	3.5	0	4	-1.8	2.9
Rep. of Korea	1	3.3	-6.5	6	4.8	4.2	12.6	0	-1.2	3.6
HKT	3.6	5.8	-4.7	9.7	7.4	3.6	9.1	2.6	1.4	6.1
Philippines	2.8	2.4	-6.2	-6.5	3.9	0.5	13	3.7	0.6	0
ANZ	-1.5	-0.3	-12.8	-2.5	1.1	-0.5	-1.7	-6	-3.6	-0.1
RestAPEC	-1.7	-0.5	-13.1	-2.7	1	-0.7	-1.8	-6.2	-3.8	-0.2
EU15	-20	-0.8	-13.4	-3	0.7	-1	-2.1	-6.5	-4.1	-0.5
RestAsia	-0.9	0.3	-12.2	-1.9	1.8	0.2	-1	-5.4	-3	0.6
ROW	-1.6	-0.4	-12.9	-2.6	1.1	-0.6	-1.8	-6.1	-3.7	-0.2

Electronics

	Singapore	Malaysia	Thailand	Viet Nam	Indonesia	PRC	Japan	Rep. of Korea	HKT	Philippines
Singapore	0	2.5	-1.8	19.2	4.8	8.1	1.6	7	-0.6	-0.2
Malaysia	3.6	0	2.2	9.9	6.2	10.5	4.7	10.9	1.8	1.1
Thailand	4.7	6.8	0	6.2	9.2	11.4	6.4	9.5	2.9	4
Viet Nam	9.8	2.8	1.9	0	5.1	12.8	13	16.9	8	0.1
Indonesia	1.6	1.9	0.4	7.9	0	8.4	2.8	8.9	-0.1	-0.7
PRC	2.9	1.8	0.2	20.6	4.1	0	5.3	13.9	1.1	-0.9
Japan	3.5	7.3	3.4	13	9.7	11.8	0	9.5	1.7	4.5
Rep. of Korea	4.3	8.1	4.1	13.8	10.6	12.7	5.2	0	2.5	5.3
HKT	-0.1	1.2	-3	17.8	3.6	6.8	0.4	5.7	-1.9	-1.4
Philippines	0.9	1.2	-0.5	7.1	3.5	7.7	2	8	-0.8	0
ANZ	0.4	-1.6	-6.3	0.6	0.7	1.3	-3.9	-5.9	-1.3	-4.1
RestAPEC	0.2	-1.7	-6.5	0.5	0.5	1.2	-4	-6.1	-1.5	-4.3
EU15	0.1	-1.9	-6.6	0.3	0.4	1	-4.2	-6.2	-1.6	-4.4
RestAsia	0.4	-1.5	-6.2	0.7	0.7	1.4	-3.8	-5.9	-1.3	-4.1
ROW	0	-1.9	-6.6	0.3	0.3	1	-4.2	-6.2	-1.7	-4.5

ANZ = Australia and New Zealand; EU15 = Austria, Belgium, Denmark, Finland, France, Germany, Greece, Ireland, Italy, Luxembourg, Netherlands, Portugal, Spain, Sweden, United Kingdom; HKT = Hong Kong, China and Taipei,China; PRC = People's Republic of China; RestAPEC = Chile, Peru, Canada, Mexico, and United States; RestAsia = Bangladesh, India, Pakistan, Sri Lanka, Cambodia, and Lao PDR; ROW = rest of world.
Source: Authors' estimates.

is driving the overall decline in Thailand's exports. However, the expansion of other export markets for Thailand in combination with declining import prices leads to a rise in GDP as well as income for the country (Table 3.6). Indeed, Thailand's GDP growth is one of the highest for the countries examined.

Indonesia, on the other hand, expands its textile exports across the board at a robust rate. Indeed, the highest export growth is within the region, specifically to Malaysia and Thailand, but Indonesia also expands its exports to the rest of Asia, EU15,[12] and the rest of APEC.[13] The large relative increase in textile exports of Japan, and to a lesser extent the Republic of Korea, are again off a fairly low export base.

A more diverse pattern is observed in the electronic sector. Again, intra-APEC Asian exports are expanding, but there is also growth in markets outside the region. Viet Nam and Indonesia are shown to have the greatest growth across the board with both countries expanding electronic exports in all markets. Malaysia, already a significant exporter of electronics, expands regional markets at the expense of those in the EU15 and the rest of world.

Toward Greater Trade

Asia's trade facilitation has greatly improved, but it must continue to do so in order to sustain economic growth and regional integration. Asia's international trade is growing in value and shrinking in weight per unit value. Exports are diversifying across new markets with smaller flows, and intra-regional trade in parts and components for regional production networks accounts for a growing share of total trade. These trends underscore the need for speed, flexibility, and information. Cross-border improvements that facilitate the expansion of trade along these lines will boost a country's export competitiveness and its efficient integration into the global economy.

The sequencing and complementarity of cross-border trade facilitation efforts are important, particularly as transport corridors develop into more diversified economic corridors. Once physical infrastructure has been built,

---

[12] EU15 = Austria, Belgium, Denmark, Finland, France, Germany, Greece, Ireland, Italy, Luxembourg, the Netherlands, Portugal, Spain, Sweden, United Kingdom.

[13] The rest of APEC here consists of the Chile, Peru, Canada, Mexico, and the United States. Australia and New Zealand, also members of APEC are included in their own category while the Russian Federation is included in the rest of the world (ROW).

developing complementary soft or ICT infrastructure, and enhancing trade facilitation at the border may be more important for trade than further investments in physical infrastructure. For example, once a two-lane highway has been built, streamlining customs facilities may boost trade more than widening it to four lanes.

As production becomes increasingly fragmented and traded internationally, cooperation among economies participating in production networks is becoming more important. The competitiveness of each country's production depends on that of the other countries in a production network as well as on the efficiency of the trading links among them. They thus have a strong incentive to cooperate with each other, particularly on reducing the costs of trading among them.

Flexibility, as well as timeliness, will become more valuable as greater trade implies greater potential vulnerability to external shocks such as financial turmoil or sharp fluctuations in fuel prices. An extended economic downturn in export markets would diminish export prices, potentially raising ad valorem trade costs and altering the prices of traded goods relative to those of nontradables. In general, one would expect the direct price effect to dominate, favoring trade in goods that are smaller, lighter, and of higher unit value. Trade finance may also be negatively affected, reducing the ability of trade to contribute to economic recovery in a region where it has been highly important in the past.

Factors such as delays in customs clearance, unofficial payments, and poor governance are particularly damaging because they impede this flexibility. They are also barriers to trade that need to be addressed through regional cooperation on trade facilitation measures. Improvements that reduce the costs of international trade are crucial for the region to realize the full gains from recent and prospective trade policy liberalization. This should be a priority in negotiations on bilateral and regional trade agreements, which can provide an added incentive and commitment to reform.

The empirical analysis presented here shows the significant gains from a reduction—even a relatively modest reduction—of trade costs. GDP in the region expands and countries move into a more diversified trading pattern. An examination of individual trends shows that when trade costs are lowered, it allows countries to move into new areas of trade. Some economies, such as Thailand in the scenario presented here, may experience an initial decline in overall exports as the economy moves out of traditional markets and into higher value-added sectors. However, such temporary adjustments are not long lived and policy makers need to be aware of this transition process and develop appropriate measures to manage the process effectively. We also see that some markets expand regionally while for others, trade facilitation facilitates trade with economies outside the region as well. However, regional market gains dominate and for those markets outside the region, the changes are not large relative to the gains between APEC Asian partners. The analysis highlights the importance of considering the direction of individual trade flows and the goods involved when planning trade facilitation policy measures and developing policies to handle the inevitable adjustment costs to a more diversified sectoral base.

References

Abe, K., and J.S. Wilson. 2009. Weathering the Storm: Investing in Port Infrastructure to Lower Trade Costs in East Asia. World Bank Policy Research Working Paper 4911. Washington, DC: World Bank.

Amiti, B., and B.S. Javorcik. 2008. Trade Costs and Location of Foreign Firms in China. *Journal of Development Economics.* 85. pp. 129–149.

Arnold, J. 2009. The Role of Transport Infrastructure, Logistics, and Trade Facilitation in Asian Trade. In J. Francois, P. Rana, and G. Wignaraja, eds. *Pan-Asian Integration: Linking East and South Asia.* Basingstoke, UK: Palgrave MacMillan.

Arvis, J.-F., M.A. Mustra, L. Ojala, B. Shepherd and D. Saslavsky. 2012. *Connecting to Compete: Trade Logistics in the Global Economy.* Washington, DC: The International Bank for Reconstruction and Development/World Bank.

Athukorala, P.-C. 2008. Recent Trends in Asian Trade and Implications for Infrastructure Development. Background Paper prepared for ADB/ADBI Flagship Study on Infrastructure and Regional Cooperation. http://www.adbi.org/research.infrastructure.regional.cooperation/ (accessed 10 May 2009).

Banomyong, R. 2008. Logistics Development in the North-South Economic Corridor of the Greater Mekong Subregion. *Journal of GMS Development Studies.* 4 (December). pp. 43–58.

Brooks, D.H. 2005. Competition Policy, International Trade, and Foreign Direct Investment. In D.H. Brooks and S. Evenett, eds. *Competition Policy and Development in Asia.* London: Palgrave Macmillan.

Brooks, D.H., and D. Hummels, eds. 2009. *Infrastructure's Role in Lowering Asia's Trade Costs: Building for Trade.* Cheltenham, UK: Edward Elgar Publishing.

Christ, N., and M.J. Ferrantino. 2009. Land Transport for Exports: The Effects of Cost, Time, and Uncertainty in Sub-Saharan Africa. http://www.usitc.gov/research_and_analysis/economics_seminars/2009/ChristandFerrantino-LandTransportforExportTheEffectsofCostsTimendUncertaintynSSAApril2009.pdf (accessed 12 May 2009).

De, P. 2009. Trade Transportation Costs in South Asia: An Empirical Investigation. In D.H. Brooks and D. Hummels, eds. *Infrastructure's Role in Lowering Asia's Trade Costs: Building for Trade.* Cheltenham, UK: Edward Elgar Publishing.

Dennis, A., and B. Shepherd. 2007. Trade Costs, Barriers to Entry, and Export Diversification in Developing Countries. World Bank Policy Research Working Paper 4368. Washington, DC: World Bank.

Djankov, S., C. Freund, and C.S. Pham. 2008. *Trading on Time*. Washington, DC: World Bank. www.doingbusiness.org/Documents/TradingOnTime_APR08.pdf (accessed 10 May 2009).

Fink, C., A. Matoo, and H.C. Neagu. 2002. Assessing the Impact of Telecommunication Costs on International Trade. World Bank Policy Research Paper 2552. Washington, DC: World Bank.

Francois, J.F., and G. Wignaraja. 2008. Economic Implications of Asian Integration. *Global Economy Journal*. 8 (3). pp. 1–45.

Hausman, W.H., H.L. Lee, and U. Subramanian. 2005. Global Logistics Indicators, Supply Chain Metrics, and Bilateral Trade Patterns. World Bank Policy Research Working Paper 3773. Washington, DC: World Bank.

Hertel, T.W., ed. 1997. *Global Trade Analysis: Modeling and Applications*. Cambridge and New York: Cambridge University Press.

Hoekman, B., and A. Nicita. 2008. Trade Policy, Trade Costs, and Developing Country Trade. World Bank Policy Research Working Paper 4797. Washington, DC: World Bank.

Hummels, D. 2009. Trends in Asian Trade: Implications for Transport Infrastructure and Trade Costs. In D.H. Brooks and D. Hummels, eds. *Infrastructure's Role in Lowering Asia's Trade Costs: Building for Trade*. Cheltenham, UK: Edward Elgar Publishing.

Hummels, D., V. Lugovsky, and A. Skiba. 2007. The Trade Reducing Effects of Market Power in International Shipping. NBER Working Paper 12914. Cambridge, MA: National Bureau of Economic Research.

Jacks, D.S., C.M. Meissner, and D. Novy. 2008. Trade Costs, 1870–2000. *American Economic Review*. 98 (2). pp. 529–534.

Kimura, F., Y. Takahashi, and K. Hayakawa. 2007. Fragmentation and Parts and Components Trade: Comparison between East Asia and Europe. *North American Journal of Economic and Finance*. 18 (1). pp. 23–40.

Limão, N., and A.J. Venables. 2001. Infrastructure, Geographical Disadvantage, Transport Costs, and Trade. *The World Bank Economic Review*. 15 (3). pp. 451–479.

Ma, L., and J. Zhang. 2009. Infrastructure Development in a Fast Growing Economy—the People's Republic of China. In D.H. Brooks and D. Hummels, eds. *Infrastructure's Role in Lowering Asia's Trade Costs: Building for Trade*. Cheltenham, UK: Edward Elgar Publishing.

Martinez-Zarzoso, I., and L. Márquez-Ramos. 2008. The Effect of Trade Facilitation on Sectoral Trade. *The B.E. Journal of Economic Analysis & Policy*. 8 (1): Article 42.

Minor, P., and M. Tsigas. 2008. Impacts of Better Trade Facilitation in Developing Countries: Analysis with a New GTAP Database for the Value of Time in Trade. Paper presented at the 11th Annual Conference on Global Economic Analysis, Helsinki, 12–14 June.

Patunru, A., N. Nurridzki, and Rivayani. 2009. Port Competitiveness: A Case Study of Semarang and Surabaya, Indonesia. In D.H. Brooks and D. Hummels, eds. *Infrastructure's Role in Lowering Asia's Trade Costs: Building for Trade*. Cheltenham, UK: Edward Elgar Publishing.

Stone, S., and A. Strutt. 2009. Transport Infrastructure and Trade Facilitation in the Greater Mekong Subregion. ADBI Working Paper 130. Tokyo: ADBI. Available at http://www.adbi.org/workingpaper/2009/01/20/2809.transport.infrastructure.trade.facilitation.mekong/ (accessed 11 May 2009).

Strutt, A., S. Stone, and P. Minor. 2008. Trade Facilitation in the Greater Mekong Subregion: Impacts of Reducing the Time to Trade. *Journal of GMS Development Studies*, 4 (December):1–20.

UNCTAD. 2008. *Review of Maritime Transport.* Geneva, Switzerland: United Nations Conference on Trade and Development.

UNESCAP. 2006. *Trade Facilitation in Selected Landlocked Countries in Asia.* Bangkok: UNESCAP.

Walkenhorst, P., and T. Yasui. 2005. Benefits of Trade Facilitation: A Quantitative Assessment. In P. Dee and M. Ferrantino, eds. *Quantitative Methods for Assessing the Effects of Nontariff Measures and Trade Facilitation.* Singapore: APEC Secretariat and World Scientific.

Wilson, J.S., C.L. Mann, and T. Otsuki. 2003. Trade Facilitation and Economic Development: Measuring the Impact. World Bank Policy Research Working Paper 2988. Washington, DC: World Bank.

World Bank. 2008. Doing Business Database. Available at http://www.doingbusiness.org/ (accessed 15 May 2009).

4

Trade Logistics and Regional Integration in Latin America and the Caribbean*

Pablo Guerrero, Krista Lucenti, and Sebastián Galarza

Introduction

As supply chains span national boundaries, the performance of each is determined by the efficiency in the management of the borders the products are crossing as well as domestic logistics performance. The close link between them has led to a convergence between transport, logistics and trade both domestically and internationally.

The last decades have seen a remarkable reduction in international barriers to trade, led in large part by multilateral trade liberalization under the World Trade Organization (WTO) as well as significant improvements in maritime transportation, freight containerization, and information and communications technology (ICT). At the same time, international trade has been widely recognized as one of the most important drivers of economic development, as seen by the experiences of the newly industrialized countries of Asia, specifically the People's Republic of China (PRC), in increasing economic output achieved in large part through export-led growth strategies. Correspondingly, countries searching to expand their markets through increased bilateral trade agreements have also begun to look within their regions. In many cases,

---

* This chapter has been previously published as an Inter-American Development Bank Working Paper No. 148 in December 2009. Sincere thanks to Kun Li from the Integration and Trade Sector of the IDB for support in updating the statistics and analysis in this current publication. This text has been edited for typographical errors and stylistic consistency.

deeper regional integration has not only increased the bargaining power of developing countries at the global level but has also created opportunities to exploit intra-regional trade and the positive links between trade and economic growth.

Recognizing the potential benefits of increased trade liberalization, countries in Latin America and the Caribbean (LAC) have embarked on a transformational process to reduce their trade barriers, increase bilateral trade agreements, and deepen integration. Since the mid-1980s, the region has reduced its average tariffs from around 40% to 8.7% in 2012[1] while its export share of gross domestic product increased from 13% to 24% during the same period.[2] In addition, during this time, the region's average growth rate of exports was 6.5%, with manufactured goods representing 16% of exports at the beginning of the period and 51% by 2012.[3] Since 1990, 226 regional trade agreements[4] have come into force across the globe with 69 of these involving LAC countries. Over half of these agreements have involved Chile (18), Peru (11), or Mexico (13). Thirty-six regional agreements signed by LAC countries have been south–south arrangements (WTO 2013). For the region, 10 intra-regional and 7 extra-regional agreements are either in force or signed since 2011 while another 6 are in negotiations (IDB 2013a).

Despite these achievements, the region continues to lag behind most industrialized countries and many developing regions in its efforts to secure the benefits from increased trade liberalization and deeper regional integration.

The region's reduction in average applied tariffs on manufactured goods (8.7%) was greater than both the world average (6.7%) for 2012 and that of middle-income developing countries (7.6%).[5] It was also considerably greater than high-income OECD countries (3.83%), with the United States having an average tariff of 2.9% and the EU-27, 1.4%.The region has been unable to maintain its share of world merchandise exports and has seen its participation drop from 11.3% in 1948 to 6.8% in 2012, while Asia increased its share from 14% to 31% in the same time period (Figure 4.1).[6]

Despite efforts toward increased regional integration, intra-regional trade within the largest trading blocs represented only 19% of total merchandise exports, compared with 27% for the Association of Southeast Asian Nations

---

[1] UNCTAD TRAINS data, 2012.
[2] World Development Indicators, 2012 (WB 2012).
[3] Footnote 2.
[4] These include Economic Integration Agreements (EIAs), Custom Unions (CUs), Free Trade Agreements (FTAs), and Partial Scope Agreements (PSAs).
[5] World Development Indicators, 2012 (WB 2012).
[6] Footnote 5.

Figure 4.1
Manufactured Exports by Regions (% of merchandise exports)

[Bar chart showing manufactured exports as % of merchandise exports across regions: Euro Area, East Asia & Pacific, South Asia, Latin America & Caribbean, Europe & Central Asia, Sub-Saharan Africa, Middle East & North Africa, for the periods 1970–1979, 1980–1989, 1990–1999, 2000–2009, 2010–2012.]

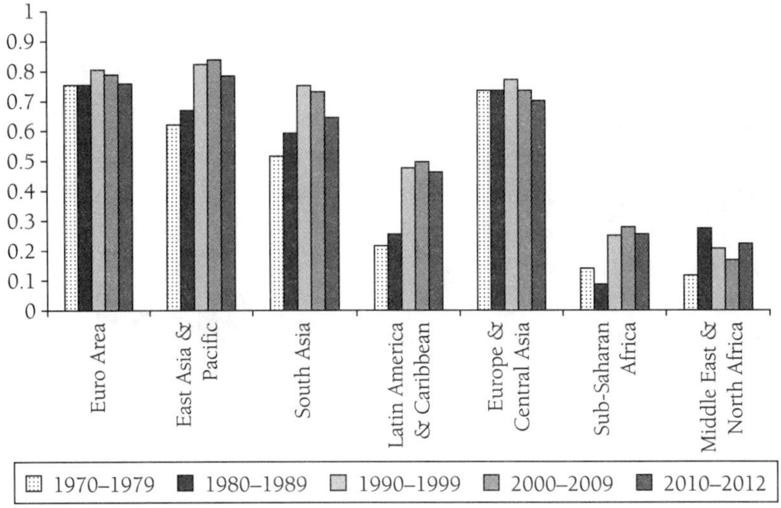

Source: World Development Indicators November 2013.

(ASEAN), 48% for the signatory countries of the North American Free Trade Agreement (NAFTA), and 62% for the European Union (EU-27) in 2012.[7] In 2008, the Union of South American Nations (UNASUR), modeled on the EU-27, was ratified by the twelve countries of South America as an intergovernmental union integrating the regional agreements in the region (the Common Market for the South (MERCOSUR) and the Andean Community of Nations (CAN)), as part of a continuing process of South American integration. The Caribbean Community (CARICOM) has not, thus far, lived up to its potential though intra-regional trade has been on the rise (Figure 4.2).

One explanation for why LAC countries have lagged in their integration into the world trading system (and with each other) is their difficulty in coping with a globalization process that is inherently transport-intensive and where supply chains are now being organized on a global scale. Technological innovations driven by transport technology developments have changed the global economic landscape, allowing countries to exploit economies of scale in both the transport and the production of manufactured goods. However, the region does not invest enough in infrastructure and logistics to benefit from these economies of scale, particularly since their investment is outpaced by those in other regions.

[7] Calculated based on Comtrade data.

Figure 4.2
Intra-Regional Exports of Major Trading Blocs (% of merchandise exports, 1990–2012)

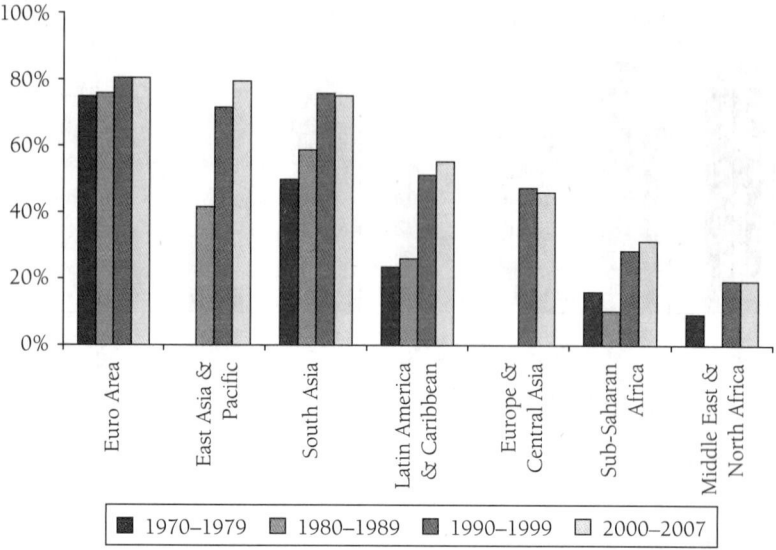

Source: IDB INT calculated based on COMTRADE.

During the past two decades, infrastructure investment in LAC has been shaped by drastic fiscal adjustment measures arising from macroeconomic crises, by incorporation of private investment in infrastructure that has not increased enough to cover the substantial decline in public financing, and by a concentration of financing in a limited number of countries and sectors.[8] In 1980, the region's coverage of productive infrastructure, including roads, electricity, and telecommunications networks was higher than in the newly industrialized countries of Asia. Today, they lead LAC by a factor of three to two. While LAC spent 1.1% of gross domestic product (GDP) in 2011 on infrastructure, down from 3.7% from 1980–1985, Asian countries invested 7%.[9] This investment is well below the needed 5% to close the infrastructure gap (IDB 2013b). A large part of this drop in investment stems from the reduction in public sector participation (1% of GDP during the 1990s) which

---

[8] According to the World Bank, between 1990 and 2003, 93% of private investment (by total project value) in LAC infrastructure went to just six countries (Argentina, Brazil, Chile, Colombia, Peru, and Mexico) and was concentrated in telecommunications and energy sectors (WB 2005).

[9] Calculated based on WDI data.

did not begin to recover until 2006, thanks to greater fiscal space emerging from prudent macroeconomic policies.

An array of performance indicators confirms that region is lagging behind most industrialized countries and several developing regions with respect to logistics. The 2012 Enabling Trade Index (ETI) overall score for LAC was 3.88 of 7, with the global average set at 4.73 (WEF 2012). Similarly, the Logistics Performance Index (LPI) overall ranking of 2.74 of 5 positions LAC countries behind those of East Asia and the Pacific in a number of areas, although it performs on average as well as Europe and Central Asia (WB 2012). Poor logistics performance has also led to higher transportation costs for the region relative to its counterparts—earlier estimates indicate that logistics costs in LAC range between 18 and 34% of product value, while the OECD benchmark is 9% (Guasch and Kogan 2006).

Increasingly, the infrastructure and freight logistics gap between LAC and other regions is being analyzed as one of the root causes of the limited potential output gains from economic and trade related policies. An early paper by Calderón and Servén (2004) suggests that if LAC countries caught up to the region's leader in terms of infrastructure quantity and quality, their long-term per capita growth gains would range between 1.1% and 4.8% per annum. Furthermore, if they caught up to the East Asian median country (Republic of Korea), the potential growth rate gains would range from 3.2% to 6.3%. This scenario requires the region to have an uninterrupted infrastructure investment rate between 5% and 7% of GDP for 20 years to maintain current infrastructure and to further expand the network.

However, achieving this requires substantial investment and sound policies, strong and robust institutions, and sensible investment planning.

As a result of underinvestment in infrastructure and poor performance in freight logistics, the LAC region is pressed to broaden its trade facilitation agenda from customs modernization to the incorporation of physical integration projects, transport services, and specialized logistic infrastructure.

Without a renewed focus on freight logistics and trade facilitation measures—including physical infrastructure and overall land use, planning for logistic corridors and multimodal transport services, and regulatory frameworks to simplify international trade procedures—the region will continue to be left out of self-reinforcing production and trade networks while transport and logistics costs will make it more difficult to compete globally.

This chapter is organized as follows: The first section focuses on the historical process of regional integration experienced by LAC countries, highlighting future concerns for deeper integration. The second section highlights recent developments in the global economy and its effects on international trade with and within LAC countries. The third and fourth sections look at the increasing importance of trade logistics and transport costs in the global economy. The fifth section analyzes the region's performance in terms of logistics and physical integration. The sixth section looks at existing regional initiatives to advance the physical integration of the region. The final section examines the future of trade logistics in LAC and the agenda to deepen regional integration, with particular emphasis placed on the actual and potential role of the Inter-American Development Bank.

Trade Agreements and Regional Integration in LAC

The postwar period has been marked by two important phenomena in the political economy of trade relations. First, globalization has changed the economic geography of the world, with increased population density particularly in urban spaces, and far better and more complex transport networks. These have led to cost reductions and just-in-time production methods. Second, regionalism has marked developments in the global trading system, driven by the same forces as globalization and by the democratization of political power and the search for stability in once-volatile areas of the world. As of July 2013, the WTO has recorded 575 notifications of RTAs (goods, services, and accessions are counted separately) and of these, 379 are in force.[10]

These phenomena are in large part a result of successive efforts to establish a rules-based world trading system. Multilateral negotiations through the General Agreement on Tariffs and Trade in 1947 led to the establishment of the WTO in 1995, whose membership is growing (159 countries to date). The reduction in tariffs across the world has significantly expanded opportunities for countries to participate in the world economy. LAC countries have been active participants in these transformational processes which deepened considerably since the 1990s, with unilateral opening of economies and increased regional trade agreements.

Latin America has had a long tradition of regional cooperation and integration strengthened in the 1960s through the rise of import-substituting industrialization (ISI)[11] development strategies and the creation of the Latin

---

[10] www.wto.org/english/tratop_e/region_e/region_e.htm

[11] ISI strategies focused on promoting infant industries through high levels of external protection, state participation, and investment regulation, with the promise of achieving export-led growth and decreased dependence on industrial countries.

American Free Trade Association (LAFTA) in South America and the Central American Common Market (CACM).[12] Regional integration provided an opportunity to deepen the potential of ISI through a larger market. This allowed the infant industries to grow in size and create production efficiencies until they were able to compete. Consequently, LAFTA and CACM became the first formal attempts to harmonize trade flows and increase regional integration in Latin America.

However, ISI policies did not establish macroeconomic stability and economic growth; the first attempt at regional integration was unsuccessful due to a complicated political and economic climate. Among many factors, the region had an intrinsic tendency for national protectionism marked by tension between the state and private sector. Trade negotiations did not provide sufficient incentives to create a rules-based system whereby the benefits accrued from increased exchange would be evenly distributed to member countries. Finally, the development of national and regional infrastructure, coupled with low levels of investment and maintenance as well as poor transport services, limited gains from increased regional cooperation.

Caribbean states had a remarkably different history of economic integration, given the late independence of many of the islands from primarily British colonial rule, which stymied the first attempts at economic integration (the West Indies Federation was established in 1958 under British dictate but collapsed with the withdrawal of Jamaica in 1962).

With independence, the Caribbean Free Trade Association was established in 1968 (modeled on the European Free Trade Association) to promote liberalized trade between its members, although few efforts were made to establish extra-regional trade relations. As a result of this, as well as of the uneven benefits accrued by its member nations, the free trade agreement was dropped in favor of the Caribbean Community (CARICOM) established in 1973. However, Caribbean integration continues to falter due to political pressures and competition between islands producing and selling similar goods and services.

In the 1990s, following what is now commonly referred to as the debt crisis and the structural reforms promoting trade and financial liberalization that ensued, LAC entered into a period of revived regionalism still present today. The policy framework established during this period set the stage for unilateral measures to reduce traditional barriers to trade while promoting open and competitive economies (Devlin and Estevadeordal 2001). Furthermore, it encouraged a development strategy based on recognition of the economic

---

[12] In 1980, LAFTA gave way to the Latin American Integration Association (or ALADI).

and political benefits of increased cooperation and trade by securing reform through institutional and rules-based arrangements.

This cooperation initially led to an increasing number of North–South reciprocal trade agreements, followed by a rethinking of traditional approaches to integration in the region. Since 1960, over 250 trade agreements have come into force, with the trend picking up strongly after 1990 (WTO 2013). Simultaneously, average tariffs in the region have declined from over 40% in the mid-1980s to about 8.7% in 2012 (Table 4.1).[13]

Table 4.1
Trade Agreements in Latin America and the Caribbean, North–South Agreements

North–South Agreements		
Participating economies/trading blocs	*Year of signature*	
North American Free Trade Agreement (NAFTA)	1994	
Canada–Chile	1997	
Mexico–European Union	1999	
Israel–Mexico	2000	
European Free Trade Association–Mexico	2001	
Canada–Costa Rica	2002	
Chile–European Union	2002	
European Free Trade Association–Chile	2004	
Republic of Korea–Chile	2004	
Panama and the Separate Customs Territory of Taipei,China, Penghu, Kinmen, and Matsu	2004	
United States–Chile	2004	
Japan–Mexico	2005	
Dominican Republic–Central America–United States Free Trade Agreement (CAFTA–DR)	2006	Free Trade Agreements
Panama–Singapore	2006	
Trans-Pacific Strategic Economic Partnership	2006	
Chile–Japan	2007	
MERCOSUR–Israel[a]	2007	
United States–Panama	2007	
Canada–Colombia	2008	
EC–CARIFORUM States Economic Partnership Agreement	2008	
European Free Trade Association–Colombia	2008	

(Table 4.1 Contd)

---

[13] TRAINS data.

(Table 4.1 Contd)

North–South Agreements	
Participating economies/trading blocs	Year of signature
Nicaragua and the Separate Customs Territory of Taipei,China, Penghu, Kinmen, and Matsu	2008
Australia–Chile	2009
Canada–Peru	2009
Peru–Singapore	2009
United States–Peru	2009
EFTA–Colombia	2011
EFTA–Peru	2011
Peru–Republic of Korea	2011
Canada–Colombia	2011
Japan–Peru	2012
US–Colombia	2012
US–Panama	2012
EU–Colombia and Peru	2013
Canada–Panama	2013
Costa Rica–Peru	2013
Costa Rica–Singapore	2013
EU–Central America	2013

Source: WTO Secretariat, RTA Database, 2013.
Note: [a] Not signed by Venezuela.

Importantly, subregional initiatives, including MERCOSUR, CAN, and CARICOM, did not limit their agreements to trade but incorporated structural aspects to reform their institutional environment and build longer-term strategic policies to compete in the world trading system. These included agreements in standards, transport, customs cooperation, services, investment, dispute settlement, labor (except for MERCOSUR), and competition, while none included agreements concerning intellectual property rights—a clause included in all North–South trade agreements with Latin America except for the Canada–Chile agreement signed in 1997 (WB 2005). Through these agreements, countries sought to enforce internal regulatory measures as well as capture the benefits of increased opportunities for export diversification, foreign direct investment, greater specialization, product differentiation, and intra-industry trade resulting from increased market access and a clear regulatory framework (Table 4.2).

Table 4.2
Trade Agreements in Latin America and the Caribbean, South–South Agreements

South–South Agreements		
Participating countries/trading blocs	Year of signature	
Central American Common Market (CACM)	1961	Customs Union
Caribbean Community (CARICOM)	1973	
Andean Community (CAN)	1988	
Southern Cone Common Market (MERCOSUR)	1994	
Latin American Integration Association (ALADI)	1980	Preferential Trade Agreements
Global System of Trade Preferences among Developing Countries (GSTP)	1989	
Chile–India	2007	
Programa de Integración y Cooperación entre Argentina y Brasil (PICAB)	1986	Free Trade Agreements
Central American Integration System (SICA)	1993	
Chile–Venezuela	1993	
Bolivia–Mexico	1994	
Group of Three (G-3)	1994	
Costa Rica–Mexico	1995	
Bolivia–MERCOSUR	1996	
Chile–MERCOSUR	1996	
Chile–Peru	1998	
Mexico–Nicaragua	1998	
Chile–Mexico	1999	
Chile–Central American Common Market (CACM)	1999	
CARICOM-Dominican Republic	2000	
Mexico-Northern Triangle of Central America	2000	
El Salvador–Mexico	2001	
Guatemala–Mexico	2001	
Chile–Costa Rica	2002	
Costa Rica–Trinidad and Tobago	2002	
MERCOSUR–Comunidad Andina	2002	
MERCOSUR–Peru	2003	
Panama–El Salvador	2003	
Bolivarian Alliance for the Americas (ALBA)	2004	
CARICOM–Costa Rica	2004	
MERCOSUR–India	2004	

(Table 4.2 Contd)

(Table 4.2 Contd)

South–South Agreements	
Participating countries/trading blocs	Year of signature
MERCOSUR–Colombia	2005
Chile–PRC	2006
Panama–Chile	2008
Panama–Costa Rica	2008
Union of South American Nations (UNASUR)	2008
Chile–Colombia	2009
Colombia–Northern Triangle (El Salvador, Guatemala, Honduras)	2009
Panama–Nicaragua (Panama–Central America)	2009
Peru–Singapore	2009
Peru–PRC	2010
Chile–Guatemala (Chile–Central America)	2010
Turkey–Chile	2011
PRC–Costa Rica	2011
Peru–Mexico	2012
Chile–Malaysia	2012
Panama–Peru	2012
El Salvador–Cuba	2012
Chile–Nicaragua (Chile–Central America)	2012
Costa Rica–Peru	2013

Source: WTO Secretariat, RTA Database, 2013.

More recently, initiatives aimed at establishing a hemispheric cross-continental market, namely the Free Trade Area of the Americas (FTAA), have met with less success. These highlight the political limitations the region faces in moving forward on a common agenda for deeper integration (Estevadeordal et al. 2003). Equally important to note are some of the potential costs of increased regional commercial integration, such as trade and investment diversion away from other world markets, conflicts arising from asymmetric development impacts of regional integration, and, perhaps most important, the administrative and institutional strain caused by a web of different trade arrangements.[14] A recent study by Estevadeordal and Robertson (2009) finds significant evidence of an increasing tariff effect (consistent with trade diversion) as a result of the proliferation of bilateral agreements in LAC.

[14] See Bhagwati and Krueger (1995).

While LAC countries are not as reliant on foreign trade as other regions, they have not been exempt from the severity of the global economic recession, despite the fact that, in 2012, exports as a percentage of GDP represent only 24% for the region, 10% below the world average and far from the Euro area (45%) and East Asia (34%).[15] Commodity prices reached record peaks, expected to drop by over 33% compared with 2008 and recover only 3% in 2010. For Central American and Caribbean countries, net commodity importers, the overall effect of declining commodity prices on their terms of trade has been positive, enabling them to maintain healthy balances in their international reserves from the low cost of fuel imports. Their external financial linkages are generally limited and the impact of the crisis was not as significant as in other areas of the region. Net commodity exporters with inflation-targeting regimes (Brazil, Chile, Colombia, Mexico, and Peru) have been adversely affected by declining commodity prices, causing their terms of trade to shift.

The importance of India and the PRC as a destination for LAC exports has increased more than 100% since 1990. Trade with the PRC has grown at an annual rate of 29%[16] since 2003, the same year that they became Brazil's largest trading partner. Overall, the growth of the PRC and India in world markets is an opportunity for LAC exporters and importers—accounting for up to 8% of LAC exports in 2004, mainly driven by the PRC. Furthermore, a recent study concluded that there is no robust evidence of substitution between the PRC's trade flows and LAC exports to third markets (Lederman, Olarreaga, and Soloaga 2007). As trade relations grow and the PRC continues to play an ever more important role in the world economy, and in LAC in particular (becoming a member of the IDB in 2008), economic cooperation with the PRC will be a source of increased value to trade relations through knowledge-sharing and technology transfers (Devlin, Estevadeordal, and Rodríguez-Clare 2006). Nonetheless, these opportunities have yet to be fully exploited, given the size of the markets served.

As a consequence of the crisis, a rise in protectionist measures has threatened recovery of world trade growth to its pre-crisis levels. From 2000 to 2012, anti-dumping initiations have averaged around 229 a year with the number of initiations clearly beginning to decline after peaking in 2001 at 372 (WTO 2012). Many countries have adopted policies to maintain production and consumption within their national borders—usually through nontariff

---

[15] World Development Indicators 2013 (WB 2013).
[16] Calculated based on COMTRADE data.

trade barriers, which are easier to disguise and more difficult to sanction, and contingency measures, including increased anti-dumping measures. Although these have proved in most cases to be transitory measures and closely linked to falling economic activity, their widespread use reduces the possibility of negotiating international arrangements and limits the rapidity and depth of substantial recovery in international trade flows. The Doha round[17] has yet to deliver on its promises, in part, because of this economic environment.

This, combined with the difficulties experienced in integrating regionally, has led to the emergence of a more sophisticated integration and trade agenda, one based on shared interests and a willingness to commit political capital. The Trans-Pacific Partnership and the Pacific Alliance are two recent regional initiatives whose membership demands commitment and investment in reforms.

Transport and Logistics Costs in International Trade and Logistic Performance in LAC

World trade patterns are constantly changing due to advances in technology, including those in the area of logistics services and transport. As technologies for manufactured production have become more available, trade in intermediate and final goods has increased, creating greater opportunities for countries to reap benefits from specialization. In 2012, intra-industry trade accounted for 24% of all trade; however, it is highly concentrated in North America, Europe, and Australia (accounting for 45% of all intra-regional trade) as well as Southeast Asia (roughly 34%), while the figure for LAC is closer to 14% (Figure 4.3).[18]

As countries increase their trade in manufactured goods and as supply chains become vertically integrated in a global production process, international trade patterns reflect increased commerce with neighboring markets with similar production and consumption capabilities. In 2012, 26% of world trade will occur between bordering countries; this accounts for 17% of all

---

[17] The WTO Doha Development Round or Doha Development Agenda (DDA) is the current trade-negotiation round which commenced in November 2001 in Doha, Qatar. Though its objective is to lower trade barriers to goods, open up services markets, and strengthen rules to mitigate against protectionism, the talks have been unable to overcome entrenched positions on major issues, such as agriculture, industrial tariffs and nontariff barriers, services, and trade remedies.

[18] Calculated based on COMTRADE SITC Rev1 5-digit data.

Figure 4.3
Index of Intra-Industry Trade by Region

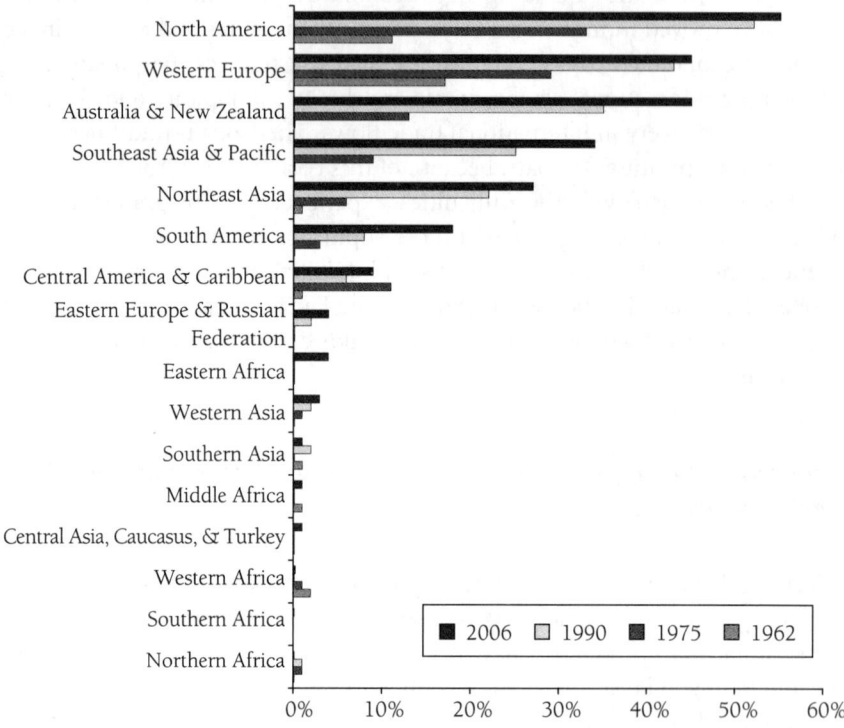

Source: Calculated based on COMTRADE SITC Rev 1. 5-dig data. Region definition is based on Brülhart (2008).

trade in LAC, 48% in North America and 32% in Western Europe.[19] In the latter countries, the benefits of a well-developed integration infrastructure and development mechanisms along the borders of each country are key to trade and freight logistic development. Another factor influencing trade patterns through technological innovations in transport is the significant rise in intermodal transport—mainly in high capacity and more efficient modes such as maritime, waterway, and railway transport—and the integration of separate transport systems through the use of at least two different modes of transportation. This has shifted the freight logistic components to the entire supply chain, as these processes are increasingly seen as whole rather than as a series of sequences, each with its particular documentation and cost structure.

[19] Calculated based on COMTRADE data: Export.

From the regulation of infrastructure and the provision of well-developed transport services, a robust and strategic approach is needed to enable better infrastructure quality and transport services. For international trade, a more efficient, reliable and secure interaction between different transport modes is of paramount importance, given the geographic space and volume the global economy now occupies. These trends further support the view that globalization has been transport-intensive, as economies of scale have affected not only production but also transport costs, further reinforcing trade in a virtuous and mutually enforcing cycle.

Over time, the main reductions in transportation costs, due to higher investments in transportation infrastructure, technological innovation, transportation reform, and lower overall trade barriers, have been in road and air transport, while maritime transport was revolutionized by containerization. In particular, innovations in air and maritime transport, the two modes of transport that have most influenced the growth of international trade and globalization, have been of particular importance. For instance, advances in technologies for air shipping—which accounts for about 40% of the value of international trade—have caused the average revenue per ton-kilometer shipped to drop by a factor of 10 between 1955 and 2004 (Hummels 2007; Rodrigue 2007). Similarly, ocean shipping, which constitutes 99% of world trade by weight, has seen its costs consistently decline during the last 20 years in large part through containerization—with estimates showing that using containers can lower shipping costs by 3%–13% (Hummels 2007)—and the advent of larger than post-Panamax vessels (the largest ships that can pass through the Panama Canal). Lower vehicle costs and the deregulation of the trucking industry have pushed road transport costs down by almost 40% during the past three decades (WB 2009).

Over the past three decades transport costs have fluctuated due to changes in the price of fuels, the uneven regulatory frameworks in which many of these industries develop, and rising concerns about security costs. Air transport has been characterized by technological developments, monopoly power of large state operators, and fluctuations in price depending on the commodity being shipped. For maritime freight operations, costs have been reduced in large part through containerization, the rise of large maritime vessels, and the advent of fewer freight lines, together with efficiency gains in port operation and infrastructure that allow for reduced direct port costs from greater storage capacity. Competition for transshipment services has also contributed to reducing the cost of international shipping while sometimes negatively affecting internal trade with higher tariffs than those offered to international freight.

Unfortunately, LAC countries have not fully benefited from positive trends in transport and logistics development. During the 1970s, the region experienced high levels of infrastructure investment relative to other regions, reaching higher coverage of productive infrastructure than East Asia by 1980. Today, many of these gains have rapidly reversed. Traditional urban settlement principles that clustered along valleys and "internal regions" have prevented countries from effectively pursuing a more systematic approach to infrastructure development and long distance land-based transport networks. As a result of a lack of combined land and territorial planning, the region underperforms in a series of indicators. This reflects a chronic underinvestment in new infrastructure and maintenance of existing projects, especially in terms of the road network, efficiency and capacity of ports, and readiness of airport infrastructure. According to the Infrastructure Quality Gap Index, which analyzes the relative needs and deficiencies of infrastructure development in the 12 LAC countries with respect to Germany, Peru, and Colombia have the largest infrastructure gaps while Chile, El Salvador, and Mexico have the narrowest (WEF 2007).

Despite improvements to the productivity of LAC ports as the result of decentralization and concessioning programs, global standards are increasing and LAC ports continue to underperform (IDB 2011).

Not surprisingly, the region continues to spend nearly twice as much to import goods, while airfreight costs in 2006 actually rose in relation to their level in 1995—with the Caribbean seeing an increase of as much as 36% (Mesquita et al. 2008) (Figure 4.4).

Figure 4.4
Total Import Freight Expenditures as a Share of Imports, 2006 (%)

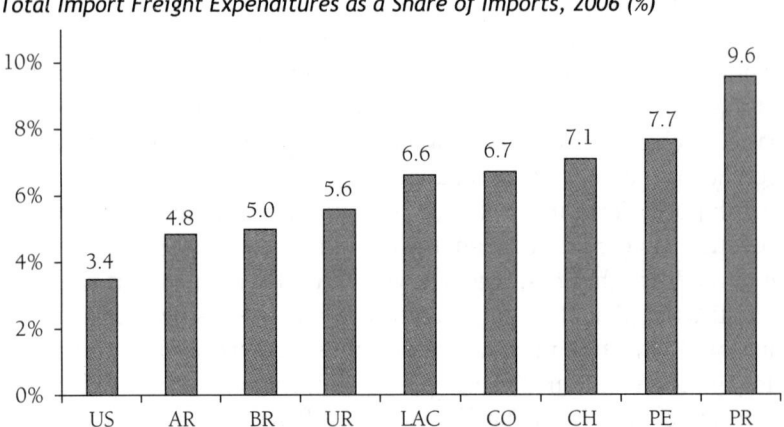

Source: Mesquita Moreira, M. et al. 2008.

The region's exports, with their reliance on abundant natural resources (including a weight-to-value ratio much higher than many capital-intensive goods) and proximity to the world's largest markets, are much more transport-intensive than competing exports. Thus LAC countries, whose economies mainly depend on the export of large and bulky raw materials, are more exposed to changes in demand as well as being more sensitive to the quality and quantity of their transport infrastructure.

Overall, about 40% of the difference in shipping prices between the region and the US and Europe can be explained by port and airport efficiencies, while only 17% of these differences are accounted for by higher tariffs. For example, LAC exports to the US are subject to ocean freight rates that are on average 70% higher than those on exports from the Netherlands. As result, for a typical LAC country, improving port efficiency to the US level would lower costs by 20%. Reducing tariff rates and increasing competition to US levels would further reduce transport costs by 9% and 4%, respectively (Mesquita et al. 2008).

Intra-regional exports largely depend on the development of transport infrastructure in general and regional integration transport infrastructure more specifically. According to recent simulations, for every dollar invested in infrastructure, the region can expect to generate $1.70 in increased economic activity, implying a $0.70 GDP gain. Countries with high intraregional trade potential and large infrastructure gaps are estimated to accrue GDP gains in excess of $2.00 for every dollar invested in transport infrastructure over the next 10 years. An average 1.1% of regional GDP invested annually in transport infrastructure development and maintenance can be expected to generate an additional 27% in exports (IDB 2011) (Figure 4.5).[20]

Further, in a recent IDB study, Colombia has most to gain from improvements to its transport infrastructure and services: a 1% reduction in ad valorem transport costs can translate into an increase in exports by 7.9% in agriculture, 7.8% in manufacturing, and 5.9% in mining. Even in Mexico where the impact across sectors was the lowest, a 1% reduction in transport costs could produce a 4% increase in exports (Mesquita et al. 2013).

In Central America economies trucking services play an essential role. They are the dominant transport mode in internal flows, with a share of over 90% of the total ton–km in the region. Trucks are also key for intra-regional trade, as the region is too small and does not have enough volumes for a dense short-distance maritime network, and international railway networks have not been

---

[20] IDB Integration and Trade Sector (IDB-INT) computable general equilibrium (CGE) model simulation (IDB 2011).

developed. Given its high share in the regional freight market, trucking services performance impacts directly on the vast majority of supply chains in Central America (IDB 2013c) (Figures 4.6 and 4.7).

Figure 4.5
Return of Investment in Transport Infrastructure Hardware

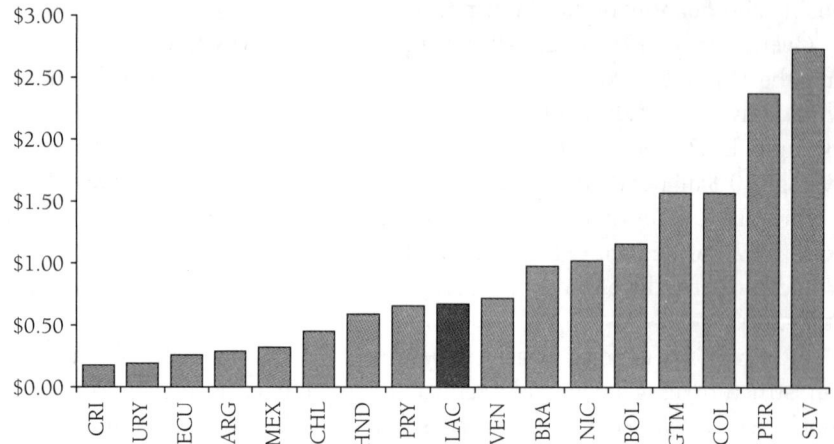

(GDP gains from each dollar invested in transport infrastructure, in dollars, through 2020.)
Source: IDB/INT CGE model, 2011.

Figure 4.6
Heavy Vehicles Average Ages—Central America and Selected Countries 2010–2012

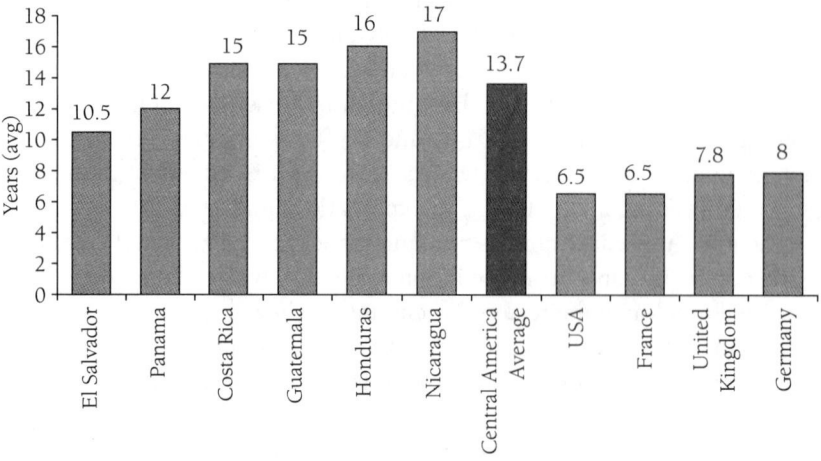

Source: Freight Transport and Logistics Database for Mesoamerica, IADB 2013.

Figure 4.7
Average Distance Traveled (km truck/year)—Central America and Selected Countries

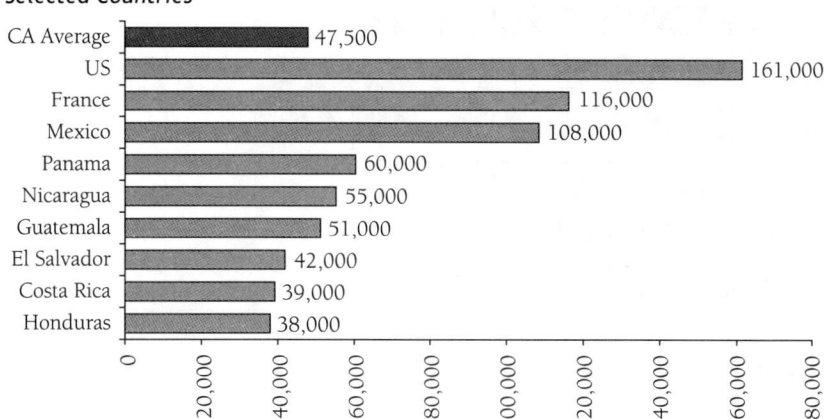

Source: Freight Transport and Logistics Database for Mesoamerica, IADB 2013.

The sector is also an important source of employment and value added for Central America's economies. Based on IADB data,[21] the transport sector makes an average contribution of 5% to regional GDP,[22] with road transportation representing a significant share of the total. Also, over 50% of companies in the sector are small (owner-operators). From this perspective, the sector's structure and performance have a significant social dimension.

In the next five years, regional GDP is expected to grow close to 4% in average, while trade volumes will increase 4.5%.[23] This scenario presents a challenge for Central America's logistics system as a whole, but is even more critical for trucking services given their dominant stance in mobility of freight in the region.

The incidence of trucking services in Central America's logistics chains coupled with forecasts of economic and trade growth in the medium term highlight the need for comprehensive modernization policies to boost the sector's efficiency (Figures 4.8 and 4.9).

These findings highlight not only the importance of improved freight logistics and transport services and infrastructure for the development of national export sectors (with corresponding productivity and output growth) but also how limited transport development has inhibited regional integration. Despite

---

[21] Freight Transport and Logistics Database for Mesoamerica, IADB 2013.
[22] Excluding Panama, where the transport sector represents 14.5% of GDP.
[23] IMF World Economic Outlook Database. (IMF 2013).

Figure 4.8
Central America Trucking: Percentage of Empty Backhauls

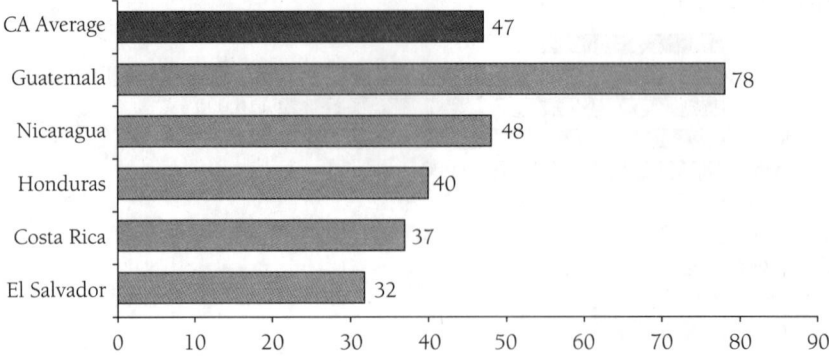

Source: Freight Transport and Logistics Database for Mesoamerica, IADB 2013.

Figure 4.9
Tariffs (US$/km/year) and Trucks Average Age—Central America and United States

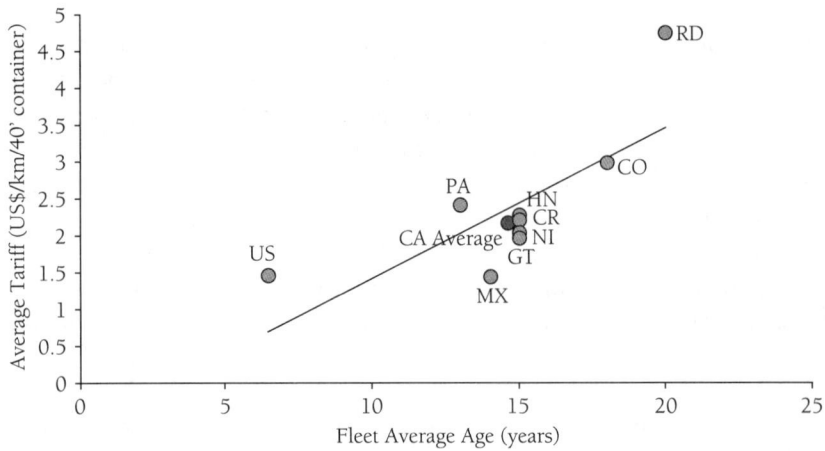

Source: Freight Transport and Logistics Database for Mesoamerica, IADB 2013.

geographical constraints and the long distance between populous urban centers, few live within 25 kilometers of a border (16% in mountainous areas) or a coastline (48% in tropical areas), respectively—figures that increase to 37% and 54% living within 75 kilometers (WB 2009). Accordingly, very few urban settlements have been developed along border regions (a contrast when compared to North American cities), and therefore few productive centers are located less than 200 kilometers from borders. Accordingly, since urban settlements house economic activities further from borders, transport costs to and from borders hinder the development of infrastructure.

After the surge of regional initiatives in the early 1990s and the corresponding progressive reduction in nontariff barriers, the region's new trade agenda needs to focus on more practical issues, centered on measures to reduce transport and logistics costs, which will increase productivity growth and competitiveness internally and externally. Potential gains from spatial economies in remote areas are limited due to the highly complex coordination needed at the regional level. Several efforts are currently under way, including the development of strategic corridors such as the Initiative for the Integration of Regional Infrastructure in South America (IIRSA) and the Mesoamerica Project.

Since the transport sector is generally characterized by high entry and maintenance costs, owning physical infrastructure consolidates economic power. In 2003, some 20% of the world's carriers owned or controlled close to 60% of global port slot capacity (WB 2009). Maritime markets have had limited competition in part due to the high entry costs into the market, compounded by the indivisibility of infrastructure facilities when providing transport services. As a result, markets for these services are rarely competitive and are usually owned by the state (in the case of seaport and airport infrastructure) or by large international companies (for transport services).

Shorter supply chain processes including just-in-time production and the outsourcing of logistics procedures have set the stage for substantial improvements in the modernization of supply chain and logistics management in sector firms. As a result, the demand for freight transport has changed substantially, incorporating the need to minimize logistics costs in line with inbound and outbound traffic, warehousing, inventory costs at different stages of the production cycle, damaged stock, and other costs associated with the physical flow of goods. Furthermore, as freight logistics technology and its associated costs are consistently present throughout the entire product life cycle, the quality of service and efficiency associated with these is of increasing importance in competitive international markets.

Nonetheless, the development of a comparative metric system and associated measurement for logistic services on international shipments is an increasingly complex process given the nature of the services, the array of procedures involved and their many combinations. As one United Nations Economic Commission for Europe study concludes, the volume of information about the link between logistics and competitiveness is growing however there is a persistent inadequacy of tools and methodologies to effectively assess the transport sector's contribution to competitiveness in the context of transport's role in supply chains (UNECE 2009). As the supply chain uses different modes of transport (maritime, air, rail, and truck) for both international and national trade and deliveries and the fragmentation of production across different countries increases the amount of freight in circulation, measuring logistics performance is neither an easy task nor one safe from controversy.

Guasch and Kogan (2006) analyzed logistic performance indicators at the macro level as well as inventory stocks for developing countries to assess their impact on countries' growth and competitiveness. Their findings in terms of logistic performance indicators show that countries in LAC spend on average two or three times as much as OECD countries on logistics; inventory stocks show that they are on average 15% of GDP, two to five times larger than OECD averages. As a result, the logistics cost as percentage of product value for LAC countries is twice that of OECD countries and the US. Overall, their results indicate LAC countries' competitiveness suffers from poor transportation services and from the large financial costs required to maintain stock at an efficient level, which affect the ability of companies to streamline internal processes (Guasch and Kogan 2006) (Figure 4.10).

Finally, it is important to recognize the development costs associated with improvements in transportation, freight logistics, and trade over the past decades. The challenge to public policy is to find ways of creating incentives

Figure 4.10
Logistics Costs as Percentage of Product Value for Selected Economies (2004)

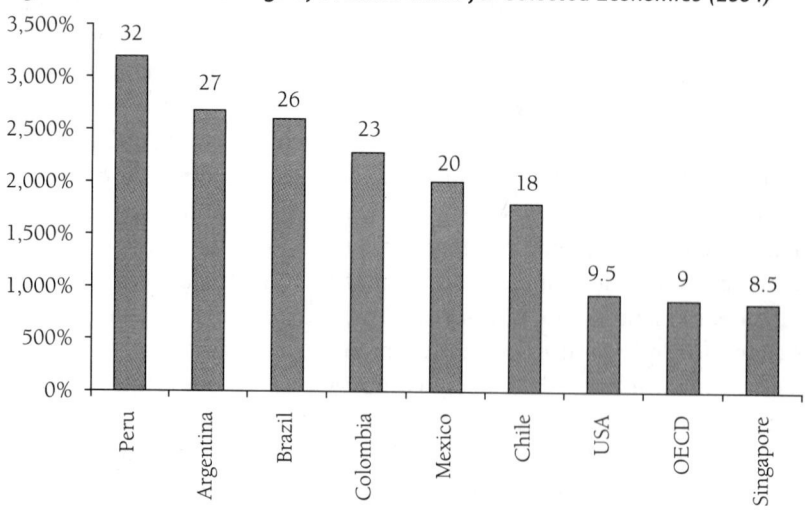

Source: Guasch, J.L. and Kogan, J. (2006).

for the transport industry to internalize these development costs and of increasing fuel efficiency and safety standards. Several estimates, including the *Stern Review* on the economics of climate change (Stern 2006), have placed the current cost of internalizing emissions well within historical variations in fuel prices. Recently, the UN Climate Change Conference in Copenhagen has shown increased political will from industrial and emerging markets to tackle emissions, with the transport sector representing close to 13.5% of total greenhouse gases. Controlling the development costs derived from transport will play an increasingly important role in the development of future trade logistics and is likely to lead to renewed economies of scale in both transport and production through increased efficiency.

Regional Initiatives to Advance the Integration Process

Despite lagging trade logistics performance in the region, there have been considerable achievements toward an integrated regional agenda and improved connectivity. LAC has undergone a process of commercial and political integration that has encouraged physical integration initiatives to ensure the connectivity of infrastructure networks. In this sense, the most important regional initiatives have been the IIRSA and the Mesoamerica Project. The objective of both initiatives is to increase intra-regional trade through trade facilitation measures and to give priority to economic geography approaches and regional planning as a means of deepening integration at the regional level.

IIRSA, the largest of these initiatives, encompasses more than 550 transport, energy, and communications infrastructure projects, organized in nine Integration and Development Hubs. Originating in 2000 with a view to advancing the physical integration of the South American continent, the IIRSA is an institutional mechanism for intergovernmental coordination that incorporates novel methodological approaches, developing a strategic vision to align the regional portfolio of infrastructure projects through increased coordination and harmonization of standards in infrastructure and border crossing services as well as infrastructure investment (Figure 4.11).

These are complemented by key initiatives aimed at unleashing potential synergies from scale economies in transport and knowledge transfer while emphasizing monitoring and evaluation procedures to recover important lessons learned and improve future performance. As a result of these initiatives, IIRSA has identified key processes for integration that require normative

Figure 4.11
IIRSA Corridors

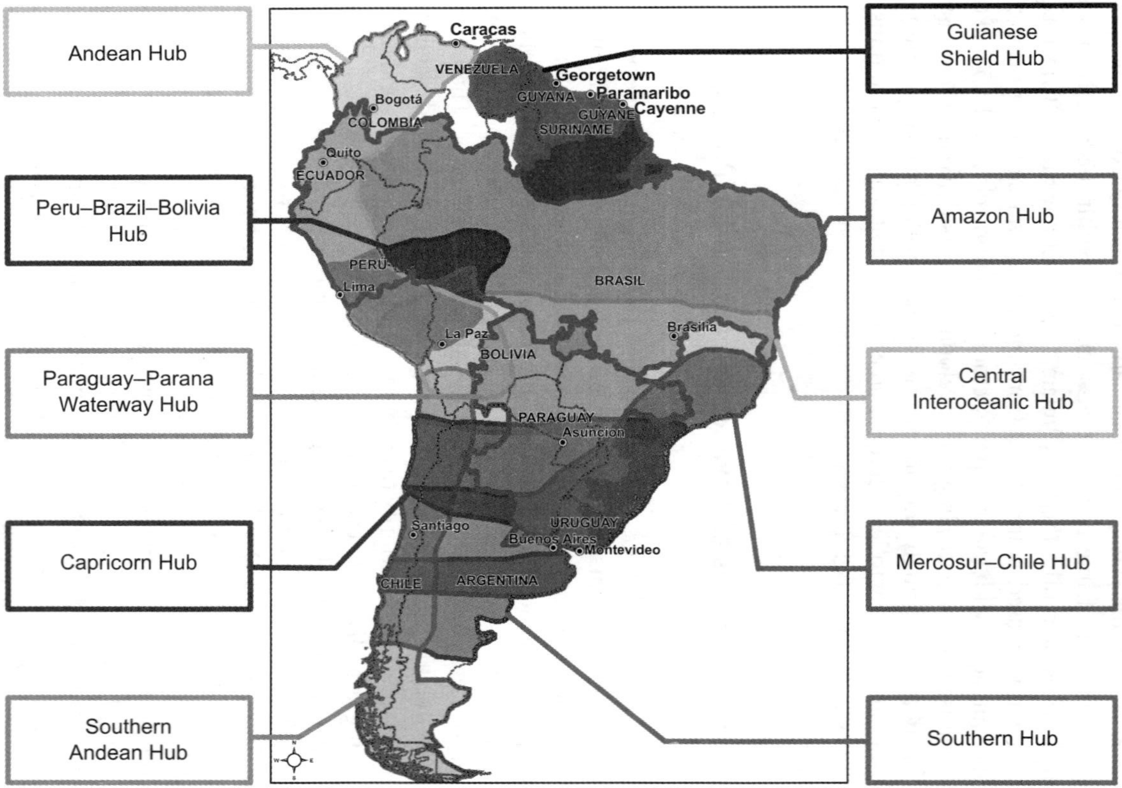

Andean Hub
Peru–Brazil–Bolivia Hub
Paraguay–Parana Waterway Hub
Capricorn Hub
Southern Andean Hub
Guianese Shield Hub
Amazon Hub
Central Interoceanic Hub
Mercosur–Chile Hub
Southern Hub
Caracas
VENEZUELA
Georgetown
GUYANA
Paramaribo
Cayenne
GUYANE
SURINAME
Bogotá
COLOMBIA
Quito
ECUADOR
PERU
Lima
BRASIL
La Paz
BOLIVIA
Brasilia
PARAGUAY
Asuncion
URUGUAY
Santiago
Buenos Aires
Montevideo
CHILE
ARGENTINA

Source: IIRSA Secretariat. www.iirsa.org.

harmonization, such as the regulation of transport and energy markets, ICT infrastructure, and border crossing management.

Importantly, the IIRSA-established financial structure has helped incorporate the private sector into transport investments with the backing of regional multilateral funding. The IDB, Andean Development Corporation, and the Fund for the Development of the River Plate Basin support more than 25% of the total investment required by projects currently in progress or finished. Furthermore, though more than 40% of its financing capital comes from public sources, public–private partnerships and the private sector contribute significantly to the resources of the program (Figures 4.12 and 4.13 and Table 4.3).

Finally, IIRSA has deepened the development of methodologies for integration projects with increased economic assessments of transnational projects, strategic environmental assessments, productive and logistic integration, and development of digital maps and geographic information systems. Productive integration has been further developed by taking advantage of potential linkages between the removal of physical barriers and increased logistic and economic integration, extending the scale of production and markets, promoting competitiveness, and taking advantage of agglomeration economies. Furthermore, the development of logistic services is helping add value to

Figure 4.12
IIRSA Project Portfolio by Sector

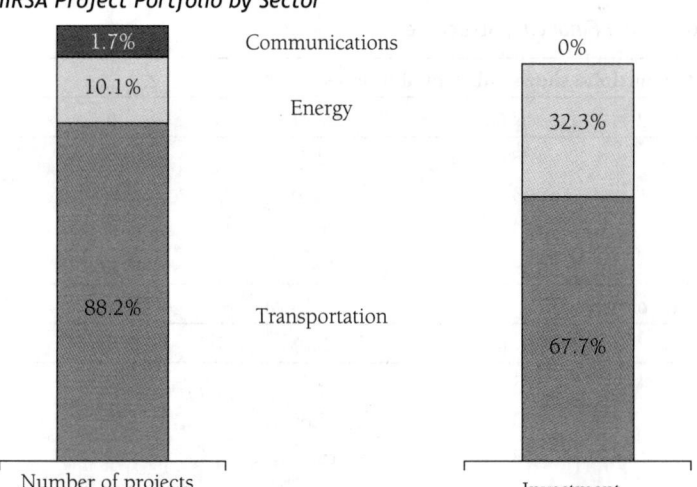

Source: http://www.iirsa.org/proyectos/Proyectos.aspx, 2013.

Figure 4.13
IIRSA Project Portfolio by Countries

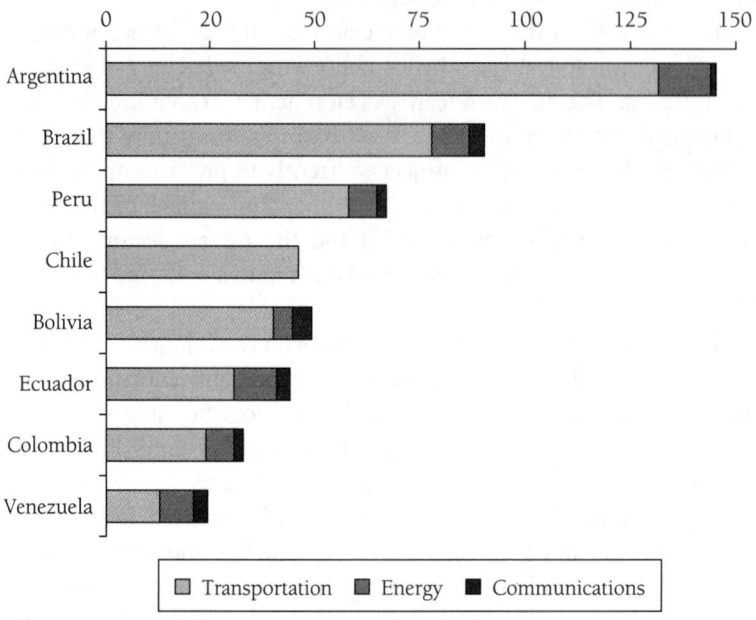

Source: IIRSA Secretariat. www.iirsa.org accessed in 2009.

Table 4.3
IIRSA Project Status and Financing Structure

Almost 70% of the portfolio shows substantial progress			
Project status	Projects (#)	US$ MM	%
Profile	138	12.5	13
Completed	53	8.5	9
In execution	175	46	48
In preparation	158	29.1	30
Financing structure of projects			
Financing	Projects (#)	US$ MM	%
Public	393	44.1	46
PPP	73	35.8	37
Private	58	16.2	17
TOTAL	524	96.1	100

Source: IIRSA Secretariat. www.iirsa.org accessed in 2014.

IIRSA projects through knowledge transfer, capacity-building initiatives, and improved local and regional institutional performance and competitiveness.

In 2008, the Mesoamerica Project was born from the original Plan Puebla Panama (established in 2001) as an effort to integrate the Central American Corridor and Mexico through infrastructure and social projects. Currently the project includes 10 countries from Mexico to Colombia and including the Dominican Republic, with over 28 projects in execution. Importantly, the initiative seeks to move beyond the physical integration of participating countries and into areas of trade facilitation and increased investment in social services, such as health, education, and environmental protection. As a result of these efforts, strong synergies have become apparent in the integration projects, particularly in the smaller countries, where infrastructure has traditionally been a bottleneck. It has integrated other regional initiatives, such as the Central American Integration System, while attracting the multilateral participation of the IDB, the Central American Bank for Economic Integration, the Andean Development Corporation, and the Secretariat for Central American Economic Integration (Figure 4.14).

Regional Agenda to Deepen Integration: The Importance of Freight Logistics in Trade Facilitation

Over the past two decades, multilateral and bilateral trade negotiations have reduced bound tariff rates and, to a lesser extent, softened nontariff barriers to trade. Increasingly, however, trade transaction costs such as those resulting from poor transport infrastructure have proved to be more costly. As a result, developing countries are being forced to rethink their trade policy agenda to take into account trade costs not covered in past rounds of negotiations. Without a renewed focus on non-policy trade costs and the relevance of freight logistics and specialized transport infrastructure to the trade facilitation agenda, developing countries will continue to be left out of self-reinforcing production and trade networks.

The incorporation of specific measures oriented toward transportation in trade facilitation has become a key policy initiative to enhance future gains from trade. Activities include both services provided by the state and the flow of freight internally and externally. Clearly, developing countries have much to gain, given the high transaction costs of their trading patterns. Trade facilitation measures focusing on customs procedures and regulatory environments can lead to improved controls, reduced administrative costs, and increased cooperation between the public and private sectors even when applying these measures implies costs (OECD 2005).

Using a sample of 75 countries (weighted toward developing economies), Otsuki, Mann, and Wilson (2003, 2004), found that improving these countries' trade facilitation records to the global average resulted in trade gains equivalent to $377 billion, representing an increase of about 9.7% in total trade—with Latin America accruing about 20% of these gains (South Asia got the largest share, 40%). A little over 40% of these gains would come from improved service sector infrastructure, while nearly 20% are due to improvements in the regulatory environment.

Firms in developing countries also witness delays in inventory holdings, an area of particular concern for countries that rely on exports of bulky natural resources with short shelf lives, as is the case for many LAC countries. The implied costs of holding inventories through tied-up capital, increases in unit costs, and diminished competitiveness can be detrimental to the development of export sectors in LAC and increases shipping delays. Guasch and Kogan (2003) found that while US businesses typically hold inventories of around 15% of GDP, inventories in Latin America and other developing regions are often twice that. In addition, if the interest rate for financing holdings is between 15% and 20%, the cost to an economy of additional inventory holdings is more than 2% of GDP (Table 4.4).

Developing reliable and efficient transport networks, affordable and available transport services, and required logistic services will help to eliminate

Table 4.4
Comparison of Average Inventory Levels, Losses to Markets, and Logistics Costs in Latin America and OECD, 2004

Inventory level in Latin America: Ratio with US inventories (mean)		
Country	Raw material	Finished products
Chile	2.17	1.76
Venezuela	2.82	1.63
Peru	4.19	1.65
Bolivia	4.2	2.74
Colombia	2.22	1.38
Ecuador	5.06	2.57
Mexico	1.58	1.46
Brazil	2.98	1.98

Source: Guasch, J.L. and Kogan, J., 2006.

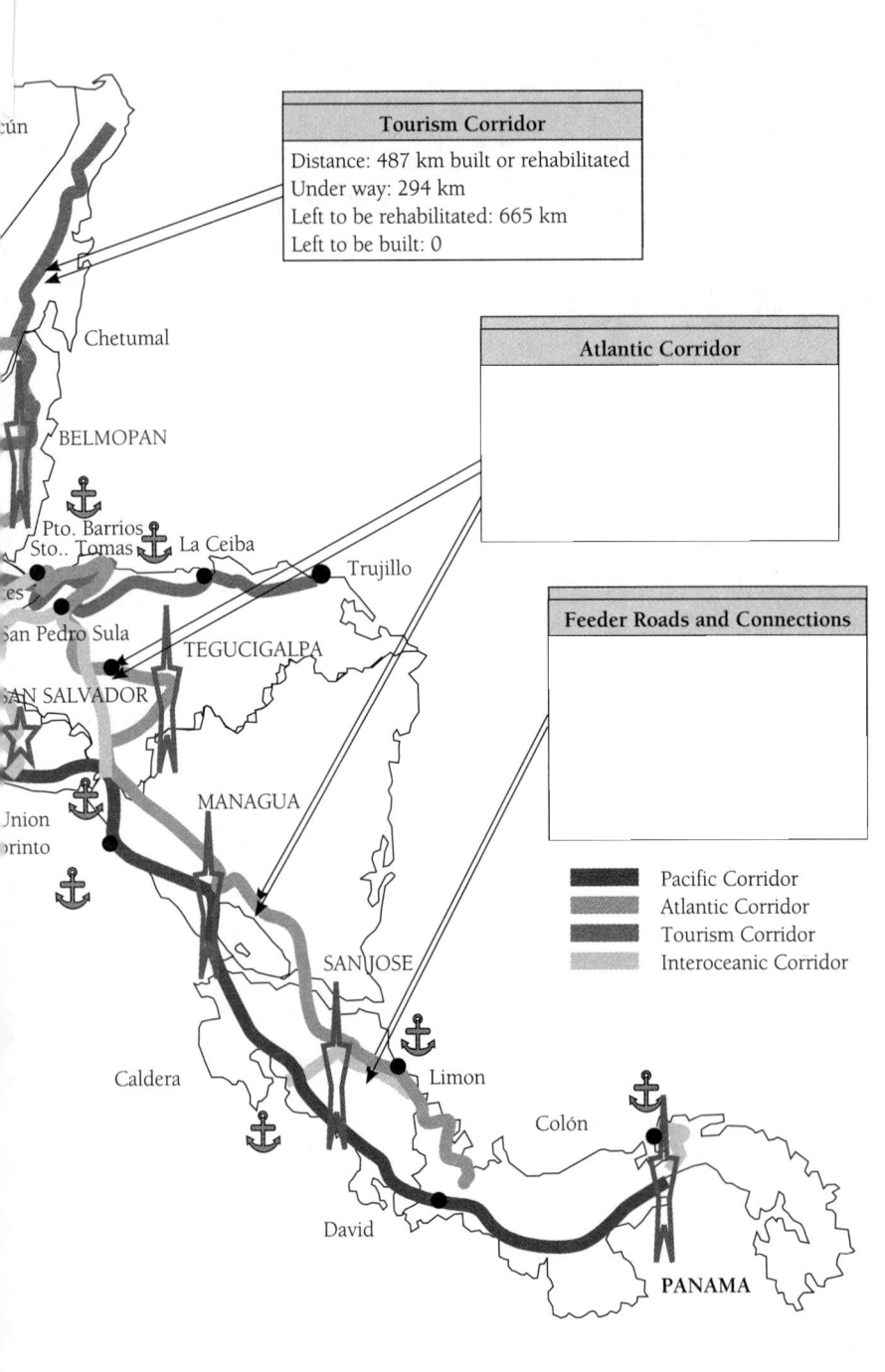

Figure 4.14
Mesoamerican Project Corridors

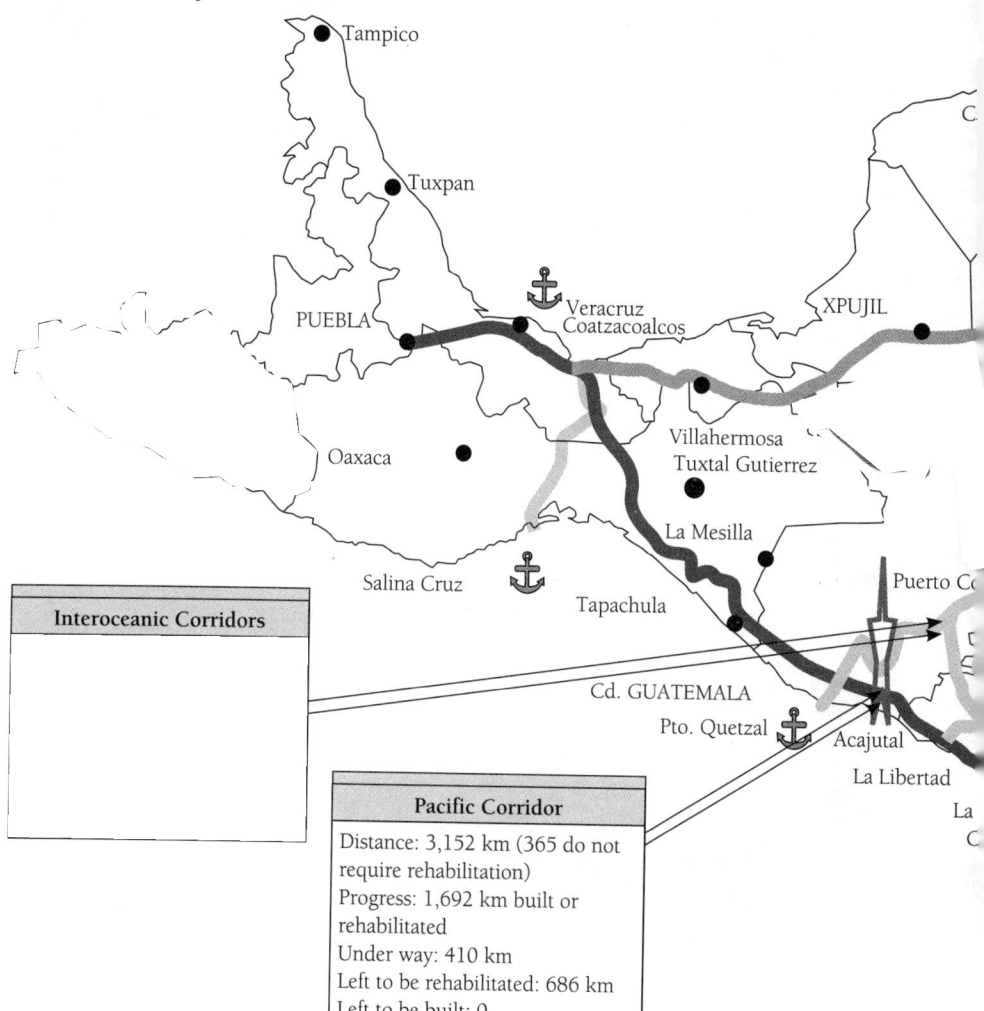

Source: Mesoamerica Project Secretariat. www.proyectomesoamerica.org.

these excess inventories. Consequently, excessive inventory costs provide a further example of how improvements in trade facilitation and freight logistic measures such as port efficiency, ICT, infrastructure, harmonization standards, and customs procedures can benefit trade through a virtuous circle that allows countries to exploit economies of scale in both transport and production.

Unfortunately, much remains to be done in order to improve the region's weak trade facilitation measures and close both the trade and infrastructure gaps with other regions.

Overall, a renewed focus on trade facilitation measures has become of increasing importance to the region's trade agenda as traditional trade restrictions have been substantially reduced and trade benefits have not been fully realized. Furthermore, through increased coordination and harmonization of customs and border procedures, trade facilitation supports efforts toward increased regional integration. Similarly, these measures tend to enhance the efficiency of revenue collection agencies and are associated with increased government revenue while at the same time incorporating the private sector into productive activities.

If better provision of transport infrastructure from the public sector and the enabling of more efficient transport services from the private sector are key to spurring national trade, investment in regional physical infrastructure projects is essential to reducing costs of international land-based transport. This is particularly true for landlocked countries and for the development of regions closer to international borders and distant from national ports.

Improving trade logistics through deepened trade facilitation measures has become of increasing importance to LAC's regional integration agenda. Given the substantial decline in tariffs and other traditional barriers to trade, logistics performance and the institutional capacity to provide it seem fundamental to expanding productivity gains and benefiting from existing trade agreements. Reforming the current institutional climate to promote much needed transformations in terms of increased human capital, private-sector development, logistic services, infrastructure quality, and increased investment in transport infrastructure is a costly and sometimes lengthy process. The challenges to public policy in designing, executing, and evaluating a successful strategy that gives priority to key issues and efficiently tackles the many problems intrinsic to the current logistics performance of LAC countries are many. Nonetheless, the future benefits of these processes are more likely to exceed their costs in most aspects of economic and political activity.

What limitations help explain the weak logistics performance in LAC countries? First, the region is underserved by a weak institutional capacity that limits its ability to cope with the demands of accessible and reliable transport infrastructure and the services provided by the state are inadequate to serve a rapidly growing trade facilitation agenda. In particular, scarce human resources, weak ICT infrastructure and regulation, and monitoring and evaluation systems adversely affect the reform agenda needed to expand institutional arrangements. Consequently, the coordination capacity of LAC countries is weak and impedes the necessary development of the logistics agenda.

Second, the region's infrastructure network in general and transport infrastructure in particular have suffered from chronic underinvestment. Estimates of the investment needs of the current infrastructure framework are 5% of the region's GDP over 20 years in order to satisfy construction and maintenance requirements, increase coverage, and tap growing demand (IDB 2013b).

Finally, the infrastructure gap in LAC countries is exacerbated by poor project management in the public sector matching a weak private sector adversely affected by chronic shortages of human resources and limited access to technology.

Restrictions of investment capital have also contributed to the underdevelopment of small- and medium-size enterprises (SMEs) as providers of logistics services. Land transportation services, mostly trucking and logistics operators, have had limited expansion and remain relatively weak performers in the logistics chain, with room to improve and modernize the industry. Another limitation on the logistics performance of SMEs is their inability to exploit economies of scale and substantial institutional roadblocks. Finally, performance across countries has remained uneven, with limitations ranging from demand-related obstacles such as freight imbalances and seasonality to a lack of harmonization in the organization of the logistics supply chain across borders. In addition, there is also significant heterogeneity within countries, especially the geographically larger countries of the region that have the highest potential opportunities to exploit scale economies and increase agglomeration. As a consequence of these limitations, the logistics gap is widening, aggravated by weak performance in multiple components of the logistics chain, engendering greater heterogeneity across LAC countries.

In response to the limitations and weak performance of LAC countries as a whole, a rethinking of the current agenda to transform trade logistics requires actions at the national, subnational, and regional level. Specifically, it requires project and program coordination in the areas of transport infrastructure and related transport services, specialized logistic infrastructure, trade policies, and, importantly, in sectors where these agendas converge.

Improvements in trade logistics must focus on the provision of basic infrastructure, particularly in the road network, in order to expand coverage and maintain quality standards. Importantly, regulations that facilitate and encourage private–public partnerships, especially for large regional infrastructure projects such as ports and railroads, need to be improved. Well-functioning specialized logistic infrastructure is also needed to ease freight handling, streamline inspection processes, and provide value-added services in areas closer to ports, airports, and border crossings. Equally important is the establishment of clear guidelines to support logistics management development for SMEs, logistic operators, and intermediaries. At the same time, services delivered by the state, including customs and border crossings and security provisions, need to be substantially improved. Additionally, efforts need to be formalized to implement institutional organizations to promote high quality logistics.

In the area of ICT, there is ample room to capture the benefits of improved routing, packing, and retrieval that could effectively reduce kilometers traveled per vehicle, contributing to reduced carbon dioxide emissions. There is also a transformation in the economic environment in which businesses work when these technologies are incorporated: job transformation (wholesalers, postal operators, and carriers/logisticians) and job creation, such as virtual links in the delivery chain, supply–demand interfacers, and suppliers of complete logistics solutions (EC 1998).

The agenda for physical integration, on the other hand, must facilitate the coordination and harmonization of standards across borders to further reap the benefits of economic agglomeration. Projects of greater potential impact must be given priority, while regional integration of infrastructure projects should be axis-based, with clear development criteria that equitably distribute the costs and benefits of integration among members. In order for this strategy to achieve its full potential impact, it must be accompanied by a significant allocation of resources.

Hence, the region must develop financial mechanisms to provide affordable financial resources for these projects, such as a common fund or earmarked resources for infrastructure integration. In this respect, the experience of the EU-27 is of particular importance: a cohesive policy for transport infrastructure was developed to allow countries to catch up to regional standards and funds were earmarked for integration projects.

Finally, in areas where agendas converge, transport and trade facilitation measures need to be deepened to allow for further coordination and gains from cooperation. Continued emphasis on key processes regarding the development and harmonization of border crossings and the regulation of diverse transport modalities is of particular importance. Furthermore, the agenda for the expansion of productive integration and intra-regional logistics services must support both national and subnational organizations in order to fully achieve the economies of agglomeration necessary to reap the most benefits from these costly reforms.

Here the IDB can support the development of a cohesive regional political and economic architecture by helping to strengthen institutional capacity at the national and subnational levels. Furthermore, the IDB can add value as a knowledge bank of ideas, thereby facilitating the coordination of thematic agendas by calling on regional experts in various fields and disciplines. Private sector reasoning should influence state-led integration. Deepening regional ties is important to the process, as are the costs of non-trade issues in regional development integration, such as transportation infrastructure. As such, there is huge potential for closing the gap between LAC regional trade and other regions worldwide by sharing experiences, drawing from state modernization and private sector development initiatives, and developing comprehensive joint approaches which incorporate territorial and transport planning and spatial and scale economies.

The IDB is prepared to spearhead many of these initiatives as an efficient vehicle for policy, projects, and regional cooperation. Importantly, the IDB's agenda has been expanded to support the coordination of national initiatives while emphasizing the harmonization of cross-border interactions. This agenda places emphasis on provision of basic infrastructure, particularly road networks; improvements in services and regulations that facilitate PPPs, like ports and railroads; improved services delivered by the state, like customs management, border crossings, and security; support for logistic management development in SMEs, operators, and intermediaries; implementation of an institutional organization for high-quality logistics; integration of "axis-based" regional infrastructure development criteria, giving priority to projects of greater regional impact; development of financial mechanisms to increase investment in key areas; and commitment to an agenda for productive integration and logistics services, supporting national and subnational organizations. Overall, these initiatives will help the region better cope with a changing international environment and allow it to exploit the positive links between trade, integration, and economic growth.

References

Bhagwati, J., and A. Krueger, eds. 1995. *The Dangerous Drift to Preferential Trade Agreements*. Washington, DC: American Enterprise Institute.

Brülhart, M. 2008. An Account of Global Intra-Industry Trade, 1962–2006. Working Paper 2008-08. Nottingham, UK: University of Nottingham.

Calderón, C., and L. Servén. 2004. The Effects of Infrastructure Development on Growth and Income Distribution. Policy Research Working Paper 3400. Washington, DC: World Bank.

Devlin, R., and A. Estevadeordal. 2001. What's New in the New Regionalism in the Americas? In Victor Bulmer-Thomas, eds. *Regional Integration in Latin America and the Caribbean: The Political Economy of Open Regionalism*. London: The Institute for the Study of the Americas, University of London.

Devlin, R., A. Estevadeordal, and A. Rodríguez-Clare, eds. 2006. *The Emergence of China: Opportunities and Challenges for Latin America and the Caribbean*. Cambridge, MA: Inter-American Development Bank and David Rockefeller Center for Latin American Studies, Harvard University.

Estevadeordal, A., D. Rodrik, A.M. Taylor, and A. Velasco, eds. 2003. *FTAA and Beyond: Prospects for Integration in the Americas*. Cambridge, MA: Harvard University Press.

Estevadeordal, A., and R. Robertson. 2009. Gravity, Bilateral Agreements, and Trade Diversion in the Americas. Cuadernos de Economia. 46. pp. 3–31.

European Commission (EC). 1998. *The Contribution of Business Services to Industrial Performance*. Luxembourg: European Commission.

Guasch, J.L., and J. Kogan. 2003. Just-in-Case Inventories: A Cross Country Analysis. Policy Research Working Paper 3012. Washington, DC: World Bank.

Guasch, J.L., and J. Kogan. 2006. Inventories and Logistic Costs in Developing Countries: Levels and Determinants—A Red Flag for Competitiveness and Growth. Policy Research Working Paper 2552. Washington DC: World Bank.

Hummels, D. 2007. Transportation Costs and International Trade in the Second Era of Globalization. *Journal of Economic Perspectives* 21(3): 131–154.

Inter-American Development Bank (IDB). 2011. Investing in Integration: The Returns from Hardware-Software Complementarities. Policy Discussion Paper. Washington, DC: IDB.

Inter-American Development Bank (IDB). 2013a. Trade and Integration Monitor 2013: After the Boom, Prospects for Latin America and the Caribbean South-South Trade. Washington, DC: IDB.

Inter-American Development Bank (IDB). 2013b. Estrategia de Infraestructura para la Competividad. Internal document.

Inter-American Development Bank (IDB). 2013c. Trucking Services in Belize, Central America, and the Dominican Republic: Performance Analysis and Policy Recommendations.

International Monetary Fund (IMF). 2013. *World Economic Outlook*. Washington, DC: International Monetary Fund.

Lederman, D., M. Olarreaga, and I. Soloaga. 2007. The Growth of China and India in World Trade: Opportunity or Threat for Latin America and the Caribbean? Policy Research Working Paper 4320. Washington DC: World Bank.

Mesquita Moreira, M., C. Volpe, and J. Blyde. 2008. Unclogging the Arteries: The Impact of Transport Costs on Latin American and Caribbean Trade. *Special Report on Integration and Trade*. Cambridge, MA: IDB and David Rockefeller Center for Latin American Studies, Harvard University.

Organisation for Economic Co-operation and Development (OECD). 2005. *The Economic Impact of Trade Facilitation*. Paris: OECD Trade Directorate.

Otsuki, T., C.L. Mann, and J.S. Wilson. 2003. Trade Facilitation and Economic Development: Measuring the Impact. Policy Research Working Paper 2988. Washington, DC: World Bank.

Otsuki, T., C.L. Mann, and J.S. Wilson. 2004. Assessing the Potential Benefit of Trade Facilitation: A Global Perspective. Policy Research Working Paper 3224. Washington, DC: World Bank.

Pablo Guerrero, Krista Lucenti, and Sebastián Galarza Mesquita Moreira, M., J. Blyde, C. Volpe, and D. Molina. 2013. Too Far to Export: Domestic Transport Costs and Regional Export Disparities in Latin America and the Caribbean. Special Report on Integration and Trade. Washington, DC: IDB.

Rodrigue, J.P. 2007. Transportation and Globalization. In R. Robertson and J.A. Scholte, eds. *Encyclopedia of Globalization*. London: Routledge.

Stern, N. 2006. *The Economics of Climate Change. The Stern Review*. London: Cambridge University Press.

United Nations Economic Commission for Europe (UNECE). 2009. Supply Chain and Logistics Implications for Transport. Informal Document No. 10. 71st Session of the Inland Transport Committee. Geneva: UNECE.

World Bank (WB). 2005. Infrastructure in LAC: Recent Developments and Challenges, eds. Marianne Fey and Mary Morrison. Report No. 32640-LCR. Washington, DC: World Bank.

World Bank (WB). 2009. *World Development Report: Reshaping Economic Geography*. Washington, DC: World Bank.

World Bank (WB). 2012. *Connecting to Compete*. Washington, DC: World Bank.

World Bank (WB). 2013. *World Development Indicators*. Washington, DC: World Bank.

World Economic Forum (WEF). 2007. *Benchmarking National Attractiveness for Private Investment in Latin American Infrastructure*. Geneva: WEF.

World Trade Organization (WTO). 2012. *Statistics on Anti-dumping: Anti-dumping Initiations*. Geneva: World Trade Organization.

World Trade Organization (WTO). 2013. *International Trade Statistics*. Geneva: World Trade Organization.

World Trade Organization (WTO). 2013. *Regional Trade Agreements Database*. Geneva: World Trade Organization.

PART II

Supply Chains

5

Supply Chain Dynamics in Asia

Ruth Banomyong

Introduction

The development of logistics services and communication technologies has revolutionized the supply chain management and has created a "global" market. Shippers and consignees require efficient logistics services that can move their goods to the right place, at the right time, in the right condition, and at the right price (Grant et al. 2006). It is, therefore, of great importance that linkages within and between Asian countries be strengthened to facilitate trade and integrate supply chains for better access to the global market.

The purpose of this chapter is first to introduce a number of key supply chain issues that impact the operations of manufacturers and traders in Asia and the rest of the world. The second objective is to illustrate the key role played by Asia-based logistics providers in managing dynamics that occur within any given supply chain. The last section of the chapter describes a case study that illustrates how supply chain decisions are made and how a particular Asian manufacturer was able to integrate itself into the global supply chain of a major car manufacturer located in the United States (US).

World markets have become increasingly "globalized." To a large extent, this reflects the fact that the majority of, if not all, countries are adjusting to the strong trade liberalization pressures observable around the world. This pressure stems from international trade agreements, including the North American Free Trade Agreement (NAFTA) and the General Agreement on Trade in Services under the auspices of the World Trade Organization.

There is also the development of trading blocs like the European Union (EU), Association of Southeast Asian Nations (ASEAN), and the Asia-Pacific Economic Cooperation (APEC). These trade policy initiatives have a common objective: to open up new trading opportunities by facilitating and enhancing international trade.

Global economic integration relies upon efficient global supply chains, but integration can only succeed if there is cooperation among trading nations. Certain countries, especially in some regions of Asia, are served by relatively few logistics service providers, under less than favorable operating conditions, and where risks are higher. For these countries, this situation results in a failure to develop their international trade potential, higher prices for imports, lower foreign exchange earnings from exports, restricted investment and employment and, thus, in limited economic growth. The logistics costs associated with the distribution of any product can account for a high proportion of its sale price (Banomyong, Cook, and Kent 2008). There is therefore, potentially, considerable scope for efficiency gains that will reduce costs, which in turn will be reflected in the price of a given product. This reduction cannot be implemented without local manufacturers and traders being in complete control of their respective supply chains.

Supply chain management is an integrative approach for planning and controlling the material flow from suppliers to end users (Carter and Ferrin 1995). It is used as a technique to create and maintain a firm's competitive advantage. The management of supply chains is important in ensuring that customers' demands are met, as well as in preventing excess in stocks that may lead to high holding costs or losses through obsolescence. One of the goals of supply chain management is to meet customer service objectives while simultaneously minimizing transport, inventory, and other associated costs (Cooper, Lambert, and Pagh 1997).

The integration of supply chains in Asia can provide a foundation for further economic cooperation and development. For some countries in Asia, inadequate transport infrastructure and high logistics service costs have constrained supply chain development and integration. Major infrastructure investments are already being undertaken in many Asian countries and more are planned (Asian Development Bank [ADB] 2007). Physical connectivity between neighboring countries will be significantly improved on the completion of these infrastructure investments. The improving infrastructure, coupled with expanded cross-border cooperation among Asian countries, will accelerate the process of integrating the Asian supply chain with the rest of the world and the global market.

Key Supply Chain Issues in Asia

Supply chains are not just confined within national borders or markets. In an international supply chain, many state agencies and, in particular, customs agencies play a very important role in the efficiency and efficacy of the supply chain. There is also a heavy reliance on specialized logistics service providers, such as freight forwarders or customs brokers who can facilitate the flows of goods across borders or even develop logistics systems for their clients. The biggest difference between domestic and international supply chains is the environment in which these chains operate.

The key role of a supply chain is to assist in the production, consumption, and distribution of goods and services. This means that goods must be produced and delivered to the market (or customer) in the right quantity, of the required quality (i.e., without defect), and at a competitive price. Integrated and seamless logistics systems can play an important role in facilitating global supply chain processes (Byrne and Markham 1991).

It is therefore important that the movement of goods can be done by combining several modes of transport from one point or port of origin, via one or more interface points, to a final point or port where one carrier or many carriers can organize the whole transport process. Integrated transport is an efficient transport system that provides physical door-to-door operations within the environment of a simple, streamlined documentation process with a single liability system. The objective of integrated transport is to provide a service that is completely reliable and predictable, and that fully meets the needs of the customer (Andersson and Hasson 1998).

However, the efficient operation of transport modes and nodal points is dependent on reduced barriers, fewer institutions, and a simplified legal regime in order to effectively implement integrated logistics operations. As trade is not possible without transport, support for integrated transport will facilitate national and international trade by ensuring an uninterrupted and smooth flow of cargo and by giving better control over the supply chain to manufacturers and traders.

Managing the Supply Chain for Enhanced Competitiveness

Asian countries are recognized for the high quality and low cost of their products. The competitiveness of internationally traded products is greatly influenced by various factors that add to the overall logistics cost within supply chains (Banomyong 2004). These factors need to be taken into account when considering Asian supply chains in order to sustain competitiveness. The main factors are:

The cost associated with the physical transfer of goods is an essential piece of information in the negotiation of an international trade transaction. To maintain a product's competitiveness, the seller must make sure that his cost is as low as possible. However, in any particular supply chain, this cost is made up of a number of cost elements corresponding to services that enable physical linkages between supply chain members. These elements cannot always be clearly quantified beforehand.

Some cost elements (i.e., direct costs) are directly related to the logistics service provided. In general, they are based on published tariffs that reflect the local market conditions, the quality of the service, and the management capacity of the service provider. These considerations depend on the state of the local infrastructure and equipment, and on the local infrastructure and/or equipment maintenance policy to provide reasonable transport services.

Other cost elements (i.e., indirect costs) are a consequence of the service provided. They build up as financial costs resulting from poor operations (e.g., low speed, unexpected delays), as additional costs (e.g., increased insurance premiums), or as "consequential costs" (e.g., sales opportunities lost because goods are not readily available). They reflect the efficiency of the service, the level of risk involved, and the capacity of the service providers to cope with administrative and operational problems.

Transit time is an important element as goods in transit cost money (Tyworth and Zeng 1998). Any reduction in transit time therefore reduces the overall cost of the delivered goods. Transit times can be improved by increasing transport speed while cargo is moving on any particular transport mode or by reducing idle time while cargo is waiting at some interface point for its next movement. A lack of proper coordination of transport operations or excessive administrative and documentary requirements can neutralize any effort or investment in increasing commercial speed.

To reduce the financial cost of their inventories, producers favor arrangements that supply the required input goods "just in time" (JIT), that is, within a short time of the item's anticipated use in production or sale (Christopher 1998). Under these conditions, time reliability is very important. Industries with tight schedule operations (i.e., JIT supply chains) cannot afford delays in delivery (Banomyong, Nair, and Beresford 1999).

Safety of goods is equally important. Any loss or damage—because of theft, mishandling, poor quality packaging, or physical damage caused by accident—will result in goods not being available at the expected time and place, or in the expected condition. The financial consequences of such non-availability, in addition to the cost of loss or damage, are similar to the time reliability consequences mentioned earlier.

Uncertainties related to issues such as schedules, breakages, loss, pilferage, and rules and regulations are faced by traders and may disadvantage exporters and importers.

Security measures are necessary to guarantee the protection of global supply chains against acts of terrorism or other unexpected threats. Beyond the loss of human life and material destruction, a terrorist attack will disrupt the flow of goods within a global supply chain. The above-mentioned considerations indicate that trading opportunities can benefit from better-organized supply chain services. To increase the competitiveness of existing supply chains, sellers and buyers must adapt their commercial practices to meet customers' supply chain requirements, and governments must provide logistics service providers with institutional, regulatory, and operational environments that can stimulate and guarantee the level of service needed for the efficient movement and storage of goods, services, and information.

Logistical activities have traditionally been among the largest costs in global supply chains. However, the most significant advances in modern logistics have not been in cost reduction, but in improved processes to move goods and materials between nations in a timely and seamless manner (Sinha and Babu 1998). Distance is critical in global supply chains, as international marketers require systems designed to handle the challenges of distance in a manner that is timely and transparent to customers (Sharma, Sahay, and Sachan 2004).

Distance in global supply chains equates to transportation speed and dependency. As a general rule, the longer the average distance of transport, the greater is the total cost of transportation. This increased transportation cost results from firms seeking to maintain flexibility while reducing or avoiding extensive inventory commitment. Improved flexibility and lower average inventories translate into an increased number of small shipments moving under positively controlled logistical operations. The distances involved and the specialized nature of international requirements have created a dependence by supply chain members on third-party providers, such as logistics service providers, capable of providing a broad range of value-added services to assure logistical continuity and supply chain integration.

A supply chain approach must encompass not only the economic, commercial, and operational aspects of the international movement of goods, but also all issues related to the facilitation of trade and the responsibility for the goods while in transit (Childerhouse et al. 2008). To take into account all interests involved in the development of a supply chain, especially in Asia, the relationships between traders, services providers, and governments must be clearly identified and proper coordination in the implementation of security measures must be established. The development of supply chains will also create a need for properly regulated logistics providers. This can result in an increased level of competitiveness for all key supply chain stakeholders.

Asian traders and manufacturers can expect the following economic and financial benefits from integrating their supply chains:

- Reduced transit time, increased time reliability, and increased security of cargo, particularly at interface points.
- Reduced transport costs (resulting from the use of modern transport-related technologies, such as ocean going containers and electronic data interchange [EDI]).
- Closer commercial relationships with services providers.
- Greater awareness and understanding of supply chain and logistics related issues influencing their trade.

Asia-based service providers can expect the following benefits:

- Increased importance of international logistics service providers and supply chain solution developers. This will be particularly useful in the development of relationships with and for recognition by governmental agencies.
- Commercial incentives to adopt new technologies, such as the internet, EDI, and radio frequency identification.
- Opportunities to further refine their marketing strategies; for example, for logistics service providers can concentrate their activities in niche operations to serve specific commodities on specific trade routes.

Asian governments will, in theory, benefit from better-integrated supply chains, as they offer an opportunity to update trade and transport related administrative procedures and regulations. An efficient and effective national supply chain will facilitate commerce with other trading partners.

Supply Chain Security

Supply chain security can be perceived as being inconsistent with the objective of facilitating international trade (Dulbecco and Laporte 2003). However, security has now become very much a part of the mainstream supply chain paradigm and can also become a trade facilitation driver.

If all firms involved in a particular supply chain were to optimize their logistical systems independently of other firms in that chain, the management of product flow across the whole chain or pipeline would likely be suboptimal. Attempts to overcome this problem have resulted in the creation of supply chain management. Supply chain management extends the principles of logistics management to customers and suppliers, crossing geographical and organizational boundaries (Banomyong et al. 2005).

Supply chain management leads to stricter requirements on the level of service related to frequency, reliability, lead time, information provision, risk of damage to cargo, security of cargo, complexity of administrative procedures, and the number of smaller consignments.

The security of the supply chain, like the efficiency of the chain, concerns both the physical flow of goods and the flow of information from origin to customer (Banomyong 2005). In a supply chain, there is no benefit if certain links or stakeholders are operating efficiently while others are not. It is the total performance of the supply chain from origin to final consumption that is relevant. Each link in the supply chain is dependent on the previous link in order to achieve continuity, synchronization, and enhanced final customer service level. The security issue is directly related to the performance measurement of any supply chain. This means that all security conditions must be met and guaranteed in order for goods to move unhindered within supply chains.

The supply chain in Asia has experienced important changes during the last 25 years and several ports in the region have come to specialize in the concentration of transshipment activities. Ocean going containers ensure flexibility of shipments. Several Asian ports are dedicated to this technology and are, as a consequence, consolidating their status as supply chain hub centers. Economic growth and development have restructured the nature and pattern of supply chains, introducing new demands within the main trading regions in Asia.

Hub centers thus require a specialized, high-capacity transshipment infrastructure. However, infrastructure is not the only dimension in nodal restructuring. Supply chain development also requires the integration of value-added services and transshipment functions at key nodal links. These key nodal links will not only further supply chain integration, but will also support the efficient distribution of manufacturers' and traders' goods and services. The security of these hub centers as nodal links in the supply chain is of critical importance.

The world has become a system of linkages in which individual nodal links are connected in intricate patterns of dependency in hub-feeder relationships, as well as in end-to-end connections that reflect the increasing trade dependencies among regions. This trade dependency is derived within a broader competitive regional environment, with the development of supply chains underlining the need for efficiency as well as security. These conditions have had, and will continue to have, an impact on the management strategies of supply chain nodes around the world (Robinson 1998).

Security has now become, along with reliability, time compression, and cost reduction, one of the necessary preconditions for high-performance supply chain management capable of guaranteeing high economic performance. The quest to achieve global supply chain efficiency and efficacy is currently leading toward the development of techniques that allow a wide variety of unforeseen events to be overcome through the use of prevention measures. This is made even more evident by the JIT paradigm and door-to-door service, which require a high level of security, low inventory levels, and efficient movements between several points of origin and destinations.

However, security comes at a cost. Supply chain security leads to an increase in logistics costs and exerts a relatively negative pressure on economic growth, especially for the Asian countries involved. Even though the cost of security is universal, much of the burden has been shifted to Asian countries by the main importing countries in the West (such as the US), whose security programs have been targeted at Asian exporters (Banomyong 2005). The short-term effect of an increase in supply chain security is relatively negative, but the medium- to long-term impact is likely to be beneficial to certified and recognized operators. This permits the creation of dedicated secure supply chains, where supply chain processes are considered to be more efficient and controlled. More security could, therefore, mean greater trade facilitation and possible expansion (e.g., as a supply chain becomes more secure, goods that are physically moved within the system benefit from greater ease of access to importing countries).

It must also not be forgotten that the cost of delays and procedures linked to the trade of goods is estimated to be between 5% and 13% of the value of goods traded (Banomyong, Cook, and Kent 2008). Security issues, if not dealt with properly, can also become a major cause of delays. Table 5.1 describes the main players involved with the security of the global supply chain.

Stakeholders are diverse, with often-conflicting objectives, but it is in the interest of all parties to improve the reliability of global supply chains by increasing security in order to avoid disruption of the system. It is important to guarantee the protection of global supply chains and their capacity to serve international markets. If a nodal link is considered secure, it is likely to benefit from increased goods traffic. However, only a uniform level of security in all supply chain nodal links will reduce the risk of disruption to global supply chains, as a supply chain is only as strong as its weakest link (Banomyong and Sopadang 2009). It is not enough to have a number of selected secure supply chain nodes if other nodes within the supply chain are not held to the same standard. The example illustrated in Box 5.1 reflects the challenges involved in securing global supply chains.

In order for traders and manufacturers to integrate into efficient and effective global supply chains, security related activities must be completely synchronized in their requirements relating to global supply chain management. Security initiatives are now considered key logistical activities, but are also very problematic, especially in an international context where the institutional framework is confusing. If a security activity fails, it will have an impact on the competitiveness of global supply chains. This is a challenge that Asian countries must overcome.

Table 5.1
Players in the Security Supply Chain

The governments	Customs have the duty to protect the national economy and society instead of merely focusing on goods control at the border.
The traders	Reliable, secure and efficient supply chain will theoretically contribute to global trade expansion.
The ports	Security will represent a critical variable in terms of competitiveness.
The service providers	Key player in terms of security as they move goods and information.
The insurance providers	Increase security less insurance premium.

Source: Adapted from Dulbecco and Laporte (2003).

Box 5.1
Secure Supply Chains: The People's Republic of China (PRC)–Europe Smart and Safe Trade Lanes

The EU concluded an agreement on Customs Cooperation and Mutual Administrative Assistance in Customs Matters with the PRC that entered into force on 1 April 2005. On 19 September 2006, the European Commission and the PRC agreed to launch a pilot project on smart and secure trade lanes, with particular emphasis on sea containers. The agreement aims to improve cooperation on supply chain security and to work toward mutual recognition and reciprocity of security measures. The pilot project initially involves the ports of Rotterdam (Netherlands), Felixstowe (United Kingdom), and Shenzhen (PRC).

As of 19 November 2007, the customs administrations of the United Kingdom, Netherlands, and PRC exchange electronic information on sea containers leaving their territory through Rotterdam, Felixstowe, and Shenzhen. This is an important step in European customs cooperation with the PRC and paves the way for reciprocity and mutual recognition of security measures. This initiative took place within the EU framework for the secure and smart trade lanes pilot project.

Both sides agreed to exchange experience and develop best practices in order to better understand and prepare the implementation of the World Customs Organization Framework of Standards to Secure and Facilitate Global Trade. They also agreed to pursue the objectives of reciprocity and mutual recognition of measures for security and facilitation to be implemented between the General Administration of Customs of the PRC and the customs authorities of the EU.

In summary, the smart and secure trade lane pilot project will allow:

- the testing of end-to-end supply chains from the point of packing containers, through the entire container journey, to the point of final destination;
- agreement on and testing of criteria for economic operators to be granted authorized economic operator (AEO) status;
- agreement on and testing of data requirements for preloading security clearance for "door to door" supply chains;
- the definition of and agreement on minimum risk rule set (profiles) and minimum control standards for customs clearance;

(Box 5.1 Contd)

(Box 5.1 Contd)

> - the testing and evaluating of information technology and technical solutions that enhance security and control systems while facilitating legitimate trade; and
> - comparison of equivalent AEO legislation in order to prepare the ground for mutual AEO recognition between the EU and the PRC.
>
> The evaluation of the first phase of the pilot project was launched in spring 2009 and should be finalized by the end of the year.
>
> *Source:* Adapted from European Commission. Security Cooperation with Third Countries. Available at: http://ec.europa.eu/taxation_customs/customs/policy_issues/customs_security/cooperation_3thcountries/index_en.htm (accessed 31 December 2009).

The Role of Logistics Providers in Handling Supply Chain Dynamics

Supply chain objectives are rarely fully met because of the individual behavior of decision makers in firms along the supply chain, as their behavior is neither optimal nor rational (Parnaby 1979). Due to the dynamic nature of the supply chain, amplifications and fluctuations occur from suppliers all the way down the chain (Sterman 1989). What is needed is a robust control system that is flexible enough to counteract any disturbances along the supply chain.

Logistics and supply chain management are seen as the fields in which logistics providers, by virtue of their particular expertise, are able to offer the most added value to transactions in the freight trade. Freight forwarders, as "logistics service facilitators," play an important role in supply chain management, as an increasing number of firms outsource their logistics function (United Nations Economic and Social Commission for Asia and the Pacific [UNESCAP] 2002). These third party logistics providers are now becoming more involved in the design, management, and control of firms' supply chains. Asia-based regional logistics providers are the best equipped to manage supply chains in Asia as they are familiar with the context in which they operate.

The selection of a logistics provider is critical to supply chain competitiveness (Hensher and Chow 1999). Third party logistics plays a pivotal role in the design and provision of an integrated supply chain that responds to the client's needs. In order to help their customers, logistics providers need to behave more like partners of their clients. Not only do logistics providers have to arrange for the transport of cargo and facilitate its clearance through customs, they also need to manage their clients' order processing. This means that logistics providers are involved not only in lowering their clients' costs by reducing waste in ordering operations, but also in integrating their clients' supply chains. The aim is to make the partnerships so tight and seamless that the logistical services provided become part of the clients' own businesses. Figure 5.1 illustrates how logistics service providers control a global supply chain.

The task of a logistics provider is to facilitate trade to the extent that the trader needs only to produce and sell the goods (or to order the goods, in the case of imports). Once this has been done the logistics provider can take over and provide every subsequent function from factory gate to final delivery. As the distance between the manufacturer (i.e., the exporter) and the distributor or retailer is often quite considerable (and vice-versa for imports), problems relating to both material and information flows are common.

Suppliers have to respond as quickly as possible to various situations within a specified time frame. If the supplier cannot do so, the multinational enterprise (MNE), as the focal firm in the supply chain, will probably choose another supplier. This creates a number of problems for manufacturers, as they not only have to manufacture goods on time, but they also need to deliver them on time (Bruisma, Gorter, and Nijkamp 2000). The problem of delivering goods on time becomes very crucial when MNEs use JIT management techniques.

The logistics provider's main role is to manage the supply chain such that goods arrive on time; however, because of limited resources and various operational constraints, logistics providers are not always able to deliver, rendering their clients less competitive.

Logistics Providers' Role in a Regional Supply Chain

Supply chain routing alternatives between Thailand and Viet Nam will now be presented and compared. The purpose of this subsection is to illustrate some of the issues logistics providers have to deal with when managing their clients' supply chains in the context of Southeast Asia. A total of three supply chain alternatives are described in Table 5.2 and illustrated in Figure 5.2. Exporters and importers are not interested in routing decisions. Their sole focus is on having their goods delivered as per the agreed upon service level and cost. It is

Figure 5.1
Role Played by Logistics Service Provider in Global Supply Chain

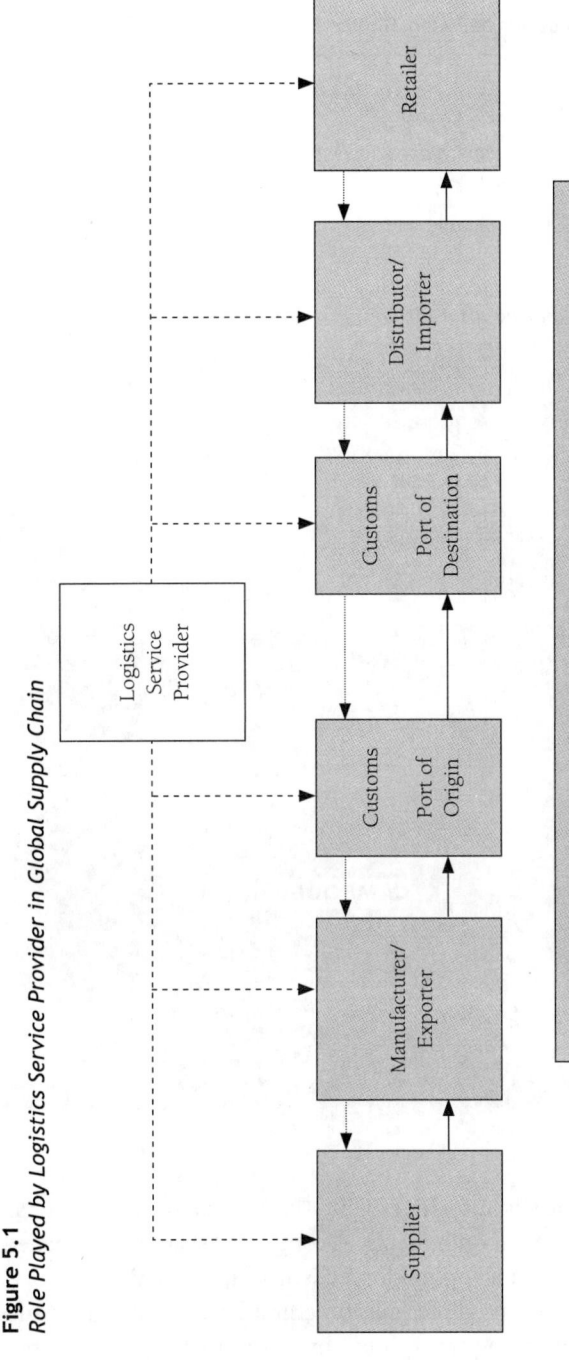

Source: Author's own rendition.

Table 5.2
Routing Alternatives between Thailand and Viet Nam

Route	Thailand	Mode	Viet Nam
1	Bangkok/Laem Chabang	Road vs. Sea	Ha Noi
2	Bangkok/Laem Chabang	Road vs. Sea	Da Nang
3	Bangkok/Laem Chabang	Road vs. Sea	Ho Chi Minh

Source: Compiled from industry sources.

Figure 5.2
Supply Chain Routing Alternatives between Thailand and Viet Nam

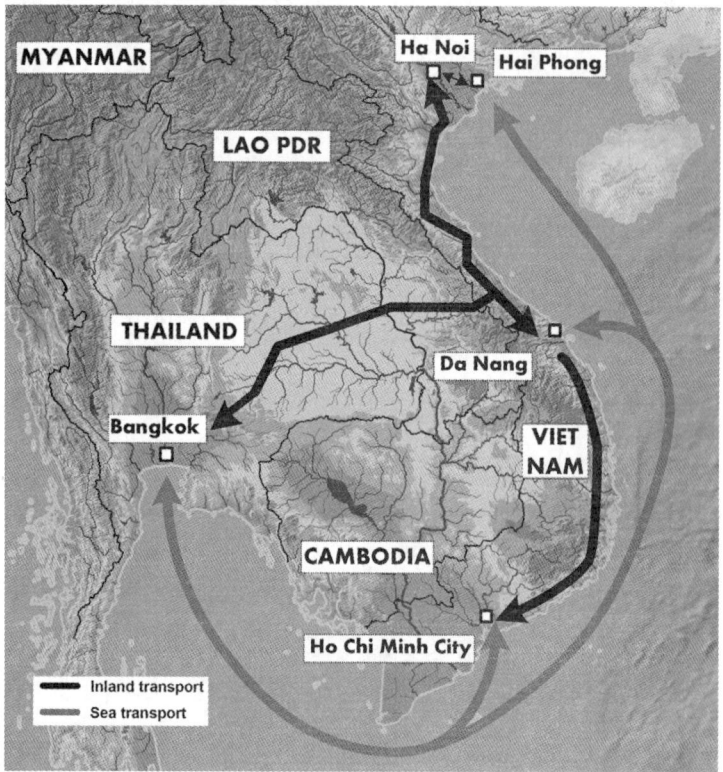

Source: Author.

the duty of the logistics provider to find the optimal solution that balances the client's cost and time requirements. A contextual scanning is needed in order to find the most suitable option for a client's supply chain.

There is currently no direct maritime link between Bangkok and Ha Noi. Freight containers being transported by sea must therefore be transshipped at Ho Chi Minh port, increasing transit time and cost. Sea transport costs (including transshipment) represent about 30% of total transport costs, but more than 70% of transit time. Trucking costs represent around 15% of total transport costs. It is interesting to note that administrative formalities can comprise up to 36% of the total cost of transportation between Bangkok and Ha Noi via the maritime route. Also, while the total cost of transport by road is 30% higher than the maritime option, it is also 80% faster.

For a shipment traveling by land between Bangkok and Ha Noi, transport has the highest activity ratio: more than 68% of total costs and 73% of total time for the whole journey. If no transloading is conducted at the border, it is possible to reduce transport costs by over $300 per twenty-foot equivalent unit.[1] Transloading does not need to be done at the Lao People's Democratic Republic (Lao PDR)–Viet Nam border.

A number of fees are levied by various related authorities in the transit of goods between Thailand and Viet Nam. This creates a problem for the land route as there is empirical evidence that the land route is likely to be selected by traders who are handling higher value and more-time-sensitive commodities. These add-on fees defeat the purpose of physically and institutionally connecting Thailand and Viet Nam via Lao PDR to facilitate trade.

The actual physical transportation of goods is not a problem in and of itself. The difficulty lies in border crossings, despite the existence of the Greater Mekong Subregion Cross Border Transport Agreement, whose objective is to reduce border crossing time to not more than 30 minutes per border.

Cost is not the sole factor taken into account in routing selection; transit time is another key component. The land route can link Bangkok to Ha Noi in just over 2 days, while the sea route takes more than 14 days due to transshipment. Even if a direct maritime link between Bangkok and Ha Noi existed, the journey would take at least 5 days to complete.

The current maritime linkage is a reflection of the relatively low volume of direct trade between Thailand and Viet Nam's northern region. If the volume of trade were higher, there would surely be direct links between the countries. The existing maritime linkage is not competitive given the time dimension and is probably only suitable for cargo that is non-time sensitive.

---

[1] On 11 June 2009, Thailand, Lao PDR, and Viet Nam held a ceremony to officially mark the implementation of a trilateral exchange of traffic rights, but the procedures are still being implemented.

Designing Supply Chains: The Role of Logistics Providers

In Asia, supply chain control processes, including production scheduling, shipment of product, and inventory maintenance, are frequently decentralized and remote from each other. The processes usually operate independently of one another and in serial order. Slow feedback from the marketplace causes scheduled production to over or under manufacture in relation to the actual demand. Another issue in the region is the relatively high cost of logistics—the result of inadequate physical facilities and cumbersome administrative barriers, coupled with a legal framework not adapted to modern international business practices (Banomyong, Cook, and Kent 2008).

Specialized middlemen, such as logistics service providers, perform critical, value-enhancing functions that benefit all the players along the supply chain and increase the supply chain's competitiveness. One of the ways Asia-based logistics providers can support the integration of supply chains for their clients and their network is by designing and developing effective supply chains and integrating multiple service suppliers into a seamless distribution system.

Limited resources and operational constraints are not unique to logistics provider operations in Asia. In each region or country in the world, various resource limitations and operational constraints exist. It is the duty of Asia-based logistics providers to make the best use of their resources within the existing physical constraints and the limited institutional framework prevalent in many Asian countries (Banomyong and Beresford 2001).

The logistics provider sees its function in the supply chain as that of a distributor. Its main role is to move goods from one end of the supply chain to the other within the constraints imposed by both clients and the commercial environment. "Customer panic" occurs when a client is faced with a difficult situation in the supply chain—usually a stockout—and is unable to rectify the situation. When a break in the supply chain occurs or is going to occur, there is a very strong risk that the whole supply chain will be immobilized, generally for a longer period that it took the break to occur (Hong-Minh, Disney, and Naim 2000). An analogy may be drawn between this type of situation and a traffic jam along a motorway. Typically, it can take up to three times longer for a traffic jam to clear than it takes one to build up.

The increased interest in managing supply chain dynamics in recent years has led to a number of research activities that have tried to verify the predicted demand amplification and information distortion. So far, most of these studies have focused on retail networks and distribution chains, neglecting the complexity introduced by product conversion in supply chains.

According to Hines, Holweg, and Sulliwan (2000), the factors affecting supply chain complexity are:

- A lack of interaction of information and material flow, causing, for example, short or late deliveries, which force firms to reschedule production.
- Interaction of whole value streams, competing, for example, for capacity at bottleneck points.
- Multiple routing of parts or products through the supply chain.
- Dynamic demand and supply patterns of particular parts or products.
- The average numbers of parts bought from each first tier company, which can range from 50 to 600 parts.
- Ordering policies and customer prioritization, which distorts demand and supply chain flows.
- Product conversion and value added within each manufacturing level of the supply chain.
- New product introduction and product retirement, which creates further instability.

Due to the complexity involved, a new system dynamics framework is necessary to gain a more comprehensive view of supply chain reality. Supply chain management in many Asian countries, such as Thailand, is still in its early stages. This is particularly true for local small and medium enterprises (SMEs) and family-owned businesses. Supply chain management practices have been widely implemented between multinational firms operating in Asian countries, but these practices have not yet reached the small- and medium-sized local suppliers (Wong and Boon-itt 2008). Supply chain performance for most local firms in Asia is weak, but has great potential for improvement because most business owners do not yet have a grasp of supply chain issues. During a supply chain assessment of many local firms, it was discovered that existing assessment tools, such as the Supply Chain Operation Reference model or the Enkawa Supply Chain Logistics Scorecard, were considered to be too complicated and too difficult to use, especially for SMEs (Banomyong 2008). This shows that many SMEs in the region are not in control of their supply chains and are subject to the influence of the focal supply chain firm, which is usually an MNE.

When members in the supply chain are rendered nonoperational, costs increase significantly and major penalties are incurred. In such situations, the players involved must find someone who is able to solve the problem of immobilization in the supply chain.

This is where logistics providers become invaluable as, through their network of overseas agents, they can monitor manufacturers throughout Asia, giving them complete control over their clients' supply chains. Some logistics providers may even act as a buffer to potential problems, creating an emergency network so that goods will arrive on time. The purpose of such an "emergency channel" is to minimize the impact of interruptions along supply chains (Jennings, Beresford, and Banomyong 2000).

The only prerequisite for a logistics provider to be able to activate an emergency channel is that the provider, or a member of the provider's network, must be physically in possession of the goods. In such cases, a solution is feasible and can be worked out at the most reasonable cost to the client. If the goods are not in a logistics provider's (or the provider's agent's) possession, however, it is almost impossible to find a solution.

The logistics provider's role is not only to organize the supply chain, but also to service it. As such, the logistics provider can be described as the "engineer" or "architect" of the supply chain. The duty of the logistics provider is not only to forecast customers' requirements, but also to provide value-added services that will contribute to the enhancement of customers' competitiveness. However, forecasting customers' requirements is not an exact science and the logistics provider must also be able to respond rapidly to unforeseen events or requests involved in the provision of logistics services to clients.

The logistics provider cannot operate successfully in isolation, but has to rely on his agency network, subcontractors, and clients. A close partnership has to be formed between the service provider and the client. This partnership, in turn, will facilitate the creation of more realistic supply chain designs and operational processes. It is the duty of the logistics provider to be aware of all the options available and to design supply chains flexible enough to cope with unforeseen events.

Today, logistics providers are faced with the daunting challenge of balancing cost minimization with clients' almost infinitely variable requirements. The outsourcing of logistics functions and JIT management techniques have forced logistics providers to design more-dynamic and more-efficient supply chains within various operational constraints. However, it is the physical aspects of the supply chain that will ultimately shape supply chain dynamics.

The successful development of basic infrastructure and the adaptation of local commercial practices to international standards through the removal of all unnecessary trade barriers are preconditions to the integration of supply chains in Asia and the rest of the world.

The challenges for logistics providers in Asia include identifying essential transport infrastructure and networks, as well as determining how to achieve and maintain an active and competitive role in providing logistics services through the integration of global supply chains.

Logistics providers located in developed Asia provide extensive logistical and supply chain management services. These services go beyond transport and distribution, catering to the needs of exporters and importers by managing all transport requirements from the point of origin of raw materials, through the manufacturing process, to delivery to the final consumer. In contrast, logistics providers in Asia's developing economies are faced with many physical and non-physical barriers to providing full door-to-door transport and other logistical services, such as inadequate banking practices, documentation, and insurance.

Logistics and supply chain management, as a discipline, is not fully developed in many parts of Asia. The main functions of logistics—purchasing, production, distribution, warehousing, inventory, and information—are available in the region, but the emphasis is generally on transportation or distribution issues. The majority of logistics providers in Asia are not currently capable of offering a higher level of value-added logistics services.

Involvement of Asian SMEs in Global and Regional Supply Chain: A Case Study

Supply chain management integrates suppliers, manufacturers, and distribution centers to get the right products to the right place at the right time and in the proper condition (Christopher and Towill 2001). As the management of supply chains improves, the potential of integrated global supply chains is starting to be realized. Eventually, raw materials will be harvested at the source, manufacturing will be performed in the locations providing the highest processing value-added, and products will be sold in the markets offering the highest prices—regardless of the geographical locations of the various members in the supply chain. A number of theories have been tested to determine how firms could devise efficient and effective global supply chain strategies (Naylor, Naim, and Berry 1999). Despite these developments, many supply chains fail to meet their performance objectives (Fisher 1997). Moreover, as illustrated in the following case study, some firms have been able to successfully compete by employing strategies that oppose those recommended for lean and agile supply chain design.

In this case study, part of the global supply chain of a US automotive seat supplier is examined. This global supply chain sourced raw materials from approved vendors in the US, transported them over a 28-day period to a cut-and-sew operation in the Northeast of Thailand, returned the completed leather seat covers to the US over another 28-day period, and delivered them to a seat assembly plant that ultimately fed into a JIT auto assembly plant in Detroit, Michigan. Despite substantially increasing the supply chain cycle time to over 12 weeks (including a 2-week holding of safety stock in both the US and Thailand), the supply chain had a competitive advantage over similar operations in maquiladoras located near the US–Mexico border that had only a 3-day transit time to the seat assembly plant.

Maquiladoras were originally formed in 1964 when the US cancelled a program that admitted Mexican workers into the US to provide labor in agriculture. Mexico initiated the Border Industrialization Program in order to replace the lost economic value of the exported labor, providing an incentive for American factories located in the US to move to Mexico to take advantage of lower labor costs. These maquiladoras enabled Mexico to accelerate its economic growth through the provision of cheap labor located in border areas (Fullerton and Barraza de Anda 2003).

Maquiladoras import at least 90% of the raw materials for components that they process. These companies assemble components into finished or semi-finished goods and then re-export them back to the US, mostly to the industrial Midwest states (Fullerton and Barraza de Anda 2003). NAFTA was expected to spur additional growth in maquiladoras, and the number has indeed increased rapidly since 1994, when the agreement went into effect. However, while NAFTA was blamed for relocating US jobs to Mexico, the primary economic force behind the rapid growth of maquiladoras was the devaluation of the peso at the end of 1994, which effectively cut labor costs (in US dollar terms) by more than 40% (Gruben 2001). Maquiladoras have been incorporated into the "lean" paradigms of automobile suppliers to provide labor cost savings while maintaining proximity to auto assembly plants based in the US Midwest.

The competitive cost advantage in the case study supply chain was achieved through a supplier in Thailand that produced leather seat covers of higher quality (with a direct economic benefit of higher yields) and at a lower labor cost than maquiladora operations in Mexico. These benefits helped offset the additional costs of safety stock, freight between the US and Asia, and potential inventory obsolescence due to a longer supply chain.

As supply chain strategies continue to be developed and refined, the characteristics of the product itself (e.g., size vs. cost), as well as the value of the labor input (e.g., quality and efficiency vs. cost), need to be incorporated into the global supply chain design and management decision-making framework in order to facilitate optimum performance. One of the main motivations for a firm to look at suppliers outside of its home country is to secure a competitive advantage through lower costs and/or higher quality products. This might be in the form of unit price reductions for items produced in low-wage markets (Trent and Monczka 2003) or of a source of products not available locally (Mansfield 2003). As an example, a significant industry relying on procurement from international sources is the US clothing industry, in which apparel and footwear are produced in low-wage regions including Asia and South and Central America. The global aspects of these supply chains include only the final link: the product may be produced entirely in the low-cost region and then shipped to distribution centers or directly to retailers in North America or Europe (Cho and Kang 2001).

"Agile" supply chains attempt to leverage the advantages of global suppliers. Industries that rely on agile supply chains require the flexibility to meet rapidly changing customer expectations, or to stay ahead of changing technologies that may quickly become obsolete. Examples of products in these industries include semiconductors and computers, for which innovation drives customer demand and responsiveness is a primary requirement (Christopher and Towill 2001). Supply chain systems for semiconductors and computers may link manufacturers and subcontractors in multiple locations in Asia or Europe to customers in the US (Bhatnagar and Viswanathan 2000; Brown, Hau, and Petrakian 2000).

Under a different paradigm, "lean" supply chains seek to stabilize the supply of raw materials and manufactured components, while eliminating waste in the supply chain. In lean supply chains, the primary driver of the system is cost. As a result, every effort is made to shorten transit times and eliminate in-process inventory or safety stock (Womack, Jones, and Roos 1990). The automobile industry, first in Japan and now also in the US, has focused on developing lean systems, categorizing suppliers based on strategic importance and requiring key firms to make regular deliveries as often as every two hours. Suppliers might relocate to Mexico to reduce labor costs while remaining within two to three days shipping time from major assembly plants in the US

Midwest. More distant global sources would not be considered if the management's goal is to create a lean supply chain.

It has also been observed that the advantages of lean and agile strategies are not mutually exclusive. Hybrid or "leagile" strategies use lean methods for high volume lines, while maintaining agility for more specialized products. These strategies make use of lean concepts up to a decoupling point in the supply chain (Banomyong, Veerakachen, and Supatn 2008; Naylor, Naim, and Berry 1999), after which agile processes are applied. Alternatively, they use lean methods in situations where demand is demonstrably stable and agile principles for the more unpredictable aspects of operations (Christopher and Towill 2001).

Another approach to determining the appropriate supply chain strategy is based not on customer requirements (e.g., responsiveness vs. low cost), but on the type of product. Using this method, agile supply chains would be used for innovative products with unpredictable demand, while functional products, with their mature life cycles, would benefit more from lean supply chains that minimize waste (Fisher 1997).

The case study presented below illustrates a deliberate, competitive supply chain strategy that involved accepting an eight-week transit time over a one-week transit time, plus an increased safety stock of four weeks, in order to utilize a more distant supplier (i.e., in Thailand instead of Mexico) offering better quality at a lower cost. This decision seems to go against the prevailing body of knowledge pertaining to lean and agile supply chains that dominates the literature today. As such, this case study can be considered an appropriate part of the iterative process in understanding the theory of globally integrated supply chain management (Eisenhardt 1989).

The Case Study

In most modern automobile assembly operations, the assembly process is limited to forming body panels and welding vehicles frames. All other components—engines, seats, instrument panels, and other electrical, mechanical, and decorative items—are supplied from external sources and then bolted onto the vehicle as it moves down the production line.

One of the most expensive and complicated subassemblies supplied to the automobile is the seat. Seats are supplied in a wide variety of colors and materials, and many other options (e.g., heaters and air bags) are available for any given vehicle model. To be able to respond to the range of permutations that are required by automakers, seat manufacturers have assembly operations that mirror the automobile assembly plants that they supply. Their operations are usually located within 30 minutes of the automobile assembly plant and are tied to the plant via EDI. The same job order that triggers the production of the automobile triggers the assembly of the seat. During the 2 hours it takes the vehicle to travel from welding shop to final assembly, the seat must be built with all the required options and sent directly to the correct location at the auto assembly plant to be installed in proper sequence in the correct automobile.

Similar to the auto plant, the seat-making operation performs little manufacturing other than forming the seat frames. All other components, such as molded foam, electromechanical parts, and seat covers, are delivered in batches and used on an as-needed basis. As a second tier supplier (supplying the first tier seat plant), the operation in Thailand was of a type referred to in the automobile industry as a "cut and sew" or "trim" operation. This refers to the process of cutting and sewing together cloth, foam, leather, vinyl, and other soft materials to form one component of an automobile seat; in this case, the seat cover.

Raw materials had to be produced by approved suppliers, who were primarily located in the greater Detroit area, or in the states adjoining Michigan. The one exception was the leather supplier, who produced and shipped its components from Omaha, Nebraska, a center of beef production and a source of raw hides. All materials were shipped in full containers and packed at the respective suppliers' locations, with the exception of a small number of items, such as thread and fasteners. Overland transportation in the US averaged three to five days from the Midwest to a west coast port, and sea shipments to Thailand took approximately 24 days, with the entire transit time averaging 4 weeks in one direction. The supply chain system was set up so that deliveries were made every week (Figure 5.3). At any one time, therefore, there was one shipment that was about to arrive in Thailand, two shipments in transit between Asia and North America, and one shipment just leaving suppliers in the US. Finished seat covers flowed back to the seat assembly plant in the Detroit area in a similar pipeline, also within a 4-week timeframe.

Safety stock was maintained in both Thailand (in the form of raw materials) and the US (in the form of completed seat covers awaiting assembly) as a contingency against a delayed shipment, and was strictly controlled to two weeks' supply. This stock level was determined based on the strategic assumption that a problem in transit could occur that might delay any one shipment, but not two consecutive shipments. Therefore, two weeks supply of inventory

Figure 5.3
Pipeline of Weekly Shipments between Thailand and the United States

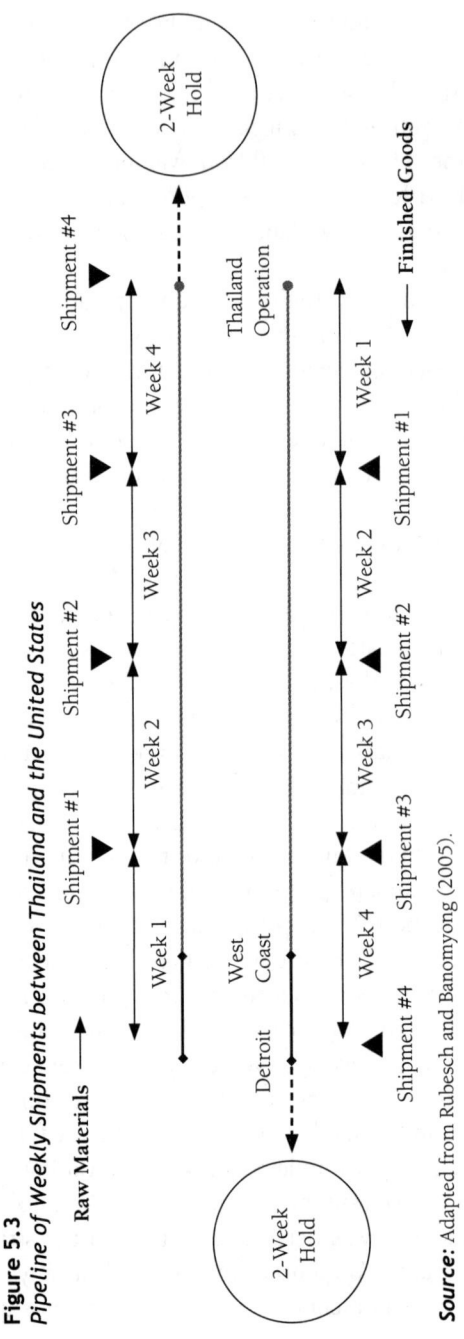

Source: Adapted from Rubesch and Banomyong (2005).

would be enough to maintain production until the next shipment arrived the following week.

The key competitive advantage for the Thailand operation was in the processing of leather. Leather is a natural product varying in grain and appearance, and contains many imperfections that cannot be used in seat covers. Each hide had to be inspected for imperfections before patterns for the various pieces could be cut in order to avoid the imperfections. The leather cutting process is time consuming and requires considerable judgment and skill by the leather cutters. The leather cutters in the Thailand operation had many years' experience and were heavily relied upon for their expertise.

The Thai plant achieved an average yield of 70%, or about 5% better than the best suppliers from Mexico, giving the Thai plant a US$14 cost advantage per seat cover over its competitors as a result of better utilization of leather. At the same time, lower wages gave the Thai plant an additional US$73 cost advantage, contributing to an overall advantage of US$87 per seat cover. Meanwhile, additional freight, inventory, an obsolescence allowance, and more durable packaging offset the cost advantage by US$39, for a net positive contribution of US$48 per seat cover (see Table 5.3 for a complete breakdown of the logistics costs involved).

The difference in production cost seems to be the main driver behind the selection of the Thai supplier; however, cost cannot be the only factor as other variables need to be included in the decision-making process of selecting suppliers. Production cost needs to be understood within the total cost framework. It is this total cost approach that illustrated the cost competitiveness of the Thai plant.

Table 5.3
Comparison of Cost Components for One Leather Seat Cover (Mexico vs. Thailand)

Cost per seat cover, complete set (US$)	Mexico	Thailand
Labor	88	15
Leather	199	185
Other materials	67	67
Packaging	2	6
Outbound logistics	4	21
Inbound logistics	2	8
Cost of inventory	–	3
Obsolescence allowance	–	9
Total Costs	362	314

Source: Adapted from Rubesch and Banomyong (2005).

Case Study Summary

The supply chain literature focuses on how customer requirements and market demand determine supply chain strategies that are responsive (i.e., agile), efficient (i.e., lean), or a combination of the two (i.e., leagile). However, the case study presented suggests that market-driven factors alone may not be sufficient to determine the optimum supply chain strategy.

Product characteristics have considerable influence over transportation options and, therefore, over supply chain strategies. For example, the size of the product with respect to its value influences whether air freight or sea freight is the most viable option, which in turn affects supply chain strategy.

The expertise, efficiency, and cost of labor as a resource in the supply chain must be considered when supply chain strategies are being determined. A labor advantage in one location relative to another—e.g., better skills or lower wages—may offset additional transportation costs so that a supply chain that uses a more distant labor source could offer advantages over one that employs labor closer to the customer market, as illustrated in the case study.

Conclusions

The purpose of this chapter was to describe a number of key supply chain issues and the key role that can be played by logistics providers within an Asian context. A case study was provided to illustrate actual supply chain dynamics and how an Asian firm might integrate into global supply chains.

Supply chain management in Asia still remains a challenge for all involved stakeholders. Asian manufacturers and traders need to be in better control of their supply chains, while most local providers are still struggling to provide value-added logistics services. Infrastructure and institutional arrangements are improving, but not quickly enough to enable successful supply chain management. Supply chain management must consider the deployment of all resources that affect customer value.

Asian policy makers need to be aware of the importance of supply chain management and of how the integration of national supply chains into regional and global supply chains can contribute to sustainable trade growth with key trading partners.

References

Andersson, T.H., and P. Hasson. 1998. Why Integrated Transport Systems? *OECD Observer*. 211. pp. 27–31.

Asian Development Bank (ADB). 2007. Logistics Development Study of the North South Economic Corridor. Manila: ADB.

Banomyong, R. 2004. Assessing Import Channels for Lao PDR. *Asia Pacific Journal of Marketing and Logistics*. 16 (2). pp. 62–81.

Banomyong, R. 2005. The Impact of Port and Trade Security Initiatives on Maritime Supply Chain Management. *Maritime Policy & Management*. 32 (1). pp. 1–11.

Banomyong, R. 2008. Developing a Logistics Performance Assessment Tool for SMEs. In A.C. Lyons, ed. *Annual Logistics Research Network (LRN) Conference Proceedings 2008*. Liverpool, UK: Chartered Institute of Logistics and Transport.

Banomyong, R., and A. Sopadang. 2009. Logistics Benchmark Study of the East West Economic Corridor. In K. Pawar and C. Lalwani, eds. *14th International Symposium on Logistics (ISL) Proceedings*. Istanbul, Turkey: University of Nottingham.

Banomyong, R., and A.K.C. Beresford. 2001. Multimodal Transport: The Case of Laotian Garment Exporters. *International Journal of Physical Distribution and Logistics Management*. 31 (9). pp. 663–685.

Banomyong, R., C. Basnet, P. Childerhouse, E. Deakins, S.M. Disney, M.M. Naim, D.R. Towill. 2005. Internationalising the Quick Scan Audit Methodology. In A. Villa and R. Pasquino, eds. *18th International Conference on Production Research Proceedings*. Salerno, Italy: University of Salerno.

Banomyong, R., P. Cook, and P. Kent. 2008. Formulating Regional Logistics Development Policy: The Case of ASEAN. *International Journal of Logistics: Research and Applications*. 11 (5). pp. 359–379.

Banomyong, R., R.V.N.P. Nair, and A.K.C. Beresford. 1999. Managing "Demand Amplification" in the Supply Studies and Chain: The Thai Forwarders' Experience. Occasional Paper 59. Cardiff, UK: Cardiff University, Department of Maritime International Transport.

Banomyong, R., V. Veerakachen, and N. Supatn. 2008. Implementing Leagility in Reverse Logistics Channels. *International Journal of Logistics: Research and Applications*. 11 (1). pp. 31–47.

Bhatnagar, R., and S. Viswanathan. 2000. Re-engineering Global Supply Chains: Alliances between Manufacturing Firms and Global Logistics Services Providers. *International Journal of Physical Distribution & Logistics Management*. 30 (1). pp. 13–34.

Brown, A.O., L.L. Hau, and R. Petrakian. 2000. Xilinx Improves its Semiconductor Supply Chain Using Product and Process Postponement. *Interfaces*. 30 (4). pp. 65–80.

Bruisma, F., C. Gorter, and P. Nijkamp. 2000. Multimodal Infrastructure, Transport Networks and the Location of Firms. *Transportation Planning and Technology*. 23. pp. 259–281.

Byrne, P.M., and W.J. Markham. 1991. *Improving Quality and Productivity in the Logistics Process: Achieving Customer Satisfaction Breakthroughs*. Oak Brook, IL: Council of Logistics Management.

Carter, J.R., and B.G. Ferrin. 1995. The Impact of Transportation Costs on Supply Chain Management. *Journal of Business Logistics*. 16 (1). pp. 189–212.

Childerhouse, P., A.J. Thomas, D.R. Towill, and R. Banomyong. 2008. An International Comparison of Supply Chain Practices and Performance: Thailand, Celtic, English and New Zealand. In K. Pawar and C. Lalwani, eds. *Proceedings of the 13th International Symposium on Logistics.* Bangkok: University of Nottingham.

Cho, J., and J. Kang. 2001. Benefits and Challenges of Global Sourcing: Perceptions of US Apparel Retail Firms. *International Marketing Review.* 18 (5). pp. 542–561.

Christopher, M. 1998. *Logistics and Supply Chain Management: Strategies for Reducing Cost and Improving Service.* Harlow, UK: Prentice Hall.

Christopher, M., and D. Towill. 2001. An Integrated Model for the Design of Agile Supply Chains. *International Journal of Physical Distribution & Logistics Management.* 31 (4). pp. 235–246.

Cooper, M.C., D.M. Lambert, and J.D. Pagh. 1997. Supply Chain Management: More Than a New Name for Logistics. *International Journal of Logistics Management.* 8 (1). pp. 1–13.

Dulbecco, P., and B. Laporte. 2003. *How can the Security of the International Supply Chain be Financed?* Clermont-Ferrand, France: Centre d'Etudes et de Recherches sur le Développement International (CERDI).

Eisenhardt, K. 1989. Building Theories from Case Study Research. *Academy of Management Review.* 14 (4). pp. 532–550.

Fisher, M.L. 1997. What is the Right Supply Chain for Your Product? *Harvard Business Review.* 75 (2). pp. 105–116.

Fullerton Jr., T.M., and M.P. Barraza de Anda. 2003. Maquiladora Prospects in a Global Environment. *Texas Business Review.* October. pp. 1–5.

Grant, D.B., D.M. Lambert, J.R. Stock, and L.M. Ellram. 2006. *Fundamentals of Logistics Management.* Berkshire, UK: McGraw-Hill.

Gruben, W.C. 2001. Was NAFTA behind Mexico's High Maquiladora Growth? *Economic Financial Review.* July: 11–21.

Hensher, D.A., and G. Chow. 1999. Interacting Agents and Discrete Choices in Logistics Outsourcing: A Conceptual Framework. In H. Meersman, E. Van de Voorde, and W. Winkelmans, eds. *Proceedings of 8th World Conference on Transport Research (WCTR).* Amsterdam: Pergamon Press.

Hines, P., M. Holweg, and J. Sulliwan. 2000. Waves, Beaches, Breakwaters and Rip Currents: A Three-Dimensional View of Supply Chain Dynamics. *International Journal of Physical Distribution & Logistics Management.* 30 (10). pp. 827–846.

Hong-Minh, S.M., S.M. Disney, and M.M. Naim. 2000. The Dynamics of Emergency Transshipment Supply Chains. Occasional Paper 66. Department of Maritime Studies and International Transport Cardiff, UK: Cardiff University.

Jennings, E., A.K.C. Beresford, and R. Banomyong. 2000. Emergency Relief Logistics: A Disaster Response Model. Occasional Paper 64. Department of Maritime Studies and International Transport. Cardiff, UK: Cardiff University.

Mansfield, B. 2003. Spatializing Globalization: A "Geography of Quality" in the Seafood Industry. *Economic Geography.* 79 (1). pp. 1–16.

Naylor, J.B., M.M. Naim, and D. Berry. 1999. Leagility: Integrating the Lean and Agile Manufacturing Paradigms in the Total Supply Chain. *International Journal of Production Economics.* 62 (1–2). pp. 107–118.

Parnaby, J. 1979. Concept of a Manufacturing System. *International Journal of Production Research.* 17 (2). pp. 123–135.

Robinson, R. 1998. Asian Hub/Feeder Nets: The Dynamics of Restructuring. *Maritime Policy and Management.* 25 (1). pp. 21–40.

Rubesch, E., and R. Banomyong. 2005. Selecting Suppliers in the Automotive Industry: Comparing International Logistics Costs. *Asia Pacific Journal of Marketing and Logistics.* 17 (1). pp. 61–69.

Sharma, D., B.S. Sahay, and A. Sachan. 2004. Modelling Distributor Performance Index Using System Dynamics Approach. *Asia Pacific Journal of Marketing and Logistics.* 16 (3). pp. 37–67.

Sinha, R.K., and A.S. Babu. 1998. Quality of Customer Service in Supply Chain System: A Diagnostic Study. *International Journal of Quality & Reliability Management.* 15 (8/9). pp. 844–859.

Sterman, J.D. 1989. Modeling Managerial Behavior: Misperceptions of Feedback in a Dynamic Decision Making Experiment. *Management Science.* 35 (3). pp. 321–339.

Trent, R.J., and M.R. Monczka. 2003. International Purchasing and Global Sourcing—What are the Differences? *Journal of Supply Chain Management.* 39 (4). pp. 26–37.

Tyworth, J.E., and A.Z. Zeng. 1998. Estimating the Effects of Carrier Transit-Time Performance on Logistics Cost and Service. *Transportation Research Part A.* 32A (2). pp. 89–97.

United Nations Economic and Social Commission for Asia and the Pacific (UNESCAP). 2002. *Training Manual on Operational Aspects of Multimodal Transport.* Bangkok: UNESCAP.

Womack, J.P., D.T. Jones, and D. Roos. 1990. *The Machine That Changed the World.* New York, NY: Macmillan.

Wong, C.Y., and S. Boon-itt. 2008. The Globalisation of Automotive Component Suppliers. In M. Morita, ed. *3rd Annual Conference for Production and Operations Management Society (POMS).* Tokyo: POMS.

6

The Internationalization of SMEs in Regional and Global Value Chains

Hank Lim and Fukunari Kimura

Background

Since the early 1990s, international production networks have developed within the Association of Southeast Nations (ASEAN) and East Asia. Extensive production networking and the regional division of labor have resulted in massive vertical intra-industry trade in parts and components within the region, effectively becoming the actual economic integration in East Asia. Figure 6.1 shows the share of intra-regional trade (exports and imports) within several economic areas. The share of intra-East Asia trade—where East Asia is defined as the 10 ASEAN countries; the People's Republic of China (PRC); Japan; Hong Kong, China; and the Republic of Korea—rose remarkably from 34.9% in 1980 to 52.4% in 2003. Surprisingly, this figure is higher than that of the North American Free Trade (NAFTA) area, which stands at 44.6%, though a bit lower than 58.7% of the European Union (EU). East Asia has no doubt achieved a high level of de facto economic integration in terms of international trade transactions within the region. The integration process has not been seriously interrupted, not even by the Asian currency crisis that occurred in the late 1990s.

However, economic integration in East Asia does not seem to have developed in an even manner. The share of intra-regional trade of the ASEAN 10 and PRC–Japan–Republic of Korea in 2003 remains at only 22.2% and 25.8% respectively, against that of East Asia as a whole (52.4%). This suggests that

Figure 6.1
Intra-Regional Trade (export and import ration in percent)

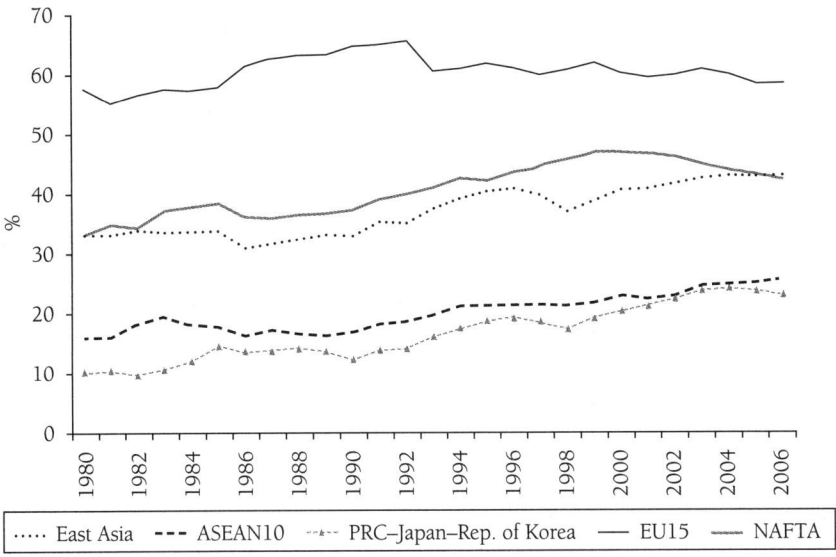

Source: IMF, Direction of Trade, CD-ROM, May 2007.

economic activity requires a large space in which to expand, such as the whole of East Asia, as spatial economists argue. Figure 6.2 shows trade shares of East Asia by partner countries or regions. Such a trend suggests that countries at relatively low-income levels have played a significant role in the expansion of the intra-regional trade in East Asia.

The trade pattern inside East Asia has changed, from a traditional pattern in which capital goods and final products, such as consumer and intermediate goods, have been traded with each other to a pattern where parts and components are traded instead. To put it differently, intermediate goods in the same industry have been actively traded among the Asian countries, expanding intra-industry and intra-regional trade. For instance, import shares of parts and components within East Asia increased from 7.2% in 1980 to 32.2% in 2003, while those of processed goods decreased from 37.3% to 28.0% in those same years. Parts and components as shares of trade have become the largest among commodity groups (Figure 6.3).

East Asia is experiencing an explosive increase in trade in intermediate goods, particularly in machinery industries, based on the international division of labor and production processes among countries at different income levels and development stages. Trade patterns, in today's global competition

Figure 6.2
Trade Share of East Asia with Partner (%)

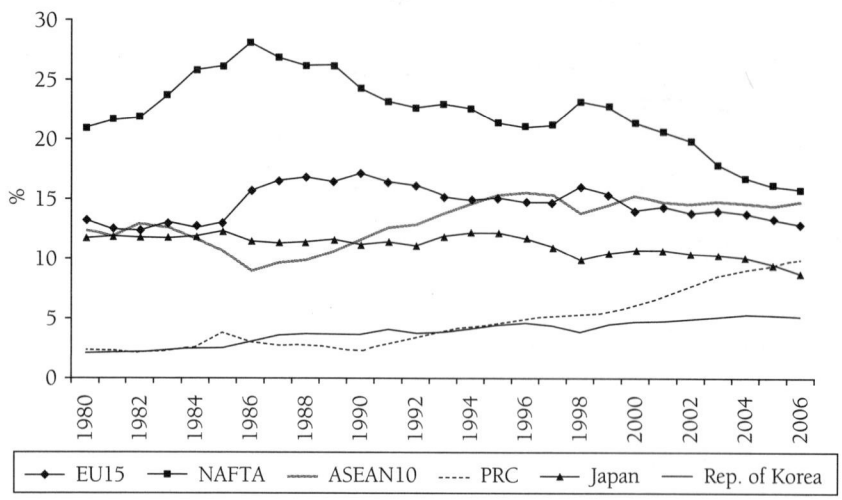

Source: IMF, Direction of Trade, CD-ROM, May 2007.
Note: East Asia consists of ASEAN10; PRC; Japan; Hong Kong, China; Republic of Korea; and Taipei,China.

Figure 6.3
Trade Pattern inside East Asia (%)

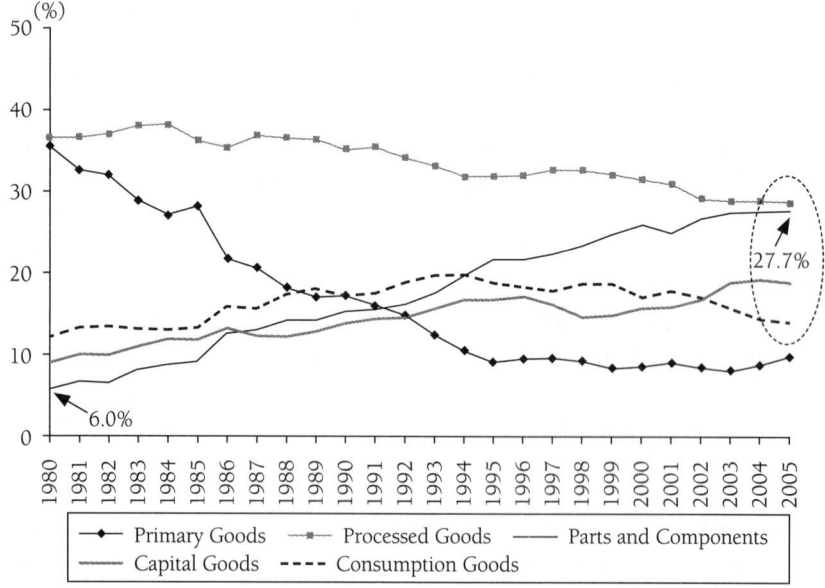

Source: Original data came from UN Comtrade database. Compiled by IDE.
Note: The values of trade goods are measured by import value on US dollar basis.

where economies of scale are a strong consideration, are quite different from the traditional ones based on the static concept of comparative advantage. The whole production process now involves sequential production blocks that are located across countries. Different stages of production are undertaken by different suppliers located in different countries. Products traded between firms in different countries are components instead of final products.

This phenomenon is known as cross-border production sharing or the fragmentation of production. Production processes are finely sliced into many stages and located in different countries in East Asia (Figure 6.4). In theory, with such vertical specialization a slight decline in trade costs would induce an increase in the trade of intermediate goods since goods may move across national borders multiple times. For example, an intermediate good is exported from country A to country B and is imported back to country A again after processing in country B. In this case, the good crosses a national border twice in country A and twice in country B. This is what actually happens in East Asia; when trade cost goes down, the competitiveness of the whole of East Asia increases greatly.

The Mechanics of International Production Networks and SMEs

Although international production and distribution networks in East Asia began to form since the beginning of the 1990s, Jones and Kierzkowski (1990) began developing the theory of fragmentation around the same time. The theory pointed out fundamental differences between the division of labor for industry and production-processes, or rather between finished products trade and intermediate goods trade, particularly within the context of the firm's decision making in cutting out production blocks and service link costs.

Figure 6.5 illustrates the original idea of fragmentation. Suppose that a large factory in the machinery industry takes care of all production processes from upstream to downstream. Such a factory is both capital and human-capital intensive and as such is likely to be located in a developed country. However, if we look at the factory in detail, we may find various production processes. Some processes are human-capital intensive and require a pool of researchers and technicians. On the other hand, some processes are highly labor-intensive and a pool of unskilled labor may suffice. Other processes may need to operate 24 hours per day in order to accelerate capital depreciation. Hence, if we can fragment production processes into several production

Figure 6.4
Production/Distribution Networks (geographical fragmentation)

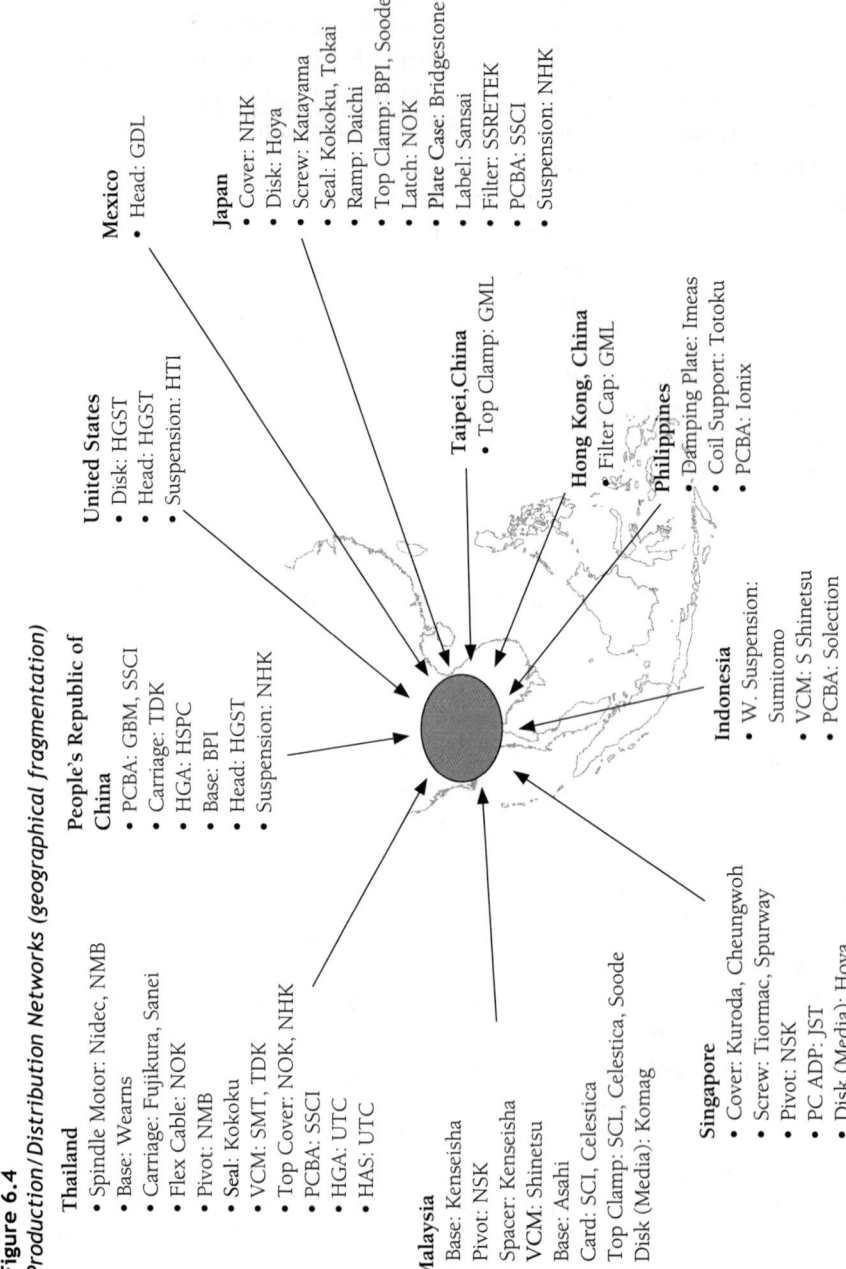

Thailand
- Spindle Motor: Nidec, NMB
- Base: Wearns
- Carriage: Fujikura, Sanei
- Flex Cable: NOK
- Pivot: NMB
- Seal: Kokoku
- VCM: SMT, TDK
- Top Cover: NOK, NHK
- PCBA: SSCI
- HGA: UTC
- HAS: UTC

Malaysia
- Base: Kenseisha
- Pivot: NSK
- Spacer: Kenseisha
- VCM: Shinetsu
- Base: Asahi
- Card: SCI, Celestica
- Top Clamp: SCL, Celestica, Soode
- Disk (Media): Komag

Singapore
- Cover: Kuroda, Cheungwoh
- Screw: Tiormac, Spurway
- Pivot: NSK
- PC ADP: JST
- Disk (Media): Hoya

People's Republic of China
- PCBA: GBM, SSCI
- Carriage: TDK
- HGA: HSPC
- Base: BPI
- Head: HGST
- Suspension: NHK

United States
- Disk: HGST
- Head: HGST
- Suspension: HTI

Mexico
- Head: GDL

Japan
- Cover: NHK
- Disk: Hoya
- Screw: Katayama
- Seal: Kokoku, Tokai
- Ramp: Daichi
- Top Clamp: BPI, Soode
- Latch: NOK
- Plate Case: Bridgestone
- Label: Sansai
- Filter: SSRETEK
- PCBA: SSCI
- Suspension: NHK

Taipei,China
- Top Clamp: GML

Hong Kong, China
- Filter Cap: GML

Philippines
- Damping Plate: Imeas
- Coil Support: Totoku
- PCBA: Ionix

Indonesia
- W. Suspension: Sumitomo
- VCM: S Shinetsu
- PCBA: Solection

Source: Hiratsuka (2006).

Figure 6.5
The Theory of Fragmentation

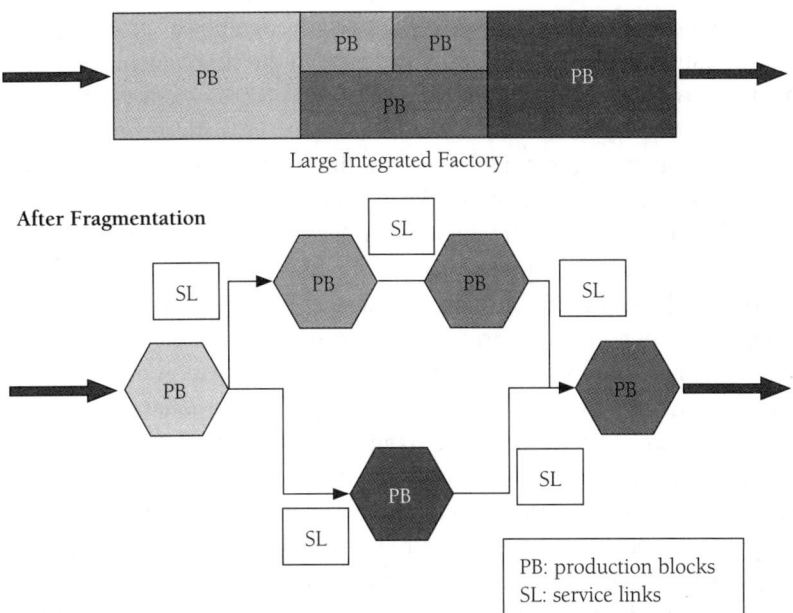

Source: Kimura 2006.

blocks and locate them in appropriate places that possess different location advantages, we may save on the total production cost. This is fragmentation.

Fragmentation of production processes makes sense when the savings of production costs in production blocks is large and incurred service link costs for connecting remotely located production blocks are small. Firms can cut out production blocks so as to exploit differences in location advantages in remote areas. However, service link costs, including transport costs and various coordination costs, should not be too large. Transactions between production blocks tend to be relation-specific in a production process.

The international production and distribution networks in East Asia have reached a high level of sophistication in that fragmentation and agglomeration occur at the same time, developing the complicated combination of intra-firm and inter-firm transactions. To analyze the sophistication of production and distribution networks in East Asia, Kimura and Ando (2005) introduced fragmentation in terms of the firm's disintegration. They also included a dimension of fragmentation in terms of geographical distance, where a firm decides whether to keep some economic activities inside the firm or to outsource them to unrelated firms (Figure 6.6). This two-dimensional framework explains the sophisticated nature of fragmentation in East Asia, where fragmentation of both intra-firm and inter-firm production processes is developed.

By introducing the idea of intimacy between geographical proximity and inter-firm transactions, the framework can explain the simultaneous development of the firm-level fragmentation of production processes and the industry-level formation of agglomeration. Inter-firm transactions are accompanied by extra transaction costs as compared to intra-firm transactions, which here are interpreted as service link costs in disintegration-type fragmentation. Such costs may be particularly high when a firm does not perfectly trust its counterpart. Short distances help such transactions by cutting down the cost of identifying and monitoring business partners as well as the cost of troubleshooting. Such forces in turn formulate industrial agglomeration in East Asia. At such a sophisticated stage of development of the formation of production networks, SMEs play a crucial role. SMEs are essential components of production networks, involved in inter-firm fragmentation in various forms such as subcontracting arrangements and original equipment manufacturer (OEM) contracts. SMEs are also essential components for industrial agglomeration. In this context, local SMEs as well as multinational SMEs can be important participants in the vertical inter-firm division of labor.

In ASEAN and East Asia, international trade in parts and components has expanded explosively, and the international division of labor in terms of production processes has developed to an unprecedented degree. At the same

Figure 6.6
Fragmentation in a Two-Dimensional Space

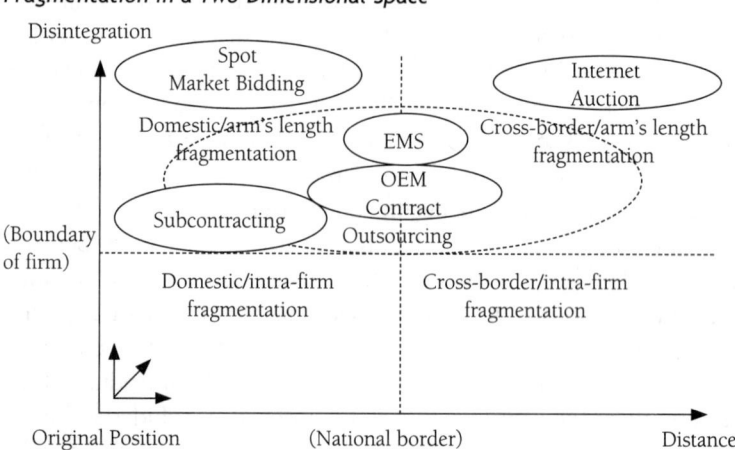

Source: Kimura and Ando (2005).

time, economic agglomeration or industrial clusters have grown in several notable places where dense vertical supply chains have formed. The fragmentation of production processes and the formation of economic agglomeration, however, are rather new phenomena starting from the late 1980s or the early 1990s. The new economic geography and fragmentation theory are extremely useful in understanding the mechanisms of agglomeration and fragmentation.

The new economic geography explains the formation of economic agglomeration in geographical space. The spatial structure of economic activities is considered to be the outcome of a process involving two opposing types of forces—agglomeration forces and dispersion forces. The geographical theory analyzes the balance of these two opposing forces that generate a variety of location patterns of economic activities.

A key property of agglomeration forces is the circular causality of economic activities. For example, an automobile assembler would attract a number of upstream suppliers, and the resulting productivity enhancement and market expansion might lead to the entry of another assembler. Such circular causality would generate a sort of economies of scale through geographical proximity.

At the same time, the growth of economic agglomeration would enhance dispersion forces. Concentration of economic activities would increase land prices and wage rates, bring severe price competition among firms, cause traffic congestion, complicate telecommunication, and generate air pollution. Due to such congestion effects, dispersion forces would be intensified.

One of the important factors that affect the balance between agglomeration forces and dispersion forces is transport cost, which includes freight costs, tariffs, nontariff barriers, and risk for exchange-rate variation. As transport costs decrease, agglomeration may grow. With a substantial decrease in transport cost, production activity may disperse instead.

There are three elements that make fragmentation possible. First, there must be production cost saving in fragmented production blocks—the firm must take advantage of differences in location advantages between the original location and a new location. Second, the cost of service links that connect remotely located production blocks, like the costs of transportation, must not be too high. Third, the cost of network set-ups must be small. When the additional cost for setting up a new plant is relatively small, the production process fragments easily. The feasibility of fragmentation, therefore, depends heavily on the nature of technologies in the industry and economic environment. New economic geography and the fragmentation theory provide insights to important factors that determine the location of economic activities in the globalizing era.

International production and distribution networks in ASEAN and East Asia are, relatively speaking, the most advanced and sophisticated in the world. East Asia has no doubt developed a favorable policy environment that is suitable for globalizing corporate activities. However, such a policy environment has been realized through accumulated profit-motivation actions by the private sector rather than being developed with well-designed strategic moves.

New economic geography and the fragmentation theory provide rich implications for policy environments in the globalizing era. New economic geography suggests a promulgation of policies that affect agglomeration forces and dispersion forces. The fragmentation theory suggests policies affecting production cost saving, service link cost, and network-set-up cost. Combined with careful consideration of policy needs that differ by development stages, it is possible to develop desirable policy packages in order to utilize globalizing forces.

The Link with Technology Transfer and Spillovers

International production and distribution networks provide various opportunities for multinational enterprises (MNEs) and local firms in developing countries to compete and cooperate with each other. Such interactions between MNEs and local firms are much more varied and intense than in a world with relatively simple North–South industrial divisions of labor. This implies that the nature of technology transfers and spillovers has evolved in the enhanced economic dynamism.

In comparison with the relocation of whole operations to least developed countries (LDCs), a MNE has a greater degree of freedom in how to cut out production blocks, which in turn yields greater flexibility in the location pattern. This means that a MNE can relocate some activities to LDCs with much smaller-commitments than in the case of relocating all activities. The consequence is that some production processes actually move to LDCs with technology advantages. From the viewpoint of hosting LDCs, such transfers require less policy than in the case of the relocation of the entire industry in the form of import-substituting foreign direct investment (FDI).

The physical movement of technology and managerial know-how to LDCs would provide more opportunities for local firms and entrepreneurs to enjoy technology transfers or spillovers. However, there is a potential difficulty that comes with these slices of value chains. Particularly at the early stage of development, fragmented production blocks do not typically engage in transactions with neighboring firms, which limits the linkage channel of technology transfers and spillovers to a particular firm. In addition, technology absorptive capacity is one of the crucial determinants for what sort of production processes will be located in LDCs, whether vertical linkage is developed, and whether technological spillovers occur. LDCs at the initial stage of industrialization typically suffer from low technology absorptive capacity.

Once LDCs reach the stage of industrial agglomeration, the perspective of technology transfers and spillovers is drastically improved. In industrial agglomeration, vertical division of labor by means of inter-firm transactions is actively conducted. Initially, such transactions tend to be among upstream and downstream MNEs. However, under severe competitive pressure, MNEs start seeking local firms to transfer technologies to local firms and entrepreneurs in order to obtain a supply of parts and components at satisfactory prices, quality, and delivery timing. Technology absorptive capacity of local firms and entrepreneurs again becomes an important determinant of the extent of technology transfers and spillovers. A key difference from traditional import substitution with heavy trade protection is the competitive pressure from international markets, which forces efficiency in MNE operations.

The spatial structure of production networks provides an important geographical consideration regarding technology transfers and spillovers. At least in the case of machinery industries with major just-in-time systems, inter-firm transactions almost always occur in geographical proximity. When a novice local firm enters international production networks, it most often occurs as a first layer transaction. This coincides with the geographical extent to which human resources can travel daily. Cross-border inter-firm transactions by local firms, such as transactions at the second or third layer of production, are rare except in cases where the firm has already established a strong reputation. Layer of production refers to different stages or phases of production.

In industries other than machinery, some adjustments are necessary. In the garment industry, for example, the speed and frequency of transactions are typically slower than that in the machinery industry, and thus longer distance transactions between MNEs and local firms may be possible. In the software industry, the geographical distance in transactions may be less important, although credibility remains important. In both cases, technological links with MNEs are crucial to the quality of work.

New Development Strategies and Technology Transfers and Spillovers

The formation of international production and distribution networks in East Asia induces a fundamental revision of development strategies for LDCs. New development strategies claim that participation in international production and distribution networks is the key to accelerating economic development in an era of globalization.

The development of international production and distribution networks in East Asia also presents a new perspective on technology transfers and spillovers. Hosting FDI generates both positive and negative effects on local firms and entrepreneurs. Negative effects stem from enhanced competition in local markets for products and labor, and technological dominance by MNEs may adversely affect the performance of local firms. On the other hand, positive effects include easier access to technology and managerial know-how for local firms and entrepreneurs. Technology transfers or spillovers may occur in the form of imitation or reverse technology, spin-off of engineers, and most notably vertical links to upstream and downstream MNEs.

A traditional development strategy known as import-substituting FDI seeks to establish vertical links between local firms and MNEs, and leverages those links to explore the possibility of technologically upgrading local firms and entrepreneurs. Such attempts often fail because the size of the local market is small and compensating incentives for MNEs such as import restrictions degrade the competitive environment. Under discretionary incentive schemes, MNEs typically have a weak incentive to make technology transfers to local firms and entrepreneurs.

Another development strategy that utilizes export-oriented FDI and does not provide a notable increase in technology transfers and spillovers insofar as the activities of MNEs are geographically segregated in narrow export processing zones (EPZs). MNEs in EPZs are exposed to international competition and pursue maximum efficiency. In this situation, the value-added slices that MNEs bring in are often very thin and limited to purely labor-intensive activities, and the enclave nature of EPZs becomes a serious obstacle to technology transfers and spillovers.

The concept of four layers of transactions has a profound implication in the context of East Asia. Developing countries at the early phase of economic development try to participate in international production networks by hosting production blocks pushed out of congested industrial agglomeration in the neighborhood. During this phase, transactions by invited production blocks occur mostly in the second layer. However, developing countries that have reached a higher phase of economic development should try to formulate efficient industrial agglomeration. In this phase, transactions in the first layer become important. Alternatively, in the context of developing economies outside East Asia, long distance transactions such as those in the third layer become important. The types of expected transactions require different policies, and have different demands for hard and soft infrastructure.

International production and distribution networks, particularly at the stage of development observed in the East Asia today, present a possibility for technology transfers and spillovers. East Asia proves that the sophistication of production fragmentation can achieve the level of industrial agglomeration in which active technology spillovers may occur. In an internationally competitive environment, some MNEs are quite willing to transfer technologies. This is a new way of pursuing technology transfers and spillovers.

One problem is that not all countries can immediately attain such a stage of development. In order to participate in international production and distribution networks, a country must host the first wave of production blocks invested by MNEs. At this stage, the operation tends to be thin in value-added processes, perhaps even thinner than in the case of traditional EPZ operations, and local vertical links are not yet established. This means that significant technology transfers or spillovers may not be expected for a while if the technology absorptive capacity of the industry is not well developed. Policy makers in LDCs must be patient in hosting FDI until a critical mass is built up, rather than hastily introducing performance requirements for technology transfers. Once the seed of industrial agglomeration has been planted, local firms and entrepreneurs will have ample opportunities for penetrating production networks, which will eventually accelerate technology transfers and spillovers.

Although these arguments require further theoretical elaboration and empirical support, they seem to be largely consistent with the literature on technology spillovers, such as Lim (2007). The literature in particular suggests that vertical input–output linkages between local firms and MNEs are the most powerful channels to accelerate technology transfers and spillovers.

The Internationalization of SMEs in Regional and Global Value Chains

Current State of SMEs in Southeast Asia

Before exploring what policies can facilitate the internationalization of SMEs in Southeast Asia, it will be useful to first examine the sector's characteristics

152 Hank Lim and Fukunari Kimura

to get a sense of the present and potential capabilities, as well as the constraints that are present. This, however, is a tricky task given the following factors: (i) a lack of timely and comprehensive information about SMEs due to a structural weakness in statistical service in many developing countries, (ii) the wide differences in economic structures and levels of development in the region, and (iii) differences in countries' definitions of SMEs.

Roles and Characteristics

With its massive size, the SME sector forms the backbone of Southeast Asia's economy. It accounts for a majority (more than 90%) of the number of all private-sector firms (Asasen, Asasen, and Chuangcham 2003) and employs a considerable proportion of the domestic workforce in each country (40%–90%). Thus, it is not surprising that Southeast Asia's SMEs play a significant economic role, albeit to varying extents (Figure 6.7). They make a substantial contribution to employment (about 40%–90%) and exports (more than 25%), and play different dynamic roles that drive economic growth and industrial development (Wengel and Rodriguez 2006). For example, SMEs in Singapore provide a flexible skilled production base that attracts MNEs; while in

Figure 6.7
Roles and Characteristics of SMEs

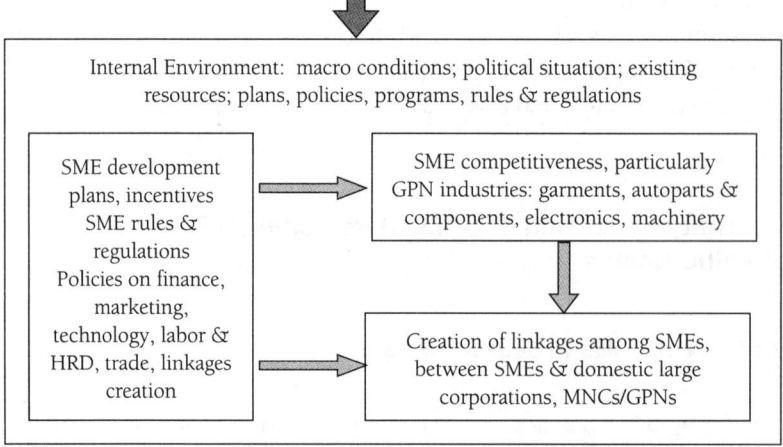

Viet Nam SMEs and rural enterprises were instrumental in the transition process from a planned to market economy.

Southeast Asia's SMEs pervade virtually all socioeconomic activities and services across urban and rural–urban areas. But there is much variation in their sectoral composition. While SMEs have an overwhelming presence in the Malaysian service sector, they are strongly represented in agriculture in Indonesia, food, beverage, and tobacco in Cambodia, and wholesale and retail trade in the Philippines (Figure 6.7).

Given the trends of rising globalization and economic integration in the Asian region, there is significant potential for the SME sector to increase its contribution to the region's development through greater participation in global value chains (GVCs). There are, however, some characteristics that are generally shared among SMEs in Southeast Asia that limit their ability to do so.

Entrepreneurism

There is a shortage of a sustainable entrepreneurial drive in the sector. This can be attributed to a weak culture of innovation, and in the high growth Asian economies an over-reliance on technologies brought in by MNCs. Entrepreneurship capabilities are crucial for SMEs to maximize their inherent comparative advantages gained from operating on a small scale, such as the flexibility to adapt to changing market demands.

Level of Expertise

The SME sector's development is also constrained by a lack of skill and expertise in organization and management, which are important for enterprises' efficiency, flexibility, and competitiveness (Asasen, Asasen, and Chuangcham 2003). The need for competent, contemporary management is compounded by the fact that drastic economic and technological developments have created new, modern ways of production and service delivery.

Related to this issue is information communication technology (ICT) capability. Although there have been no comprehensive studies done on the extent of adoption of ICT in the SME sector in Southeast Asia, preliminary data suggest that a huge number of SMEs in Southeast Asia have yet to establish an online presence and networking facilities (Asasen, Asasen, and Chuangcham 2003). This can be partly attributed to a lack of awareness and know-how and limited access to ICT infrastructure, hardware, and software.

Networking

There has been minimal clustering and network forming among SMEs, activities that, as many scholars agree, can help small firms overcome some of the barriers they commonly face, such as difficult access to information, markets, and inputs (Giuliani, Pietrobelli, and Rabellotti 2005). This may be due to an inward-looking mentality that is typical among the family enterprises that account for a large proportion of the sector. To illustrate, more than 90% of SMEs in Cambodia are single proprietorship businesses, owned by an individual or family (Baily 2007). In Malaysia, micro-establishments represent 79.4% of SMEs (Normah 2006). Linkages also require fundamental shifts in business strategies that SMEs may not be able to achieve because of a lack of resources and knowledge.

Access to Finance

SMEs in most Southeast Asian economies have been having difficulty gaining access to finance for a long time. This can be attributed to imperfections in the financial markets and a lack of critical primary and secondary markets such as those for SME equity and bond financing. The formal banking sector remains the dominant source of credit for local businesses in the region. Worsening the problem, the current economic crisis has increased risk aversion and decreased liquidity. In response, governments have made substantial efforts to allocate formal-sector resources to support SMEs through measures such as subsidies and safeguarding banks. However, success has been spotty. Thus, SMEs are still struggling to secure long-term bank loans, working capital and bridge financing.

The Process of SME Integration into Global Value Chains

This section examines the three main frameworks that researchers have used to understand how firms internationalize and the consequent implications on government policy for SMEs. This will help shed light on the relevant motivating factors for these trends. Although the frameworks define internationalization as the process in which firms increase their involvements in overseas operations, the focus here is on SMEs and their participation in GVCs.

GVCs are evolving tiered structures. The main role is played by a lead firm that manufactures the final product. This firm is supported by a small number of preferred first tier suppliers, which are also supported by other suppliers, and so on, forming a tiered structure (Figure 6.8). It is generally easier to enter a network as a lower-tier supplier. But this position tends to be unstable as other suppliers can easily replace the original supplier by offering better comparative advantages such as lower costs (Abonyi 2005). Therefore the challenge for SMEs is not only to try to enter GVCs, but to move up the tiers by increasing the value content of their activities.

Admittedly, the frameworks presented below are theoretical and distinct. However, all of them have found some empirical evidence in past studies (e.g., Etemad and Wright 2003; Lloyd-Reason et al. 2005), suggesting that harmonizing the different approaches instead of viewing them as contradictory can

Figure 6.8
How SMEs Fit into Global Value Chains

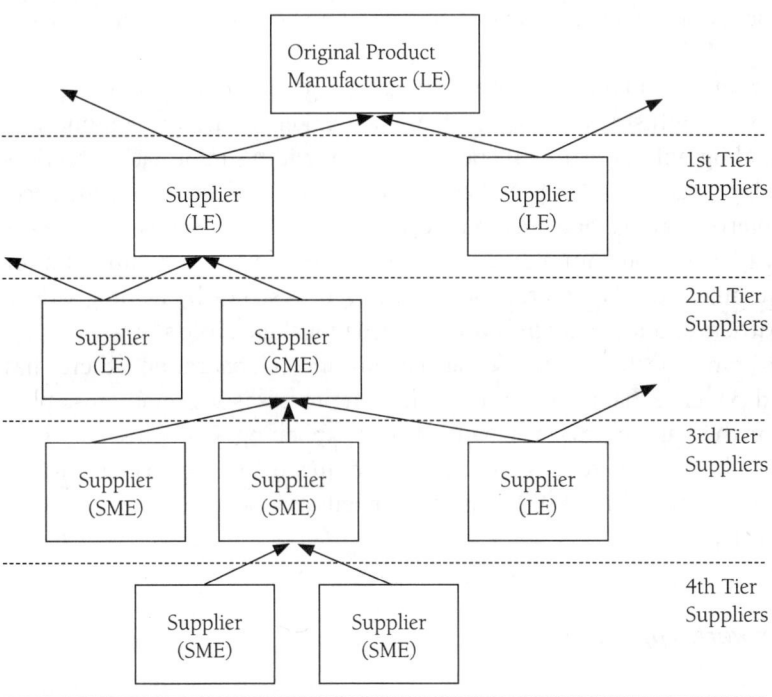

LE = Large enterprise; SME = Small or medium enterprise
Source: Abonyi, 2005.

help guide analyses of SME internationalization. Indeed, the theories seem to be interrelated. They all state that knowledge of foreign markets is a fundamental driver of overseas expansion, although they attribute the acquisition of it to different sources.

The Stage Approach

According to the stage model, internationalization can be seen as an incremental process where different stages follow each other in a logical order (Luostarinen 1994). The assumption is that a firm's knowledge about foreign markets and commitment to expanding overseas will consequently affect its business decisions and activities. As a firm's international involvement increases, so does its overseas knowledge and commitment, thus starting an expansionary cycle. The process has been described as "a gradual acquisition, integration and use of knowledge about foreign markets and operations and a successively increasing commitment to foreign markets" (Johanson and Vahine 1977: 36).

Governments can therefore play a critical "triggering" role by enacting policies to boost SMEs' knowledge of overseas markets and their commitment to expanding abroad. This can be done by providing information services and raising awareness about the benefits of internationalization, for instance. Once enterprises have branched out beyond national boundaries, the process is likely to gain momentum on its own. It then becomes more important for the government to play the role of facilitator, for instance by helping reduce entry barriers and lowering the cost of international expansion.

With rapid technological advancement and globalization, there has emerged evidence that the internationalization process is accelerating—a phenomenon the stage approach is inadequate in explaining. Though small, there have even been an increasing number of ventures that are global at start-up (Oviatt and McDougall 1997). This phenomenon is better explained by the following two models.

The Network Approach

Proponents of the network approach view internationalization as a natural development resulting from the process of establishing, improving, maintaining, and dissolving relationships with individuals and firms (Johanson and

Mattson 1988). A firm's network of both local and overseas relationships is seen as a crucial form of capital as it can create trust, raise access to information, and increase the firm's ability to mobilize resources. As firms internationalize, the number and strength of relationships in their network increases, bringing more benefits and helping them integrate further into GVCs.

In line with this theory, studies have found that SMEs rely heavily on their networks for many activities when internationalizing, particularly in obtaining market knowledge and looking for opportunities (Mohibul and Fernandez 2008). Thus, a firm that wants to internationalize must first understand the market in which it operates—the environmental conditions and business relationships (Madsen and Servais 1997)—before finding ways to strengthen and utilize its network.

Facilitating the formation of relationships and linkages within local firms and between local and foreign firms should therefore be an essential component of policies helping SMEs internationalize. The government can, for example, assist SMEs in identifying foreign business partners.

International Entrepreneurship Theory

International entrepreneurship theory (IET) states that the basis for a firm's internationalization is international entrepreneurship, which is defined as the discovery, enactment, evaluation, and exploitation of opportunities across national borders to create future goods and services (Oviatt and McDougall 2005). Discovery refers to finding opportunities. Enactment entails seizing opportunities and acquiring a competitive advantage, and evaluation is used to assess the actions taken.

This framework is especially relevant in the current age of technology, where SMEs can make use of cheap and easy ways of getting information and communicating with other countries to help them expand their activities abroad. The approach is also useful in understanding international new ventures, which from inception strive to build competitive advantage from the use of their resources and the sale of outputs in various countries (Oviatt and McDougall 1994) and therefore defy the traditional stage theories of internationalization.

Research on IET suggests that the entrepreneurial qualities of SME leaders are key to a firm's internationalization, particularly in the early phases (Etemad and Wright 2003). However, as the business expands further, it gains more knowledge and expertise, and so the characteristics of the enterprise begin to exert more influence. Government policies aimed at helping SMEs internationalize, should thus include the promotion of entrepreneurism, as well as encouraging and helping SMEs explore the usages and opportunities of technology.

Fostering Local Firms and Entrepreneurs

How to foster local firms and local entrepreneurs in the competitive environment is a big concern for developing countries. In the past, direct or indirect protection for local firms was taken for granted as part of the infant industry protection argument. But now in the globalization era, local firms must compete with gigantic MNEs in the open market from the beginning. Determining what sort of industrial policies or SME policies would be justifiable is one of the most controversial topics among development economists.

SMEs play pivotal roles in the functioning of international production networks and economic agglomeration. There are certainly ways to foster local firms or SMEs by utilizing globalizing forces.

There is evidence that local firms are participating in production and distribution networks, particularly in machinery industries. An empirical study of Thailand, based on an industrial survey, obtained interesting research findings. First, between MNEs and SMEs there have been positive spillovers and linkage effects in the machinery industry, but not in other industries so far. Second, the impact of trade liberalization differs from industry to industry. Trade liberalization has increased productivity in the machinery industry and labor-intensive industries. Third local firms in machinery industry in particular have received the largest benefits from trade liberalization.

Another example of the link between MNEs and local firms can be found in Penang, Malaysia. In Penang, many indigenous enterprises have developed through linkages with foreign electronics companies. Indigenous enterprises are participating in producing not only parts and components but also industrial equipment. Foreign assemblers operating in Thailand are also gradually outsourcing to indigenous suppliers. Most of the indigenous enterprises that have linked with MNEs are SMEs. Some of them have succeeded in the global market place, serving customers in Asia and Pacific region and worldwide.

Economic integration has provided business opportunities not just in production and distribution networks, but also in capturing enlarged markets. For example, a Malaysian electrical appliance firm is expanding OEM production outsourced from MNEs and in the process of increasing production of

OEM, the firm is able to expand to integrated ASEAN market. It is notable in agricultural products, including food and beverage, that ASEAN enterprises have shown a big presence. A Philippine food and beverage industry firm has expanded its business to overseas in Australia, PRC, Indonesia, and Viet Nam. A leading Thai agro-based company expanded its business into Cambodia, PRC, India, Indonesia, Malaysia, Myanmar, Singapore, Viet Nam, and other countries.

Such indigenous enterprises have succeeded in establishing linkages with MNEs and thus have expanded their businesses in the integrated global market.

Prior to the Asian financial crisis in 1997, rapid and dynamic economic growth in East Asia was facilitated through market-driven forces. Various regional economic cooperation initiatives and schemes were introduced, including an agreement on the ASEAN Free Trade Area (AFTA) in 1992 that came into full operation by the end of 2003. However, in the past the impact of ASEAN-initiated regional cooperation was negligible because ASEAN economies were basically competing in the same product range and their main export markets were to non-ASEAN countries. Recently, however, there is clear evidence to indicate that the impact of AFTA has encouraged production networking in Thailand, Viet Nam, and other ASEAN economies on some intermediate and consumer goods. Some economists claimed that in reality economic integration has proceeded in East Asia, even in the absence of effective implementation of AFTA and other regional bilateral trade and investment agreements. The nature and characteristics of de facto economic integration are important for policy discussion to understand how far integration has been realized and what sort of integration has been achieved so far. Understanding such fundamental issues would be helpful for policy makers to design regional and bilateral free trade agreements (FTAs) in order to facilitate and accelerate the development of regional production networks. The development of vertical production networks has certainly been supported by trade liberalization efforts. On the other hand, the trade regime in East Asia is still far from a single production base and a single market. Substantial barriers in service trade still remain in East Asia. The development of vertical production networks, as well as remaining trade barriers, affects the nature of the on-going process of legal economic integration in East Asia.

It is vitally important to understand the extent of the influence of the GVC and legal regional trade agreements (RTAs) on regional production networking. Global business corporations have extended their production, material, and resource sourcing and markets beyond their domestic economies. Because of the pressure of integration, competition, and just-in-time (JIT) production system, which is based on timely delivery of spare parts and component to minimize the inventory costs, East Asia is now fully connected into a GVC system in which it produces the world production output. The importance of production networking, clustering (agglomeration), and fragmentation must be factored in de facto regional FTAs. There are some studies related to the importance of this issue. A future study should examine specific trade and investment areas and sectors.

The Impact of Subregional and Bilateral FTAs on Production Networking

Economic integration in terms of production networking or value chains has not benefited much from formal RTAs. The basic weaknesses of the ASEAN Free Trade Area (AFTA), ASEAN Economic Community (AEC), ASEAN Investment Area (AIA), and ASEAN Framework Agreement on Services (AFAS) are that there are too many exceptions on key sectors of ASEAN economies. Furthermore, the standardization and harmonization of rules and regulations has been inadequate. Transportation, infrastructure, and institutions to implement those trade and investment agreements are also absent or inadequate.

Production network and regional economic integration are accelerating in Southeast and Northeast Asia within the framework of GVCs and expanding production networks in East Asia. These trends are being driven by competition, the rise of the PRC and India, the political stability of the region relative to other regions, and the availability of productive labor forces and resources, all buttressed by individual countries' macroeconomic regimes and liberal trade and investment regimes that promote economic development.

Despite many distortions and inefficiencies in implementing ASEAN regional cooperation schemes, there are many cumulative positive effects on the rapidly emerging production networking and agglomeration of industry in East Asia. The clustering of the automobile and parts industry in Thailand, the clustering of the electronic industry in Malaysia, and the knowledge-based industry cluster in Singapore are cases in point. Indirectly, positive and business-friendly policies and institutional environments in Southeast Asian countries have contributed to the emergence of industrial clustering, agglomeration, and production. Further and enhanced efforts to accelerate and integrate existing agreements in goods, services, and investment are vitally important for ASEAN economies to meet the challenges and opportunities related to the rise of the PRC, India, and the accelerating trend of GVC development. In the case of Cambodia, Lao People's Democratic Republic (Lao PDR), Myanmar, and Viet Nam (CLMV), these countries require development assistance in addition to ASEAN regional economic integration. Without adequate development assistance, trade and investment liberalization would not be sufficient for these countries, perhaps with the exception of Viet Nam, to benefit from the emerging production networking and industrial clustering in Southeast Asia.

Economic integration through regional and bilateral FTAs can enhance regional production networking if policy makers can minimize the distortions related to regional and bilateral FTAs in East Asia. Since 2000, bilateral FTAs and subregion FTAs have proliferated throughout East Asia. These bilateral FTAs are based on reciprocal preferential tariff schemes. Both parties choose their own sensitive list. This implies that, for example, the ASEAN–PRC FTA (ACFTA) is counted as 10 separate bilateral FTAs between PRC and the 10 ASEAN countries. The degree of market access faced by an ASEAN exporter varies according to the ASEAN destination markets. This means that there are 45 bilateral preferential trade relationships within 10 ASEAN countries. In the same way, the ASEAN–Japan FTA, ASEAN– Republic of Korea FTA, and ASEAN–India FTA are each 10 separate bilateral FTAs. ASEAN–CER (Closer Economic Relation of Australia and New Zealand) constitutes 20 bilateral FTAs. In total, 105 ASEAN FTAs are enforced and/or under negotiation. Any ASEAN exporter faces different preferential treatments based on destinations. Baldwin (2006) has called the overlapping FTA problem the East Asian "noodle bowl syndrome." Potentially, 16 countries would produce 120 bilateral FTAs in the region.

Different FTA strategies by individual countries may create severe overlapping FTA problems. Because of the different FTA strategies taken by each country, there is much heterogeneity in exclusion lists, tariff rates, rules of origin (ROO), dispute settlement mechanisms, mutual recognition, competition policy, and other norms and regulation among existing multilateral FTAs in Asia. The overlapping FTAs can complicate tariff rates and ROO for the same products, according to the destination. It is commonly agreed that the costs arising from the ROO are expected to increase substantially when there are overlapped FTAs and RTAs.

Other than a lack of FTA, there are other crucial impediments to East Asia's bilateralism. First of all, with the exception of a few countries, East Asia has failed to form high level FTAs in terms of trade liberalization. Typically, reduction in agricultural trade barriers is important for narrowing development gaps, however, agricultural products tend to be excluded from most Asian preferential tariff treatments.

Moreover, the bilateral FTAs in East Asia have addressed trade liberalization in goods, but liberalization in service trade has not progressed much.

As a result, economic integration in East Asia still remains "shallow." Benefits from integration are limited since there are many border-related barriers other than tariffs.

The policy environment for trade facilitation in East Asia varies considerably by country. For example, custom clearance time is quite different among countries. Custom procedures are still complicated and lack transparency in many East Asian countries. This means that the policy space to facilitate trade, or reduce trade costs, is very large. If trade facilitation measures such as simplification and harmonization of customs procedure, paperless trading, and mutual recognition are improved, they will reduce trade costs and expand production networks by a considerable extent.

The enhancement of logistic infrastructure system, including that of the institutional system, is an issue to be challenged by East Asian policy makers in order to realize deep integration, since it serves to facilitate trade and location of production. A study on cross-border trade facilitation for ASEAN countries by the Japan External Trade Organization (JETRO) (2008) finds that goods between Bangkok and Ha Noi, for example, have been transported mainly by sea, which does not fit the JIT production operation prevailing in other parts of East Asia. The JETRO study suggests that if logistic infrastructure systems, such as road networks, transportation terminal facilities, and legal institutions, are developed and established, then the volume of trucking transportation would increase. In a different context, land transportation clusters and volume would increase between Singapore, Malaysia, and Thailand if the three countries would agree to standardize their long-haul trucking system to facilitate cross-border trade and the JIT production network among the three most developed ASEAN economies.

Emerging Business Opportunities for SMEs in the Region

MNCs have expanded their production, material, and resource sourcing and markets beyond their domestic economies. Because of the pressures of integration, competition, and JIT production systems, the region is fully connected into a GVC system that churns out output for the global marketplace.

As a result, globalization provides new opportunities for developing economies to enter international trade through production sharing and outsourcing. Since the early 1990s, international production networks have developed in ASEAN and East Asia, and gradually spread to India, Australia, and New Zealand, driven by market forces and facilitated by regional, subregional, and bilateral FTAs.

Signs of congestion in economic agglomeration in East Asia are beginning to appear, and dispersion forces have started to influence industrial location. There has been a substantial increase in production costs due to agglomeration and the resulting difficulties in securing labor, land, and other factors of production. In particular, labor-intensive and land-intensive production processes tend to shift location. Therefore, regional economic integration has set off dynamic growth impulses through global and regional production networking. In turn, this process has been facilitated by industrial agglomeration and fragmentation in sequential order. Differences in wage levels and land prices between more developed and less developed economies in the region create economic opportunities for narrowing the development gap and affect the spillover effect of growth to other neighboring economies. Their geographical proximity to growth centers would be a drawing point to less developed region but drastic reductions in the set up cost and the service link cost as well as improving policy environments would be required.

Latest Trends in SME Businesses in Asia and the Pacific

Globalization and regional integration processes are increasing in terms of speed and space. Countries that are able to take advantage of these two underlying fundamental forces have been growing faster and more sustainably. At the same time, economic openness and domestic trade and investment liberalization have dramatically increased competition in the domestic, regional, and global marketplace. Larger and efficient companies are normally able to leverage these new opportunities and challenges in domestic markets as well as across external markets. This challenging new economic environment tends to put SMEs at a disadvantage compared to large and medium-sized enterprises. However, there is empirical evidence to indicate that SMEs continue to develop and prosper in some economies.. For example, SMEs in Japan; Republic of Korea; Taipei,China; Hong Kong, China; and Singapore are doing well and expanding. SME growth is not restricted to these countries but also increasingly in Thailand (automobile and electronic), Malaysia (electronic), Philippines (electronic, ICT), India (ICT, services), Australia, and New Zealand (ICT, services).

The fact is that large enterprises (LEs) and SMEs are the two important drivers of development in the developing Asia and Pacific region. While MNEs and domestic LEs have been playing an important role in accelerating the industrialization process, SMEs provide the crucial industrial linkages to set off a chain reaction of broad-based and sustainable development. Without SMEs as subcontractors and suppliers of intermediate inputs to MNEs and domestic LEs, industrial growth in developing countries would not be able to realize sustainable increase in domestic value-added, employment, productivity, and industrial linkages. In the globalizing era of the borderless marketplace, buttressed by regionalization and liberalization, SMEs provide an important source of domestic employment creation and resilience against more volatile external economic fluctuations, and serve as a mechanism for local capacity building.

SMEs play a pivotal role in the functioning of international and regional production networks. There are certainly ways to foster local firms and SMEs by utilizing globalizing market forces and regional economic integration; the issue is how to provide a critical linkage between SMEs and the large local companies and MNCs. Successful cases in Singapore and other countries have proven that governments play a vital role in ensuring a competitive market structure, providing relevant and effective technical upgrading, marketing information and management, consortium financing, and clustering (economies of scale) to SMEs.

While trade and investment liberalization and globalization are detrimental to the domestic growth of SMEs, there are counter-policy measures that can be implemented to synergize the negative effects of globalization and regionalization to result in a more dynamic, rapid, and sustainable regional economic development. The development of SMEs in the region is important as success in this effort will go a long way toward reducing regional and domestic income gaps, creating a balance of income and employment, and securing sustainable human and social security. To achieve this, there is a need to improve SMEs' international competitiveness through SME promotion policies, financing, and the tax system. SMEs can be sharpened in their ability to compete through improvement of competitiveness due to research and development, improvement of quality control, and skill. To upgrade the production process and capture a larger share of value-added, the government should promote the development of local parts and supplier industries. This seems an effective avenue to increase the domestic content of MNCs operating in the country. The development of domestic suppliers would require a package of technical assistance, including the provision of training to develop the skills of local suppliers together with access and availability of finance along with increased linkages between SMEs and large enterprises.

As regional production networking becomes more important as a source of economic growth, outsourcing and subcontracting will offer increasing opportunities for SMEs to capitalize on regional economic integration. Alternative and important emerging business opportunities for SMEs are the advent of Internet businesses and the widespread use of electronic and computer business design. Because of the electronic and computer revolution in business management and practices, many SMEs in Singapore and Hong Kong, China are expanding their business operation from homes and other flexible arrangements. Such flexibility in doing business comes about due to the infinite business opportunities offered through the borderless cyberspace world. This new mode of doing business reduces business and transaction costs enormously.

SMEs are also expanding very rapidly in the service sector of tourism and specialized marketing to newly emerging markets beyond the domestic market as the process of regional economic integration. Regional integration is further facilitated through reduction in tariff and nontariff barriers and the harmonization of standards and customs procedures. In addition, free movement of capital and skilled professionals would facilitate the formation of an integrated single market and production base.

As regional integration is broadened and deepened toward a single market and production base, competition and market size increase at the same time. This is a positive effect of regional integration. Without a corresponding increase in the efficiency of local firms and SMEs, regional integration cannot be sustained as there will be more domestic opposition due to increased economic and social instability and unemployment. This is the crux of regional economic integration that underpins its sustainability, that it must not only increase efficiency but also provide positive and acceptable benefits to every constituent member within the free trade area or economic community.

With the processes of regional cooperation and economic integration, economies tend to experience higher economic growth. However, the higher rate of gross domestic product (GDP) growth may not be accompanied by a higher rate of employment. With globalization and regional integration, there is a tendency that the rate of increase of output (GDP) and the rate of increase of employment to not be proportionally linked. In other words, a country may have a much higher rate of increase in output than the rate of increase in employment. In addition, regional integration may tend to increase income disparity among members of the preferential trading area, if some countervailing measures are not properly instituted. In this respect, the development of viable and sustainable SMEs provides an effective measure to counter the negative effects of globalization and regional economic integration.

Therefore, improving the competitiveness and capability of SMEs is vital for the sustainability of regional economic integration. There are manifold elements required to improve the competitiveness of SMEs. Countries at different stages of economic development require different core policy instruments aimed at improving their SMEs' capability development. Experience drawn from successful SME development in the Republic of Korea; Taipei,China; and Singapore indicates that technology and industry upgrading are the core measures that must be continually implemented in order to stay competitive, in addition to clustering and improved marketing capability.

These economies set up central institutions to monitor and diffuse new technologies and provided technological services that SMEs could not provide for themselves. These included material testing, inspection and certification of quality, instrument calibration, establishment of repositories of technical information, patent registration, research and design, and technical training. The Singapore Institute of Standards and Industrial Research has an incubator scheme that allows SMEs and innovators to make use of the Institute's space, equipment and technical advice, and provides common facilities for local firms to do research and development. These services are not given free, but are offered at affordable rates due to economies of scale and clustering effects. These three countries also provided training and management consultancy facilities for SMEs along with subsidized credit, tax incentives, and financial guarantees to capital market imperfections. As for technology upgrading, cost sharing was adopted to ensure that companies take the programs seriously.

Trade facilitation and technical assistance are normally attached with regional and bilateral FTAs. For example, the AEC has the Initiative for ASEAN Integration (IAI) to narrow the development gap between the more developed six ASEAN countries and CLMV countries. Equally, the ASEAN–PRC FTA, ASEAN–Japan FTA, ASEAN– Republic of Korea FTA, have preferential treatment and development assistance extended to less developed economies. Asia-Pacific Economic Cooperation (APEC) has an economic and technical (Eco-Tech) program as an integral part of the process of trade and investment liberalization in the Asia-Pacific region. Regional cooperation and integration among countries with differing stages of economic development must be accompanied with development assistance, technological transfer and enhancing capability schemes in order to be effective and sustainable. International division of labor and specialization has become an important feature of international and regional trade and investment patterns and the development of technological capability of SMEs is an integral policy of liberalizing trade and investment regime. Regional economic integration opens up opportunities and challenges for policy makers to provide industrial and technological upgrading to SMEs.

Summary and Conclusion

The importance of SMEs in the age of globalization, production networking, and regional economic integration is well documented and firmly established in the literature. The central question is why some countries have successfully transformed and established viable, competitive, and sustainable SMEs development while the majority of other developing countries have failed. The answer is complex and requiring of country-specific, sectoral level analysis as well as the examination of economic, political, social, and cultural elements in a dynamic context. However, some elements can be used as basic policy guidelines for developing SMEs.

Successful cases of SMEs development in Japan; Republic of Korea; Taipei,China; Hong Kong, China; Singapore; Thailand; Malaysia; India; and many other economies have adopted long-term comprehensive, coordinated and consistent policies. Often, empirical evidence shows that correct policy measures for SMEs in developing countries are not coordinated among relevant ministries, agencies, and organizations, which in the long run results in inconsistent policies. Therefore, governments and responsible agencies must develop "best practices" on the ideal business environment, training and upgrading, financing, marketing and management, sub-contracting, and networking and monitoring mechanisms to ensure that SME policies are efficiently and effectively carried out. Successful case studies invariably indicate that effective collaboration between government, trade associations, education, and training institutions is important in reducing cost for human resource development and capacity building.

Likewise, the dissemination of information through the effective use of available ICT should be maximally used. In this context, the establishment of national and regional corporate credit information and database and credit guarantee system in the region should be given high priority. The establishment of such database and credit information would contribute significantly to the problem of trade financing and other financing aspects of SMEs.

Globalization and regional integration require the healthy and sustainable existence of SMEs and their development in the region. The proliferation of bilateral and subregional FTAs has created duplication and overlapping of ROOs and other trade and investment rules and regulations that would increase the transaction cost of doing business in the region, affecting SMEs adversely. It is necessary to create a conducive business environment through the provision of standardization of products and services, rules and regulations and a seamless market infrastructure in the region.

References

Abonyi, G. 2005. Integrating SMEs into Global and Regional Value Chains: Implications for Subregional Cooperation in the Greater Mekong Sub region. Paper prepared for UNESCAP, Bangkok.

Asasen, C., K. Asasen, and N. Chuangcham. 2003. A Proposed Policy Blueprint for the ASEAN SME Development Decade 2002–2012. REPSF Project, 02/005.

Bailey, P. 2007. Cambodian Small and Medium Sized Enterprises: Constraints, Policies and Proposals for their Development. Paper presented at the third workshop for the ERIA Related Joint Research of SME Project, IDE-JETRO, Bangkok, November.

Baldwin, R. 2006. *Managing The Noodle Bowl: The Fragility of East Asian Regionalism*. Geneva: Graduate Institute of International Studies.

Etemad, H., and R.W. Wright. 2003. Internationalisation of SMEs: Toward a new paradigm. *Small Business Economics*. 20. pp. 1–4.

Giuliani, E., C. Pietrobelli, and R. Rabellotti. 2005. Upgrading in Global Value Chains: Lessons from Latin America Clusters. *World Development*. 33 (4). 549–573.

Hiratsuka, D. 2006. *ERIA Test Run Project Institute of Developing Economies*. Tokyo: ERIA.

JETRO. 2008. *2007 Survey of Japanese-Affiliated Firms in ASEAN and India*. Tokyo: JETRO.

Johanson, J., and J.E. Vahine. 1977. The Internationalization Process of the Firm: A Model of Knowledge Development and Increasing Foreign Market Commitment. *Journal of International Business Studies*. 8. pp. 35–40.

Johanson, J., and L.G. Mattson. 1988. Internationalization in Industrial Systems: A Network Approach. In N. Hood and J. Vahlne, eds. *Strategies in Global Competition*. London: Croom Helm.

Jones, R., and H. Kierzkowski. 1990. The Role of Services in Production and International Trade: A Theoretical Framework. In Jones, R., and A. Krueger, eds. *The Political Economy of International Trade: Essays in Honor of Robert E. Baldwin*, pp. 31–48. Oxford: Basil Blackwell.

Kimura, F. 2006. International Production and Distribution Networks in East Asia, 18 Facts, Mechanics and Policy Implications. *Asian Economic Policy Review*. 1 (2): 326–344.

Kimura, F., and M. Ando. 2005. Two-dimensional Fragmentation in East Asia: Conceptual Framework and Empirics. *International Review of Economic and Finance (special issue on "Outsourcing and Fragmentation: Blessing or Threat")* 14: 317–348.

Lim, H. 2007. Regional Economic Cooperation and Production Networks in Southeast Asia. Presented at the ISEAS-IDE Joint Workshop. Singapore.

Lloyd-Reason, L., A. Damyanov, O. Nicolescu, and S. Wall. 2005. Internationalization Process, SMEs and Transitional Economies: A Four-Country Perspective. *International Journal of Entrepreneurship and Innovation Management.* 5 (3–4). pp. 206–226.

Luostarinen, R. 1994. *Research for Action: Internationalization of Finnish Firms and their Response to Global Challenges.* UNU World Institute for Development Economies Research. Helsinki: UNU/WIDER.

Madsen, T.K., and P. Servais. 1997. The Internationalization of Born Globals: An Evolutionary Process? *International Business Review.* 6 (6). pp. 561–583.

Mohibul, I.M., and A. Fernandez. 2008. *Internationalization Process of SMEs: Strategies and Methods.* Unpublished Master's Thesis, Malardalen University, Sweden.

Normah, M.A. 2006. *SMEs: Building Blocks for Economic Growth.* Paper presented at the National Statistics Conference, Department of Statistics, Malaysia. September.

Oviatt, B., and P. McDougall. 1994. Toward a Theory of International New Ventures. *Journal of International Business Studies.* 25 (1). pp. 45–64.

Oviatt, B., and P. McDougall. 1997. Challenges for Internationalization Process Theory: The Case of International New Ventures. *Management International Review.* 37(Special Issue). pp. 85–99.

Oviatt, B., and P. McDougall. 2005. Defining International Entrepreneurship and Modeling the Speed of Internationalization. *Entrepreneurship Theory & Practice.* September. pp. 537–553.

Wengel, J., and E. Rodriguez. 2006. SME Export Performance in Indonesia after the Crisis. *Small Business Economics.* 26. pp. 25–37.

7

Regional Integration Behind the Border: Applying a Value Chain Approach

*Grant Aldonas**

Introduction

Globalization has fundamentally altered the conduct of international trade, the organization of production, and the basis of international commercial competition. Trade, once characterized by arm's length transactions between independent buyers and sellers in different countries, is now driven by, and takes place within, the companies operating on a global basis or within the broader reach of their supply chains (Dymond and Hart 2008: 13). For individual firms, their ability to add value as a part of such supply chains determines their success and their survival.

The accelerating integration of world markets allows global firms to organize production on a globally efficient basis. Operating a global supply chain has become a competitive necessity, which has altered the structure of global enterprises. Rather than operating as single vertically-integrated multinational firms located in one country exporting goods produced entirely in their home market, global firms increasingly organize themselves on a horizontal basis, serving as the hub of a network of suppliers located in a number of different countries.

* The following chapter is substantially drawn from the one authored by Grant Aldonas, Alberto Trejos, and Philip Schwagel for the Inter-American Development Bank. The responsibility of any errors or omissions in adapting that approach to the challenge of developing a regional integration strategy that reaches beyond the border is the author's own. This text has been edited for typographical errors and stylistic consistency.

In effect, what globalization has done is soften the boundaries of these enterprises. They now operate more as economic ecosystems, rather than simple linear sequences of steps in a production process. The interaction among the various stakeholders in this ecosystem is "thicker" and more frequent than the conventional linear representation of a supply chain conveys.

As the hub of a network of suppliers, the global firm mobilizes the capital, talent, and ideas needed to produce goods or services for a global market. It also coordinates the interaction among the various suppliers in the product's value chain needed to produce a final product for consumer sale—from research and development to design and manufacturing all the way through to distribution, retail sales, and after-sales service. Only industries (fewer every day) that produce physically untradeable goods or services are unaffected by these forces.

Organizing production on a global basis offers such enterprises economies of scale and efficiencies that make them cost competitive in virtually any market (Dymond and Hart 2008: 13). They are, as a result, driving the cost efficiencies that deliver the benefits of globalization to consumers' doorsteps around the world. They also compel their competitors to go global to compete.

These global networks of suppliers have become the new basis for global competition among firms. Successful management of a global supply chain has become "a defining source of value generation" for the globally-engaged firm. By the same token, the lack thereof becomes a critical liability. As these global supply chains increasingly dominate much of global trade, they have, in effect, become the market.

This dynamic has deep implications for both regional integration and development. It is difficult to point to a development success that has not relied heavily on access to export markets as one of the principal ways of both raising incomes and driving change. Indeed, regional integration strategies adopted by firms in both Latin America and Asia have largely been designed with that objective in mind.

To the extent that the dynamic unfolding in global markets redefines the terms of "market access," regional integration strategies designed to help member countries reach global markets have to adjust as well. In this new environment, market access depends not only on the ability to be productive and competitive in specific activities, but also on the ability to link effectively with other suppliers in a global chain. A sound regional integration strategy must facilitate that linkage—it must provide a policy environment that encourages the economic eco-system essential to local firms' participation in such global supply chains.

This remarkable shift in industrial organization should lead us to ask whether the conventional perspective on regional integration and trade policy fully captures the unfolding dynamic in global markets? The answer is that it does not and that the unfolding changes in global markets will require a different approach to regional integration that takes the new competitive dynamic into account.

From a development perspective, the rapid integration of markets globally and the rising dominance of world trade by competing supply chains requires us to think of trade and development as a single process that connects individuals to markets—at first locally and regionally, but eventually on a global basis.[1] Thinking in terms of development solely within a developing country makes less sense in light of the globalization of the world economy, particularly when a developing country's economic competitiveness and standard of living may be eroding by virtue of its lack of engagement in the broader world economy.

The increasing share of world trade dominated by global supply chains should also lead us to consider how policy makers could best make use of the same tools used by globally-engaged firms to think about their own operations. That is particularly important with respect to their sourcing decisions and how they connect producers in developing countries to global markets. The challenge that presents is how to use those tools in a way that would inform the judgment of policy makers in developing countries, as well as international financial institutions like the Inter-American Development Bank (IDB), the Asian Development Bank (ADB) and development assistance agencies, on the priorities the country might wish to address as part of a regional integration strategy.

The following discussion outlines an analytical approach to address this challenge. It reviews the tools used by global business in analyzing their own operations and suggests how those tools might be applied to the challenge of building a stronger regional platform from which local producers can compete in global markets.

---

[1] Dymond and Hart (2008: 22) capture this point well in highlighting the cost of internal barriers to trade in Canada inhibiting stronger economic performance because they "impede Canada's participation in global value chains, and lock Canadians into the limited opportunities of the small domestic market".

Analytical Approach

The analytical approach suggested here applies the tool most commonly used by global businesses in making their own strategic decisions about sourcing—a value chain map. Global businesses use such maps to identify each step in the process of producing and marketing their goods and services on world markets to assess how to reduce costs at every stage.

The same tool, however, can also be used to identify the internal and external barriers limiting the ability of a country or region's producers to participate in such value chains. Conventionally, trade policy and regional integration strategies have focused on barriers to exports (i.e., those obstacles that hinder the export of goods and services to particular markets). By the same token, the conventional approach to removing those barriers involves trade negotiations, either within a multilateral forum such as the World Trade Organization or in regional or bilateral trade arrangements.

In today's global markets, however, market access is defined less by conventional tariff and nontariff measures. It will, instead, depend on the ability of local producers to meet the commercial standards of global buyers and integrate their business processes with those of the buyer and the other suppliers in the buyer's value chain.

The first step in the analytical approach involves mapping the value chain to identify the costs and weaknesses that undercut the competitiveness of local firms or inhibit their efficient integration into the web of suppliers and customers along the value chain. The reason for this step flows directly from the perspective of the globally-engaged firms that manage the value chain and make its sourcing decisions. Those firms have a compelling interest in managing the cost side of their businesses to remain competitive in world markets.

At each stage in a value chain, a producer purchases inputs and then adds value. The producer's value-added becomes part of the cost of the next stage of production. The eventual price to the consumer is the sum of the value added by everyone in the supply chain, including the requisite return on capital demanded by investors in each producer (i.e., profit) at each stage of production. Firms examine each stage in the production process to determine how they can lower costs and raise quality by working with existing suppliers or seeking alternative sources of supply.

Seen in that light, the focus of global firms on mapping the barriers that might impede connecting potential suppliers to their network of suppliers is critical due to the impact it has on costs at each stage of production and the delay and uncertainty such barriers can create for production throughout the entire value chain. In that sense, the value chain map not only holds the key to the globally-engaged firm's profitability, but also defines the parameters that their suppliers must meet to participate as part of a network of suppliers.

In essence, the map helps explain why, even when informational barriers are overcome, trade opportunities are often unavailable to entrepreneurs who face hurdles in bringing their goods to the market. These barriers are adding cost to the globally-engaged firm's supply chain. To be competitive and able to host the firms that successfully interact in one segment of the value chain, a country must have both productive conditions and available inputs that allow the activities within each stage of production to be carried out profitably, and a business climate that allows the links between successive stages to be efficient, cheap, and safe.

Applied to the question of regional integration, the value chain map would perform a similar function. It would help identify the barriers, whether internal or external, that hinder the ability of regional producers to become a part of global value chains serving external markets. These barriers may lie within the links of the value chain, in which case the local firms must invest in process improvements that will allow them to integrate successfully into such value chains. On the other hand, the barriers may also lie between successive links in the value chain, relating less to the competitiveness of the individual local enterprise and more to the internal weaknesses in the business climate or to costs and delays in the process by which companies interact with international suppliers, service providers, and end-customers.

The second stage in the analytical framework involves using the value chain map to collect information on barriers affecting each stage of production by product within a country and within a region. That data is essential to the application of an econometric framework (described next) that would provide a single, consistent measure of effect of the barriers, whether internal or external, on the ability of local producers to integrate into the global value chains that would take their goods and services to world markets.

The needed information would include, for example, information on changes in the nature of the value chain of production over time (e.g., information regarding improvements in the efficiency of a port over time or data reflecting a decline in the quality of roads over time and the impact that has on time to market). This can then be added to data on trade flows over time, with the model predicting trade flows in a given year and the ups and downs of the trade barriers over time being used in the econometric application to assess the impact of such changes. If improvements in roads, for example, tend to occur at the same time as strong exports (after taking into account the "normal" influences of exports), this would suggest that road improvements are an important positive influence on trade flows.

In reality, it will be difficult at the outset to obtain such data on changes in barriers over time for the simple reason that the data might not have been kept in previous years for the trade barriers of most interest. Having said that, one of the benefits of adopting the analytical framework is precisely to begin the process of collecting data on what really matters in terms of sourcing decisions—something that conventional trade statistics alone do not do.

Another example of the type of data needed involves information on the value chain of production across items within a country. This would require data for only a single time period, but it would be information across several or a range of products. The empirical model could then be applied to gauge the extent to which higher-than-expected trade flows were associated with products that had relatively low barriers within their value chains.

The third stage in the analytical framework involves the application of econometric measures to the data collected on obstacles at various stages of the value chain. Gravity equations are valuable in that they help quantify the effect of barriers imposed on exports by transit cost and distance, and reduce those barriers to a single measure that allows policy makers to assess where they might get the greatest return on investment in lowering barriers to trade, whether internal or external, that inhibit access to global markets. Similarly, reducing the barriers that create friction and raise costs in a supply chain to a common measure would also help inform the IDB's or ADB's judgment, and that of development assistance agencies, in their efforts to work with local officials on their regional integration and development strategy.

Previous work done for the World Bank by Djankov, Freund, and Pham (2006) takes a significant step in that direction, by introducing the impact of time spent in shipping, as opposed to shipping costs alone, as an element to consider. What we propose here goes further, by not only looking into costs, delays, and risks related to international shipping in and out of the country, but also to domestic barriers to the efficient operation of value chains. These barriers may have different impacts across sectors, and hence cross-industry. The empirical model could, as result, gauge the extent to which higher-than-expected trade flows were associated with products that had relatively low barriers within their value chains.

What that requires, in the first instance, is an empirical model that explains trade flows. Significantly, the focus here is on the ability of enterprises in a country or region to integrate into the global value chains that make up the global market, as opposed to a simpler measure of export competitiveness that might be examined for purposes of trade negotiations. That means that the model should address both imports and exports to assess the obstacles in the flow of components and other inputs to local producers as well as the flow of their finished work to be integrated into the global buyer's value chain.

The framework suggested here is based on the well understood gravity model, in which the volume of trade flows of particular types of items depends on the economic size of the trade partners, their physical distance and other measures of transportation costs, and political economy factors such as the existence of a bilateral or multilateral trade agreement or a common border. This provides the baseline onto which to add information about the value chain of production and barriers at different stages of the production process.

Intuitively, the model is used to predict what trade between two nations in a particular product "should be." Additional information is then added on the particular type and magnitude of barriers affecting a product to gauge the impact of barriers, whether internal, at the border, or external on both inbound and outbound trade flows (imports and exports).

The output of the model is thus an estimate of the incremental impact of particular types of barriers to trade, where the barriers to be examined will depend on the available data. Once the model has been estimated, simulations can be carried out that show the quantitative impact on trade of policy reforms that remove or reduce particular barriers.

The model to be estimated can be represented as follows, where an example of the equation involved is of exports of an item from country A to country B:

$$\text{Exports}_{AB} = \text{GDP}_A + \text{Population}_A + \text{Distance}_{AB} + \text{Remoteness}_A + \text{Landlock}_A + \text{Time}_A + \varepsilon_{AB}$$

In this stylized model, the dependent (left hand side) variable is the quantity (volume) of exports of the particular item. This depends on the gross domestic product (GDP) and population of the exporting country, A, the distance from country A to country B, a measure of the remoteness of country A in terms of its being physically isolated from global centers of economic gravity, an indicator as to whether country A is landlocked, and a measure of the time it takes to move a product from the factory to the main port for exports from country A.

As expected, bigger and richer countries tend to export more, while distance and remoteness from other countries and groups of countries tends to reduce exports, as does being landlocked. The coefficient on the last variable, time, then indicates the impact in reducing exports of an additional day of transit from factor to port—that is, the cost of delay.

The model can be estimated using a variety of appropriate data. For example, data on exports of a common item can be collected for many countries to many destinations, and this cross-country variation used to isolate the impact of an additional delay of time on trade in that product on average across countries. The precise econometric specification would then be adapted to take into account the cross-country nature of the data—for example, by adding country-specific "dummy" variables to control for factors idiosyncratic to each nation; this provides for an "apples-to-apples" comparison of the data across disparate nations (some of which, for example, might export a lot of a particular item while others might export very little). The estimated impact coefficient of the effect of time on exports can then be used in conjunction with the actual days of delay for each country to calculate the trade-reducing impact on a country-by-country basis.

Alternately, data on exports and barriers facing a variety of products can be collected for a single country, whether in a single or small number of years, or if possible, over a period of time. Estimating the data for a single country then shows the impact of delays more narrowly focused within that nation.

The key to estimate the model, regardless, is to have variation across at least one dimension—over time or across products. It could be quite difficult to gather the needed information on trade and transportation barriers over time, since detailed records might not, as yet, be available going backward in time. This suggests that a cross-product approach might be more fruitful, at least in the near term. Data would be needed on the steps and barriers involved in the value chain of production for a range of items; the impact of these barriers can then be assessed within a nation.

The methodology can be applied for both exports and imports and, of course, the exports from one nation are the imports of another. But, as highlighted previously, understanding the competitive effects of the barriers on imports is just as important as barriers to exports in that import barriers can contribute significantly to the cost of local production.

The basic outline of this empirical methodology has been successfully used by the World Bank's Doing Business project to estimate the impact on exports of additional days of delay in getting a good from the factory to its port of embarkation. Using data on trade flows across 126 countries, the World Bank finds that each day on average that a product is delayed within a nation in its transit from factory to port reduces trade by 1%. This impact is statistically significant and quantitatively meaningful: each day of delay is as costly for trade as if the countries involved—the origin of the items and the destination—were an additional 70 km in distance. As expected, the impact of shipping delays is especially salient for time-sensitive products such as perishable agricultural items.

The results of the World Bank project suggest that developing nations could usefully focus on reducing barriers to trade that stand between products and markets—delays in getting goods to market matter for trade and thus for national income and well-being. This applies whether the barriers relate to exports or imports—delays matter whether they are between the importing vessels and consumer or between the domestic producer and potential export destinations in other nations.

Perhaps most significantly for purposes of the trade policy choices that countries in both Latin America and Asia are contemplating, the analysis outlined here will illustrate that the reduction in barriers behind the border are every bit as important, if not more important, as the elimination of conventional trade barriers (i.e., tariff- and nontariff measures in principal export markets) specific to the region's exports.

Case Study: Mapping the Peruvian Value Chain for Perishable Agricultural Products

In the work completed for the IDB, we constructed a value chain map based on existing literature regarding the perishable agricultural products industry and conducted interviews with a number of key participants in the Peruvian perishable products industry itself to detect the main links and the sources of the key inputs at each stage of the process (Aldonas and Trejos 2010). We focused on perishable agricultural products for four reasons:

1. Peru had already established a successful industry in the sector, particularly in the case of asparagus, which suggested that improving the efficiency of each stage in the value chain could offer significant benefits, both to existing export crops such as asparagus, but also to newer products such as avocados.
2. By their nature, perishable products are sensitive to any delays introduced into their production, harvest, processing, shipping, and distribution, which could reduce the competitiveness of Peruvian agricultural products in global markets. Therefore, the innovative contribution of a value-chain approach—one that looks between production stages and to interrelated processes, rather than thinking of each firm as acting in isolation—is particularly relevant to the sector.

3. Reducing barriers to production, distribution, and sale of perishable products offered a way to generate significantly higher returns for producers who otherwise are limited in their potential scale to serving local markets.
4. Smaller scale producers, who make up a significant share of the producers whom the Peruvian policy makers would most like to connect to wider markets, are also most likely to suffer from the added cost that barriers to trade impose, whether internal or external, due to their lack of scale and the inability to pass those costs on to consumers in the highly competitive environments in which they operate.

The description and analysis of the value chain allowed us to identify some areas in which domestic reform or the removal of external trade barriers could improve the prospects for Peruvian entrepreneurs to compete successfully in global markets. That includes those areas where assistance from the IDB or other institutions, such as the World Bank in the context of the Aid for Trade initiative, might contribute to lowering the cost of accessing markets through targeted support for improving the physical and institutional infrastructure needed to connect existing Peruvian entrepreneurs to markets, improve the export performance, and allow new and initially small entrants to establish the links already enjoyed by their predecessors.

We assessed the key strengths and weaknesses in the value chain serving Peru's perishable agricultural products industry by identifying the barriers and costs that prevent higher competitiveness and the entrance of smaller producers, into the export value chain of perishables. We approached that challenge from two different angles. One involved drawing on the databases of the barriers Peruvian producers confront in producing and bringing goods to the international market that have been developed by the World Bank in the context of its Doing Business series. The World Bank Doing Business reports document barriers entrepreneurs face in doing business in a variety of developing country markets, including Peru. The World Bank's data set offers a useful reference point for a more in-depth analysis of the barriers in Peru specifically.[2]

---

[2] The World Bank's (2008) data set does have some limitations for our purposes. It focuses primarily on tasks such as starting a business or paying taxes, rather than focusing exclusively on the barriers to trade that a Peruvian entrepreneur would actually face in connecting to markets. In addition, where the World Bank's data does address processes directly affecting the ability of Peru's farmers to gain access to markets, it focuses on barriers they face in connecting to markets as a producer, while ignoring the barriers that would

To supplement the World Bank's Doing Business data set, we also met with Peruvian producers, Peruvian officials, logistics companies, and potential buyers to gain a better sense of the steps involved in bringing Peruvian perishables to market. We also analyzed the dataset in the World Economic Forum's *World Competitiveness Report* (2009).

Our work allowed us to produce a rough map of the value chain connecting Peru's producers to local, regional and global markets, both as producers and as consumers. The outbound map helps illuminate internal barriers to trade in Peru and external barriers Peruvian producers face—those imposed by the market (e.g., commercial standards) or by foreign governments (e.g., tariffs, quotas, phytosanitary standards, etc.).[3]

The inbound value chain map details the same process from the perspective of the individual Peruvian entrepreneur as a consumer acquiring inputs for the production of perishables in Peru. That map will help policy makers understand how their own tariff and nontariff barriers to trade, as well as processes like customs clearance and physical barriers like poor roads or ports, may raise the cost and limit the ability of local entrepreneurs to connect to and compete in local, regional, and global markets.

In one sense, this initial value chain map serves as a benchmark. Gathering information on and analyzing changes in the nature of the value chain over time would offer Peruvian policy makers and the IDB a means of measuring progress in connecting Peruvian producers to export markets, and give them an indication of the obstacles to regional integration. As noted previously in outlining the analytical framework, information collected in succeeding years on the obstacles identified in the initial mapping exercise (e.g., changes in the efficiency of ports or the quality of roads over time). This can then be added to data on trade flows over time, with the model predicting trade flows in a given year and the ups and downs of the trade barriers over time being used in the econometric application to assess the impact of such changes.

Perhaps most significantly from the perspective of defining "regional integration beyond the border," the process also allows illustrating barriers within the country, either in the form of obstacles to competitive production, or impediments to an efficient link between domestic firms that act as successive

---

inhibit connecting to markets as a consumer in ways that would lower production costs and improve competitiveness.

[3] The value chain analysis, in fact, helps underscore that, in today's global marketplace, commercial standards may play a far more important role than individual national trade barriers in defining whether or not goods or services will enter the global stream of commerce.

links of the chain. Policy makers can then identify missing pieces, in the form of absent public goods, externalities, or shortfalls in the supply of specific services or inputs. Often, appropriate policy is directed at creating the incentives and conditions for those missing pieces to emerge.

In addition to examining the connections between the links in the value chain, we also attempted to offer some assessment of the strength of each link. We relied on the numbers used by the World Economic Forum in its annual competitiveness report, combined wherever possible with data from those companies we interviewed as part of the project. We supplemented that analysis with existing information on similar industries and an inventory of nontariff measures in the region, including those affecting Peru's producers of perishable agricultural projects.

The resulting picture helped clarify which actions by Peruvian policy makers and the IDB have the greatest potential to improve the prospects of Peruvian producers accessing global markets—whether those actions involve domestic reforms, infrastructural investment, satisfying global buyers' commercial standards, or negotiation with foreign trading partners to lower export barriers.

To facilitate the exposition, we have broken down the value chain for exporting perishables into two segments: those that supply raw materials and services to agricultural producers and processors are the "upstream" half, and those who work and deliver the output to the international market make up the "downstream" half. We also focused on sanitary and phytosanitary requirements and transportation because they relate in very direct ways to the issue of what steps are involved in regional integration behind the border.

Upstream in Peru's perishable agricultural products sector, producers buy directly machinery, equipment, and agro-industrial tools, plus irrigation implements, fences, fuels, and packaging materials, including bales, cardboard, labels, etc. Some of these inputs (especially chemicals, tools, and equipment) are imported from foreign firms that have local representation and permanent local stocks. Although each brand may have only one representative, importer, or distributor, there are enough providers in the market of most of these inputs and services for there to be intense competition across brands. The number of participants in each segment of the chain, as the figure illustrates, is quite high, except in the case of fuel, which is such a generic commodity that only four providers, plus the threat of additional competition, are enough to provide some market discipline. Other inputs, such as cardboard, bands, towels, asparagus holders, and basic fertilizers are mostly provided by local producers, although this does not imply that markups are necessarily smaller.

182 Grant Aldonas

In services, competition is even more intense. In this case, the "service" sector consisted mostly of local consultants, many of them on retainer by producer associations, chambers, or even the government, who provide technical assistance for the growth and protection of crops, for example. Several certification bodies (for instance, INDECOPI) decide on technical norms; verification of origin is extended by Servicio Nacional de Saneamiento Ambiental ([SENASA], National Agricultural Sanitary and Phytosanitary Service) (a government body); other public sector departments are in charge of lab tests, SPS (Sanitary and Phytosanitary Measures), food safety, etc.

In the case of the upstream processes, the resulting value chain map looks like as it is shown in Figure 7.1.

In general, the value chain map helps provide an overview of the competitiveness of different stages. As the number of suppliers reflects, the supply of many of the major inputs and services is sufficient and competitive, and the

Figure 7.1
Agro-Exports Supply Chain—Upstream

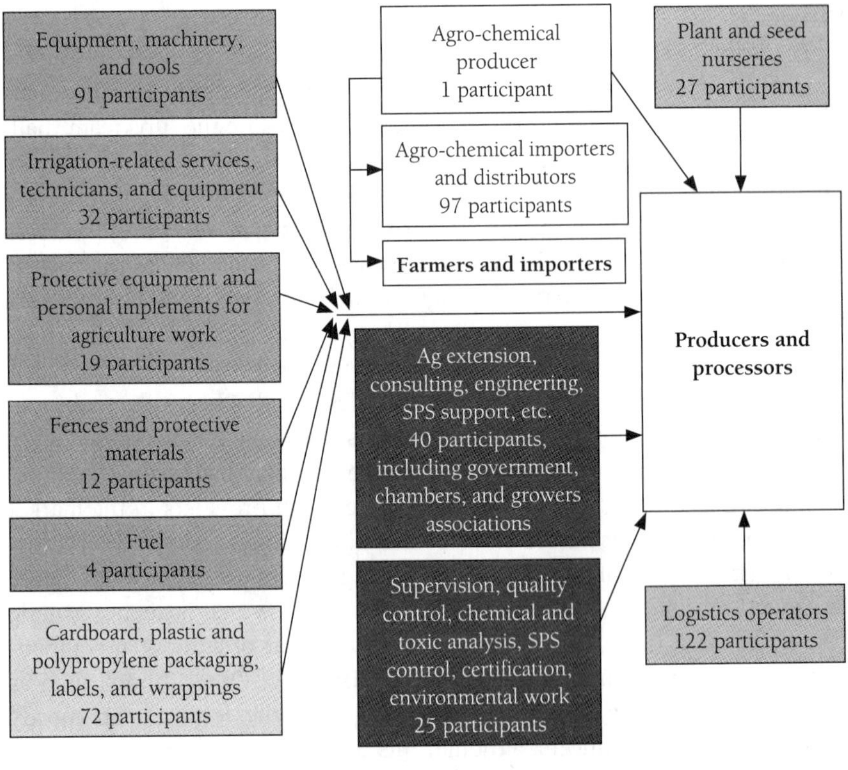

Upstream Suppliers	Intermediaries	Producers
Equipment, machinery, and tools — 91 participants	Agro-chemical producer — 1 participant	Plant and seed nurseries — 27 participants
Irrigation-related services, technicians, and equipment — 32 participants	Agro-chemical importers and distributors — 97 participants	
Protective equipment and personal implements for agriculture work — 19 participants	Farmers and importers	Producers and processors
Fences and protective materials — 12 participants	Ag extension, consulting, engineering, SPS support, etc. — 40 participants, including government, chambers, and growers associations	
Fuel — 4 participants	Supervision, quality control, chemical and toxic analysis, SPS control, certification, environmental work — 25 participants	Logistics operators — 122 participants
Cardboard, plastic and polypropylene packaging, labels, and wrappings — 72 participants		

Source: Interviews.

levels of quality and times of delivery have improved significantly over the last few years (and vary across specific products, as we illustrate later).

There were, however, three exceptions to this rule that are worth highlighting here, particularly as they relate to regional integration behind the border. The first involved quality control, including toxicological analysis, which is critical to exports destined for developed markets, especially Europe. In Peru, there are no labs that can do the required analyses, resulting in delays of 10–15 days, and additional costs, incurred by the need to take these samples to labs in Chile. In one sense, regional integration, as well as Peru's export competitiveness, would be encouraged if there were a single regional set of requirements and the Chilean labs established operations in Peru and elsewhere throughout the relevant region.

The second exception involved SENASA—the part of the Ministry of Agriculture that is in charge of, among other things, issuing sanitary certificates and collaborating with, among others, INDECOPI, in setting technical norms for the production of fruits and vegetables. According to the interviewed parties in the private sector, these institutions do an acceptable job, but the lack of growth in SENASA's budget or staff and the lack of investment in new technologies represent a potential serious choke point given that the quantity of exports has trebled. This meant that the processing of certificates, which are required by importers and which used to be very quick and adequate, was delayed and prone to errors, resulting in still further delays.

This second exception highlights a different sort of challenge for regional integration behind the border—one that has limited the utility of a number of free trade arrangements to date—namely the investment in institutions required to implement such an arrangement and ensure that regional progress is not slowed by the weakest link in the institutional chain.

The third exception involved mark-ups in the sale of some inputs and services, which can be quite high, especially in chemical products such as fertilizers and pesticides. This led many large producers to become direct importers, mostly from the People's Republic of China, and producer's associations to act as direct buyers as one of the services they deliver. These arrangements proved inefficient (usually there is a delay, little local stocks, lack of services and technical support connected to the imported product, a deviation of the attention and resources of the local organizer, etc.); they only existed due to the very high prices that create a need to circumvent the local representative of the foreign brand.

Peru has developed innovative arrangements among its producers as a means of reducing the inefficiencies inherent in the current arrangement.

Those innovations raise a third potentially interesting area for exploration in terms of regional integration behind the border—that of developing and extending innovations like Peru's to producers throughout a particular region as a means of improving the region's competitiveness, increasing the value of the clusters of high quality production within the region, and taking advantage of the network externalities that would flow from such market dynamics.

Regarding shipping and port costs, Peru was and is quite competitive, whether compared with its immediate neighbors or with other developing regions in the world. There is, on the other hand, some room for improvement. It takes less time and less paperwork (although more money) to process imports and exports than for the average Latin American competitor. And although the cost per container, at $875, is 28.8% lower than the regional average, and 18.1% cheaper than the OECD average, we should remember that among Peruvian exports, bulky items with large volume-to-value ratios are more prominent than in other countries, and, therefore, shipping costs are still high. Furthermore, Chile, a fairly relevant competitor in fresh produce, still beats Peru on all these counts.

Of course, origin certification and the meeting of high sanitary standards and strict technical norms are very important for Peru, and explain a significant portion of the higher cost and delay compared with some other countries (Table 7.1). It would hardly be beneficial for the perishable exports sector to waive those requirements for the sake of expediency, losing marketability, value, and product differentiation. At the same time, seen from the perspective of regional integration behind the border, the adoption of a single regional set of rules that squared with those used by global buyers and the region's principal export markets would yield efficiencies that would benefit Peru's producers as well as producers in the rest of the region.

Given Peru's relative strength in terms of meeting the necessary sanitary and phytosanitary standards, however, an effort aimed at reducing the time and cost of port and terminal processing and document preparation seems like a more urgent investment. Recent work estimates that one day of extra delay in the export process implies roughly 1% less export volume, and that this effect is even larger for time-sensitive products, with a limited storage life.[4] In economic terms, the extra three days of waiting for export processing

---

[4] Djankov, Freund, and Pham (2006) run a regression of a geography model in which, in addition to distance and shipping costs, delays in the process of exports and imports are counted as an independent variable. They find statistically significant and actually quite large coefficients for the explanatory power of time into the volume of exports. The effects are larger when only perishable products are considered.

Table 7.1
Cost and Delay for Processing Foreign Trade at Border

Region or country	Number of documents for export	Days to clear exports	Cost for exports per container	Number of documents for import	Days to clear imports	Cost for imports per container
Peru	7	24	875	8	25	895
East Asia & Pacific	6.7	23.3	902.3	7.1	24.5	948
East Europe & Central Asia	7.1	29.7	1649.1	8.3	31.7	1822.2
Latin America	6.9	19.7	1229.8	7.4	22.3	1,384.30
Middle East & North Africa	6.5	23.3	1024.4	7.6	26.7	1204.8
OECD	4.5	10.7	1069.1	5.1	11.4	1132.7
South Asia	8.5	33	1339.1	9	32.5	1487.3
Sub-Saharan Africa	7.8	34.7	1878.8	8.8	41.1	2278.7
Colombia	6	14	1690	8	15	1640
Chile	6	21	745	7	21	795
Panama	3	9	729	4	9	879
Ecuador	9	20	1345	7	29	1332

Source: Doing Business 2009, World Bank.

put Peru to the south of Chile: farther from the European and North American markets where their competing produce is directed.

Problems at the border are, of course, only one aspect of the country's competitiveness and business climate. Internal barriers affect the profitability and volume of exports as well. Those include a broad range of areas, including the general business climate relative to a country's competitors; the quality of institutions and infrastructure; macroeconomic stability; basic education; the efficiency of the goods and labor markets; the ability of local firms to innovate and adopt new technologies and business processes; and the degree of concentration of market power, especially in the process of distributing imported goods.[5]

Even the bureaucratic barriers to starting a company can have an impact, as well as opening up additional opportunities for corruption. Anecdotal

---

[5] See generally World Economic Forum, The Global Competitiveness Report 2008–2009 and Global Competitiveness Index Ranking 2008–2009.

evidence from Peru reinforces that point. It suggests that it is actually impossible for a small business to do certain things consistently within the law, a finding that is consistent with the work begun in Peru by Hernando de Soto (1989) roughly two decades ago.[6]

While such items are commonly thought of as issues of internal reform, they would benefit from the adoption of a coherent strategy for regional integration behind the border. Peru's process involves many more steps than those of many of its neighbors that would be likely partners in a regional arrangement. Adopting a regional integration strategy that looked behind the border would create an opportunity for Peru to remove those steps and improve its competitiveness along with that of the region without losing much if anything from the perspective of the prudential policies such measures may have originally been designed to serve.

What this points toward is the value of a regional integration strategy that does, in fact, address the obstacles to value chain participation behind the border. Properly understood, the implications of Peru's institutional weaknesses relative to its competitors imply that Peru must compete in the global markets on the basis of cost, rather than product differentiation, specialization, or productivity, all of which would pay greater dividends in terms of economic growth and development. This largely explains why most Peruvian fruit and vegetable exports are still unprocessed traditional products.

Many of the findings with respect to the downstream value chain in Peru's perishable agriculture production mirrored those affecting the upstream value chain. For that reason, we focused on a different use of the methodology suggested—one that is designed to illuminate the trade-offs implicit in the policy and funding choices any country or group of countries make as part of a regional integration strategy that reaches behind the border.

The following Figure 7.2 illustrates the other half of the general value chain for perishable exports. Downstream from farmers, we also find several segments of the value chain that involve sufficient providers to guarantee competition, world-comparable prices and quality, allowing output to reach the foreign final consumer in an effective and competitive way. Over 300 companies are direct exporters, in addition to a number of producers and processors

---

[6] According to the World Bank's Doing Business Report, it takes 65 days, 10 separate legal/documentary procedures, and nearly 3 months of the average income, to open a new firm. Readers may remember that *The Other Path*, Hernando de Soto's seminal work on understanding the cost of bureaucratic burdens and forced informality on the productivity and success possibilities of the poor, was based on documenting the massive cost of operating a business within the law in his native Peru.

Figure 7.2
Peru Agro-Export Supply Chain—Downstream

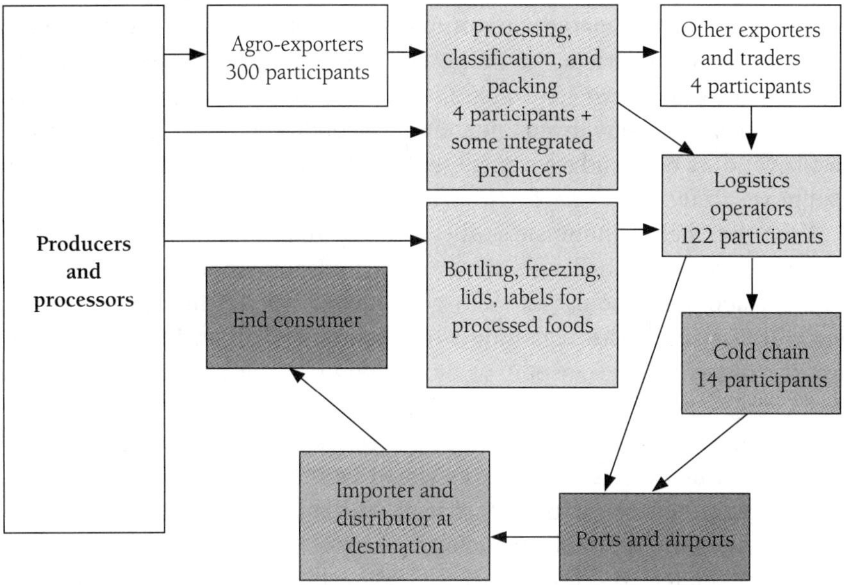

```
                    ┌──────────────────┐    ┌──────────────────┐    ┌──────────────────┐
                    │  Agro-exporters  │───▶│   Processing,    │───▶│  Other exporters │
                    │  300 participants│    │ classification,  │    │   and traders    │
                    └──────────────────┘    │    and packing   │    │  4 participants  │
                  ▲                         │  4 participants +│    └──────────────────┘
                  │                         │  some integrated │              │
                  │                         │    producers     │              │
                  │                         └──────────────────┘              ▼
┌────────────┐    │                                               ┌──────────────────┐
│            │────┘                                           ───▶│     Logistics    │
│ Producers  │                              ┌──────────────────┐  │     operators    │
│    and     │─────────────────────────────▶│    Bottling,     │  │ 122 participants │
│ processors │                              │ freezing, lids,  │  └──────────────────┘
│            │         ┌──────────────┐     │   labels for     │              │
│            │         │ End consumer │     │ processed foods  │              ▼
└────────────┘         └──────────────┘     └──────────────────┘  ┌──────────────────┐
                             ▲                                    │    Cold chain    │
                             │                                    │  14 participants │
                             │                                    └──────────────────┘
                       ┌──────────────┐                                   │
                       │ Importer and │                                   │
                       │ distributor  │◀────┌──────────────────┐◀─────────┘
                       │at destination│     │ Ports and airports│
                       └──────────────┘     └──────────────────┘
```

Source: Interviews.

themselves. There are also 122 logistics operators that serve the perishables sector in the process of getting their output to foreign markets.

Some of the processors or the packaging plants of agricultural output in the chain are either owned by the larger individual agricultural producers, or by associations, groups or cooperatives; only a handful of processing plants are stand-alone businesses. This means that this link in the chain is usually very fluid.

In some cases, the availability of a cold chain is a key to add value to the resulting output. Several different companies would participate in the different aspects of the logistics for a single exporter. Some of these are cargo or shipment consolidators, either acting as intermediaries to provide smaller quantities and larger variety to foreign buyers, or as shipping agents putting together the cargo of different producers to share a single container.

The importance of the cold chain helps illustrate the trade-off alluded to previously. One of the key challenges in this value chain is the perishability of the products. Any delay raises costs considerably. That affects the relevant choices for warehousing and transport of the goods and, more importantly for purposes of public policy and any eventual regional integration strategy, a potential implicit choice between two different export sectors.

With respect to asparagus, for example, the distributor in the importing country should receive the cargo within 4–5 days of the crop collection, to take full value of market opportunities. Shipping by sea, which is more common for Peru's fruits, would be cheaper than shipping by air, but sea transport takes between 13–16 days, which sharply reduces the option value of the crop significantly. Even under optimal conditions, asparagus can hardly last beyond 21 days and even small oscillations in temperature and humidity can prove costly.

What this helps illuminate is the potential tradeoffs for Peruvian policy makers. Peru faces challenges in terms of transportation linkages affecting both air and seaborne cargo. With government budgets limited, it may be forced to make choices regarding where its transportation budget is spent. Improvements in air transport would redound to the benefit of asparagus producers—one of Peru's success stories in terms of integrating its production into global markets. Improvements in sea transport would, instead, contribute to fruit exports—an area in which Peru has considerable room for diversification of its exports. In that sense, the choice of how Peru spends its transportation budget implicitly involves a choice between a development and integration strategy based on intensive exploitation of the existing advantage it holds in asparagus production or a strategy of export diversification, which is likely to draw many more producers into contact with global markets.

Seen in that light, the example of Peru's asparagus and fruit industries also helps highlight the need for reaching beyond the mapping of obstacles in the value chain toward econometric modeling of the impact of those barriers. Peruvian policy makers would be in a far better position to assess the costs and benefits of either approach to transportation noted previously if they had a common means of measuring the current costs of doing business as usual, as well as the value of specific improvements in the infrastructure.

Conclusion

The analysis above suggests a number of further steps worth taking. The next step, in the case of the Peruvian example discussed above, would involve a review of the preliminary results with Peruvian officials and local entrepreneurs to ensure that the results conform to and benefit from their intimate knowledge of both the local market and the administrative side of the equation. This step in the process would be used both as a means of ensuring accuracy and as a device for gathering additional information at a more refined level.

The successful conclusion of that step in the process would then lead to the data collection needed to do the econometric modeling and the use of the model outlined previously to measure the individual obstacles in the value chain by a single comparable measure such as cost or time to market. Applying the econometric model would offer policy makers a means of measuring the expected return on investment from any policy intervention they might choose.

Beyond the application of the methodology outlined previously, there are a number of other analytical steps that might contribute to a more coherent regional integration strategy that reaches behind the border and results in deeper economic integration as well as improvements in export competitiveness on global markets. One would involve benchmarking Peruvian perishables, for example, against other Peruvian export successes. Mapping the supply chain of existing successful enterprises would allow Peruvian policy makers and the IDB to evaluate progress in perishable agricultural products against those benchmarks. It might also help illuminate how existing successful enterprises overcame the barriers to trade found elsewhere in the Peruvian economy in order to connect themselves to local, regional, and global markets.

This analytical step could also take the form of benchmarking Peru's perishables sector against producers in other countries (Costa Rica, Brazil, and Chile come to mind). Analyzing the value chains in perishable agricultural products in other countries might offer instructive examples of how other countries succeeded in building profitable and sustainable export sectors in perishables that include a greater share of small- and medium-sized exporters.

The discussion above highlights the fact that value chains such as that serving the perishable agriculture sector in Peru do not exist in isolation. The value chain here is, in turn, served by other value chains. To the extent warranted by the basic supply chain analysis (i.e., the extent to which either sector represents one of the high value barriers to be addressed), it would also make sense to apply the supply chain analysis to particular sectors that are known facilitators of both exchange and broader development goals.

What such an analysis would illuminate would be the inefficiencies (and therefore higher costs) involved in delivering services, such as finance and telecommunications, that are absolutely essential to enable Peruvian producers of perishables and other products to access export markets. Those sectors have their own supply chains and it may prove helpful to apply a similar analysis to the delivery of those key services as well as the supply chains of product and services markets.

The final step in completing the analysis would involve using the value chain analysis in developing both a country's or a region's trade negotiating strategy and its regional integration strategy. The supply chain analysis outlined previously offers a means of identifying those foreign trade barriers the removal of which in future negotiations would generate the greatest return for a country's or region's exports.

At the same time, the value chain analysis could serve the purpose of assessing where changes behind the border would contribute to the ability of its producers to integrate successfully on a regional basis, as well as integrating into global markets. As the discussion above reflects, many of the challenges that Peruvian producers of perishable agricultural products face are the delays engendered by domestic institutions and problems with physical infrastructure, which raise both costs and uncertainty—the two factors that are of the highest concern to potential global buyers of Peru's products.

References

Aldonas, G., and A. Trejos. 2010. *Connecting People to Markets: Methodologies for Integrating Trade and Development Goals*. Inter-American Development Bank.

De Soto, H. 1989. *The Other Path: The Invisible Revolution in the Third World*. US, New York: Harper & Row.

Djankov, S., C. Freund, and C. Pham. 2006. Trading in Time, World Bank Policy Research Working Paper No. 3909, World Bank, Washington, DC.

Dymond, W., and M. Hart. 2008. Navigating New Trade Routes: The Rise of Value Chains and the Challenges for Canadian Trade Policy. *Commentary*. 259. pp. 13–22.

World Bank. 2008. Doing Business–Measuring Business Regulations data set, International Finance Corporation, World Bank, Washington, DC. Available at http://www.doingbusiness.org.

World Economic Forum. 2009. Global Competitiveness Reports for 2008–2009. Available at http://www.weforum.org/issues/global-competitiveness.

PART III

Asia–LAC Relations

8

PRC's Outward FDI to Latin America: Trends and Motivations*

Gloria O. Pasadilla

Introduction

Since 2000 the People's Republic of China (PRC) has developed into an important source of direct investment for developing countries. Asia is the PRC's top investment destination, while Latin America is in second place as a recipient of Chinese outward foreign direct investment (OFDI) stock. The Latin American countries and sectors the PRC invests in, as well as possible motivations for its investments, are subjects worth exploring. The first section discusses the general trend in the PRC's OFDI and investment motivations, while the second section focuses on OFDI in Latin America.

General Trends

Following its success in attracting inward FDI, the PRC has embarked on a "go global" strategy. From zero overseas FDI in the 1970s, the PRC had accumulated US$317 billion of OFDI stock overseas by the end of 2010, becoming the eighth largest source of FDI stock and fifth in FDI flow in the world. The combined 2010 OFDI flows of the PRC and Hong Kong, China put them

---

* In this report, "US$" refers to US dollars.

on par with the United States (US). Yet, despite the PRC's steady accumulation of OFDI, being a latecomer to the outward investment game, its share in global investment stock is a minuscule 1.6%, compared to the US share of 24%, and the United Kingdom's (UK) 8%.[1]

Of the US$317 billion of Chinese OFDI stock in 2010, 72% was in Asia and 14% was in Latin America and the Caribbean (LAC). Europe, Africa, Oceania, and North America trail far behind with an aggregate share of 14% as shown in Figure 8.1(a). Hong Kong, China receives 63% of Chinese OFDI in Asia, leaving 9% distributed over the rest of the region, of which 4.1% is in ASEAN member economies. Chinese investments in LAC, excluding those in offshore financial centers such as the Cayman Islands and the British Virgin Islands, amount to only 1% of Chinese OFDI stock, while the combined OFDI in the Cayman Islands and British Virgin Islands is 13% as seen in Figure 8.1 (b). This investment pattern reveals the concentration of Chinese investments to a few offshore financial centers (including Hong Kong, China), which together take 85% of Chinese outward investments as given in Figure 8.1 (c). It also suggests that the true breakdown of the destination of Chinese OFDI is virtually unknown because financial investments to offshore centers usually get deflected either to ultimate host countries and/or back to the PRC as FDI inflow, a phenomenon known as round-tripping (Box 8.1).

In investment modalities, Chinese OFDI is increasingly using mergers and acquisitions (M&As) as a vehicle compared to the earlier use of joint ventures and the establishment of Chinese subsidiaries overseas. Table 8.1 shows how M&As increased from a meager US$109 million in 1988–1989 to US$29,201 billion in 2010, a rise from 14% to 42% of Chinese OFDI outflows. In 2006 and 2008, the majority of Chinese OFDI took place via M&A, most of which targeted companies in North America and the European Union. Cross-border M&As are typically used for Chinese OFDI in technology and communications and in natural resources sectors, as a way to quickly acquire advanced technology, sales networks, brand names, and other strategic assets overseas (OECD 2008). Because of the business sophistication involved, M&As are mainly used by Chinese multinational enterprises (MNEs) while smaller investors use the establishment of sales offices and/or joint ventures to enter markets.

---

[1] PRC's share in world stock of FDI is likely higher if unrecorded outward investments by private Chinese enterprises were properly captured. Chinese OFDI is famously underestimated because the official data from the ministry of commerce only include officially approved and registered investments. Most private enterprises do not apply for approval for their outward investments, especially reinvested foreign earnings, and thus escape the PRC's official statistics (OECD 2008).

Figure 8.1
Chinese Stock of OFDI

(a) Share of Host Regions (%)

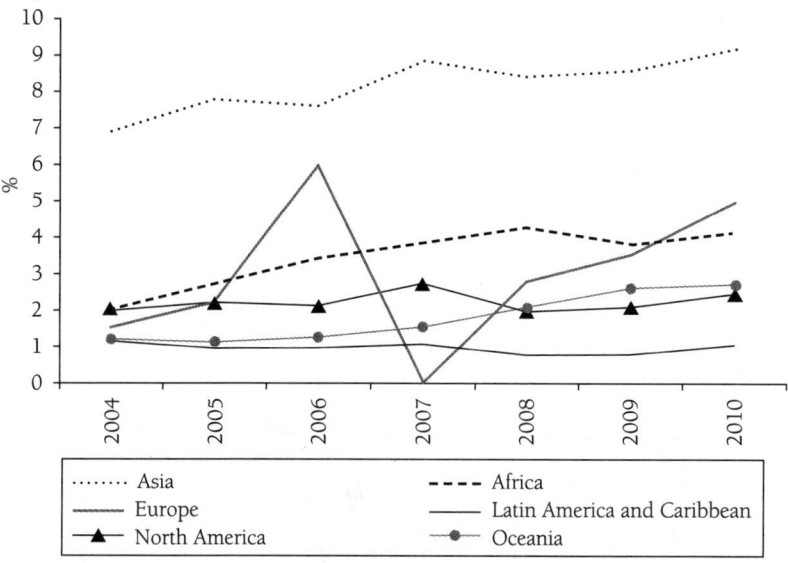

*excluding Hong Kong, China; Cayman Islands; and British Virgin Islands

(b) Hong Kong, China, and OFCs

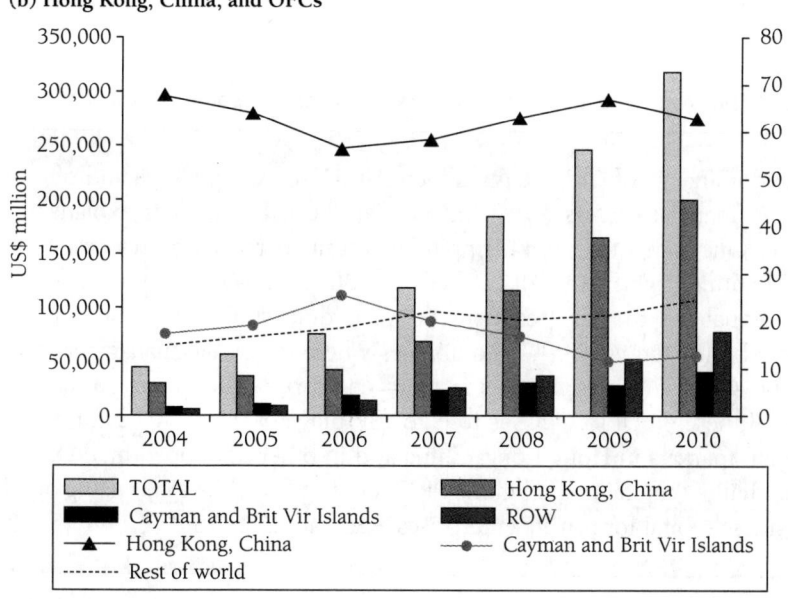

(Figure 8.1 Contd)

(Figure 8.1 Contd)

(c) By Host Regions

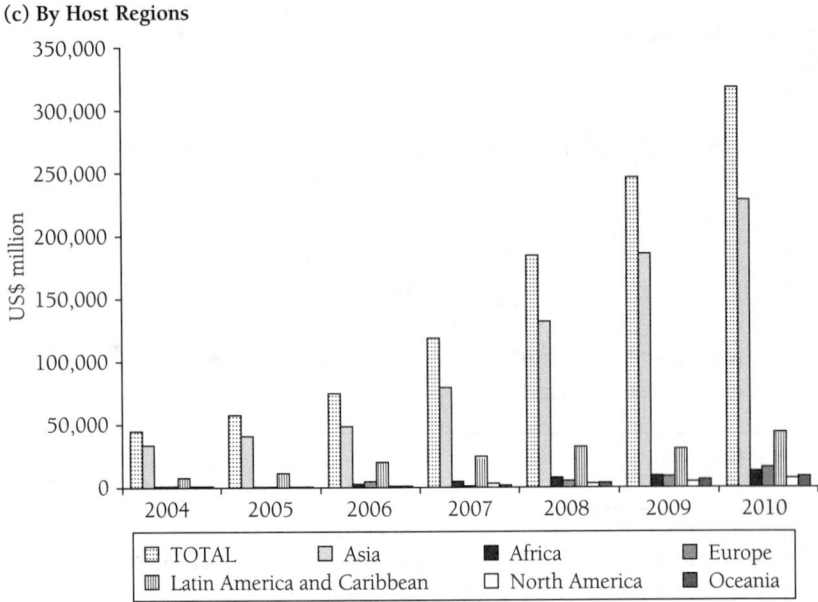

OFC = offshore financial center; OFDI = outward foreign direct investment.
Source: Ministry of Commerce, PRC (2011).

Box 8.1
Chinese OFDI, the Offshore Financial Centers, and Round-Tripping Investments[a]

> The dominance of Chinese investments in Hong Kong, China and offshore financial centers (OFC) in the Caribbean has various explanations. One is that the round-tripping investments receive a preferential tax treatment given to FDI in the PRC. But in 2008, a new Chinese law equalized the tax treatment between domestic investments and those by foreign established companies where the actual management body is located in the PRC as resident enterprise. Another reason for the Chinese OFDI to OFCs is to take advantage of the more advanced capital markets in Hong Kong, China and in other developed markets. The shallow capital market in the PRC does not allow the easy raising of business capital for private enterprises that want to expand.

(Box 8.1 Contd)

(Box 8.1 Contd)

> Some illustrations of how Chinese firms, usually non-state-owned-enterprises, use their OFC investments are outlined below:
>
> (a) PRC company XYZ incorporates a holding company in the British Virgin Islands or Cayman Islands, and then orchestrates an acquisition of its own PRC-based company XYZ. The holding company becomes based abroad but a significant part of its operations is in the PRC. Being based in the OFC allows it to more easily raise capital on foreign capital markets. Usually following an initial public offering, its access to bank borrowing also improves. From their perch, they can also do strategic acquisitions in other countries, or buy other PRC-based companies that are themselves held by offshore holding companies.
> (b) PRC company ABC is incorporated in the Cayman Islands as a holding company. To take advantage of the PRC's preferential tax treatment of investments from Hong Kong, China over other OFCs, it established two holding companies in Hong Kong, China to hold its interests in subsidiaries based in the PRC and wind up two holding companies in the British Virgin Islands.
>
> [a] Adapted from Sutherland et al. (2010).

Large Chinese MNEs that are administered by the central government's ministries and agencies do the bulk of Chinese outward investments. Available data of outward investments by central state-owned-enterprises (SOEs) show their share to be an average of 85% of the total stock of Chinese OFDI in 2004 and 2005. The remainder is shared by SOEs administered by regional governments[2] and non-SOEs that are either private or owned collectively. In 2004, private firms accounted for a mere 1.5% of the PRC's outward FDI flow (Cheng and Ma 2010).[3] Central government SOEs enjoy considerable support including favorable financing, direct and indirect subsidies, and low interest loans from state-owned banks, making them "fearsome" international

---

[2] For example, Lenovo is owned by the Beijing regional government, TCL by Shanghai.
[3] Please see Footnote 2 on the limitations of Chinese FDI data for a possible underestimation of OFDI by private firms in the PRC.

Table 8.1
M&A in the PRC's OFDI (US$ million)

	1988–1989 average	1990–1991 average	2000–2002 average	2005	2006	2007	2008	2009	2010	2011[a]
PRC's net purchases	109	430	3,561	3653	12,090	−2,282	37,941	21,490	29,201	13,476
% share of OFDI flow	13.9	16.7	43.6	29.79	68.56	−8.61	67.86	38.02	42.44	–

Source: OECD (2008) for 1988–2002 data; UNCTAD (2011) for 2005–2011 data and MOFCOM (2011) for OFDI flows.
Note: [a]January–May

competitors (Salidjanova 2011). Given the major role of the government through its control over the SOEs,[4] Chinese OFDI has often been seen as motivated by commercial as much as by political interests. Some Chinese MNEs take great pains to distance themselves from the government and project themselves as private firms to minimize concern over their investment bids.

Reasons for Chinese OFDI

On the macroeconomic front, the government has good reason to adopt a "go global" strategy. Capital outflow, through direct investment or portfolio investment, is seen as a way to reduce pressure for the renminbi to revalue in the face of vigorous capital inflows and persistent trade surpluses. The very low returns from US Treasury securities, of which it held US$1.1 trillion as of September 2011, is another reason for the PRC's foray into higher risk but higher return OFDIs.

On the microeconomic front, Chinese enterprises, by learning from foreign partners, have reached a level of maturity to be able to operate businesses abroad. Excess capacity in some sectors is another push factor for Chinese enterprises to diversify operations and to explore new markets overseas. Chinese OFDI is also motivated by the search for natural resources to meet growing domestic demand for energy, minerals, and other commodities. Other OFDI are for the purpose of acquiring strategic assets such as advanced technology, brand names, and customer and distribution networks (OECD 2008).

Sectoral compositions reveal the motivations of Chinese enterprises. In 2010, the top two sectors where Chinese OFDI stock are placed are in the services sectors—leasing and business services with US$97.2 billion (31% of total OFDI stock), and banking and financials with US$55.3 billion (17%), of which 81% is in banking, and 19% is in insurance, securities, and other financial sectors. By the end of 2010, Chinese state-owned commercial banks had established 59 branch offices and 17 affiliated institutions in 34 countries, including Japan, the UK, and the US (MOFCOM 2011).

Mining comes in third with US$44.7 billion, followed by two more service sectors: wholesale and retail trade, and transport and storage. Curiously,

---

[4] The government holds non-tradable shares of the SOEs; their board members and managers are government appointed; they have relatively easy access to government subsidies and cheap loans; and their operations are not threatened by bankruptcy and takeover (OECD 2008).

manufacturing, which is a PRC strength, only places sixth with an OFDI of US$17.8 billion. This investment composition suggests that Chinese OFDI aims primarily to support PRC's import and export activities and to seek resources to meet domestic demand. Arguably, even the latter is ultimately meant to also support the export of manufactured goods.

Chinese Investments in LAC

Chinese overseas investments in LAC is second to Asia, but the offshore financial centers of the British Virgin Islands and the Cayman Islands capture 92% of the total stock (more than US$40 billion). The rest of Latin America receives only 8%, with Brazil topping the list with less than half of 1% (US$924 million). Peru follows with 0.21% (US$654 million) and Venezuela 0.13% (US$417 million) (Figure 8.2). Total investment in LAC excluding OFC is US$3.4 billion, or 1.1% of the total stock of Chinese OFDI worldwide. Though insignificant relative to total Chinese outward investment, annual Chinese FDI flows to the region have been increasing at an annual average

Figure 8.2
Chinese OFDI Stock in Latin America and the Caribbean, 2010

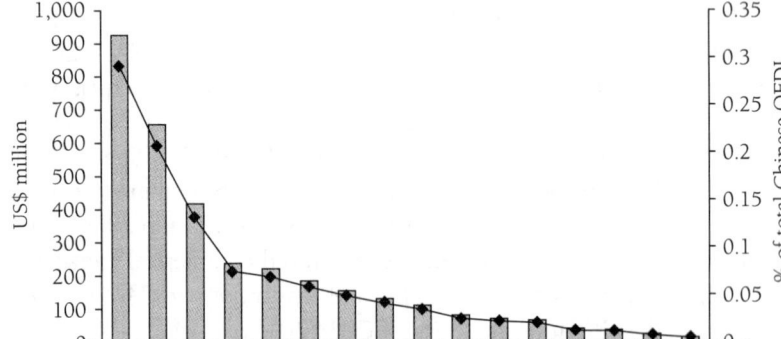

SVC = Saint Vincent and Grenadines
Source: MOFCOM (2011).

of 39% since 2004. With a trillion dollars of Chinese foreign reserves parked in low-yield US Treasury debts that can be rechanneled to OFDI and with an expanding Latin American regional market, the investment growth potential is high.

Various reports of sectoral distribution of Chinese OFDI in LAC is patchy but the Inter-American Development Bank (IDB) (2010) notes that the fact that Chinese investments are heavily concentrated in the Southern Cone[5] (i.e., Argentina, Brazil, Chile, Peru), the investments must be of the resource-seeking variety. These investments seek secure access to the supply of natural resources either by investing directly in mines or agricultural land or by developing the infrastructure around them. For example, in Peru, mining accounts for almost 100% of Chinese investments. In Chile, investments are in agriculture, forestry, and mining. In contrast, in Brazil, the PRC has a more diversified portfolio, with manufacturing taking a significant share.

Lack of more detailed sector distribution of Chinese OFDI precludes a deeper analysis of the nature of the investments in LAC. What follows in the discussion below is an analysis of various sources of (unofficial) data collected by various organizations. First, we look at Greenfield investment information collected by fdimarkets.com based on publicly announced information. Then we analyze information of investments by major Chinese MNEs that has been tracked by the Heritage Foundation.[6]

Table 8.2 shows samples of investments of the top 10 Chinese company investors in LAC that have Greenfield investments. The top 10 Chinese companies account for 37% of all projects from the PRC. The sample of projects show that investments vary: from establishment of subsidiary banks in Brazil to construction of water treatment facilities near a mining plant; from setting up a headquarter office for the LAC market and establishment of dealerships to the construction of R&D facilities.

Of the 129 Greenfield investment projects in LAC recorded from January 2003 to September 2011, 23 (about 18%) were from Chinese mining companies. Automotive OEM (original equipment manufacturer) companies have 22 projects (17%), while firms engaged in communications have 20 (16%). The coal, oil, and natural gas sector and the industrial machinery and equipment sector each have 9 projects, while Chinese financial companies have 8 projects (Figure 8.3).

---

[5] South America is the resource-rich part of LAC compared to Central America and the Caribbean.

[6] This information is downloadable from www.heritage.org/research/reports/2011/01/china-global-investment-tracker-2011.

Table 8.2
Greenfield Investments of Top Company Investors in Latin America and the Caribbean

Company	No. of LAC projects	Sector of co.	Main business activity of co.	Sample of projects (completed and announced)
China National Petroleum (CNPC)	9	Coal, oil, natural gas	Manufacturing	2009: $1 B joint venture to build crude oil refinery in Costa Rica 2010: $4.5 B refinery expansion in Cuba; to commence in 2011 2003: $70 M Drilling and exploration of Aracapi-Parahuacu fields in Ecuador
ZTE	9	Communications	Manufacturing	2009: $4 M for construction of a training center in Bogota, Colombia in partnership with the Javeriana University. 2011: Multi-services facility for telecom research and development, local logistics, and customer service to serve South America
Huawei Technologies	7	Communications	Manufacturing	2011: $300 M to establish a research and development center in Campinas, Brazil. 2009: $5.7 M for production of transmission equipment and other electronic components in Brazil 2006: US$20 million for a new Training Centre and Operations hub in Mexico City
SAIC Chery Automobile	5	Automotive OEM	Manufacturing	2009: To open headquarters, manufacturing plant and 55 car dealership in Brazil for Chery car
China Minmetals Group	3	Metals	Mining	2004: $2 B for copper and aluminum production 2009: Galeno copper mine in Peru (unknown amount)

Great Wall Motors (GWM)	3	Automotive OEM	Manufacturing	2010: To build passenger cars, special utility vehicles, multi-purpose vehicles and pickups in Brazil and Venezuela by 2013
Industrial and Commercial Bank of China (ICBC)	3	Financial services	Business services	2011: Announced plan to establish a subsidiary, a full service bank in Sao Paulo, Brazil under the name ICBC do Brasil Banco Multiplo.
China Development Bank	3	Financial services	Business services	2009: To open a representative office in Brazil (and Venezuela) to invest in ports, steel mills and energy.
Beiqi Foton Motor	3	Automotive OEM	Manufacturing	2010: $12 M Mexican subsidiary to manufacture light trucks for domestic market 2010: $4 M to establish a new light trucks assembly plant in Colombia
Aluminium Corporation of China (Chinalco) (Chalco)	3	Metals	Mining	2008: $24 M, water treatment in copper mining in Peru; 2009: $2.15 B to develop the Toromocho copper mine in Peru

Source: Author's calculations based on data from fdimarkets.com

Figure 8.3
Distribution of Projects by Sector

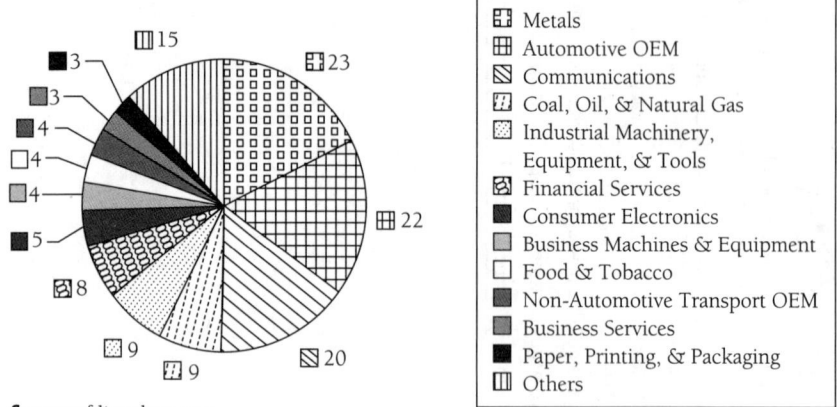

Source: fdimarkets.com

In terms of type of business activities, manufacturing firms have the most Greenfield projects, 60 out of 129, or 46% of the total, followed by firms engaged in sales, marketing, and support with 21 projects, and mining or extraction with 13 projects. Business services, usually associated with financial services firms, have 11 projects. The remaining projects are in education, retail, design, development and testing, and logistics, distribution and transportation, among others[7] (Figure 8.4).

Another set of information is from the Heritage Foundation, which tracks the top Chinese MNEs' worldwide investment activities. From 2003 to June 2011, Chinese investment (Greenfield and M&A) totaled US$61.6 billion, or about 16% of Chinese OFDI. This far exceeds the official data reported by the Ministry of Commerce, PRC (MOFCOM) where outward investment to LAC (sans OFCs) only exceeds US$3 billion, or 1.1% of total Chinese OFDI. One explanation is that the MOFCOM data does not include investments in 2011 while the Heritage Foundation does, so in some sense they are not strictly comparable.[8] Another plausible explanation is that, because this data tracks

---

[7] While the pattern of investments in LAC appears different from the overall sectoral distribution of Chinese investments around the world, the comparison is unwarranted. The above discussion of sector distribution refers to number of investment projects in LAC while earlier analysis used total outward investment value. There, the value of manufacturing investment pales in comparison to those in business and leasing services as well as financial services.

[8] Total value of investments in LAC decreases to US$55.3 billion if 2011 investments are excluded, a minor difference from the total, but a major difference from the official estimates as of 2010.

Figure 8.4
Distribution of Number of Projects by Business Activity

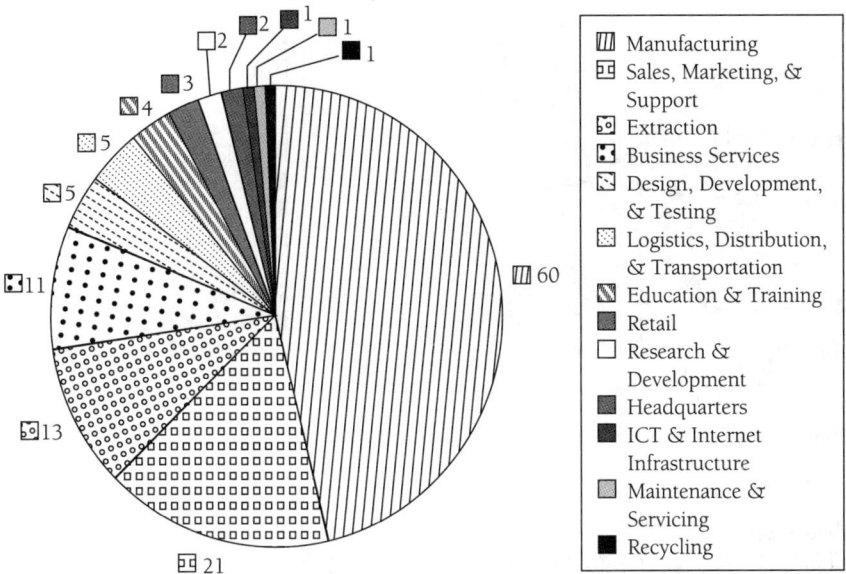

Source: www.fdimarkets.com

corporate information, it might have accounted for the final destination of investments that were coursed through Hong Kong, China or the Cayman Islands and the British Virgin Islands. If correct, this potentially makes the Heritage Foundation data superior to the official estimates as far as the breakdown of the destination of Chinese investment is concerned. Another plausible explanation is that the Heritage Foundation data includes values of stock acquisitions that may not be considered "investment" in the official data because the official record of investment only accounts for acquisitions that exceed 10% of equity share.

For what it is worth, the unofficial information shows that Brazil takes a third of total Chinese OFDI in LAC with more than US$18 billion, a share that is close to the official estimate from MOFCOM of 28%. However, while Peru is the next biggest recipient of Chinese OFDI according MOFCOM data, the Heritage Foundation puts Argentina second to Brazil with 23%, then Venezuela (15%), Peru (12%), and Ecuador (10%) (Figure 8.5).

In sectoral distribution, Chinese investment in LAC is heavily concentrated on energy and metals (copper and steel), which together account for almost 60% of the total value of investments, each taking 38.1% and 21.8% shares, respectively. Transport, particularly railway construction in Argentina and

Figure 8.5
Chinese OFDI to Latin America and the Caribbean

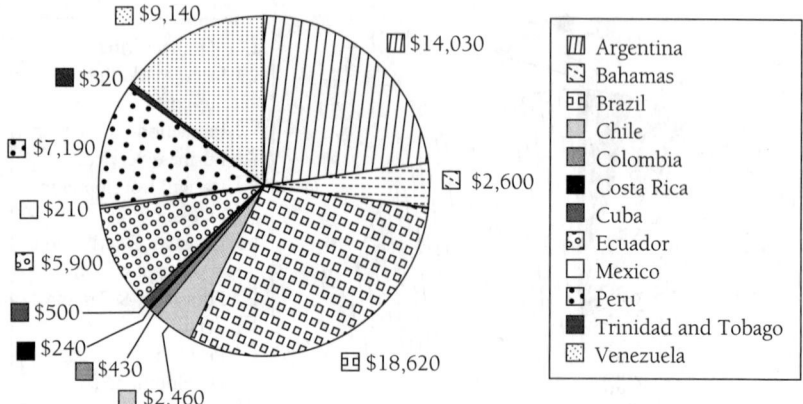

Source: Author's calculations based on data from Heritage Foundation website (accessed 24 Nov 2011). See Footnote 7.

Figure 8.6
Chinese OFDI to Latin America and the Caribbean by Sector

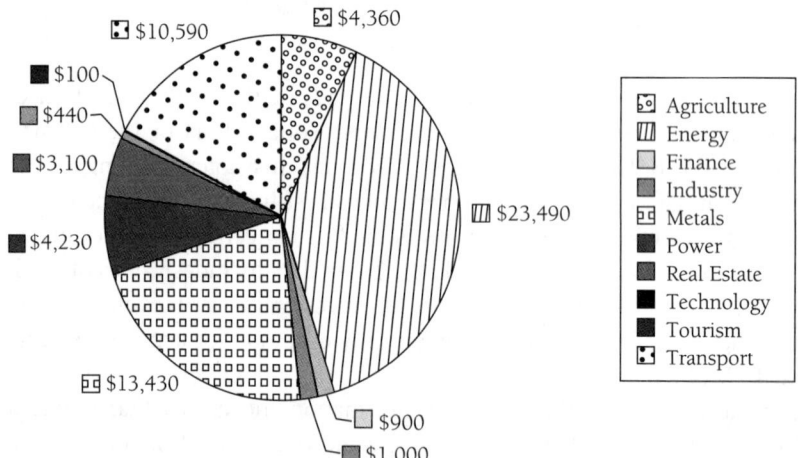

Source: Author's calculations based on Heritage Foundation data. See Footnote 7.

Venezuela, is third with a 16% share. Agriculture and hydropower each has 7% of investments in LAC while real estate takes 5% (Figure 8.6).

In summary, while total Chinese OFDI is relatively strong in the services sector according to official data, in LAC, the concentration is heavily tilted toward energy and natural resources. Considering the growing demand for these products in the PRC's domestic market, prospects of further enhanced investments in the region appear bright.

Impact on Exports

It might be too soon to expect a significant increase in exports from the Chinese investments in Latin America. According to the database of fdimarkets.com, many of the investments, especially from mining and energy companies, expect operations to start in late 2011, while others in 2013 or later. Hence, while Figures 8.7 and 8.8 show an increase in LAC exports of mineral fuel and lubricants (SITC 3) and metals and ores (SITC 27, 28, and 68) to the PRC, the high growth has been due to strong Chinese demand starting in 2003 and not yet due to increased LAC capacity from Chinese investments in these sectors.

For manufacturing, communication, or financial services sector investments, the target market is either the domestic market or the regional or Latin American market. This is true for the auto and appliance manufacturing industries, as well as for telecommunication equipment manufacturing.

Figure 8.7
Latin America and the Caribbean Exports to the PRC of Ores and Metals

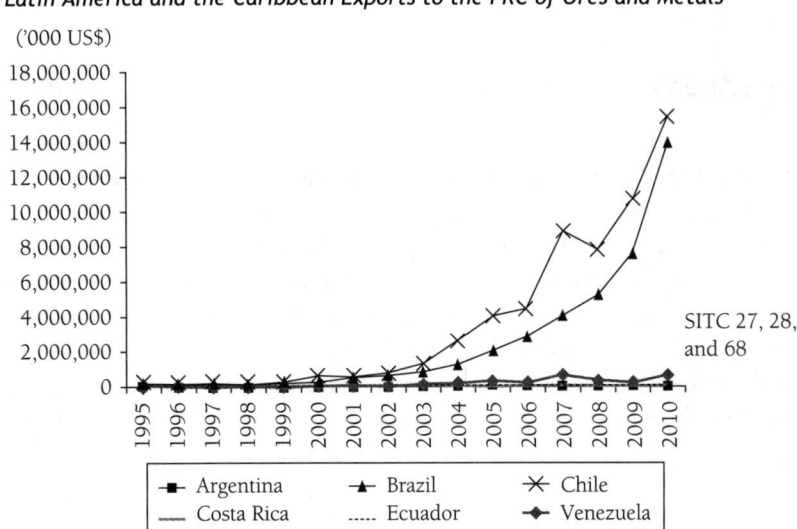

Source: UN COMTRADE.

Figure 8.8
Latin America and the Caribbean Exports to the PRC of Mineral Fuels, Lubricants, and Related Items

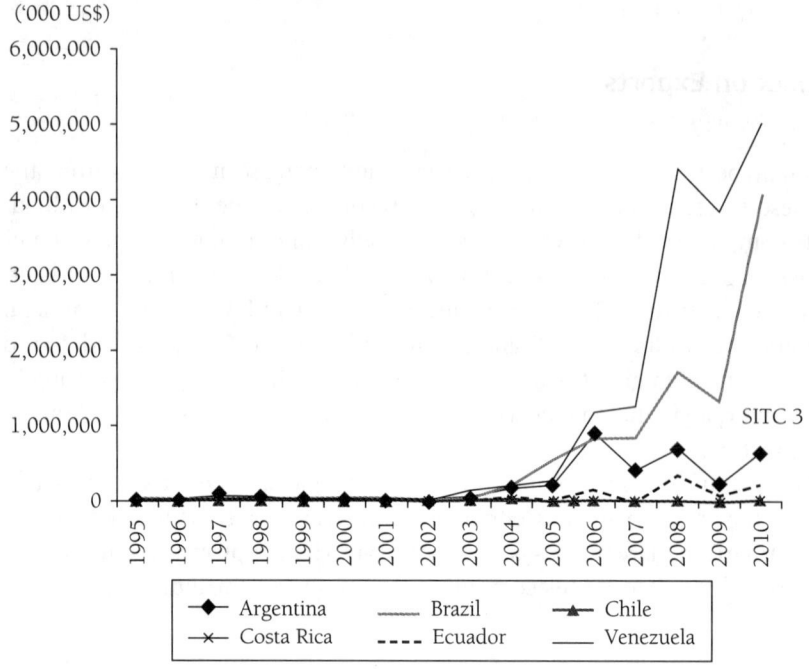

Source: Author's calculations based on UN COMTRADE data.

Looking Ahead

Considering the PRC's high surplus savings and its need to secure food, energy, and other raw materials to fuel its economy, Latin America will remain an attractive location for the PRC's OFDI. But beyond the natural resources endowment, Latin America also has a growing domestic market that is attractive for market-seeking investments such as investments in automobiles and consumer goods. These will fuel further Chinese investments in LAC. Latin America's challenge is to capitalize on this bonanza and to boost Chinese FDI spillover into the economy.

References

Cheng, L., and Z. Ma. 2010. China's Outward Foreign Direct Investment. In R. Feenstra and S. Wei, eds. *China's Growing Role in World Trade*. Chicago: University of Chicago Press.

IDB. 2010. *Ten Years after the Take-off: Taking Stock of China–Latin America and the Caribbean Relations*. Washington, DC: Inter-American Development Bank.

MOFCOM. 2011. 2010 Statistical Bulletin of China's Outward Foreign Direct Investment. Available at http://hzs.mofcom.gov.cn/accessory/201109/1316069658609.pdf (accessed 23 July 2014).

OECD. 2008. China's Outward Direct Investment. In *OECD Investment Policy Reviews: China 2008*. Paris: Organisation for Economic Co-operation and Development.

Salidjanova, N. 2011. Going Out: An Overview of China's Outward Foreign Direct Investment. *USCC Staff Research Report*. United States–China Economic and Security Review Commission.

Sutherland, D., A. El-Gohari, P. Buckley, and H. Voss. 2010. The Role of Caribbean Tax Havens and Offshore Financial Centers in Chinese Outward Foreign Direct Investment. Available at http://gdex.dk/ofdi10/Dylan%20Sutherland%20%20-%20et%20al.pdf (Accessed 20 October 2011).

9

Asia–Latin America FTAs: An Instrument for Interregional Liberalization and Integration?

Ganeshan Wignaraja, Dorothea Ramizo, and Luca Burmeister

Introduction

Before 2000 there was a limited economic relationship between Asia and Latin America[1] through either trade or FTA-led economic cooperation. Starting in the early 2000s, however, total trade growth between Asia and Latin America accelerated, driven by differences in demand conditions, factor endowments, trade policy, and the rise of giant emerging economies (ADB and IDB 2009; ADB, ADBI, and IDB 2012; Rosales and Kuwayama 2012). The 2008 global financial crisis temporarily disrupted Asia–Latin America trade growth but a rebound appears underway. Market-led integration has been followed by growing economic cooperation though free trade agreements (FTAs). Since the first Asia–Latin America FTA emerged in 2004, an average of two FTAs have taken effect every year between countries of the two regions, bringing the total number in effect to 22 (as of October 2013).

Growing Asia–Latin American economic ties have attracted attention in the literature on trade and regional integration. Research has focused on important

---

[1] Defined as the members of the Organization of America States (OAS), except the United States and Canada.

issues in the economic relationship between Asia and Latin America including drivers of interregional integration, the pattern of specialization in production and trade, tariffs and other barriers to interregional integration, the impact of competition from the People's Republic of China (PRC) on manufacturing in Latin America, and trade policy responses of Latin American governments to imports from the PRC and India (for a sample see Chami-Batista 2004; Devlin, Estevadeordal, and Rodríguez-Clare 2006; Jenkins, Peters, and Moreira 2008; Medalla and Balboa 2010; and Facchini et al. 2010; Rosales and Kuwayama 2012). However, relatively little attention has been paid to liberalization under interregional FTAs. The few exceptions include a study on the economic implications of large interregional FTAs between Asia and Latin America using a computable general equilibrium model which reported gains for both regions under different scenarios (Krasniqi et al. 2011). Some studies have explored the evolution of trade agreements between the two regions (Medalla and Balboa 2010; Rosales and Kuwayama 2012). Other studies have explored the drivers and content of interregional FTAs (e.g., Kawai and Wignaraja 2009; Gonzalez-Vigil and Shimizu 2012; Wignaraja and Lazaro 2010), but more work is needed on liberalization under recent agreements based on a comprehensive approach covering goods, services, and regulatory barriers.

This chapter suggests new criteria to assess liberalization in FTAs and painstakingly analyzes the coverage of all 22 Asia–Latin America FTAs in effect between 2004 and October 2013. It adopts a comprehensive approach to studying legal texts of agreements and examines liberalization in traditional areas like goods and services as well as regulatory barriers or new issues in trade policy. It also attempts to quantify the results, where appropriate and possible. This type of exercise goes beyond the bounds of a narrow single discipline based study and inevitably required inter-disciplinary analysis blending concepts and methods in applied international economics and international trade law. New issues in trade policy are defined here as the so-called Singapore issues (investment, government procurement, trade facilitation, and competition policy) and provisions on intellectual property rights (IPRs).

The detailed review finds that goods and services are generally well covered in most FTAs, but there is variation in the inclusion of provisions to liberalize regulatory barriers or new issues. Thus, room exists for improvement in new Asia–Latin America FTAs on regulatory barriers, notably commitments on Singapore issues and provisions on IPRs. Additionally, this chapter highlights the best Asia–Latin America FTAs and identifies key policy priorities to maximize gains from interregional integration in the future.

The structure of the chapter is as follows. By way of background, the next section briefly accounts for the increasing trade and investment flows between Asian and Latin American countries. The third section discusses trends in Asia–Latin America FTAs and explanations. The fourth section provides an overview of our evaluation of the scope and depth of Asia–Latin America FTAs. The fifth and sixth sections discuss the details of provisions pertaining to goods, services, Singapore issues, and IPR. The seventh section suggests priorities to support FTA-led integration between the two regions. The last section concludes.

Trade and Investment Growth and Key Economies

Several aspects of trade and investment flows between Asia and Latin America can be highlighted as background for the analysis of interregional FTAs: (i) growth of interregional trade flows before and after the 2008 global economic crisis; (ii) factors underlying interregional trade; (iii) key economies in interregional trade; and (iv) growth of interregional foreign direct investment (FDI) flows.

Growth of interregional trade flows. Figure 9.1 shows total trade flows between Asia and Latin America from 1990 to 2012 as well as a breakdown of Asia to Latin America exports and Latin America to Asia exports. These are readily available from the International Monetary Fund (IMF) Direction of Trade Statistics. The development of interregional trade between Asia and Latin America is characterized by two distinct periods of growth. Two decades ago, there was relatively little total intra-regional trade (about US$48 billion in 1990) between the two regions. The 1990s and early years of the 21st century exhibited an annual average growth of 8.3%. The turning point in Asia and Latin America trade occurred in 2004 and annual average trade growth rapidly accelerated to 28.9% between 2004 and 2008. Not coincidentally, it was in the same year that the first two Latin America–Asia FTAs came into effect (Republic of Korea–Chile; Taipei,China–Panama). In 2009, the effects of the global economic crisis impacted trade between Asia and Latin America, with total trade falling sharply from US$293 billion in 2008 to US$252 billion in 2009, representing a 14% decrease in trade. Both regions, however, rebounded strongly from the crisis and interregional trade grew at 36.9% per year between 2009–2011. In 2012, interregional trade reached

Figure 9.1
Trade Flows between Asia and Latin America, 1990–2012 (US$ billion)

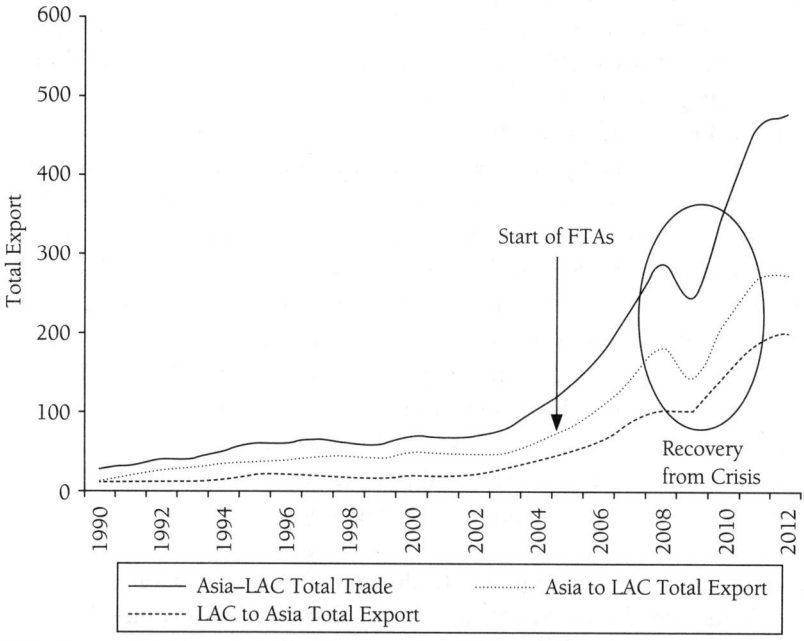

FTA = free trade agreement, LAC = Latin America and the Caribbean.
Source: Estimated from International Monetary Fund Direction of Trade Statistics (accessed October 2013).

an all-time high of US$478 billion, nearly a ten-fold increase over 1990. Figure 9.1 also shows that Asia typically experienced a trade surplus with Latin America as indicated by higher levels of Asia to Latin America exports relative to Latin America to Asia exports.

Factors underlying interregional trade. Comparative advantage, demand, and policies have influenced interregional trade growth. Differences in factor endowments have laid the basis for trade between the two regions. Latin America has an abundance of natural resources and agricultural goods while Asia is scarce in natural resources. Some Asian economies (e.g., the PRC and India) have low cost labor and capital while others—Japan; the Republic of Korea; and Taipei,China—have capital and industrial technology. Accordingly, specialization has occurred according to comparative advantage with Asian economies exporting manufactures of different factor intensities in exchange for primary commodities and semi-finished manufactures from

Latin America. Latin America's main exports to Asia include food, minerals, fuels, metals, and wood. Asia, by comparison, exports a wide range of manufactures to Latin America. Over time, with accumulation of factors and appropriate public policies, each region's comparative advantage is likely to deepen within existing advantages and shifts into other areas.

Furthermore, rapid economic growth in Asia and Latin America in the last decade or so, along with rising industrial demand and an increasing middle class, has led to increased exchanges of manufactures for commodities trade between the two regions. National economic policies have also played a role in interregional trade growth. Latin American economies liberalized their trade and investment regimes in the late-1980s and led to resource allocation according to comparative advantage, with natural resources and agricultural goods gaining ground as the region's premier exports. Meanwhile, Asia's higher export dynamism in manufactures is due to early adoption of outward-oriented development strategies, high rates of savings and investment, attraction of FDI, investment in modern infrastructure, and investment in human capital and technological capabilities, among others.

Key economies in interregional trade. A handful of economies in both regions underpin the growth in interregional trade. The Peoples' Republic of China (PRC) is a key driver behind this development and its impact has been closely analyzed (see Devlin, Estevadeordal, and Rodríguez-Clare 2006; Jenkins, Peters, and Moreira 2008; Rosales and Kuwayama 2012). Latin America has yet to replicate the relatively strong growth of the early post-war era, while most Asian countries, particularly the PRC, have grown rapidly. Some of the explanations for the growth gap between the two regions include Asia's higher levels of export dynamism, manufacturing capability, educational attainment, investment in cost-competitive infrastructure and logistics, and savings and investment.

Figure 9.2 shows trade flows from PRC and rest of Asia to Latin America between 1990 and 2012. The PRC's trade with Latin American countries had grown markedly since 1990. In 1990, the PRC's share of Asia–Latin America total trade was only 5.2%. This figure rose to an average of 11.9% during 1990–2003 and markedly to an average of 40.3% in 2004–2011. By 2012, PRC–Latin America trade had reached US$233 billion or 48.8% of total Asia–Latin America trade. This development allowed the PRC to overtake Japan as the most important Asian trading partner of Latin America. Figure 9.3 shows the major Asian traders with Latin America between 1990–2012 (as a share of Asia's total trade with Latin America) and Figure 9.4

Figure 9.2
Trade Flows from Asia and PRC to Latin America, 1990–2012 (US$ billion)

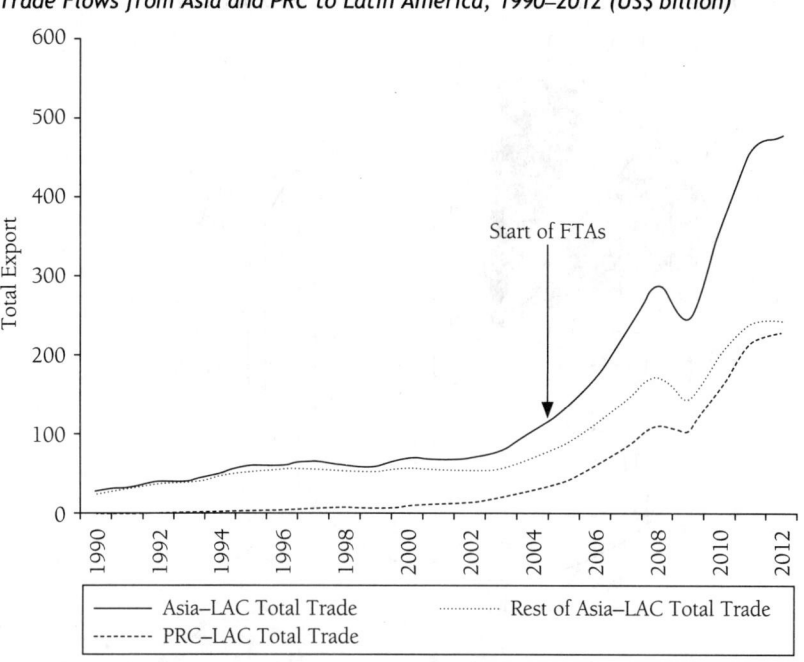

FTA = free trade agreement, LAC = Latin America and the Caribbean, PRC = People's Republic of China.

Source: Estimated from International Monetary Fund Direction of Trade Statistics (accessed October 2013).

shows major Latin American traders with Asia. As expected, Asia's largest economies—the PRC and Japan—are Asia's largest traders with Latin America. Over the period 1990–2012, the PRC accounted for 36.6% of total Asian trade with Latin America while Japan made up 24.2%. This compares with 13.9% for the Republic of Korea; 5.1% for Singapore; 4.4% for Taipei,China; 4.2% for Hong Kong, China; and 4.2% for India. Other Southeast Asian and South Asian economies, even relatively large economies like Indonesia and Pakistan, seem to hardly trade with Latin America.

Likewise, Latin America's largest economies are the major traders with Asia. Brazil and Mexico are key trade partners comprising 27.1% and 29.8% of Latin America's total trade with Asia, respectively (Figure 9.4). Meanwhile, Chile accounts for 12.9% and Argentina for 7.1%. Three other Latin America countries (Venezuela, Peru, and Columbia) have shares of less than 5% each.

Figure 9.3
Top Asian Traders with Latin America, 1990–2012 (% of total trade)

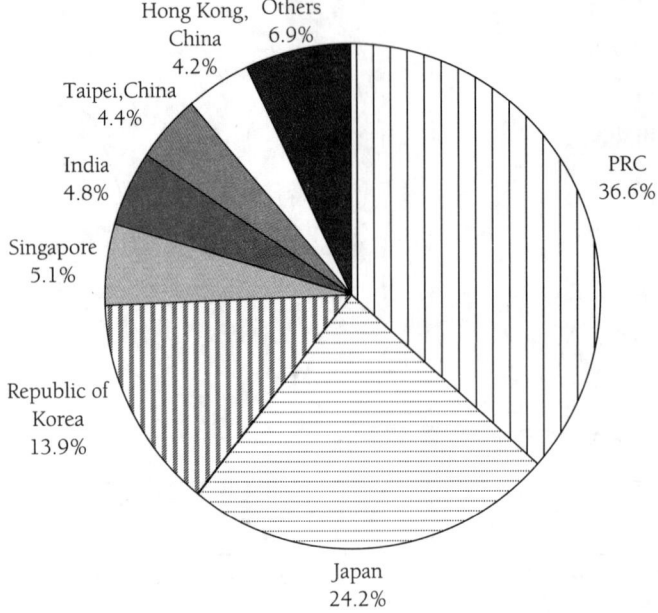

PRC = People's Republic of China.

Source: Estimated from International Monetary Fund Direction of Trade Statistics (accessed October 2013).

Notes: 1. Trade refers to total trade or the total value of exports plus the total value of imports for the 22-year period.
2. Data for Taipei,China, retrieved from Taipei,China Bureau of Foreign Trade.

Central American economies, for instance, have negligible shares of Latin America's trade with Asia.

Growth of interregional FDI flows. Although time series data on FDI flows between Asia and Latin America dating to 1990 are not available from international sources, data from 2003 onwards are provided by FDI Intelligence and shown in Figure 9.5. Some features of interregional FDI flows can be mentioned. First, annual average interregional FDI flows grew from a small base at 5.1% during 2003–2012, which is considerably slower than the growth rate of interregional trade over the same period. During same period, annual average interregional FDI flows were US$18.1 billion and cumulatively interregional inflows amounted to US$176.2 billion. Second, the cumulative data mask a notable spike in interregional FDI flows in 2008 which can be

Figure 9.4
Top Latin American Traders with Asia, 1990–2012 (% of total trade)

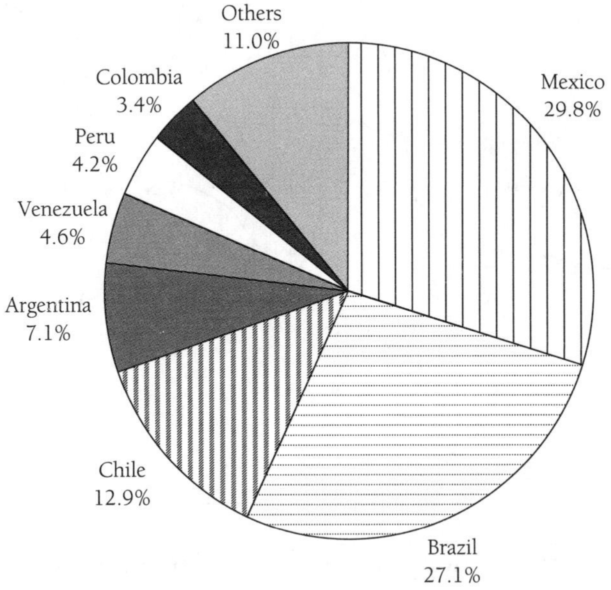

- Mexico 29.8%
- Brazil 27.1%
- Chile 12.9%
- Others 11.0%
- Argentina 7.1%
- Venezuela 4.6%
- Peru 4.2%
- Colombia 3.4%

Source: Estimated from International Monetary Fund Direction of Trade Statistics (accessed October 2013).
Notes: 1. Trade refers to total trade or the total value of exports plus the total value of imports for the 22-year period.
2. Data for Panama in 2011 were removed due to a discrepancy.

attributed to companies in Asia and Latin America initiating new FDI projects in key sectors (such as metals; oil, coal, and natural gas; renewable energy; automotives; food; and financial services) in each other's regions.

Third, a breakdown of total interregional FDI flows shows that the majority of flows during 2003–2012 went from Asia to Latin America (cumulatively US$153.9 billion) while Latin America to Asia flows were relatively small (cumulatively US$22.3 billion). Furthermore, there was a modest increase in Asia to Latin America FDI flows during 2009–2011 (US$17.6 billion per year) compared with 2003–2008 (US$15.9 billion per year). Meanwhile, Latin America to Asia FDI flows remained constant at US$2.5 billion per year in 2003–2008 and US$2.4 billion per year between 2009 and 2012. Fourth, as with trade flows, major economies from both regions seem to drive FDI flows. For instance, Japan accounts for 30.5% of cumulative Asian FDI flows to Latin America during 2003–2012, the PRC for 26.5%, and the Republic of Korea for 9.7%. Meanwhile, Brazil alone makes up a staggering 49.9% of Latin American

Figure 9.5
FDI Flows between Asia and Latin America, 2003–2012 (US$ billion)

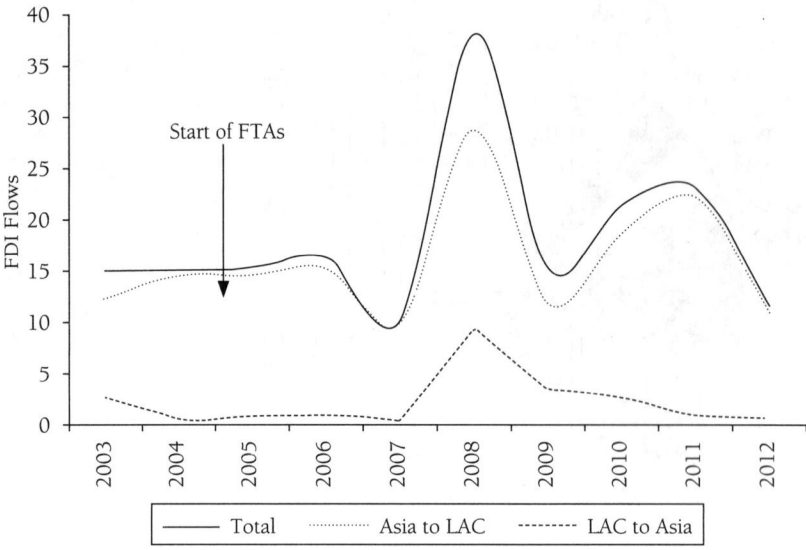

FDI = foreign direct investment, FTA = free trade agreement, LAC = Latin America and the Caribbean

Source: Estimated from fDi Intelligence (accessed October 2013).
Note: Figures include estimates by fDi Intelligence.

FDI to Asia. Further research is needed to explain the underlying patterns and drivers of interregional FDI flows. Such research can profitably focus on factor endowments, market size, corporate strategies of multinational corporations, country risk, FDI promotion, and business environments.

Growth of Asia–Latin America FTAs

The 1990s witnessed the establishment of several regional economic cooperation institutions involving Latin American countries, such as MERCOSUR, the North American Free Trade Agreement (NAFTA), and various developments in intra- and interregional bilateral trade relations (Estevadeordal and Suominen 2009; Foxley 2010; IDB 2002). In contrast, Asia is a latecomer to formal regional integration; for several decades, FTAs were virtually nonexistent in the region. Instead, Asian countries expanded trade through market-led integration without any formal arrangements except for regional schemes such as Asia-Pacific Economic Cooperation (APEC) and the Association of Southeast Asian Nations (ASEAN) Free Trade Area (AFTA). International trade policies at the national level were anchored in outward-oriented development strategies, high domestic savings rates, the creation of strong infrastructure, and investment in human capital. A long period of market-driven expansion of trade and foreign domestic investment (FDI) emerged, during which Asia increasingly became a global production center with deep and diverse technological capabilities—what Baldwin (2006) aptly called "factory Asia" and others refer to as the global factory. Shortly after the turn of the 21st century, this simple story of outward orientation and export success was augmented by a change in the nature of Asian countries' international trade policies toward FTAs (ADB 2008; Chia 2010; Kawai and Wignaraja 2010). Today, Asia is at the forefront of global FTA activity (WTO 2011).

While Asia–Latin America FTAs are of relatively recent origin, there has been a steady expansion in intra-regional FTA activity. Between 2004 and 2013, an average of two agreements took effect every year, with a total of 22 FTAs as of October 2013 (Annexure 1). Four are signed and pending implementation, an additional six Asia–Latin America FTAs are under negotiation, and 11 more are being proposed, see Annexure 1.[2] Presuming that the four FTAs pending implementation and the six FTAs under negotiation will be concluded by the end of the decade, a total of 32 FTAs between economies in the two regions will be in force in 2020 (Figure 9.6).

The leaders in Asia–Latin America FTA activity have been Chile (8 FTAs), Peru (5), and Panama (2) on the Latin American side, and Taipei,China (4), Singapore (4), PRC (3), India (2), Japan (3), and Republic of Korea (2) in Asia.

With few exceptions, Asia and Latin America's biggest traders and investors in Asia–Latin America economic ties are the same countries that have participated in Asia–Latin America FTAs. Tables 9.1 and 9.2 show that 81.5% of Latin American trade with Asia is conducted by the 13 countries that participate in one or more FTAs with Asian countries and 96% of Asian trade with Latin America involves Asia's 10 FTA players. Likewise, the same 13 Latin American economies with FTAs have undertaken 67.3% of Latin America's FDI with Asia and the same 10 Asian economies with FTAs have conducted 93.46% of Asia's FDI with Latin America.

---

[2] An FTA is considered to be "under negotiation" when the parties have had the first round of talks. A "proposed FTA" is when parties are considering a free trade agreement, establishing joint study groups or joint task force, and conducting feasibility studies to determine the desirability of entering into an FTA.

Figure 9.6
Growth of Asia–Latin America FTAs, 2004–2020

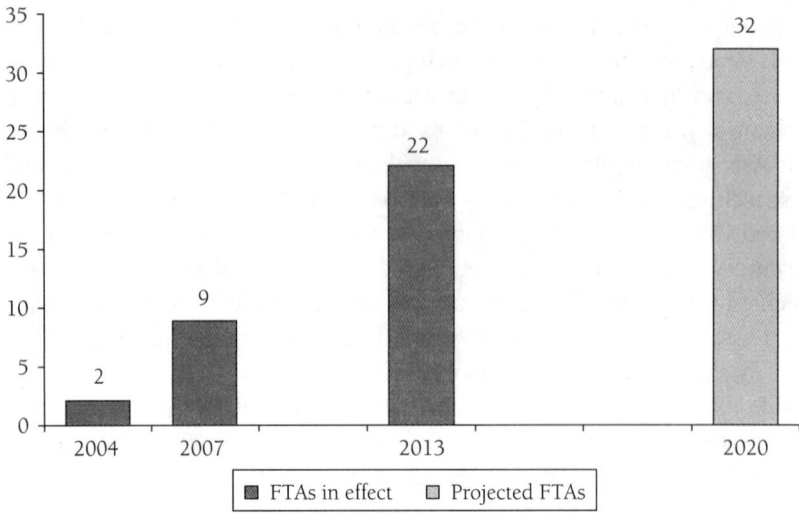

FTA = free trade agreement.
Source: Authors' compilation.

The data, thus, suggests a link between interregional trade and FDI flows and interregional FTAs, particularly in the last 5 years or so. Trade and investment activity between the two regions was initially market-led in response to the factors discussed in the previous section. Nonetheless, many residual regulatory impediments (e.g., tariffs, nontariff barriers, and cumbersome FDI regulations) still remained, which affected Asia–Latin America trade and investment flows. Accordingly, some governments of both regions concluded FTAs to reduce such barriers. These agreements seem to have had several effects. First, by putting in place some interregional rules, FTAs have contributed to building greater business confidence and trust for future trade and investment flows between the two regions. Second, as the next section shows, FTAs have contributed to liberalization in some trade and regulatory barriers. Third, trade agreements have laid the foundations for a process of trade and investment integration and liberalization between the two regions in the long-run. Over time, the conditions are being created to support existing players to expand trade, investment, and FTAs activity between the two regions as well as for new players to forge interregional economic ties. FTAs are by no means a perfect trade policy instrument and the possible costs and challenges of trade agreements are discussed in the concluding section.

Table 9.1
Shares of Latin American Countries' Trade and Investment with Asia and Number of FTAs, 1990–2012

	Share of trade 1990–2012 %	Share of investment 2003–2012 %	No. of FTAs
Chile	11.9	4.05	8
Peru	3.9	0.32	5
Panama	0.4	0.44	2
Mexico	28.6	6.32	1
Brazil	25.5	49.92	1
Argentina	6.8	6.13	1
Paraguay	0.9	NA	1
Costa Rica	1	NA	1
Uruguay	0.8	0.11	1
Guatemala	0.8	NA	1
El Salvador	0.3	NA	1
Nicaragua	0.2	NA	1
Honduras	0.3	NA	1
Countries with FTAs	**81.5**	**67.3**	
Countries without FTA	**18.5**	**32.7**	

FTA = free trade agreement.

Sources: Estimated from International Monetary Fund Direction of Trade Statistics (accessed October 2013), fDi Intelligence (accessed October 2013), and Taipei,China Bureau of Foreign Trade.
Notes: 1. Share of trade refers to the share of total trade of each Latin American country with Asia divided by the total trade of Latin America with Asia.
2. Share of investment refers to the share of total investment amount of each Latin American country with Asia divided by the total investment amount of Latin America to Asia.
3. Investment figures include estimates by fDi Intelligence.
4. NA means data not available.

Similarly, the number of FTAs alone does not indicate the importance of FTAs to economic activity or trade at the national level. It is difficult to measure how much a country's trade is covered by FTA provisions because of exceptions and exclusions contained in many agreements. Furthermore, official statistics on utilization rates of FTA preferences in Asia are hard to come by and published data on the direction of the services trade do not exist. Nevertheless, by making the bold assumption that all trade in goods between two countries is covered by an FTA (if one exists), indicative estimates can be obtained. Figures 9.7 and 9.8 show the share of an economy's trade with

Table 9.2
Shares of Asian Economies' Trade and Investment with Latin America and Number of FTAs, 1990–2012

	Share of trade 1990–2012 %	Share of investment 2003–2012 %	No. of FTAs
Taipei,China	4.4	1.91	4
Singapore	5.1	0.84	3
PRC	36.6	26.36	3
Japan	24.2	30.52	3
Republic of Korea	13.9	9.66	2
India	4.8	9.70	2
Thailand	2.5	0.13	1
Australia	1.9	16.10	1
New Zealand	0.6	0.15	1
Brunei Darussalam	negligible	NA	1
Malaysia	2.2	0.01	1
Countries with FTAs	96	93.46	
Countries without FTA	4	6.54	

FTA = free trade agreement, PRC = People's Republic of China.

Sources: Estimated from International Monetary Fund Direction of Trade Statistics (accessed October 2013), fDi Intelligence (accessed October 2013), and Taipei,China Bureau of Foreign Trade.
Notes: 1. Share of trade refers to the share of total trade of each Asian country with Latin America divided by the total trade of Latin America with Asia.
2. Share of investment refers to the share of total investment amount of each Asian country with Latin America divided by the total investment amount of Latin America to Asia.
3. Investment figures include estimates by fDi Intelligence.
4. NA means data not available

its FTA partners relative to that economy's trade with the world. For every Asian country reviewed, the trade share with its Latin American FTA partners relative to the world did not exceed 2% in 2012. However, the trade share of Latin American countries with Asian FTA partners relative to the world reached as high as 35.1% in 2012 (e.g., Chile). Indeed, Asia is a major market for Latin American countries, and as mentioned earlier, at least 30 Asia–Latin America FTAs are expected to be in force by 2020. As a result, the trade coverage of Asia–Latin America FTAs is also expected to rise significantly.

The following discussion provides four key explanations as to why Asia–Latin America FTAs have proliferated in recent years, and why they will continue to do so in the years ahead (see ADB and IDB 2009; Kawai and Wignaraja 2009; and Krasniqi et al. 2011).

Figure 9.7
Asia's FTA Trade Coverage with Latin American Countries, 2004–2012

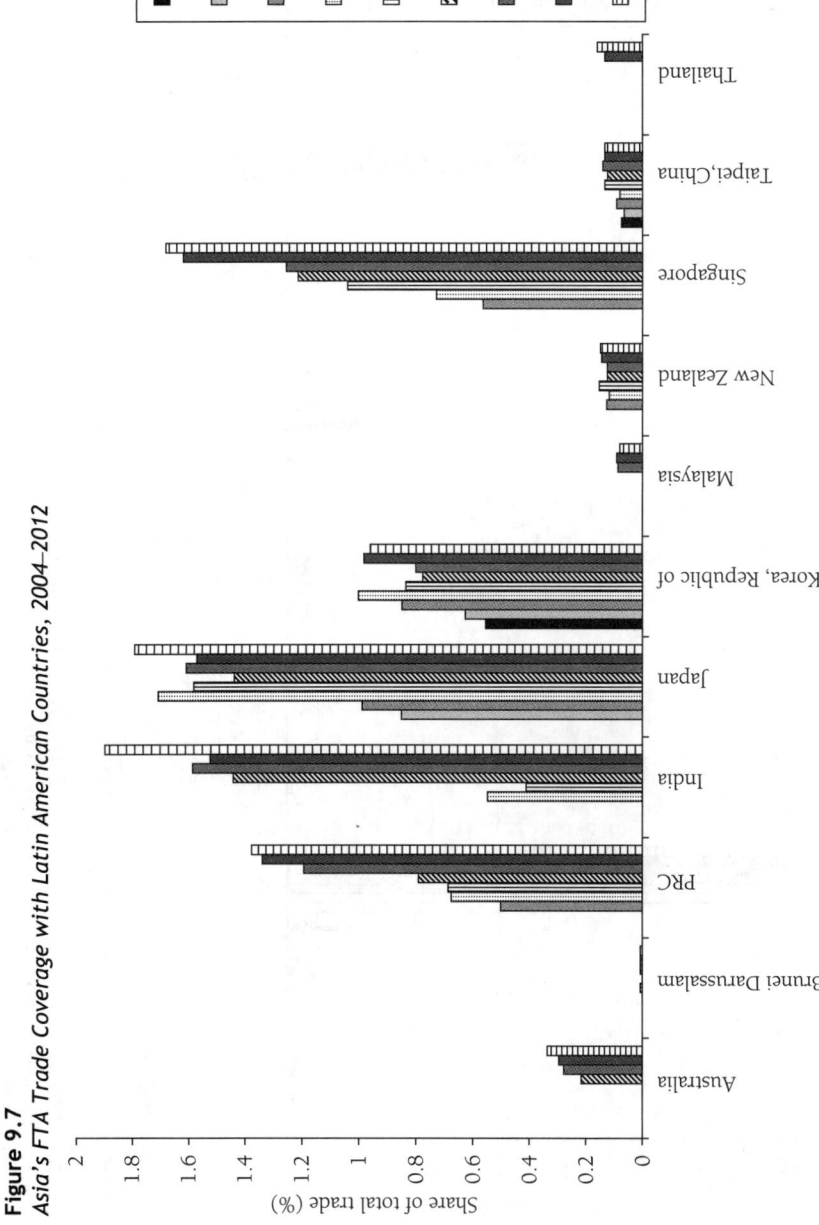

FTA = free trade agreement, PRC = People's Republic of China.

Sources: Estimates based on International Monetary Fund Direction of Trade Statistics (accessed October 2013) and Asian Development Bank Asia Regional Integration Center FTA database (accessed October 2013).

Figure 9.8
Latin America's FTA Trade Coverage with Asian Economies, 2004–2012

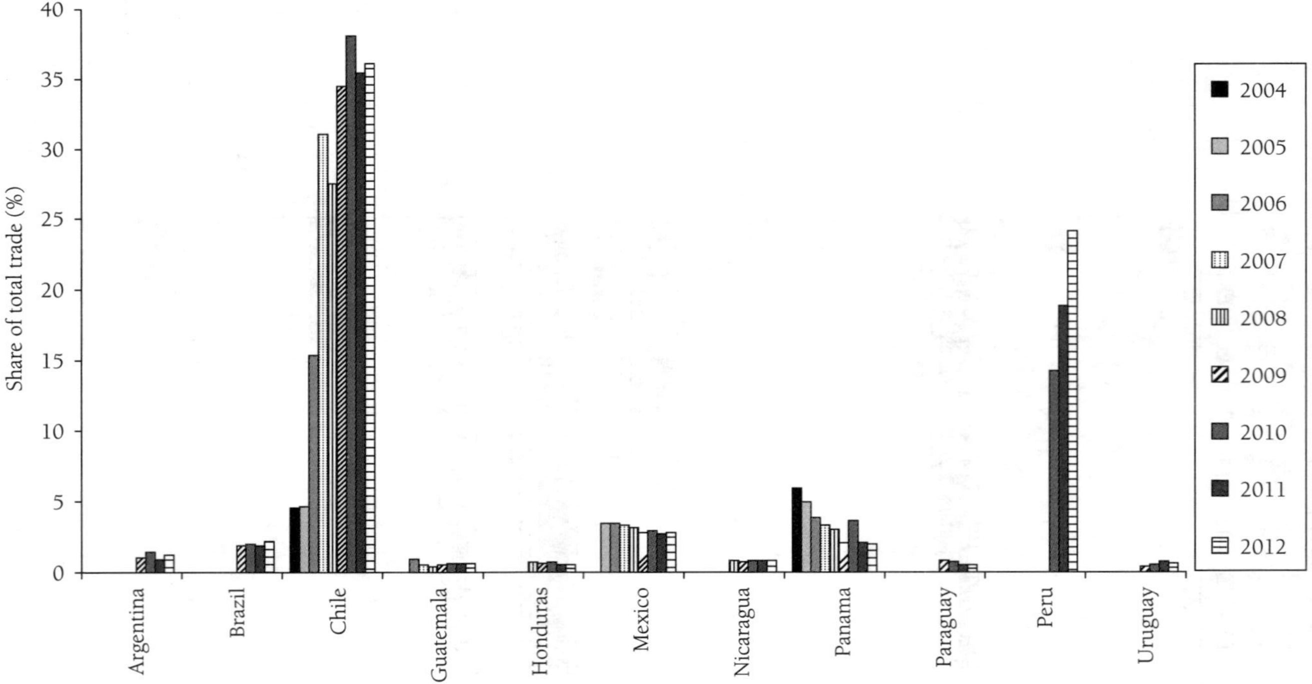

FTA = free trade agreement.

Source: Estimates based on IMF DOTS (accessed October 2013) and Asian Development Bank Asia Regional Integration Center FTA database (accessed October 2013).

Notes: 1. Only covers FTAs in effect for that year. The Trans-Pacific Strategic Economic Partnership (TPP/P4) includes Brunei Darussalam, Chile, New Zealand, and Singapore; however, data on trade between Brunei Darussalam and Chile for 2004–2010 are listed as zero in the International Monetary Fund (IMF) Direction of Trade Statistics (DOTS).
2. Data for Panama in 2011 were removed due to discrepancies.

Market-driven integration through trade. In the 1960s and 1970s, several economies in East and South East Asia adopted outward-oriented, market friendly development strategies. These strategies resulted in falling trade and investment barriers as well as increases in inward investment and exports. In the 1980s, Latin American countries typically abandoned inward-oriented import substitution strategies associated with lackluster economic performance in the region in favor of market-oriented reforms. Policy reforms included trade and capital liberalization, and privatization. The high tariff rates of Latin American countries fell sharply to around 10%–14% in the span of a decade. Capital market liberalization led to greater inward FDI flows to Latin America than in the past. In both Asia and Latin America, market-driven economic integration requires further liberalization of trade and FDI, and the harmonization of policies, rules, and standards governing trade and FDI. Policy makers in the two regions are increasingly of the view that FTAs, if given wider scope, can support expanding trade and FDI activities through the further elimination of cross-border impediments and other such harmonization efforts. Thus, FTAs can be part of a supporting policy framework for deepening production networks and supply chains formed by global multinational corporations and emerging Asian firms.

European and North American economic regionalism. The shift in US trade policy from multilateralism and bilateralism to regionalism in the 1990s contributed to the spread of regionalism in Latin America. The membership of Mexico in NAFTA led some countries such as Chile to express interest in joining, while Brazil and Argentina established a subregional trade agreement, MERCOSUR, to respond to NAFTA and increase their negotiating power. Furthermore, the European Union's (EU) expansion into Central and Eastern Europe, the creation of a monetary union in the euro area, and incipient moves toward an FTAA (Free Trade Area of the Americas) motivated Asian countries to adopt FTAs. Governments feared that the two giant trading blocs of Europe and North America might dominate rules-setting in the global trading system, thereby marginalizing Asia. Increasingly, policy makers have realized the need for (i) stepping up the pace of integration to improve international competitiveness by exploiting economies of scale and (ii) strengthening their bargaining power through a collective voice on global trade issues. FTAs can help insure against the periodic difficulties of multilateral trade liberalization, such as slow progress in the World Trade Organization's (WTO) Doha Round and a perceived loss of steam in the APEC process.

Increase in actual interregional trade and investment. Increasing cooperation in trade and investment between Latin America and Asia also facilitated the proliferation of Latin America–Asia FTAs. Specifically, the PRC's growing role in Latin American trade and investment has contributed to the increase in interregional FTAs, particularly in the aftermath of the global economic crisis. The PRC's "engagement in the region may be a reflection of the country's interest in securing access to natural resources to fuel its economic growth, but the Latin American market is also a destination for exports of Chinese manufactures" (ECLAC 2008). Meanwhile, Brazil is the Latin American country with the highest levels of investment in Asia, focusing primarily on the energy sector.

Slow progress in the WTO Doha Round. Countries have increasingly pursued FTAs due to the stalled WTO negotiation process. Hailed as a round of negotiations to promote trade-led growth in poor countries, the WTO Doha Development Round began in November 2001. The talks have largely focused on liberalization in two key areas: agricultural and non-agricultural goods market access. In essence, developed countries were being asked to accelerate the pace and scope of reductions in agricultural tariffs and subsidies, and developing countries were being asked to reduce tariffs for industrial goods and liberalize trade in services. As the prospects for agreeing on these issues and successfully concluding the round has diminished over the years, pro-business Latin American and Asian countries turned their attention to bilateral and plurilateral FTAs for the continued liberalization of trade in goods and services, as well as the adoption of the Singapore issues, which are currently beyond the scope of the WTO.

Scope and Depth of Asia–Latin America FTAs: An Overview

To the best of our knowledge, very few studies have attempted to assess the content of Asia–Latin American FTAs. In part, many of these agreements are of recent origin and academic attention has yet to turn to them. Assessing the scope and depth of Asia–Latin America FTAs is also a difficult exercise for at least three reasons. First, the legal texts of interregional FTAs are often not in the public domain and may not be in English even if available. Second, it requires detailed and often painstaking examination of legal texts of agreements for which a training in international trade law is vital. Furthermore, a background in international economics is useful to quantify and aggregate the contents of a sample of agreements and map patterns. Third, an internationally accepted methodology for assessing the scope and depth of the commitments in FTA texts is absent. An inter-disciplinary analysis blending international law with international economics seems to offer fruitful insights and a way forward. Drawing on methods used in Plummer (2007), Fink and Molinuevo (2008), ADB and IDB (2009), and Wignaraja and Lazaro (2010), this chapter developed some simple legal and economic criteria for assessing the scope and depth of Asia–Latin America FTAs.

Accordingly, this chapter evaluates each of the 22 Asia–Latin America FTAs in 3 key areas:

(i) the speed and coverage of tariff liberalization based on the criteria for FTAs in the General Agreement on Trade and Tariffs (GATT),
(ii) the number of service sectors covered based on the criteria in the General Agreement on Trade and Services (GATS), and
(iii) the coverage of "new issues" such as IPRs and the Singapore issues (investment, government procurement, trade facilitation, and competition).

An evaluation of the scope of coverage for all three topics provides an overall picture of the scope and depth of commitments in the 22 Asia–Latin America FTAs and allows us to identify those that best promote deeper economic integration through: (i) a high level of tariff liberalization in goods, (ii) comprehensive liberalization in service sectors, and (iii) substantive provisions that address new issues. The overall depth of each Asia–Latin America FTA is classified as being high, medium, or low. High depth FTAs are those that have relatively fast tariff liberalization schedules, some or comprehensive services coverage, and "new age" deep integration provisions for new issues. Medium depth FTAs are those that have relatively fast tariff liberalization schedules, some or comprehensive services coverage, and moderate or limited deep integration provisions. Low depth FTAs are those that have gradual tariff liberalization schedules, comprehensive, some or limited/excluded services coverage, and limited or shallow integration provisions.

An overview of the results is given in Figure 9.9 with detailed analysis presented in the following sections.

The majority of the Asia–Latin America FTAs ascribe to relatively fast liberalization and also incorporate comprehensive provisions on services. The prevailing approach of the FTAs to deeper integration issues such as intellectual property rights (IPRs) and the Singapore issues remain moderate and these chapters need stronger commitments, obligations, and substantive provisions

Figure 9.9
Distribution of Approaches to Tariff Liberalization, Services Coverage, and New Issues

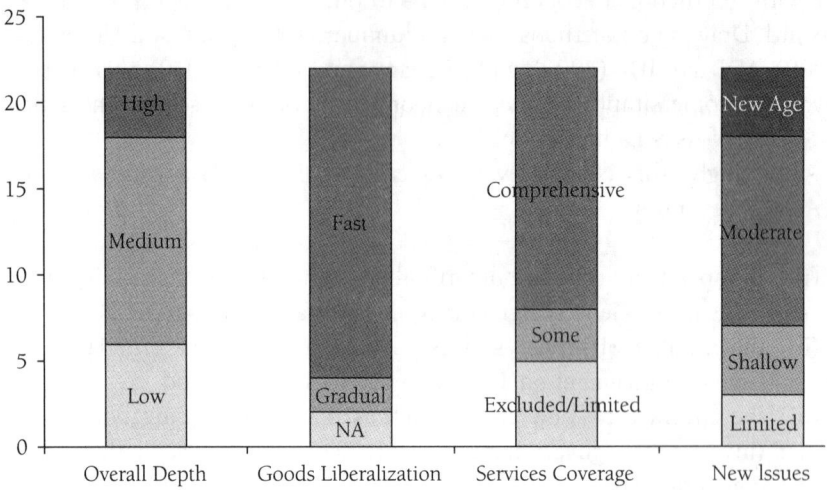

Source: Authors' calculations.

to attain a higher quality. Overall, four Asia–Latin America FTAs stand out and are deemed to be of high depth and represent the "gold standard" of FTAs. Twelve are deemed medium and six are low.

The four high quality FTAs are the Republic of Korea–Peru FTA (2011), Trans-Pacific Strategic Economic Partnership Agreement or Pacific 4 (TPP or P4) (2006), Australia–Chile FTA (2009) and Singapore–Costa Rica FTA (2013) are discussed in detail immediately below. These four FTAs liberalize trade in almost all goods with few exceptions and within a reasonable and defined time frame of ten years or less. The liberalization of trade in services is comprehensive in all four FTAs and they all provide for the automatic inclusion of newly liberalized service sectors. The four FTAs also include meaningful provisions on new issues that promote greater economic integration among all parties, thereby securing the highest possible economic welfare gains from increased trade.

The Republic of Korea–Peru FTA (2011) aims to eliminate all tariffs over a 10-year period on all products, with the exception of 107 agricultural and marine products deemed sensitive such as rice, beef, onions, and garlic. The FTA also includes liberalization in the five key service sectors. Furthermore, the FTA has above standard provisions on deeper integration issues and in particular provides strong investment protection measures and greater investment market access.

TPP/P4 (2006) comprises four original member countries: Brunei Darussalam, Chile, New Zealand, and Singapore. Five more countries—Australia, Malaysia, Peru, the United States (US), and Viet Nam—are currently negotiating to join (these negotiations are discussed in more detail later in the "Challenges" section). The market liberalization component of TPP/P4 saw the elimination of duties on the majority of tariff lines upon the agreement's entry into force. In the case of Singapore, 100% of tariff lines were liberalized immediately. Chile undertook to liberalize 89.3% of domestic exports upon entry into force with an additional 9.7% tariffs eliminated in three years. Overall, TPP/P4 liberalized 98.9% of all domestic exports upon entry into force in 2009, and will eventually reach 100% by 2015. TPP/P4's chapter on trade in services is ambitious, comprehensive, and binds parties to their existing levels of liberalization as well as to the application of any future liberalization in most sectors. The investment chapter also includes strong commitments and the same applies to the other new issue areas such as government procurement, trade facilitation, competition, and IPRs. For instance, the government procurement chapter imposes significant measures that maximize competition among member parties and decrease the cost of doing business for both government and industry.

The Australia–Chile FTA (2009) grants tariff elimination on all goods traded, including sugar, which is deemed a sensitive good, by 2015. Upon entry into force, tariffs on about 92% of tariff lines representing about 97% of total trade will be reduced to zero. Although not all key service sectors are covered in the agreement, the FTA provides export opportunities in many services areas such as mining and energy technology, engineering and consulting services, information technology, tourism, agriculture, and the food and wine industry. The investment chapter is characterized by strong legal protection and transparency provisions to provide certainty and security for cross-border investments. The government procurement chapter secures non-discriminatory treatment and transparent and fair procedures for entities in both countries.

The Singapore–Costa Rica FTA (2013) grants both parties duty free access for all goods. For Costa Rica exports to Singapore, this applies already upon entry into force of the agreement. Costa Rica, in turn, eliminates 90.6% of its tariff lines at entry into force of the agreement with the remaining tariffs lines being eliminated within 10 years. The services chapter is comprehensive as well and liberalizes sectors across the board. Key areas of interest for Singaporean companies include construction services, private education services, and hotel and restaurant services. The agreement finally covers new issues extensively, in particular with strong commitments on government procurement, intellectual property rights, trade facilitation and investment.

Goods and Services Liberalization

Goods liberalization. The WTO criteria for FTA's liberalization of the goods trade states that "where duties are eliminated with respect to substantially all the trade between the constituent territories ... and ... the plan or schedule for its formation is within a reasonable length of time" (GATT Article XXIV). The meaning of "substantially all trade" remains contentious. An FTA that eliminates 85% of either or both members' total tariff lines is often regarded as covering substantially all trade. Following paragraph 5(c) of Article XXIV, the WTO interprets a "reasonable period of time" as one that does not exceed 10 years except in extraordinary cases (GATT Article XXIV: 5). Thus, an FTA that eliminates 85% of tariff lines within ten years is classified as a relatively fast approach to tariff liberalization, while others are considered gradual.

Seventeen out of the 22 Asia–Latin America FTAs in effect for which data on tariff liberalization are available have a relatively fast approach to tariff liberalization.[3] FTAs with a relatively fast approach to tariff liberalization have typically resulted in increased market access in goods and improved bilateral trade flows. The Republic of Korea–Chile FTA is a case in point. Here, the Republic of Korea undertook to eliminate tariffs on 93.6% of its tariff lines, impacting 99% of its imports from Chile within 10 years (WTO 2005, 2008). The Republic of Korea's tariff elimination schedule saw the immediate liberalization of virtually all industrial products, which contributed to a 220% increase in imports from Chile. Similarly, upon entry into force of the Japan–Mexico FTA in 2005, 3,367 (or 37%) of Japan's tariff lines immediately became duty-free for imports from Mexico (WTO 2009). The remaining tariffs are being progressively eliminated and by 2015 trade in nearly all products between the two economies will be free of duties. In 2007, exports from Japan to Mexico increased 10.5%, while Japan's imports from Mexico increased 11.8%.

Although most Asia–Latin America FTAs liberalize tariffs in a relatively fast manner, they also contain temporary or permanent exclusions lists. Under the Japan–Chile Economic Partnership Agreement (EPA), nearly 30 lines are subject to tariff quotas,[4] including meat and meat preparations (e.g., beef, beef

---

[3] The Thailand–Peru and Taipei,China–El Salvador–Honduras agreements have gradual approaches to tariff liberalization. The India–MERCOSUR and India–Chile PTAs tariff liberalization is not applicable and even more limited as very few tariff lines are programmed for full tariff elimination and furthermore establish margins of preference for only a few hundred products.

[4] The use of both an import tariff and an import quota in which imports below a certain quantity enter at a low (or zero) tariff while imports above that quantity enter at a higher tariff.

scraps, pork, chicken), rice, processed foods (e.g., milk cream and powder, yogurt, and other dairy products such as cheese and curd), and fish products, primarily tuna. Similarly, in the Taipei,China–El Salvador–Honduras FTA, approximately 20% of tariff lines are either excluded from liberalization in a 10-year timeframe or considered as sensitive and free from any reduction commitments. These include agricultural products (e.g., processed pork, fowl meat, tea, and rice husks), fish products (e.g., fresh and chilled fish), prepared foodstuffs and beverages (e.g., milk), and transportation (e.g., passenger cars). The Thailand–Peru FTA only commits 70% of total tariff lines to liberalization and excludes a wide range of goods, such as agricultural products (e.g., meat such as pork and poultry, dairy, coffee, rice, copra, coconut and palm oil, and tobacco), fish products (e.g., fish fillet and fish meat) and finally durable goods (e.g., travel goods, handbags, wallets, jewelry cases, woven fabrics, bicycles, and used goods). In the Republic of Korea–Chile FTA (2004), Chile excluded washing machines and refrigerators on its tariff liberalization schedule for Korean exports. Likewise, the Republic of Korea refused to grant any form of tariff concession on Chilean exports of rice, apples, and pears. Meanwhile, the PRC–Peru FTA (2010) specifically excludes used goods, including reconstructed, repaired, remanufactured, or refurbished goods.

India–Chile PTA only adopts a positive list of tariff elimination and accords margin of preference[5] ranging from 10% to 50% on 296 Indian products exported to Chile and 266 Chilean products imported by India. The tariff concession only applies to certain tariff lines pertaining to specific goods under key product groups such as pharmaceuticals, chemicals, and machineries. In effect, the tariff concession excludes most goods under these product groups and other major product groups such as mineral fuels, printed books and manuscripts, silk yarns and woven fabrics (except for other fabrics containing 85% or more by weight of silk or of silk waste), and agricultural products except for certain types of meat (e.g., pork and poultry, fresh, chilled, and processed).

Overall, agriculture products remain highly sensitive and are often found on the exclusions lists of FTAs, as is the case with the PRC–Chile FTA (2006), which excludes almost all agriculture products. While traded goods in many Latin American and Asian countries remain sensitive for a variety of economic or cultural reasons, in general, tariff line exclusions should be minimized to promote trade and harmonization.

---

[5] The percentage by which specific imports from a trade partner country are accorded lower tariffs than the MFN rate (the tariff level that a GATT/WTO member imposes to other members).

Services liberalization. GATS Article V imposes three requirements on WTO members that must be satisfied when concluding an FTA: (i) substantial sectoral coverage, (ii) elimination of substantially all discrimination in the sense of national treatment, and (iii) prohibition on increasing barriers against nonmembers as a result of a new FTA (see Fink and Molinuevo 2008). Strict conformity to GATS requires compliance with all three conditions. In practice, however, it is difficult to assess conformity of an FTA with GATS Article V. A practical way forward is to focus on (i) and to interpret substantial sectoral coverage to mean that a comprehensive FTA should cover five key sectors at least (see Wignaraja and Lazaro 2010). Employing the GATS classification list of 12 service sectors, we follow a simple three-tier classification in determining the quality of an FTA based on service sector liberalization:

(i) **Comprehensive coverage of services.** FTA covers the five key sectors of GATS (business and professional, communications, financial, transport, and labor mobility and entry of business persons).
(ii) **Excluded or limited coverage of services.** FTA either excludes the services trade or provides only general provisions, or covers only one of the key sectors listed in (i).
(iii) **Some coverage of services.** FTA is not otherwise classified as comprehensive or excluded, and would typically cover between two and four key sectors and some minor sectors.

A service sector is deemed covered if at least one party includes GATS or GATS-plus commitments, while not considering the number of sub-sectors, volume of trade affected, or the four modes of supply. This classification system is employed in analyzing the extent of services coverage for each of the 22 Latin America–Asia FTAs under review. Results are presented in Figure 9.5 given earlier.

The 14 Asia–Latin America FTAs classified as comprehensive are Republic of Korea–Chile FTA (2004); Taipei,China–Panama FTA (2004); Japan–Mexico EPA (2005); Singapore–Panama FTA (2006); Taipei,China–Guatemala FTA (2006); Trans-Pacific Strategic EPA (2006); Japan–Chile EPA (2007); Taipei,China–El Salvador–Honduras FTA (2008); Taipei,China–Nicaragua FTA (2008); Australia–Chile FTA (2009); Singapore–Peru FTA (2009); Republic of Korea–Peru FTA (2011); Japan–Peru (2011); and Singapore–Costa Rica FTA (2013). Taipei,China; Japan; and Singapore are the Asian leaders in terms of degree of service coverage in Latin America–Asia FTAs. The same can be said of Chile and Peru on the Latin American side. There are three agreements with some coverage on services: People's Republic of China–Chile FTA (2006); People's Republic of China–Peru FTA (2010); People's Republic of China–Costa Rica FTA (2011). Thus, all 22 FTAs under review, except India–MERCOSUR PTA (2009), India–Chile PTA (2007), Thailand–Peru FTA (2011), Malaysia–Chile FTA (2012), and Chile–Viet Nam FTA (2012), cover services. The key service sectors covered in the majority of the FTAs between Asia and Latin America are labor mobility and entry of business persons.

Overall, Asia–Latin America FTAs provide substantial coverage in services. However, some sub-sectors of business, communications, transport, financial services, tourism and education services are excluded from coverage of key obligations such as national treatment, local presence, and market access. The Latin American countries in the FTAs discussed typically exclude from national treatment sub-sectors in tourism services, recreational services, and the sub-sector radio-television broadcast services. In contrast, the exclusion list of Asian economies comprised mostly of sub-sectors in business services, transport services, distribution services, and education services. Examples of exclusions from national treatment are illustrated in Box 9.1.

Regulatory Barriers, New Issues, and Deep Integration

Various terms have been coined to define provisions dealing with regulatory issues that often lie beyond the scope of the WTO, including "WTO plus," "deep integration," and "new issues." In discussing deep integration, this chapter uses the term new issues to describe IPRs and the four Singapore issues. Several studies have emphasized the importance of including new issues in FTAs because they foster deeper economic integration among countries (Fiorentino et al. 2009; Kawai and Wignaraja 2009, 2010; WTO 2011). Competition policy, government procurement, and investment provisions are key factors in facilitating FDI inflows and the development of production networks. Moreover, provisions on trade facilitation and logistics development help reduce trade-related transaction costs. Lastly, as technology and knowledge are integral parts of goods and services that are traded across borders (e.g., medicine, electronics, films, books, and computer software), IPR protection can promote international trade and greater economic integration.

New issues are discussed next in greater detail than tariffs and services. First, because the commitments present a more mixed and complex picture. Second, because obligations on new issues are key to deepening integration.

Box 9.1
Exclusions from National Treatment in Services in Asia–Latin America FTAs

Taipei,China–Panama FTA: Panama exclusions include the education sector and sub-sectors in tourism (travel agencies) and communications (transmission of radio and televisions programs). Taipei,China, excludes internal waterway transport, cabotage, and pilotage under transport services and other sectors.

Singapore–Panama FTA: Panama excludes education and certain sub-sectors in distribution (retail sales), recreational and cultural services (musicians and artists), transport (passenger and freight road transport services and air transport), and professional services (lawyers). Singapore excludes specific sub-sectors in business services (architectural services, financial auditing, tax-related services, professional engineering, and real estate services), education services (training of doctors), health and social services (medical and pharmacy services), and transport services (air and maritime transport services).

Japan–Peru EPA: Peru's list of reservations includes sub-sectors in communications (radio and television broadcasting, audio-visual, and radio-broadcasting), business services (legal, architectural, and advertising), transport services (air and aquatic transport), and recreational, cultural, and sporting services (bullfighting, circus, and national artistic audio-visual production services). Japan's exclusions include notary public, services incidental to mining (e.g., mining and quarrying), and freight-forwarding business (excluding freight forwarding business using air transportation).

Taipei,China–Nicaragua FTA: Nicaragua excludes for example certain business services (public accounting and auditing, and notary public), communications (professional radio and television broadcast services), transport services (land and maritime transportation, and repair and maintenance services in air transport), tourism services (hotel, restaurants, tour guides, car rental, and other tourism related activities), construction and engineering services (services related to construction). In contrast, Taipei,China, has a shorter exclusion list comprised of fisheries and aquaculture services, air transport auxiliary services under transport services, and public welfare.

For each of the new issues, this chapter develops some simple legal and economic criteria to assess the extent and depth of the coverage, and determine whether the agreements-related provisions are (1) above standard, (2) standard, or (3) non-existent (no provisions). Then, a cumulative evaluation of the level of deep integration will be provided and the FTA with regard to deep integration is deemed (i) new age, (ii) moderate, (iii) limited, or (iv) shallow.

Investment. Growth in cross-border investment flows now exceeds growth of international trade in goods and world gross domestic product and FDI has been a key driver of economic development around the world. The rise in FDI has spurred export manufacturing and the formation of regional production networks in East Asia, which has played an important role in connecting the region to global supply chains. Asian countries—specifically the PRC, Japan, and Republic of Korea—already have substantial investments in Latin America and are pursuing additional investment opportunities in the region.

While international investment flows are an important aspect of the global economy, no overarching multilateral agreement on investment exists.[6] Without a unified body of rules, investment provisions in FTAs are important to promote an open and competitive investment climate that facilitates investment flows and foster greater economic integration between the parties (UNCTAD 2004, 2006). In this chapter, investment chapters in FTAs are classified according to the level of liberalization (market access) and regulation (protection) they provide. Provisions on liberalization include most-favored nation (MFN) status and national treatment at both pre-establishment and post-establishment, and prohibition of performance requirements. Regulatory and legal protection provisions may include a dispute settlement mechanism, fair and equitable treatment, free transfers on investment-related transactions and capital movements, expropriation and compensation for loses, and restrictions on nationality requirements for senior management and boards of directors. Thus, the following parameters were established to evaluate the quality of investment chapters in Latin America–Asia FTAs based on their coverage of key investment principles and the substantive provisions of an investment chapter:

---

[6] The existing multilateral agreements—the WTO Trade-Related Investment Measures (TRIMs) Agreement, Mode 3 (commercial presence) of the GATS, Agreement on Trade-Related Aspects of Intellectual Property Rights (TRIPS), Government Procurement Agreement (GPA), and Agreement on Subsidies and Countervailing Measures (ASCM)—address certain aspects of investment rules in a disaggregated manner.

(i) **Above standard.** An FTA investment chapter that includes all liberalization and regulation provisions mentioned earlier.
(ii) **Standard.** An FTA investment chapter that embodies the core principles of investment liberalization and protection by including two key provisions: (i) post-establishment national treatment and MFN treatment, and (ii) regulation on expropriation and compensation for losses.

Fourteen of the twenty-two Asia–Latin America FTAs under review have an investment chapter.[7] Ten of these can be regarded as above standard,[8] while four met only the standard provisions.[9] The analysis of the investment chapters also shows that six of the eight FTAs that lack an investment chapter involved developing countries in both Asia and Latin America.[10]

Competition. Competition policy is a broad set of measures and instruments employed by governments to prevent distortions of competition and anti-competitive behavior, and achieve a more efficient allocation of resources in liberalized markets. A well-functioning market free of anti-competitive practices enables businesses to take full advantage of liberalization, increase trade, and spur growth. Typically, anticompetitive behavior includes anti-competitive horizontal arrangements between competitors, misuse of dominant market power (e.g., predatory pricing), anticompetitive vertical arrangements between businesses, and anticompetitive mergers and acquisitions.

---

[7] Taipei,China–Panama FTA (2004); Japan–Mexico EPA (2005); Singapore–Panama FTA (2006); Taipei,China–Guatemala FTA (2006); Taipei,China–El Salvador–Honduras FTA (2008); Taipei,China–Nicaragua FTA (2008); Australia–Chile FTA (2009); Singapore–Peru FTA (2009); Republic Korea–Peru FTA (2011); Republic of Korea–Chile FTA (2004); Japan–Chile EPA (2007); PRC–Peru FTA (2010); PRC–Costa Rica FTA (2011); Singapore–Costa Rica FTA (2013). The PRC–Costa Rica FTA adopts an existing bilateral investment treaty between the two countries, which although inclusive of key provisions, precludes more liberalization and regulation provisions than any other Latin America–Asia FTA investment chapter.

[8] Taipei,China–Panama FTA (2004); Japan–Mexico EPA (2005); Singapore–Panama FTA (2006); Taipei,China–Guatemala FTA (2006); Taipei,China–El Salvador–Honduras FTA (2008); Taipei,China–Nicaragua FTA (2008); Australia–Chile FTA (2009); Singapore–Peru FTA (2009); Republic of Korea–Peru FTA (2011); Singapore–Costa Rica FTA (2013).

[9] Republic of Korea–Chile FTA (2004); Japan–Chile EPA (2007); PRC–Peru FTA (2010); and PRC–Costa Rica FTA (2011).

[10] PRC–Chile FTA (2006); India–Chile PTA (2007); India–MERCOSUR PTA (2009); Thailand–Peru FTA (2011); Malaysia–Chile FTA (2012); Chile–Viet Nam FTA (2012). The other FTAs without an investment chapter are TPP/P4 (2006) and Japan–Peru EPA (2012).

The following criteria were used to evaluate the competition chapters of Asia–Latin America FTAs:

1. **Above standard.** In addition to standard competition provisions, specific obligations to adopt or maintain competition laws, possibly including a definition of anticompetitive behavior.
2. **Standard.** General obligations to take measures against anticompetitive behavior plus commitments to promote competition among businesses and cooperation in enforcement activities.

Two of the twenty-two Asia–Latin America FTAs are considered above standard—Trans-Pacific Strategic EPA (2006) and Singapore–Peru FTA (2009)—in that they specifically obligate members to adopt or maintain a competition law. In addition, they contain comprehensive administrative obligations relating to cooperation and coordination. Twelve FTAs contain general obligations of varying degrees relating to competition and are thus considered standard.[11] These typically prohibit anticompetitive business practices in general, ensure that there are avenues for complaints over unfair practices, and obligate the relevant authorities to commit to cooperation with one another to facilitate enforcement and share best practices. The FTAs between Chile and Singapore and Chile and the Republic of Korea adopt an approach that is focused on cooperation between the competition authorities of the concerned parties. The chapters on competition in these two agreements include definitions and objectives, as well as provisions for notification, coordination of enforcement, consultations in the event that the important interests of one party are adversely affected in the territory of the other party, the exchange of information and protection of confidentiality, technical assistance, public and private monopolies and exclusive rights, and dispute settlement. Eight of the twenty-two FTAs under review have no competition-related provisions.[12]

Government procurement. Government procurement policies are relevant to international trade when foreign suppliers participate in domestic government

---

[11] Republic of Korea–Chile FTA (2004); Taipei,China–Panama FTA (2004); Japan–Mexico EPA (2005); Singapore–Panama FTA (2006); Japan–Chile EPA (2007); Taipei,China–Nicaragua FTA (2008); Australia–Chile FTA (2009); PRC–Peru FTA (2010); Republic of Korea–Peru FTA (2011); PRC–Costa Rica FTA (2011); Japan–Peru EPA (2012) and Singapore–Costa Rica FTA (2013).

[12] Taipei,China–El Salvador–Honduras FTA (2008); India–MERCOSUR PTA (2007); PRC–Chile FTA (2006); Taipei,China–Guatemala FTA (2005); India–Chile PTA (2007); Thailand–Peru FTA (2011); Malaysia–Chile (2012).

procurement markets. The WTO and APEC regulate procurement through a set of rules and principles for establishing efficient procurement systems. The WTO GPA is a plurilateral agreement between 15 WTO members based on principles of national treatment and transparency (see Anderson et al. 2011).[13] APEC has established a set of voluntary non-binding principles to advance liberalization of government procurement markets and increase transparency and effective competition. An efficient procurement system founded on the principles of non-discrimination and transparency can ensure the optimal use of public funds.

Building on GPA rules and APEC principles, government procurement chapters in FTAs should include obligations and provisions ensuring (i) reasonable scope of commitments (ii) non-discriminatory treatment, and (iii) transparent procurement procedures and due process. The scope of commitments in government procurement chapters determines to what extent substantive rules and obligations are applied. Non-discriminatory treatment ensures that suppliers from all FTA parties are treated equally in the spirit of open and effective competition. A key provision of non-discriminatory treatment is "national treatment" ensuring that each party to the agreement accords the goods and services of suppliers from other parties treatment that is "no less favorable than that accorded to domestic goods and services."[14] Finally, in accordance with APEC[15] standards on government procurement, a transparent procurement system is characterized by the proper documentation of rules and the availability of relevant information to all interested parties in a timely manner through an open and commonly used platform.

Based on the above discussion, two criteria were developed to assess the quality of government procurement chapters in Asia–Latin America FTAs, according to the inclusion of provisions embodying the core principles of non-discrimination and transparency:

1. **Above standard.** The government procurement chapter embodies the core principles of non-discrimination and transparency by including a

---

[13] Parties to the GPA are mostly developed economies. The 27 countries of the European Union (EU) are considered to be a single signatory. No Latin American country is a signatory to the GPA. In Asia, only Japan; the Republic of Korea; Singapore; and Taipei,China, are signatories.

[14] See WTO's Agreement on Government Procurement Article 3.

[15] At their meeting in Santiago, Chile, in November 2004, APEC leaders endorsed the Transparency Standards on Government Procurement, which are based on the transparency provisions of the APEC Non-Binding Principles on Government Procurement, and adopted the standards as part of the Leader's Transparency Statement.

reasonable wide scope of commitments and covering all key affirmative obligations on non-discrimination (e.g., national treatment, qualification of suppliers, tendering procedure, and prohibition of offsets) and transparency. The chapter also covers substantial obligations going beyond the GPA (GPA-plus) such as electronic and e-government procurement, ensuring integrity, small and medium-sized enterprises (SMEs) development, cooperation and training, and establishment of a single market.
2. **Standard.** The government procurement chapter includes a provision on the scope of commitments and all key affirmative obligations on non-discrimination and transparency. It may or may not include a basic GPA-plus provision such as e-government procurement and clauses to establish cooperative measures.

Out of the 22 Asia–Latin America FTAs, 10 have chapters on government procurement.[16] Among these, 7 qualified as having above standard government procurement chapters.[17] The Asian countries in these 7 Asia–Latin America FTAs are all GPA signatories, while none of the Latin American countries are. Despite the non-accession to the GPA of these Latin American countries, their FTAs conform to the core principles of non-discrimination and transparency, and include obligations beyond those set by the GPA. Three Asia–Latin America FTAs have a standard government procurement chapter.[18] Specifically, the government procurement chapters of Japan's FTAs with Mexico and Chile adopt the language of the GPA in most key provisions, as Japan is a GPA signatory.

Trade facilitation. The WTO defines trade facilitation as "the simplification and harmonization of international trade procedures," including "activities, practices, and formalities involved in collecting, presenting, communicating, and processing data required for the movement of goods in international

---

[16] Republic of Korea–Chile FTA (2004), Japan–Mexico EPA (2005), Singapore–Panama FTA (2006), Trans-Pacific Partnership (TPP/P4) (2006), Japan–Chile EPA (2007), Australia–Chile FTA (2009), Singapore–Peru FTA (2009), Republic of Korea–Peru FTA (2011), Japan–Peru EPA (2012) and Singapore–Costa Rica FTA (2013).

[17] Republic of Korea–Chile FTA (2004), Singapore–Panama FTA (2006), TPP/P4 (2006), Australia–Chile FTA (2009), Republic of Korea–Peru FTA (2011), Japan–Peru EPA (2012) and Singapore–Costa Rica FTA (2013).

[18] Japan–Mexico EPA (2005); Japan–Chile EPA (2007); Singapore–Peru FTA (2009).

trade" (WTO 2011).[19] Numerous empirical studies have shown that even a miniscule decrease in trade transaction costs, such as burdensome customs procedures, can yield tremendous welfare gains (Engman 2005, Hummels 2001). Hence, it is crucial that customs and related procedures, which are at the heart of trade facilitation, adhere to best practices and remain consistent with GATT and WTO rules and regulations.

For the purpose of our study, we follow the five key principles in trade facilitation propounded in the study of Willie and Redden (2007), which embody the proposed WTO measures and APEC NBPs in trade facilitation: (i) transparency, (ii) simplification, (iii) harmonization, (iv) cooperation, and (v) use of modern technology. A meaningful trade facilitation policy includes specific measures to put these principles into effect. Based on the above considerations, criteria have been developed to evaluate the extent that Asia–Latin America FTAs uphold the key principles of trade facilitation:

1. **Above standard.** Customs procedure or trade facilitation chapter covers all five key principles and includes relevant measures for implementation.
2. **Standard.** Customs procedure or trade facilitation chapter covers three or four of the five key principles and includes relevant measures for implementation.

Of the 22 Asia–Latin America FTAs in effect, 19 have a customs procedure chapter or provisions on trade facilitation.[20] In most of these FTAs, trade facilitation provisions are found in the chapter for customs procedures instead of there being a separate and distinct chapter for trade facilitation. On the basis of the above criteria, 11 out of 19 Latin America–Asia FTAs with customs procedure chapter or provisions on trade facilitation qualify as above standard.[21] Eight Asia–Latin America FTAs are classified as having standard

---

[19] This definition does not include nontariff barriers (NTBs) to trade, such as sanitary and SPS, or instruments to protect social and environmental standards.

[20] Singapore–Panama FTA (2006); TPP/P4 (2006); Japan–Chile EPA (2007); Taipei,China–Nicaragua FTA (2008); Australia–Chile FTA (2009); Singapore–Peru FTA (2009); PRC–Peru FTA (2010); Republic of Korea–Peru FTA (2011); Republic of Korea–Chile FTA (2004); Taipei,China–Panama FTA (2004); Japan–Mexico EPA (2005); PRC–Chile FTA (2006); Taipei,China–Guatemala FTA (2006); Taipei,China–El Salvador–Honduras FTA (2008); PRC–Costa Rica FTA (2011); Thailand–Peru FTA (2011); Japan–Peru EPA (2012); Malaysia–Chile (2012) and Singapore–Costa Rica FTA (2013).

[21] Singapore–Panama FTA (2006); TPP/P4 (2006); Japan–Chile EPA (2007); Taipei,China–Nicaragua FTA (2008); Australia–Chile FTA (2009); Singapore–Peru FTA

customs procedure or trade facilitation chapters.[22] We also observed that Asia–Latin America FTAs embody the key principles of trade facilitation in varying degrees with respect to incorporating relevant measures. For example, while the Republic of Korea–Chile FTA (2004) and the Taipei,China–Panama FTA (2004) contain only two measures on transparency (advance rulings and review mechanism), several other FTAs[23] include three measures on transparency (e.g., publication of laws and regulations, advance rulings, and review mechanism). The same variations on relevant measures can be seen with the other four principles.

Intellectual property rights. IPRs are exclusive rights that enable the holders of such rights to exclude others from using protected technology or property. IPRs are necessary to reward creators, stimulate innovation, and promote economic development. In some instances, however, IPRs can increase prices and limit access to goods and technology. Striking the right balance between stimulating innovation on the one hand and providing public access to knowledge and goods on the other is of critical importance. IPRs encompass a wide range of different rights with different purposes, effects, and costs. While the primary purpose of patents, copyrights, and industrial design is to stimulate innovation and creativity in technology and the creative arts, the purpose of trademarks and geographical indications is advertising, ensuring that other companies cannot free ride on brand-building efforts, and to facilitate information to consumers about the origin and quality of products. Some countries are net users of patented machines and pharmaceuticals, and some are exporters. Some benefit from slack copyright protection for software, movies, and music, while some benefit from access to using trademarks or geographical indications. Therefore, the international regulation of intellectual property, whether through the WTO or FTA, must be flexible enough to leave governments the space needed to implement optimally-balanced IPR protection policies.

(2009); PRC–Peru FTA (2010); Republic of Korea–Peru FTA (2011); Japan–Peru EPA (2012) and Singapore–Costa Rica FTA (2013).

[22] Republic of Korea–Chile FTA (2004); Taipei,China–Panama FTA (2004); Japan–Mexico EPA (2005); PRC–Chile FTA (2006); Taipei,China–Guatemala FTA (2006); Taipei,China–El Salvador–Honduras FTA (2008); PRC–Costa Rica FTA (2011); Thailand–Peru FTA (2011); Malaysia–Chile (2012).

[23] Singapore–Panama FTA (2006); Taipei,China–Nicaragua FTA (2008); Singapore–Peru FTA (2008); Australia–Chile FTA (2009); Republic of Korea–Peru FTA (2010); PRC–Peru FTA (2010); and PRC–Costa Rica FTA (2011).

The Agreement on Trade Related Aspects of Intellectual Property—commonly known as the TRIPS Agreement—entered into force in 1995 and is the most comprehensive multilateral agreement concerning intellectual property.[24] IPR provisions in bilateral and regional FTAs that extend protection beyond that of TRIPS are referred to as TRIPS Plus. These include higher standards of protection (e.g., extending copyright protection from the 50 years mandated in TRIPS to 70 years), enhancing the scope of IPRs (e.g., expanding IPRs to goods and services not covered by TRIPS such as life forms and plant varieties), or by requiring more extensive enforcement procedures (e.g., stronger criminal remedies and border measures). Whether an FTA contains one or more TRIPS-Plus provisions is a key determinant of its level of IPR protection. The criteria used to evaluate the level of IPR protection in FTAs is as follows:

1. **Above standard.** FTA that contains one or more TRIPS-plus provisions.
2. **Standard.** FTA that contains IPR provisions that do not exceed those of the TRIPS Agreement.

Fourteen of the twenty-two Asia–Latin America FTAs contain IPR commitments.[25] In fact, each of these 14 FTAs contains one or more TRIPS-plus provisions. Thus, there are no FTAs with an IPR chapter classified as standard. The key TRIPS-plus provisions concern enforcement, which is a priority for Asian countries exporting goods and services that use advanced technology, and securing expanded protection of geographical indications, which is a priority for a number of Latin American countries. The TRIPS Agreement requires protection of geographical indications, but does not list which ones are eligible for the protection. All 14 FTAs offer the same level of protection as the TRIPS Agreement but regulate geographical indications in more depth by including an annexure numerating the specific geographical indications of each party that must be protected in the other party's territory.

The most comprehensive FTA with respect to IPR is the Republic of Korea–Peru FTA, which in addition to strong regulation on geographical indications

---

[24] The TRIPS Agreement was adopted on 15 April 1994 as Annex 1C of the Final Act of the Uruguay Round of Multilateral Trade Negotiations creating the WTO. Available at http://www.wto.org/english/docs_e/legal_e/27-trips.pdf

[25] Republic of Korea–Chile FTA (2004); Taipei,China–Panama FTA (2004); Japan–Mexico EPA (2005); PRC–Chile FTA (2006); Taipei,China–Guatemala FTA (2006); TPP (2006); Japan–Chile EPA (2007); Taipei,China–Nicaragua FTA (2008); Australia–Chile FTA (2009); PRC–Peru FTA (2010); Republic of Korea–Peru FTA (2011); PRC–Costa Rica FTA (2011); Japan–Peru EPA (2012); and Singapore–Costa Rica FTA (2013).

and enforcement, also expands copyright protection to 70 years after the death of the creator of the copyrighted work. The FTAs that do not regulate IP are Singapore–Panama FTA (2006); India–Chile PTA (2007); Taipei,China–El Salvador–Honduras FTA (2008); India–MERCOSUR PTA (2009); Singapore–Peru FTA (2009); Thailand–Peru FTA (2011); Malaysia–Chile (2012) and Chile–Viet Nam FTA (2012).

Summary of regulatory barriers and new issues. Throughout the evaluation of regulatory barriers and new issues, the same classifications were used for each specific issue: above standard, standard, no provision. A cumulative evaluation of the level of deep integration resulted in the FTAs deemed (i) new age, (ii) moderate, (iii) limited, or (iv) shallow. The overall results are presented in Figure 9.6 above and the individual agreements in Annexure 2. The 22 Asia–Latin American agreements appear to vary in terms of coverage of new issues. Some strengths and weaknesses of the set of agreements studied here can be mentioned as follows.

Nineteen agreements have a customs procedure chapter or provisions on trade facilitation. In this area in particular, a harmonized approach among the FTAs is advisable. Intellectual property is dealt with in 14 out of 22 FTAs, and all 14 agreements have one or more TRIPS-plus provisions. Ten FTAs have above standard investment chapters and therefore strong commitments on both liberalization and protections. Two FTAs directly mandate countries to adopt or maintain competition law and are above standard, while other FTAs encourage countries do so. Overall, competition is the deep integration issue that is lacking the most in Latin America FTAs (as in FTAs in general). Ten agreements have government procurement chapters and seven are above standard. The Asian countries in these seven Asia—Latin America FTAs are all GPA signatories, while none of the Latin American countries are. Although there is room for improvement it is encouraging that government procurement increasingly is featured in FTAs.

Key Policy Priorities

The growth in the number of Asia–Latin America FTAs creates an opportunity for future gains from further interregional integration. This deepening of trade between the two regions is attended by some key challenges that have to be surmounted if these gains are to be realized. This chapter identifies five key policy priorities that will help spur FTA-led integration between Asia and

Latin America: (i) promoting FTAs that provide deep integration, (ii) forming an interregional trade agreement between Asia and Latin America, (iii) ensuring firm-level use of FTAs, (iv) addressing the "noodle bowl" problem, and (v) pursuing structural reforms.

Priority 1: Promoting FTAs that Provide Deep Integration

New age FTAs that comprehensively address WTO-plus issues are becoming more common globally (Fiorentino et al. 2009; Freund and Ornelas 2010). Evidence presented here has notable deep integration elements, but room for improvement exists. The inclusion of WTO-plus provisions, particularly the four Singapore issues, is desirable in all future Asia–Latin America FTAs. Competition policy and investment provisions are integral ingredients in facilitating FDI inflows and the development of production networks. High costs of interregional trade due to nontariff barriers and poor transportation infrastructures are impediments to deeper economic ties between Latin America and Asia. Inclusion of provisions on trade facilitation, harmonization of customs procedures, standards and logistics development would help lower transactions costs in conducting trade. Properly addressing government procurement promotes transparency and deepens market access. Cooperation provisions—along the line of the APEC economic and technical cooperation (ECOTECH) agenda—would stimulate technology transfer and industrial competitiveness.[26]

Priority 2: Toward the Formation of an Interregional Trade Agreement

An interregional FTA is an important means to consolidate the plethora of bilateral and plurilateral agreements between the two regions and better align global and regional rules of existing Asia–Latin America FTAs (see ADB et al. 2012). Such an FTA would confer a range of economic benefits: (i) increase market access to goods, services, skills, and technology; (ii) increase market size to permit specialization and realization of economies of scale; (iii) facilitate the FDI activities and technology transfer of MNCs; and

---

[26] ECOTECH is the APEC schedule of programs designed to build capacity and skills in APEC member economies to enable them to participate more fully in the regional economy and the liberalization process. See http://www.apec.org for more information.

(iv) permit simplification of tariff schedules, rules, and standards (Chia 2010). Moreover, a large grouping would offer insurance against protectionist sentiments that pose a risk to Asia's trade and recovery.

In the last few years, a proposal for an interregional FTA through a Free Trade Area of the Asia-Pacific (FTAAP)[27] has been under serious discussion in trade fora in some Asian and Latin American countries. Since 2007, the FTAAP has been consistently proposed at APEC Summits. Above all, the FTAAP could increase the two-way trade of partner countries in a significant manner, build regional integration and also be a useful way of reviving the stalled Doha Round (Bergsten 2007; Hufbauer and Schott 2009). The formation of the FTAAP, however, is expected to take many years and involve studies, evaluations, and negotiations among all 21 potential member economies. Given that the number of APEC member economies is so large, a smaller group could be more feasible to initiate the process. The recently emerging TPP is enjoying increasing momentum among a growing number of countries sympathetic to its goal of high-standard liberalization (Markheim 2008).

The original TPP, also known as the Pacific Four (P4) agreement, is a plurilateral FTA agreed upon in 2006 between Brunei Darussalam, Chile, New Zealand, and Singapore. Led by the US, negotiations to expand membership began in March 2010 with Australia, Peru, the US, and Viet Nam. Malaysia joined the negotiations in November 2010. The parties aim to agree on a comprehensive 21st century FTA that comprehensively covers tariffs and services in addition to new issues such as investment, intellectual property, government procurement, competition policy, and labor and environmental regulations. The agreement is also expected to enforce strict regulation of state-owned enterprises (SOEs) and produce innovative initiatives to harmonize regulatory systems to free up global supply chains. A broad outline of the Agreement was unveiled at the APEC summit in Hawaii in November 2011.[28] TPP is the only current initiative to include several countries in both Asia and Latin America, and can be an important opportunity to serve as a Pacific trade bridge. Under the agreement's accession clause, it has the potential to grow to include many other nations. In June 2012, Canada and Mexico were invited to join the TPP talks. Japan has also expressed interest but has

---

[27] FTAAP covering APEC members (Australia; Brunei Darussalam; Canada; Chile; PRC; Hong Kong, China; Indonesia; Japan; Republic of Korea; Malaysia; Mexico; New Zealand; Papua New Guinea; Peru; Philippines; Russian Federation; Singapore; Taipei,China; Thailand; United States; and Viet Nam.

[28] See the broad outlines of the agreement at the USTR website http://www.ustr.gov/about-us/press-office/fact-sheets/2011/november/outlines-trans-pacific-partnership-agreement

not joined partly due to domestic politics. Other countries such as Costa Rica, Panama, Philippines, Republic of Korea, and Indonesia have been mentioned as possible future parties.

Various pros and cons have been articulated about TPP in academic and policy circles in Asia and Latin America. The pros are well known. Through other countries joining, the TPP could help expand and strengthen economic and strategic ties among select APEC members and lay the foundation for a wider FTAAP. TPP can thus foster trade and investment integration across the Pacific. Although many current and potential TPP countries already share FTAs, TPP could address a potential future noodle bowl problem in the future by simplifying and streamlining customs procedures, tariff lines, and ROOs (rationalizing, adopting coequals, upgrading origin administration, and harmonizing). By consolidating the numerous agreements in force, and together with initiatives on regulatory harmonization, TPP can particularly benefit SMEs. The cons include TPP members having to agree to more far reaching liberalization standards in traditional areas (such as agriculture and services) than in existing agreements, TPP members possibly taking on commitments in areas beyond trade policy (such as labor and the environment), the challenge of mitigating adjustment costs from widespread liberalization and new commitments, and the political and economic consequences of PRC (the world's second largest trader) not joining the TPP.

Looking ahead, TPP complements the ASEAN-centric approaches to regional integration in Asia, which is known as the ASEAN+3 (or +6) discussions (Kawai and Wignaraja 2010).[29] The two processes are not mutually exclusive, and the ASEAN+3 or +6 approach could create synergies with the TPP approach through useful discussions that lead to liberalizing trade and avoiding protectionism. Whichever avenue is taken, it is important to accelerate the liberalization of goods and services, and trade and investment, and reduce behind-the-border barriers while pursuing domestic reforms. A harmonious approach would see a convergence between the two processes, which would be a win-win solution for the entire Asia-Pacific community. In the end, any interregional agreement could be a series of linked agreements with variable coverage of members and issues.

The possibility of significant benefits from interregional FTAs has been indicated by studies based on a computable general equilibrium (CGE) model, which has produced estimates of potential welfare gains to members,

---

[29] The 10 ASEAN countries plus the PRC, Japan, and Republic of Korea (ASEAN+3) and Australia, India, and New Zealand (ASEAN+6).

losses to non-members, and sector-level gains and losses. Depending on the CGE model and data sources used, these studies differ somewhat in their estimates of welfare gains and losses. Generally, these studies indicate that there would be significant gains to members from an interregional FTA (Gilbert et al. 2004; Francois and Wignaraja 2008). Meanwhile, losses to non-members would be negligible. Krasniqi et al. (2011) examined the effects of trade integration between Asia and Latin America, using scenarios with and without the Republic of Korea and Japan, and found that such trade integration could increase welfare by about 20% on average. Petri, Plummer, and Zhai (2011) found that TPP and FTAAP are competitive routes but will create incentives for the US and PRC to consolidate tracks into a region-wide agreement. They found that both tracks can create additional trade volume of US$742 billion by 2025. Finally, Park et al. (2010) analyze the effects of FTAAP on APEC members and find that FTAAP could provide welfare gains of US$50–US$70 million. CGE studies also indicate that larger agreements in terms of membership and issues covered would bring bigger welfare gains than agreements with less members and limited coverage of issues. Furthermore, a comprehensive transregional FTA covering a range of issues implies better alignment of compatibilities between global and regional rules in Asia–Latin America FTAs. Ideally, the three issues covered in this chapter—tariff liberalization, services liberalization, and deep integration—could form the heart of such an agreement.

Priority 3: Ensuring Firm-Level Use of FTA Preferences

Well-designed and comprehensive FTAs provide numerous benefits, including preferential tariffs, market access, and new business opportunities. Previous studies at the country and industry levels, however, suggest that FTA preference utilization rates—based on shares of export value enjoying preferences—are modest in Asian countries (Baldwin 2006; World Bank 2007). Some even view FTAs as discriminatory and a drain on scarce trade negotiation capacity in developing countries (Bhagwati 2008).

Eight comprehensive surveys of exporting firms conducted between 2007 and 2012 by ADB and several partner researchers in Japan, the PRC, the Republic of Korea, Singapore, Thailand, the Philippines, Indonesia, and Malaysia shed light on the use of FTA preferences (Kawai and Wignaraja 2011 for results of six surveys). Asian exporting firms tend to utilize FTA preferences more frequently than previously thought and may even be increasing their utilization rate. Of the 1,281 Asian sample firms, around 32% use FTA preferences. When plans for using FTA preferences are also factored in, 56% of all Asian firms either use or plan to use FTA preferences. PRC, Indonesian, and Japanese firms are the highest users of FTA preferences, indicating the growing importance of FTAs at the firm level. Firms in Asia—in particular in the PRC, the Republic of Korea, and Japan—have plans in place to increase the use of FTA preferences. While these findings are encouraging, room for improvement exists in FTA preference use at the firm level in Asia.

Surveys of private firms in Latin America carried out by the IDB found that nearly all exporting firms make use of preferential agreements, with the only deviation occurring in countries which did not have FTAs with their principal trading partners (Harris and Suominen 2009; WTO 2011). The difference in Latin America comes from a long history of preferential trading arrangements dating back to the 1960s, which was also a time of high MFN tariffs, creating a sizable incentive to master the procedures of qualifying for preferential duty rates. Asia, in contrast, is a relative newcomer to FTAs with most agreements coming in the mid-2000s and countries are already applying low MFN tariffs following outward oriented trade strategies.

Use of FTAs can be encouraged by raising awareness of (i) FTA provisions, including the phasing out of tariff schedules; (ii) margins of preference at the product level; and (iii) administrative procedures for rules of origin (ROOs). Business associations and governments could make information on how to use FTAs more transparent, particularly for SMEs. Practical ideas include frequent seminars with SMEs, television programs directed at businesses, and dedicated websites and telephone help lines. More generally, institutional support systems for businesses, particularly for SMEs, need to be improved. Existing support systems for exporting under FTAs are of varying quality and utilization rates. Business and industry associations will have to play a greater role in providing members with support services for exporting under FTAs. Upgrading SME technical standards, quality, and productivity could be useful so that they can participate more fully in regional production networks driven by large firms.

Priority 4: Addressing the "Noodle Bowl" Problem

ROOs are another potentially challenging aspect of the surge in the number of Latin America–Asian FTAs. These are devices to determine which goods will enjoy preferential tariffs in order to prevent trade deflection among FTA members (Estevadeordal and Suominen 2006). The multiplicity of bilateral trade agreements, such as the growing number of Asia–Latin America FTAs, have generated a complicated, inconsistent set of ROOs, sparking concerns about what the attendant rules and administrative procedures would imply for the cost of doing business. Indeed, the firm-level surveys in Latin America that show high levels of FTA utilization, also show that firms do face challenges in utilizing multiple FTAs simultaneously, limiting their ability to leverage preferences to diversify their export markets (Harris and Suominen 2009). Multiple ROOs pose a severe burden on SMEs, whether exporting directly to FTA partners, or when integrated into multinationals' supply chains, which can be constrained by ROO. In Asia, it is predominantly seen as a future challenge according to firm-level data presented in Kawai and Wignaraja (2010, 2011). Originally termed a "spaghetti bowl" of trade deals (Bhagwati 1995), this phenomenon has become widely known as the "noodle bowl" effect in Asia.[30]

Supportive measures—such as encouraging rationalization of ROOs and upgrading their administration—can mitigate any negative effects of the "noodle bowl" problem in the future. Gains are possible from simplifying the preferential trading system through harmonizing ROOs and the procedures for calculation and certification of compliance, and cumulation provisions that allow for more efficient, sophisticated supply chains without jeopardizing eligibility for preferences. Likewise, it would be useful to adopt international best practices in ROO administration. These may include introducing a trusted trader program that would allow successful applicants to self-certify origin, expanding the use of business associations issuing certificates of origin for a fee, increasing use of information technology based systems of ROO administration, and training SMEs to enhance their capacity to use FTAs.

Priority 5: Pursue Structural Reforms

There is a consensus that a general emphasis on markets for resource allocation and promotion of greater competition on domestic markets encourages efficiency in developing countries. Where market imperfections and institutional bottlenecks arise, however, intervention through domestic structural

---

[30] Others suggest that the depiction of multiple FTAs as a complicated noodle bowl is misleading, arguing on the contrary, that this plethora of bilateral trade agreements may be creating an order of a different sort by building the foundation for a stronger regional trading system (Chia 2010; Petri 2008).

reforms may be required in Asian and Latin American countries. Indeed recent research suggests that some aspects of regulatory policies (e.g., procedures required to start a business) in Asian and Latin American countries have improved between 2005 and 2012, but an unfinished agenda remains particularly in some less outward-oriented Latin American economies (ADB, IDB, and ADBI 2012). However, there is no one-size-fits-all strategy for domestic structural reforms. Key ingredients of domestic structural reforms—open trade and investment policies, streamlining of business procedures, measures to encourage export competitiveness, improvement of infrastructure and education, and capacity building—need to be modified and sequenced to suit individual country needs and priorities. As the 2008 global economic crisis and the 1997–1998 Asian financial crisis indicate, financial markets also require adequate regulation to avert financial crises. Likewise, interregional FTAs should be designed to effectively lock-in domestic structural reforms rather than affording prolonged protection to inefficient production.

Conclusion

The 2008 global financial crisis and the growing impetus toward more South–South cooperation seems to have accentuated the growing economic relationship between Asia and Latin America since the early 2000s. This relationship was initially market-led by the private sector who responded to falling trade and investment barriers and increasing business opportunities across vast geographical space separating the two dynamic regions. A handful of large countries in both regions have forged a promising interregional economic relationship but many players are absent or only participating below potential. Furthermore, interregional investment has grown but lags interregional trade growth and is largely from Asia to Latin America. More recently, market-led interregional trade and investment has been followed by growing numbers of interregional FTAs concluded between governments to reduce trade and behind the border regulatory barriers.

This chapter suggested new economic and legal criteria to comprehensively study the extent of liberalization in goods, services, and regulatory barriers in 22 Asia–Latin American FTAs in effect in mid-2013. The contents of new, complex interregional FTAs are not widely understood and little attention has been given in the literature to studying liberalization under interregional FTAs. An inter-disciplinary approach was adopted here—blending methods from international law and applied international economics—to quantify and assess the extent of liberalization under different interregional FTAs. The criteria and methodology used in this chapter may be usefully refined in future studies.

The evaluation of agreements suggests that progress has been made in reducing trade and regulatory barriers using FTAs, but more needs to be done in future FTAs to solidify and expand the process of deep integration between the two regions. It was found that traditional areas such as goods and services are typically well covered in interregional FTAs. Relatively fast liberalization and comprehensive provisions on services characterize most interregional FTAs. Many interregional FTAs also extend beyond trade in goods and services to support deeper integration through the Singapore issues and provisions on IPRs. Four FTAs (the Republic of Korea–Peru FTA, Trans-Pacific Strategic Economic Partnership Agreement, Australia–Chile FTA, and Singapore–Costa Rica FTA) are of particular high depth while six offer low depth. Another twelve FTAs are deemed medium depth and nine of these follow the same formula: Relatively fast tariff liberalization, comprehensive commitments of services, and moderate obligations on some new issues. Some Asia–Latin America FTAs, however, adopt a somewhat cautious approach to liberalization of sensitive regulatory barriers in areas such as investment, competition, and government procurement. This caution reflects the influence of domestic business interests and lobbies. By putting in place some interregional rules, FTAs have also helped build greater business confidence and trust which is vital for future interregional trade and investment flows.

There are benefits as well as costs with FTAs between Asia and Latin America. The chapter also noted several challenges with existing Asia–Latin America FTAs including insufficient depth in some agreements, variable rates of FTA used by business, and the risk of a noodle bowl effect.

With no end in sight for the WTO Doha Round and questions remaining about the efficiency of the trade negotiating function of the WTO, the numbers of Asia–Latin America are projected to rise to about 32 by 2020. Further improvement is needed in five key areas to make future interregional FTAs more effective as a liberalizing instrument. The future policy agenda includes: promoting deep integration FTAs, forming a comprehensive interregional FTA, raising FTA use by business, addressing the noodle bowl problem, and pursuing domestic structural reforms. Strong partnerships between government, business, and regional institutions are vital to design and implement this ambitious policy agenda.

Bibliography

ADB and IDB. 2009. *Comparative Perspectives on Trans-Pacific Trade, Integration, and Development*. Available at http://idbdocs.iadb.org/wsdocs/getdocument.aspx?docnum=2246322&bcsi_scan_9688b637a46568db=1WLerGKhl/m6amyTU+0Xa+1zO0QCAAAA0EQ6BQ==&bcsi_scan_filename=getdocument.aspx (accessed 18 July 2014).

ADB, IDB, and ADBI. 2012. *Shaping the Future of the Asia and the Pacific and the Latin America and the Caribbean Relationship*. Tokyo and Washington DC: Asian Development Bank Institute and Inter-American Development Bank.

ADB. 2008. *Emerging Asian Regionalism*. Manila: Asian Development Bank.

ADB. 2012. Asia Regional Integration Center (ARIC). Free Trade Agreement and Integration Indicators database. Available at www.aric.adb.org (accessed June 2012). Available at http://idbdocs.iadb.org/wsdocs/getdocument.aspx?docnum=549983 (accessed 18 July 2014).

Anderson, R., A.C. Muller, O.L. Kodjo, J. Pardo De Leon, and P. Pelletier. 2011. Government Procurement Provisions in Regional Trade Agreements: A Stepping Stone to GPA Accession. In Sue Arrowsmith and Robert D. Anderson, eds. *The WTO Regime on Government Procurement: Challenge and Reform*. New York: Cambridge University Press. Available at http://www.criticaltheology.ac.uk/pprg/documentsarchive/fulltextarticles/wtobookchapter1.pdf (accessed 21 July 2014).

Baldwin, R. 2006. Multilateralizing Regionalism: Spaghetti Bowls as Building Blocks on the Path to Global Free Trade. *The World Economy*. 29 (11). pp. 1451–1518.

Bergsten, C.F. 2007. Toward a Free Trade Area of the Asia Pacific. *Policy Briefs in International Economics No. PB07-02 (February)*. Peter G. Peterson Institute for International Economics. Washington, DC.

Bhagwati, J.N. 1995. US Trade Policy: The Infatuation with FTAs. *Columbia University Discussion Paper Series No. 726*. New York: Columbia University.

Bhagwati, J.N. 2008. *Termites in the Trading System: How Preferential Agreements Undermine Free Trade*. Oxford, UK: Oxford University Press.

Chami-Batista, J. 2004. Latin American Export Specialization in Resource-Based Products: Implications for Growth. *The Developing Economies*. XLII (3). pp. 337–370.

Chia, S.Y. 2010. Regional Trade Policy Cooperation and Architecture in East Asia. ADBI Working Paper Series No. 191 (February). Asian Development Bank Institute. Tokyo.

Devlin, R., A. Estevadeordal, and A. Rodríguez-Clare, eds. 2006. *The Emergence of China: Opportunities and Challenges for Latin America and the Caribbean*. Washington, DC: Inter-American Development Bank.

ECLAC. 2008. *Opportunities for Trade and Investment between Latin America and Asia-Pacific: The Link with APEC*. Santiago, Chile: ECLAC.

Engman, M. 2005. The Economic Impact of Trade Facilitation. OECD Trade Policy Working Paper No. 21, TD/TC/WP (2005)12/Final. Paris: OECD.

Estevadeordal, A., and K. Suominen. 2006. Mapping and Measuring Rules of Origin around the World. In O. Cadot, A. Estevadeordal, A. Suwa-Eisenmann, and T. Verdier, eds. *The Origin of Goods: Rules of Origin in Regional Trade Agreements*. Oxford, UK: Oxford University Press.

Estevadeordal, A., and K. Suominen. 2009. *Bridging Regional Trade Agreements in the Americas*. Washington, DC: Inter-American Development Bank.
Facchini, G., M. Olarreaga, P. Silva, and G. Willmann. 2010. Substitutability and Protectionism: Latin America's Trade Policy and Imports from China and India. *The World Bank Economic Review*. 24 (3). pp. 446–473.
Fink, C., and M. Molinuevo. 2008. East Asian Free Trade Agreements in Services: Key Architectural Elements. *Journal of International Economic Law*. 11 (2). pp. 263–311.
Fiorentino, R.V., J. Crawford, and C. Toqueboeuf. 2009. The Landscape of Regional Trade Agreements and WTO Surveillance. In R. Baldwin and P. Low, eds. *Multilateralizing Regionalism: Challenges for the Global Trading System*. Cambridge, UK: Cambridge University Press.
Foxley, A. 2010. *Regional Trade Blocs: The Way to the Future*. Washington, DC: Carnegie Endowment for International Peace.
Francois, J.F., and G. Wignaraja. 2008. Economic Implications of Asian Integration. *Global Economy Journal*. 6 (3). pp. 1–46.
Freund, C., and E. Ornelas. 2010. Regional Trade Agreements. World Bank Policy Research Working Papers. 5314. Washington, DC: World Bank.
GATT. 1994. Understanding on the Interpretation of Article XXIV of the General Agreement on Tariffs and Trade (GATT) 1994. Article XXIV: 5.
Gilbert, J., R. Scollay, and B. Bora. 2004. New Regional Trading Developments in the Asia-Pacific Region. In S. Yusuf, M.A. Altaf, and N. Nabeshima, eds. *Global Change and East Asian Policy Initiatives*. Washington, DC: World Bank.
Gonzales-Vigil, F., and T. Shimizu. 2012. The Japan-Peru FTA: Antecedents, Significance and Main Features. IDE Discussion Paper No.335. Available at: http://ir.ide.go.jp/dspace/bitstream/2344/1120/1/ARRIDE_Discussion_No.335_gonzalez.pdf (accessed 18 July 2014).
Harris, J., and K. Suominen. 2009. Business Costs of the Spaghetti Bowl in Latin America. Paper presented at LAEBA meeting on ADB/ADBI/IDB FTA Impacts Studies. 26 January. Tokyo (mimeo).
Hufbauer, G., and J. Schott. 2009. Fitting Asia-Pacific Agreements into the WTO System. In R. Baldwin and P. Low, eds. *Multilateralizing Regionalism: Challenges for the Global Trading System*. Cambridge, UK: Cambridge University Press.
Hummels, D. 2001. *Time as a Trade Barrier* (unpublished). Department of Economics, Purdue University.
IDB. 2002. *Beyond Borders: The New Regionalism in the Americas*. Washington, DC: Inter-American Development Bank.
Jenkins, R., E.D. Peters, and M.M. Moreira. 2008. The Impact of China on Latin America and the Caribbean. *World Development*. 36 (2). pp. 235–253.
Kawai, M., and G. Wignaraja. 2009. Global and Regional Economic Integration: A View from Asia. IDB-INTAL. 29 (13) 35–46. Available at http://www.iadb.org/intal/icom/29/eng/pdf/i_INTAL_I&T_29_2009_Kawai_Wignaraja.pdf?bcsi_scan_9688b637a46568db=0&bcsi_scan_filename=i_INTAL_I&T_29_2009_Kawai_Wignaraja.pdf (accessed on 5 October 2011).
Kawai, M., and G. Wignaraja. 2010. Asian FTAs: Trends, Prospects, and Challenges. Asian Development Bank Economics Working Paper Series No. 226.
Kawai, M., and G. Wignaraja. 2011. *Asia's Free Trade Agreements: How is Business Responding?* Cheltenham, UK: Edward Elgar.

Krasniqi, V.B., A. Bouet, C. Estrades, and D. Laborde. 2011. Trade and Investment in Latin America and Asia: Lessons from the Past and Potential Perspectives from Further Integration. IFPR Discussion Paper 01060. International Food Policy Research Institute.

Markheim, D. 2008. America Should Support the Trans-Pacific Strategic Economic Partnership. Web Memo. No. 2178 (December). Washington, DC: Heritage Foundation.

Medalla, E.M., and J.D. Balboa. 2010. Prospects for Regional Cooperation between Latin America and the Caribbean and Asia and the Pacific Region: Perspective from East Asia. *Philippine Institute for Development Studies (PIDS) Discussion Paper Series No. 2010–12*.

Park, I., S. Park, and S. Kim. 2010. A Free Trade Area of the Asia Pacific (FTAAP): Is It Desirable? MPRA Paper. No. 26680. Available at: http://mpra.ub.uni-muenchen.de/26680/ (accessed on 26 January 2012).

Petri, P. 2008. Multi-track Integration in East Asian Trade: Noodle Bowl or Matrix? *Asia Pacific Issues*. 86 (October). pp. 2–4.

Petri, P., M. Plummer, and F. Zhai. 2011. The Trans-Pacific Partnership and Asia-Pacific Integration: A Quantitative Assessment. East-West Center Working Papers. Economic Series. 119 (October). pp. 1–15.

Plummer, M. 2007. Best Practices in Regional Trade Agreements: An Application to Asia. *World Economy*. 30 (12). pp. 1771–1796.

Rosales, O., and M. Kuwayama. 2012. *China and Latin America and the Caribbean: Building a Strategic Economic and Trade Relationship*. Santiago: Economic Commission for Latin America and the Caribbean (ECLAC).

UNCTAD. 2004. International Investment Agreements: Key Issues Volume I. UNCTAD/ITE/IIT/2004/10. Available at http://www.unctad.org/en/docs/iteiit200410_en.pdf?bcsi_scan_9688b637a46568db=0&bcsi_scan_filename=iteiit200410_en.pdf (accessed 18 July 2014).

UNCTAD. 2006. Investment Provisions in Economic Integration Agreements. UNCTAD/ITE/IIT/2005/10. Available at http://www.unctad.org/en/docs/iteiit200510_en.pdf?bcsi_scan_9688b637a46568db=0&bcsi_scan_filename=iteiit200510_en.pdf (accessed 18 July 2014).

Wignaraja, G., and D. Lazaro. 2010. North–South vs. South–South Asian FTAs: Trends, Compatibilities, and Ways Forward. UNU-CRIS Working Paper. W-2010/3. Bruges, Belgium: UNU-CRIS.

Wille, P., and J. Redden. 2007. A Comparative Analysis of Trade Facilitation in Selected Regional and Bilateral Trade Agreements and Initiatives. In ESCAP's *Trade Facilitation Beyond the Multilateral Trade Negotiations: Regional Practices, Customs Valuation and Other Emerging Issues—A Study by the Asia-Pacific Research and Training Network on Trade*. New York, NY: United Nations. Available at http://artnet.unescap.org/pub/tipub2466_chap2.pdf (accessed 22 July 2014).

World Bank. 2007. Trade Issues in East Asia: Preferential Rules of Origin. Policy Research Report, East Asia and Pacific Region (Poverty Reduction and Economic Management). Washington, DC: World Bank.

World Trade Organization (WTO). 2005. Factual Presentation: FTA Between Korea and Chile. WT/REG169/3.

World Trade Organization. 2008. Trade Policy Review of Republic of Korea: Report by the Secretariat. WT/TPR/S/204. Available at www.wto.org/english/tratop_e/tpr_e/s204-00_e.doc (accessed 22 July 2014).

World Trade Organization. 2009. Trade Policy Review of Japan: Report by the Secretariat. WT/TPR/S/211. Available at www.wto.org/english/tratop_e/tpr_e/s211-00_e.doc (accessed 22 July 2014).

World Trade Organization.2011. *World Trade Report 2011. The WTO and Preferential Trade Agreements: From Coexistence to Coherence.* Geneva: World Trade Organization.

Annexure 1

Status of Asia–Latin America FTAs (October 2013)

In Effect
1. Republic of Korea–Chile FTA(2004)
2. Taipei,China–Panama FTA (2004)
3. Japan–Mexico EPA (2005)
4. People's Republic of China–Chile FTA (2006)
5. Singapore–Panama FTA (2006)
6. Taipei,China–Guatemala FTA (2006)
7. Trans-Pacific Strategic EPA (2006)
8. Japan–Chile EPA (2007)
9. India–Chile PTA (2007)
10. Taipei,China–El Salvador–Honduras FTA (2008)
11. Taipei,China–Nicaragua FTA (2008)
12. Australia–Chile FTA (2009)
13. India–MERCOSUR PTA (2009)
14. Singapore–Peru FTA (2009)
15. People's Republic of China–Peru FTA (2010)
16. Republic of Korea–Peru FTA (2011)
17. People's Republic of China–Costa Rica FTA (2011)
18. Thailand–Peru FTA (2011)
19. Japan–Peru FTA (2012)
20. Malaysia–Chile FTA (2012)
21. Chile–Viet Nam FTA (2012)
22. Singapore–Costa Rica FTA (2013)
Signed (Not in Effect)
23. Taipei,China–Paraguay FTA (2004)
24. Pakistan–MERCOSUR PTA (2006)
25. Hong Kong, China–Chile FTA (2012)
26. Republic of Korea-Colombia FTA (2013)

Under Negotiation

27. Singapore–Mexico FTA (2000)
28. Republic of Korea–Mexico SECA (2006)
29. Taipei,China–Dominican Republic FTA (2006)
30. Trans-Pacific Partnership (2010)
31. Thailand–Chile FTA (2011)
32. Japan–Colombia FTA (2011)

Proposed

33. New Zealand-Mexico FTA (2002)
34. India–Colombia PTA (2004)
35. India–Uruguay PTA (2004)
36. India–Venezuela PTA (2004)
37. Republic of Korea–MERCOSUR PTA (2004)
38. Australia–Mexico FTA (2006)
39. Thailand–MERCOSUR FTA (2006)
40. Australia–Colombia (2009)
41. Indonesia–Chile FTA (2009)
42. Republic of Korea–Central America FTA (2010)
43. People's Republic of China–Colombia FTA (2012)

Source: Authors' compilation.

Annexure 2

New Issues in Asia–Latin America FTAs in Effect

FTA	Government Procurement Chapter	Investment Chapter	Trade Facilitation Chapter	Competition Policy	Intellectual Property Rights	New Issues (overall)[31]
1. Republic of Korea–Chile FTA (2004)	Above Standard	Standard	Standard	Standard	Above Standard	Moderate
2. Taipei,China–Panama FTA (2004)	No Provision	Above Standard	Standard	Standard	Above Standard	Moderate
3. Japan–Mexico EPA (2005)	Standard	Above Standard	Standard	Standard	Above Standard	Moderate
4. PRC–Chile FTA (2006)	No Provision	No Provision	Standard	No Provision	Above Standard	Limited
5. Singapore–Panama FTA (2006)	Above Standard	Above Standard	Above Standard	Standard	No Provision	Moderate

[31] In the overall determination, no provision is given 0 points, a standard provision 1 point and above standard 2 points. FTA is classified as new age combined score ranges from 8–10 points, moderate with a range of 5–7, limited with a range of 2–4, and shallow with a range of 0–1.

Asia–Latin America FTAs

FTA	Government Procurement Chapter	Investment Chapter	Trade Facilitation Chapter	Competition Policy	Intellectual Property Rights	New Issues (overall)
6. Taipei,China–Guatemala FTA (2005)	No Provision	Above Standard	Standard	No provision	Above Standard	Moderate
7. TPP/P4 (2006)	Above Standard	No Provision	Above Standard	Above Standard	Above Standard	New Age
8. Japan–Chile FTA (2007)	Standard	Standard	Above Standard	Standard	Above standard	Moderate
9. India–Chile PTA (2007)	No Provision	No Provision	No Provision	No Provision	No Provision	Shallow
10. Taipei,China–El Salvador–Honduras FTA (2008)	No Provision	Above Standard	Standard	No Provision	No Provision	Limited
11. Taipei,China–Nicaragua FTA (2008)	No Provision	Above Standard	Above Standard	Standard	Above Standard	Moderate
12. Australia–Chile FTA (2009)	Above Standard	Above Standard	Above Standard	Standard	Above Standard	New Age
13. India–MERCOSUR PTA (2007)	No Provision	No Provision	No Provision	No Provision	No Provision	Shallow
14. Singapore–Peru FTA (2009)	Standard	Above Standard	Above Standard	Above Standard	No Provision	Moderate
15. PRC–Peru FTA (2010)	No Provision	Standard	Above Standard	Standard	Above Standard	Moderate
16. Republic of Korea–Peru FTA (2010)	Above Standard	Above Standard	Above Standard	Standard	Above Standard	New Age
17. PRC–Costa Rica FTA (2011)	No Provision	Standard	Standard	Standard	Above Standard	Moderate
18. Thailand–Peru FTA (2011)	No Provision	No Provision	Standard	No Provision	No Provision	Shallow
19. Japan–Peru EPA (2012)	Above Standard	No Provision	Above Standard	Standard	Above Standard	Moderate
20. Malaysia–Chile FTA (2012)	No Provision	No Provision	Above Standard	No Provision	No Provision	Limited
21. Chile–Viet Nam FTA (2012)	No Provision	No Provision	No Provision	No Provision	No Provision	Shallow
22. Singapore–Costa Rica FTA (2013)	Above Standard	Above Standard	Above Standard	Standard	Above Standard	New Age

Source: Authors' compilation.

Annexure 3

Asia–Latin America FTAs—Approaches to Tariff Liberalization, Services Coverage, and Deep Integration (New Issues)

FTA	Level of Development[32]	Tariff Liberalization	Services Coverage	New Issues	Overall Quality
1. Republic of Korea–Chile FTA (2004)	Advanced–Developing	Relatively Fast	Comprehensive	Moderate	Medium
2. Taipei,China–Panama FTA (2004)	Advanced–Developing	Relatively Fast	Comprehensive	Moderate	Medium
3. Japan–Mexico EPA (2005)	Advanced–Developing	Relatively Fast	Comprehensive	Moderate	Medium
4. People's Republic of China–Chile FTA (2006)	Developing–Developing	Relatively Fast	Some	Limited	Medium
5. Singapore–Panama FTA (2006)	Advanced–Developing	Relatively Fast	Comprehensive	Moderate	Medium
6. Taipei,China–Guatemala FTA (2006)	Advanced–Developing	Relatively Fast	Comprehensive	Moderate	Medium
7. Trans-Pacific Strategic EPA (2006)	Advanced–Developing	Relatively Fast	Comprehensive	New Age	High
8. Japan–Chile EPA (2007)	Advanced–Developing	Relatively Fast	Comprehensive	Moderate	Medium
9. India–Chile PTA (2007)	Developing–Developing	NA	Excluded or Limited	Shallow	Low
10. Taipei,China–El Salvador–Honduras FTA (2008)	Advanced–Developing	Gradual	Comprehensive	Limited	Low
11. Taipei,China–Nicaragua FTA (2008)	Advanced–Developing	Relatively Fast	Comprehensive	Moderate	Medium
12. Australia–Chile FTA (2009)	Advanced–Developing	Relatively Fast	Comprehensive	New Age	High

[32] Based on IMF definition.

FTA	Level of Development	Tariff Liberalization	Services Coverage	New Issues	Overall Quality
13. India–MERCOSUR PTA (2009)	Developing–Developing	NA	Excluded or Limited	Shallow	Low
14. Singapore–Peru FTA (2009)	Advanced–Developing	Relatively Fast	Comprehensive	Moderate	Medium
15. People's Republic of China–Peru FTA (2010)	Developing–Developing	Relatively Fast	Some	Moderate	Medium
16. Republic of Korea–Peru FTA (2011)	Advanced–Developing	Relatively Fast	Comprehensive	New Age	High
17. People's Republic of China–Costa Rica FTA (2011)	Developing—Developing	Relatively Fast	Some	Moderate	Medium
18. Thailand–Peru FTA (2011)	Developing–Developing	Gradual	Excluded or Limited	Shallow	Low
19. Japan–Peru EPA (2012)	Advanced–Developing	Relatively Fast	Comprehensive	Moderate	Medium
20. Malaysia–Chile FTA	Developing–Developing	Relatively Fast	Excluded or Limited	Limited	Low
21. Chile–Viet Nam FTA (2012)	Advanced–Developing	Relatively Fast	Excluded or limited	Shallow	Low
22. Singapore–Costa Rica FTA (2013)	Advanced–Developing	Relatively Fast	Comprehensive	New Age	High

Source: Authors' compilation.

10

Prospects for Regional Cooperation between Latin America and Caribbean and Asia and Pacific:* Perspective from East Asia

Erlinda M. Medalla and Jenny D. Balboa

Introduction

The economic success of the East Asian region in the past decades shows that regional cooperation and integration, supported by both open trade and regional cooperation, is a key factor for sustained growth and development. East Asia's phenomenal rise makes it a model for economic success in developing economies. It also showed that closer cooperation with neighbors could be beneficial to member economies as regional integration facilitates specialization and economies of scale. Regional cooperation is also a critical force in addressing common issues such as energy security, food security, environmental degradation, and human security issues, among others.

At the national level, regional cooperation helped lock-in reforms within domestic economies that led to the creation of a coherent and efficient

---

* Asia and the Pacific refers to Australia, Brunei Darussalam, Cambodia, PRC, Indonesia, Japan, Republic of Korea, Lao PDR, Malaysia, Myanmar, New Zealand, Philippines, Singapore, Thailand, Viet Nam.

Latin America refers to Argentina, Bolivia, Brazil, Chile, Colombia, Costa Rica, Cuba, Dominican Republic, Ecuador, El Salvador, Guatemala, Honduras, Mexico, Nicaragua, Panama, Paraguay, Peru, Uruguay, and Venezuela.

Caribbean refers to Anguilla, Antigua and Barbuda, Aruba, Bahamas, Barbados, British Virgin Islands, Cayman Islands, Dominica, Grenada.

environment for doing business within that economy. At the global level, regional cooperation helped Asia, especially its developing economy members, secure a role in decision making for various issues relating to the region's economy and politics. In a lot of ways, Asia's outstanding economic performance can be attributed to its pursuit of open and flexible regionalism.

While regional cooperation had been explored as early as the 1960s and regional economic integration initiatives had been initiated by ASEAN (Association of Southeast Asian Nations), which lead to the signing of the ASEAN Free Trade Agreement (AFTA) in 1992, East Asia-wide cooperation was not seriously pursued in the region until after the Asian financial crisis in 1997. The Asian financial crisis prompted negotiations for bilateral and plurilateral agreements in the East Asian region and led to the creation of institutions for regional cooperation, particularly the ASEAN+1, ASEAN+3 (APT), and the East Asian Summit (EAS). These regional cooperation initiatives helped spur trade, investment, and financial reforms that deepened Asia's growing and wide-ranging regional links. Most recently, the scope and depth of cooperation had deepened to include cooperation to manage regional risks and addressing common issues. Area-wise, the scope had also expanded to include economies outside of East Asia, as shown by the recent negotiations for the Regional Comprehensive Economic Partnership (RCEP), an RTA that involves countries in East Asia and India, with potential for further expansion in South Asia. At the same time, several economies in East Asia are exploring the possibility of joining the Trans-Pacific Partnership (TPP) Agreement that will further expand the scope of interregional cooperation.

Latin America and the Caribbean, on the other hand, did not display the same success as the Asia and Pacific region in integrating their economies and securing a stronger role in the global economy. Unlike the Asia and Pacific region, and in particular East Asia, the Latin America and Caribbean region had not shown the same level of enthusiasm for open regionalism and had not been aggressive enough in looking for third markets (United Nations Economic Commission for Latin America and the Caribbean [UNECLAC] 2008). Latin American markets had been fragmented and the business environment needs to be improved to make it more attractive for foreign direct investment (FDI).

The idea of linking the dynamic Asia and Pacific region with Latin America and the Caribbean had been explored in various fora. The main challenge for establishing this connection is how to strengthen trade and investment links between the two regions. Lack of coherent and sustained policies, poor infrastructure support, and high transportation costs have also dampened previous attempts to integrate the two regions.

There are many opportunities for growth and development between the two regions once appropriate policies and support systems are in place. Efforts to expand trans-regional cooperation would not only be valuable for improving the regional value chain, but could also help enhance innovation and competitiveness, especially for Latin America and the Caribbean. Interregional cooperation between the two regions would be very challenging since they are divided by substantial geographic distance and are characterized by profound disparities in economics, politics, culture, and history. Nonetheless, it is certainly worth considering, given the mutual benefits that can be derived from this cooperation.

This chapter explores the potential for regional cooperation between the Asia and Pacific region and Latin America and the Caribbean from the perspective of East Asia. The first section provides a brief background on changing patterns of regionalism. The second section gives a background on Asian regionalism and the factors for its success. The third section deals with prospects for interregional cooperation between the Asia and Pacific region and Latin America and the Caribbean. The fourth section provides the conclusion and some recommendations to strengthen partnership and cooperation between the two regions.

The Changing Global Architecture and Regionalism: A Background

Global economic integration was hastened after World War II, as the period of peace and reconstruction made possible the increase of economic activities. Foreign trade steadily climbed and by 1960, the total ratio of foreign trade to gross domestic product (GDP) stood at 25%. Multilateral trade negotiations under the General Agreement on Tariffs and Trade (GATT) and technological developments further accelerated globalization, resulting in liberalization of trade and investments and improvements in infrastructure, creating a climate more conducive for foreign trade and freer flow of FDI (Urata 2002). Alongside these changes was the development of regional coalitions, as countries considered to be natural trading partners cooperate and formed economic blocs.

The evolving regional coalitions radically changed the global economic landscape after World War II. Formation and expansion of these regional blocs had a huge impact on trade activities worldwide. The form and structure of the regional blocs continued to evolve since the 1960s as a result of various economic and political events that enabled so-called natural economic groups and strategic partners to gravitate toward each other (Evans et al. 2004).

The 1960s was characterized by a bipolar economy, with the United States and Europe dominating global trade. A number of closely connected developing countries were linked to the dominant blocs, which either were formed because of geographic proximity, or were former colonies, or had developed a strategic partnership in the course of the cold war. The two leading world trade blocs accounted for 80% of global trade. The European bloc was closely linked with countries in Africa and former colonies. On the other hand, the United States tied up economically with Latin America and the Philippines. Britain still retained leadership in small Asian cluster consisting of former colonies, the PRC and the rest of the Middle East. In the early post war years, developing countries traded much more with Europe or the United States and not as much among themselves.

A realignment of global trading pattern took place in the 1970s, creating three distinct blocs and two clusters, with more fragmentation in trading arrangements. It showed splintering from the European and US blocs and increasing diversification of trade. It also marked the emergence of East Asia as a new trade bloc and a major player in the world market as it increasingly captured a larger share in total world trade. The changes were triggered by the increasing size and influence of the Japanese economy, continuing GATT trade rounds to open economies, and the onset of unilateral trade policy liberalization associated with structural adjustment policies in these countries.

The 1980s reinforced the developments in the previous decade and marked the emergence of East Asia as an important trade bloc. It prompted the emergence of East Asia as a major economic player. The East Asian economic bloc expanded its membership in the succeeding decades to include Australia and New Zealand, further increasing its total world trade share. On the other side of the globe, it was also during this decade that the South American bloc started to gain momentum as intra-regional trade increased in Latin America, accounting from Argentina, Paraguay, Uruguay, and Brazil increased trade shares in the region. African trade was also gaining strength as trade with South Africa and its near neighbors, Malawi and Zimbabwe, expanded.

The 1990s consolidated the gains from the previous decades and established East Asia as an economic powerhouse, changing the global economic landscape from bipolar to multipolar with the emergence of the East Asian region as the third bloc, alongside EU and North America. East Asia's growth was further propelled by the rise of the PRC and its accession to WTO in 2001. Trading patterns and economic relations between and among the different blocs also became more diversified, with the appearance of two other trade blocs, MERCOSUR and SACU. In the succeeding decades, the world witnessed the phenomenal rise of East Asia as an economic powerhouse, fuelled by the rise of the PRC and the Newly Industrialized Economies (NIEs) in East and Southeast Asia.

These new regional blocs are distinct from its predecessor in the postwar years. Whereas old regionalism created closed economic blocs, the new regionalism developed in the recent decades is a response to the rapid global transformation and increasing need to collectively respond to global issues. The new regionalism is also characterized by an "open system"—taking into account WTO rules and other multilateral institutions—which makes it more compatible with an increasingly interdependent world. Moreover, regional cooperation had also been important in solving economic, social and environmental issues. Following the Asian financial crisis in 1997 and the Global Financial Crisis of 2008, regional cooperation institutions in East Asia had played an important role in managing and alleviating the impact of the crisis (Table 10.1).

Overview of Asian Regionalism

The core of Asian regionalism is East Asia, where economic cooperation started and first gained success. Huge amounts of literature had been devoted to understand and emulate the economic success of East Asia. While obstacles remain in terms of human resource, infrastructure, and governance, East Asia has undoubtedly taken an important role in the global economy. East Asia's share of world output had risen substantially over the past two decades, overtaking the US and capturing a large size of world exports, matching that of North America (Drysdale 2005).

The growth and deepening integration of the East Asian region has been shaped by three huge waves of trade and industrial transformation. The first wave occurred with the rise of Japan and its emergence as a major industrial power. The second wave was led by the NIEs of Northeast and Southeast Asia in the late 1970s and 1980s. The third wave was pushed by the rise of the People's Republic of China (PRC). These three major time periods restructured the economic architecture of East Asia, making it an economic powerhouse and cornering almost a quarter of world output (Drysdale 2005).

Intra-regional trade in East Asia had grown more rapidly and steadily than any other region in the world. In ASEAN, intra-regional trade was less than

Table 10.1
Analytical Framework for Regional Cooperation

	Manage regional spillover and externalities	Provide regional public goods	Address regional coordination problems
Trade and Investment	Establish compatible product standards	Maintain an open, predictable and fair framework for trade and cross-border investment	Represent regional views in global trade and investment forums
			Facilitate investment in infrastructure (hard and soft) for connectivity
Financial Markets	Establish rules to protect against financial contagion	Establish institutions and reserves to avert and manage financial crises	Represent regional views in global financial forums
	Establish compatible financial regulations	Improve the legal and informational environment for regional investment	Develop compatible trading platforms and institutions
Macroeconomic Policy	Coordinate macroeconomic and exchange rate policies	Monitor macroeconomic activity, trends, and risks	Facilitate solutions to global imbalances and other macroeconomic issues
Social and Environmental Policy	Control cross-border environmental externalities	Prevent or manage spread of diseases and other public threats	Generate concerted commitment to Millennium Development Goals
	Ensure fair treatment of migrant workers	Pool know-how and experience on policy making	Promote social progress through regional collaboration in social issues
		Share environmental technology	

Source: ADB (2008).

20% in 1980. By 2012, the figure grew to 27%. Intra-regional trade in ASEAN + 3 countries also increased from 30% in the 1980 to 42% in 2012. Intra-regional trade in East Asia had grown faster than that of European Union and NAFTA in the past two decades, although EU and NAFTA still have higher intra-regional trade figures than any region in the word. However, it is worthy to note that East Asian intra-regional trade is approaching the levels of North American Free Trade Agreement (NAFTA) (Table 10.2).

Trade and investment had been East Asia's economic lifeblood and its source of growth. Investment inflows to the Asia and Pacific region surpassed North America in recent years. Export and import in merchandise trade is

Table 10.2
Asia-Pacific Intra-Regional Trade by Geographic Grouping[a] (percentage of the region's total trade)

Geographic grouping	1980	1985	1990	1995	2000	2003	2006	2012
Within ASEAN (10)[b]	17.9	20.3	18.8	24	24.7	26.6	27.2	27.6
Within ASEAN+3[c]	30.2	30.2	29.4	37.6	37.3	39	38.3	42.8
Within ASEAN+3 + Hong Kong, China and Taipei,China	34.1	37.1	43.1	51.9	52.1	55.4	54.5	
Memo: European Union (27)	61.5	60.0	66.8	66.9	66.3	68.1	65.8	62.4
NAFTA	33.8	38.7	37.9	43.1	48.8	47.4	44.3	44.1
MERCOSUR	11.1	7.2	10.9	19.2	20.7	14.7	15.7	16.2
Andean Community (5)[d]		3.3	5.4	12.4	10.8	10.8	9.1	8.5
CACM[e]		…	12.1	15.6	17.5	17.6	10.1	17.4

ASEAN = Association of Southeast Asian Nations, CACM = Central American Common Market, MERCOSUR = Common Market of the South, NAFTA = North American Free Trade Agreement.
Source: Economic Commission for Latin America and the Caribbean, on the basis of the United Nations Commodity Trade Statistics Database; with updates from the authors.
Notes: [a] The share in intra-regional trade is defined as the percentage of intra-regional trade with respect to the total trade of the region in question, based on export data. It is calculated as follows: Xii / {(Xiw + Xwi)/2}, where Xii refers to exports from region i to the same region, Xiw represents exports from region i to the world, and Xwi represents world exports to region i. A higher percentage indicates a higher level of dependency on intra-regional trade.
[b] ASEAN (10) consists of Brunei Darussalam, Cambodia, Indonesia, Lao People's Democratic Republic, Malaysia, Myanmar, Philippines, Singapore, Thailand and Viet Nam.
[c] ASEAN+3 includes the 10 ASEAN countries plus the People's Republic of China, Japan and the Republic of Korea.
[d] Andean Community (5) includes the Bolivarian Republic of Venezuela.
[e] Due to a different methodology used, the coefficient of CACM intra-subregional trade differs substantially from that shown in Figure 4.10.

among the highest in the world and has overtaken NAFTA in terms of trade volume and share in world total. Similarly, the Asia and Pacific region has been a top investment destination, with the ASEAN+6 receiving the biggest FDI inflow in 2012 and consistently showing as the third most important economic bloc in terms of FDI stock and inflow. Despite the global financial crisis in 2008, the Asia and the Pacific region also showed resilience in terms of growth of its international trade, with export growth in ASEAN+6 showing an average of 6.7% growth rate per annum for the period 2008–2012 and the SAARC region showing 10.1% growth rate between 2008–2012. In contrast, average export growth rate of Europe and North America from 2008–2012 were only at –0.5% and 3.5%, respectively (Tables 10.3 and 10.4).

Table 10.3
Inward Foreign Direct Investment

	FDI stock US$ million 2012	FDI stock % of GDP				FDI net inflow US$ million 2012	FDI net inflow % of GDP			
		1990–1995	1996–2000	2001–2005	2006–2012		1990–1995	1996–2000	2001–2005	2006–2012
Asia and the Pacific										
ASEAN	1,319,242	20.4	36.7	42.9	17.7	111,294	3.5	4.5	3.8	4.8
ASEAN+3	2,504,715					244,009				
ASEAN+6	3,423,006					329,422				
ECO	395,274	5.4	9.1	13.8	29.5	39,171	0.5	0.8	1.9	2.6
SAARC	269,347	2	4.5	5.8	9.3	28,641	0.3	0.7	1	2.0
Latin America & Caribbean	2,310,630	10.5	18.1	32	34.2	126,266	1.2	3.9	3.3	3.9
Other world regions										
Africa	629,632	14.4	21.3	28.1	29.5	50,041	0.9	1.7	2.8	3.1
Europe	8,849,964	10.7	16.7	31.9	44.0	289,249	1	3.3	2.8	3
North America	4,570,442	8	10.8	14.5	24.2	213,123	0.7	2.3	1	1.7
Other countries/areas	614,454	11.6	12.4	16.6	29.6	48,319	0.6	1.3	2.7	4.3
World	22,812,698	9.3	14	21.5	30.4	1,350,926	0.9	2.7	2	2.6

ASEAN = Association of Southeast Asian Nations, ECO = Economic Cooperation Organization, FDI = foreign direct investment, GDP = gross domestic product, SAARC = South Asian Association for Regional Cooperation.
Source: For 1990–2005, figures from Statistical Yearbook for Asia and the Pacific 2008 (Table 20.1) (UNESCAP 2008) http://www.unescap.org/stat/data/syb2008/20-Financing-for-development.asp. For 2012, figures from UNESCAP website (unescap.org) (accessed 12 November 2013).

Table 10.4
Growth in International Trade

	Average annual growth rate of imports of merchandise % per annum				Average annual growth rate of exports of merchandise % per annum			
	1990–1995	1995–2000	2000–2006	2008–2012	1990–1995	1995–2000	2000–2006	2008–2012
Asia and the Pacific								
ASEAN	15.6	0.6	10.1	6.8	16.2	5.5	10.1	6.1
ASEAN+3				6.9				5.7
ASEAN+6				6.9				6.7
ECO		5.1	18.4	3.5		7.2	18	2.1
SAARC	9.1	5.3	20.5	10.1	11.4	6.7	15.9	10.1
Latin America & Caribbean	12.8	8.4	8.3	5.2	11.6	9.2	11.1	5.5
Other world regions								
Africa		1	13.3	5.8		6.5	10.2	2.7
Europe	4.4	3.1	11.6	-1.5	6.1	2.1	11.4	-0.5
North America	8.1	9.9	7.2	2.1	8.3	6.4	5.1	3.5
Other countries/areas		5.1	10.1	4.4		9	12.3	6.1
World	7	4.7	10.9	2.9	7.7	4.3	10.9	3.2

ASEAN = Association of Southeast Asian Nations, ECO = Economic Cooperation Organization, SAARC = South Asian Association for Regional Cooperation.
Source: Statistical Yearbook for Asia and the Pacific 2008 (Table 21.3) (UNESCAP 2008) http://www.unescap.org/stat/data/syb2008/21-International-trade.asp. For 2012, figures from United Nations Economic and Social Commission for Asia and the Pacific website (unescap.org) (accessed 12 November 2013).

The industrial and trade transformation of East Asia over the last half-century has been driven by policy initiatives and market forces that opened up trade and investments in the East Asian countries. This created the opportunity to dynamically link the East Asian economies to the international production chain and also provided an environment conducive for sustained FDI flow.

The initial phase of liberalization took place in the 1980s and 1990s, as countries in East Asia began liberalizing trade and FDI policies and deregulating domestic economic activities. Countries in East Asia embarked in both unilateral liberalization and as part of the commitment made to the World Bank and International Monetary Fund (IMF) to create more comprehensive structural reform policies in exchange for economic assistance during the Asian financial crisis. Liberalization activities were also stimulated with the realization by the East Asian countries that liberalization and deregulation would promote economic growth.

Meanwhile, policies toward FDI liberalization started around the mid-1980s as countries began to realize that FDI inflows would promote economic growth. Some of the measures undertaken were the reduction of the number of sectors and industries on the negative list and relaxing the limits on foreign equity ownership. A number of economies also introduced tax holidays or tax breaks to encourage more FDI inflow (Urata 2008).

As regionalization developed, liberalization of trade and FDI also further progressed in East Asia. In 1992, ASEAN member countries created the ASEAN Free Trade Area (AFTA), which was designed to enhance trade and FDI flow in the region. AFTA is considered to be the centerpiece of the ASEAN economic integration policy and provided the impetus to explore sub-regional cooperation.

Another regional framework that facilitated trade and FDI liberalization in East Asia is the Asia Pacific Economic Cooperation (APEC). APEC provided the venue for East Asian countries to engage North America, South America, and Oceania in economic dialogue and to create a venue to discuss issues vital to economic development in the region. Though participation is voluntary, the Bogor goals[1] outline full liberalization of trade and FDI by 2010

---

[1] The APEC Economic Leaders Declaration of Common Resolve signed in Bogor, Indonesia on 15 November 1994, or commonly known as Bogor Goals, commit to sustain free and open trade and investment in the Asia Pacific by reducing barriers to trade and investment and by promoting the free flow of goods, services and capital among economies. It sets the target of creating free and open trade and investment in the region no later than 2020, with industrialized countries achieving this goal in 2010, and developing economies no later than 2020.

for members with developed economies and by 2020 for member with developing economies—these goals have been well integrated in member countries' economic agenda. To date, APEC's member countries have made significant strides in liberalizing trade and FDI.

Several studies have been devoted to understanding the shape of East Asia's economic architecture (Kawai 2007; Nanto 2008; Soesastro 2006; Urata 2008). Analysts agree that the development of the East Asian regionalism is propelled by three factors: (i) market-driven economic integration, (ii) negotiated trade liberalization initiatives, and (iii) the regional financial cooperation initiatives following the Asian financial crisis. The East Asia integration process started as market-led integration and progressed into an institution-led process as East Asia pursued bilateral and plurilateral free trade agreements (FTAs) and financial cooperation initiatives.

De Facto Economic Integration in East Asia

The market-driven forces of cross-border trade, FDI, and finance pushed the initial phase of economic integration in East Asia. The simultaneous expansion and reinforcement between trade and FDI, otherwise known as the trade–FDI nexus (Kawai 2007; Urata 2001), was largely determined by the establishment of regional production networks and supply chains by multinational corporations (MNCs). This phenomenon became known as "Factory Asia" (Soesastro 2006). By the end of 1990s, the intensity of regional trade in East Asia was already comparable to that of the EU and NAFTA. East Asia was also slowly veering away from its dependence on the US and European markets. This dependence is expected to further decline as demand for final products within East Asia continues to grow (Kawai 2007).

Meanwhile, rapid FDI inflows into East Asia are largely attributable to favorable economic environment and the abundant supply of high-quality, low-wage labor. FDI inflows to East Asia over the past decades have grown rapidly, even at a faster rate than the region's growth in trade.

Many of these FDI movements were intra-regional, from Japan and the NIEs to ASEAN and the PRC, as well as from ASEAN and to the PRC. MNCs specializing in manufacturing played an important role in enhancing economic integration. The increasing number of MNCs from Japan, and later on, from the NIEs, were key factors in linking East Asia to the global production chain since they tend to divide their production process into several sub-processes and relocate them in different countries in accordance to their comparative advantages. Such business arrangements have promoted vertical intra-industry trade within East Asia for capital equipment, parts and components, intermediate inputs, semi-finished goods, and finished manufactured products (Kawai 2007).

The PRC plays a key role in the international product fragmentation and the regional production network in general. The PRC's dynamic role on intra-regional trade has changed the structure of East Asia, and to a large extent created a positive, boost for ASEAN's competitiveness.

The PRC will likely exert more influence in the region in the future, as it poses to have more important role in the spread of FDI as well as intra-regional trade. About half of the increase in East Asia's share in world trade has been accounted for by the PRC. The rise of the PRC has further expanded "Factory Asia" and established what is referred to as the new pattern of "triangular trade" involving increased Chinese imports from East Asia and Chinese exports to third markets (Soesastro 2006).

In addition to trade and investment integration, financial markets are also rapidly integrating as a result of the deregulation of domestic financial systems, the opening of financial services, and the progressive relaxation of capital and exchange controls. Commercial banks in developed countries have begun operating abroad and consequently portfolio investments have strengthened linkages among the region's financial markets. At the same time, commercial banks in emerging economies have also expanded operations with their neighbors.

De Jure Integration: Proliferation of Free Trade Agreement in East Asia

East Asia is a dynamic participant in FTAs. As of September 2012, 138 FTAs had been concluded. This is a big increase from the small number of mere 15 FTAs in the region in the year 2000 (Figure 10.1). There are a number of reasons behind the surge in FTA in East Asia. While the growth of FTAs in East Asia typically is seen as a response to the sluggish progress of WTO negotiations, there are other reasons for rapid FTA uptake, such as keeping up with the expansion of FTAs in other parts of the world, promoting domestic structural reforms, avoiding financial crises, and responding to rivalry among East Asian economies over regional market access (Urata 2008).

Figure 10.1
FTAs in East Asia, 2000 and 2012

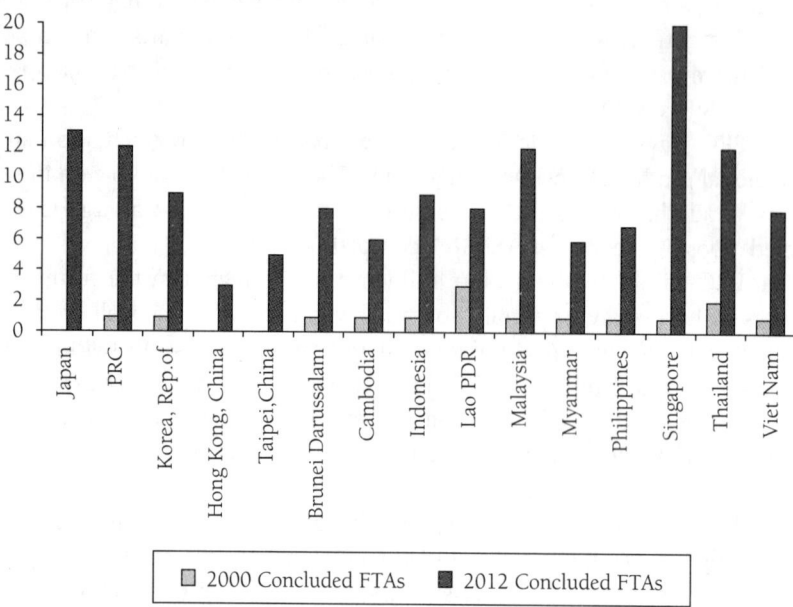

FTA = free trade agreement, Lao PDR = Lao People's Democratic Republic.
Source: Kawai and Wignaraja (2013).
Note: The above figures are FTAs both signed and in effect.

Lately, there is also an ongoing trend to seek partnership outside of the Asian region, particularly with India, EU, US, and South America. Japan, Republic of Korea, and PRC had been actively engaged in bilateral agreements and had become dynamic FTA movers in the world.

A significant development in FTA undertakings in the region is the start of negotiations of the Trans-Pacific Economic Partnership Agreement otherwise known as the TPP, and of the Regional Comprehensive Economic Partnership Agreement (RCEP). The TPP started as a free trade agreement between the four Pacific governments of Brunei Darussalam, Chile, New Zealand, and Singapore which was signed on 3 June 2005 and came into force on 1 January 2006. The TPP Agreement aims to create a free trade agreement that could serve as a model within the Asia-Pacific region. It is open to accession of APEC economies, subject to terms agreed among the parties. In September 2008, the US Trade Representative announced that the US will negotiate entry into the TPP agreement. Australia, Peru, and Viet Nam also announced that they want to be part of this FTA. There is also a strong support from Chile for

Republic of Korea to join in this agreement. The TPP is seen as a possible pathway for the creation of a wider Free Trade Area in APEC (FTAAP). By November 2011, broad outlines of a more comprehensive and deeper TPP had been discussed by leaders of Australia, Brunei Darussalam, Chile, Malaysia, New Zealand, Peru, Singapore, Viet Nam, and the United States. Significant progress had been made on the negotiations and participating countries are now on the way of concluding the comprehensive agreement in time for its accelerated track in 2013.

Meanwhile, the Regional Comprehensive Economic Partnership (RCEP) Agreement was initiated during the 19th ASEAN Summit in November 2011. It is a comprehensive FTA scheme involving the 10 ASEAN countries and its FTA partners, Australia, the PRC, India, Japan, Republic of Korea and New Zealand, and covering trade in goods, services, investment, economic and technical cooperation, intellectual property, competition and other key issues. Negotiations for RCEP started in early 2013 and are scheduled to end in 2015.

Kawai (2007) described the East Asian FTAs as either bilateral (between two countries) or plurilateral (agreement among three or more countries), outward-oriented (seeking partnership outside of the region), with WTO-Plus coverage of issues beyond trade and services liberalization, particularly trade facilitation, investment, government procurement, and competition, and consisting of multiple ROOs, as most FTAs in East Asia take on a combination of three types of ROO rather than applying a single rule.

Additionally, Kawai noted that East Asian FTAs have cooperation components that aim to address the asymmetry in economic size and development between partner countries. Japan's bilateral initiative, called the Economic Partnership Agreement (EPA), is referred to as a "new age FTA" and typically includes trade facilitation and cooperation. Likewise, the PRC's bilateral FTAs with individual ASEAN countries focus on economic and technical cooperation, with a more lenient schedule for tariff liberalization.

Recap on Asian Regionalism

In East Asia, there seems to be cautious approach and a deliberate effort to stay within WTO principles and open regionalism. East Asian countries appear to be mindful of the need for RTAs as building blocs for regional multilateralism. RTA initiatives in East Asia tend to work within a regional cooperation framework in order to seek solutions, opportunities, and institutions to address issues beyond trade and investments, such as social and environmental issues in the region.

Asian regionalism is characterized by open, gradual, and flexible systems that are responsive to the region's varying economic, political, and cultural realities. It does not follow a single track or fixed deadline, but rather is multi-track and multi-speed in order to account for the economic and political diversity of the member economies. Asian regionalism also takes on a bottom up approach. This means encouraging the countries, gradually, to make the necessary conditions for economic cooperation, e.g., creating subgroups or working groups that will address common domestic issues that impede regional cooperation. While some analysts refer to this as shallow integration, these characteristics have been lauded as necessary and desirable features of the Asian regionalism model to provide the foundation for wider collaboration and deeper partnerships in the long run (ADB 2008).

Asian regionalism is the product of economic interaction and outward-oriented growth strategies, reinforced by the integration of both policy and technology. The Asian financial crisis in 1997 highlighted the deep connections among economies in the region. The crisis has been referred to as the watershed of regionalism in Asia and exemplified the interdependence of the countries in the region. It also showed the importance of creating sound institutions and good governance to sustain economic growth (ADB 2008).

Regional Financial Cooperation and Integration

Sustained regional growth and integration in trade and investment increase the need to strengthen the regional financial architecture. Indeed, several financial cooperation and integration initiatives have been undertaken in the region.

Even before the 1997 crisis, ASEAN finance ministers had already agreed to work together on three important issues: strengthening the supervisory and regulatory framework of the banking sector, liberalizing the financial services, and evaluating the utility of the ASEAN Swap Arrangement (ASA) (Soesastro 2006).

Following the crisis, interest in financial cooperation intensified. Efforts toward increased risk management made East Asia the first region to actively pursue measures to establish regional monetary and financial cooperation. The regional economies embarked on several initiatives to strengthen the regional financial architecture, consisting of regional economic surveillance, liquidity support facility, and the development of the Asian bond market (Kawai 2007).

Several regional surveillance measures were launched in East Asia following the financial crisis. One of the most important of these measures is the ASEAN+3 Economic Review and Policy Dialogue (ERPD) process, which was launched in May 2000. The ASEAN+3 ERPD aims to prevent another financial crisis by creating channels for information sharing, assessment of economic conditions and policies, and potential for collaboration on financial, monetary, and fiscal issues of common interest.

The Chiang Mai Initiative (CMI) is considered to be the centerpiece of the liquidity support facility in East Asia and aims to address short-term liquidity needs in the event of a financial crisis or contagion and to supplement the existing financial arrangements. The CMI has two elements: the ASA and the network of 16 bilateral swap arrangements (BSAs) among ASEAN+3 members. Programs to link the CMI with IMF programs are currently underway to supplement the region's limited capacity to produce and enforce adjustment programs in the event of a crisis.

The idea of creating a regional bond fund crystallized after the 1997 financial crisis as East Asia saw the need to develop local currency bond markets as a means to lessen the region's heavy dependence on banks. The basic idea was to create a channel to mobilize the region's vast pool of savings directly toward investment in the region's long-term financial stability without going through financial centers outside of the region. Among the initiatives undertaken at the regional level are the Asian Bond Fund (ABF) initiative and the Asian Bond Markets Initiative (ABMI). Both were under the auspices of Executives' Meeting of East Asia and Pacific Central Banks (EMEAP) and the finance ministers of ASEAN+3. Alongside these initiatives are the APEC finance ministers' process and the Asia-Cooperation Dialogue (ACD) process, both of which aim to support the Asian bond market development.

Interregional Cooperation: Prospects for an East Asia–LAC Economic Partnership

The Asia and Pacific region and Latin America are characterized by wide disparity economically, politically, and culturally. The Asia and Pacific region is densely populated, accounting for more than 60% of the global population. In stark contrast, Latin America's share in world population is only 2% of the total global population. ASEAN+6 population alone comprise 48% of world population. Asia and the Pacific's population will continue to increase in 2020 and 2030, although the share of ASEAN+6 to total world population will decrease from 48% to 46%. Asia and the Pacific's huge population and vast market potential will remain to be formidable in the next couple of decades and can provide vast opportunities for investors from Latin American countries.

Asia and Pacific region's share to total world GDP in 2011 was more than 30%, surpassing North America and Europe. Latin America, however, constitutes a modest 8% of total world output. ASEAN+3's share to world GDP alone is at 26%, which is more than Europe and North America's GDP at 22% and 21% respectively. In terms of world merchandise trade the Asia and Pacific region is responsible for more than a quarter of the world's total at 28%, while Latin America's share is only 5%. In world services trade, Asia likewise commands almost a quarter of trade in services at 22%, while Latin America and the Caribbean's share remained small at 3% (Tables 10.5–10.8).

Until recently, economic relations between the Asia and Pacific region and Latin American and Caribbean countries were weak and the two regions did not have much opportunity for dialogue and cooperation. APEC has become the forum for this opportunity, facilitating information exchange between the two regions.

Tariff barriers remain as impediment to increasing trade between the two regions. While average tariff rates have significantly fallen over the past years in the two regions, the average regional most favored nation (MFN) tariff in Latin America and Caribbean is higher than in the East Asia and Pacific average, especially for agricultural products. Japan and Republic of Korea, however, remain to have very high tariff walls on its agriculture sector (Table 10.9).

The PRC's entry into the global economy added a new dynamism to the Asia and Pacific region and Latin America's relationship. Table 10.10 shows the ranking of PRC, Japan and Republic of Korea as trade partners in Latin American countries. The highlighted figures show improvement in the trade relationship with Latin America. The table shows that for the two mentioned periods, PRC showed the most improved trade relationship and plays an important role in increasing trade relations between the two regions. As of 2007, the PRC gained significant market share in 21 economies and had become one of the top 5 exporters to Argentina, Brazil, Chile, and Mexico. The PRC was also a top importer of goods from Latin American and Caribbean countries, ranking among the top 5 importers in all 23 countries listed in the table (Table 10.10).

Table 10.5
Population

	Total population million							Share to total world population %						
	1990	1995	2000	2005	2012	2015	2030	1990	2000	2005	2012	2015	2020	2030
Asia and the Pacific														
ASEAN	443	484	524	561	596	632	721	8.0	9.0	9.0	9.0	9.0	9.0	9.0
ASEAN+3	1,774	1,891	1,976	2,053	2,132	2,210	2,347	33.0	32.0	32.0	31.0	30.0	29.0	28.0
ASEAN+6	2,663	2,868	3,041	3,205	3,364	3,521	3,857	50.0	50.0	49.0	48.0	48.0	47.0	46.0
ECO	445	486	526	563	596	630	717	8.0	9.0	9.0	9.0	9.0	9.0	9.0
SAARC	1,135	1,260	1,382	1,499	1,607	1,714	1,994	21.0	23.0	23.0	23.0	23.0	24.0	24.0
Latin America & Caribbean	98	112	125	143	165	183	231	2.0	2.0	2.0	2.0	3.0	3.0	3.0
Other world regions														
Africa	290	324	357	387	419	452	541	5.0	6.0	6.0	6.0	6.0	6.0	6.0
Europe	282	297	315	331	347	361	403	5.0	5.0	5.0	5.0	5.0	5.0	5.0
North America	1,135	1,260	1,382	1,499	1,607	1,714	1,994	21.0	23.0	23.0	23.0	23.0	24.0	24.0
Other countries/areas	98	112	125	143	165	183	231	2.0	2.0	2.0	2.0	3.0	3.0	3.0
World	5,320	5,714	6,174	6,916	7,324	7,716	8,424							

ASEAN = Association of Southeast Asian Nations, ECO = Economic Cooperation Organization, SAARC = South Asian Association for Regional Cooperation.
Source: 2012 data exported from United Nations Economic and Social Commission for Asia and the Pacific website (unescap.org) (accessed 13 November 2013) (UNESCAP 2008).

Table 10.6
GDP

	GDP PPP million 2005 US$			Average GDP growth rate %			Share to world GDP %		
	1990	2005	2011	1991–2001	2000–2005	2005–2010	1990	2005	2011
ASEAN	1,030,435	2,143,933	2,883,229	4.6	5.1	5.3	2.9	4.2	4.2
ASEAN+3	6,044,366	10,742,668	18,143,744	5.4	5.2	5.2	17.1	26.1	26.6
ASEAN+6	7,573,194	17,254,742	23,005,908	5.0	5.0	4.6	21.5	33.1	33.8
ECO	1,199,462	2,048,622	1,882,396	2.4	5.4	4.4	3.4	4.0	2.8
SAARC	1,366,045	3,142,074	4,819,464	5.5	6.6	7.6	3.9	2.7	7.1
Latin America & Caribbean	3,022,185	4,775,278	6,028,319	2.9	2.6	3.6	8.6	6.9	8.8
Africa	1,251,887	2,137,743	2,750,528	2.6	5.3	5.7	3.5	4.0	4.0
Europe	10,680,386	14,281,737	15,323,989	2.2	2	1	30.3	22.9	22.5
North America	8,711,322	13,696,300	14,469,877	3.5	2.4	0.7	24.7	21.6	21.2
Other countries/areas	649,536	1,439,612	1,747,138	4.5	4.3	4.6	1.8	2.7	2.6
World	35,289,990	56,440,993	68,119,677	2.8	2.9	2.3	100.0	100.0	100.0

ASEAN = Association of Southeast Asian Nations, ECO = Economic Cooperation Organization, GDP = gross domestic product, PPP = purchasing power parity, SAARC = South Asian Association for Regional Cooperation.
Source: United Nations Economic and Social Commission for Asia and the Pacific website (unescap.org) (accessed 19 November 2013) (UNESCAP 2008).

Table 10.7
Merchandise Trade, 2012 (US$ billion)

	Import		Export	
	Value	World share	Value	World share
ASEAN	1,221,456	6.6	1,253,514	6.8
ASEAN+3	4,444,954	23.9	4,648,765	25.4
ASEAN+6	5,233,515	28.2	5,236,115	28.6
ECO	427,993	2.3	427,720	2.3
SAARC	602,014	3.2	354,617	1.9
Latin America & Caribbean	1,132,236	6.1	1,119,715	6.1
Africa	602,947	3.2	625,664	3.4
Europe	6,312,007	34.0	6,336,034	34.6
North America	2,812,034	15.1	2,002,614	10.9
Other countries/areas	935,404	5.0	1,492,772	8.1
World	18,567,000	100	18,323,000	100

ASEAN = Association of Southeast Asian Nations, ECO = Economic Cooperation Organization, SAARC = South Asian Association for Regional Cooperation.
Source: United Nations Economic and Social Commission for Asia and the Pacific website (unescap.org) (accessed 19 November 2013) (UNESCAP 2008).

Table 10.8
Services, 2012 (US$ billion)

	Import		Export	
	Value	World share	Value	World share
ASEAN	273,483	6.7	271,794	6.3
ASEAN+3	833,199	20.3	710,642	16.3
ASEAN+6	1,034,601	25.2	921,047	21.2
ECO	49,106	1.2	57,249	1.3
SAARC	137,982	3.4	154,319	3.6
Latin America & Caribbean	195,662	4.8	130,140	3.0
Africa	161,700	3.9	89,600	2.1
Europe	1,627,773	39.6	2,003,099	46.1
North America	511,944	12.5	692,622	15.9
Other countries/areas				
World	4,105,700	100	4,346,900	100

ASEAN = Association of Southeast Asian Nations, ECO = Economic Cooperation Organization, SAARC = South Asian Association for Regional Cooperation.
Source: United Nations Economic and Social Commission for Asia and the Pacific website (unescap.org) (accessed 19 November 2013) (UNESCAP 2008).

Table 10.9
Tariff Trade Restrictiveness Index (TTRI)

	MFN applied tariff all goods 2006–2008	MFN applied tariff agricultural 2006–2008	MFN applied tariff non-agricultural 2006–2008
People's Republic of China	5.33	11.40	5.05
Republic of Korea	8.20	65.30	4.40
Japan	4.75	29.36	1.37
ASEAN Average	4.60	6.51	4.57
East Asia & Pacific Average	4.89	8.23	4.69
Latin America & Caribbean Average	7.84	13.34	6.97
World	7.19	13.54	6.48

ASEAN = Association of Southeast Asian Nations, MFN = most favored nation.
Source: World Bank World Trade Indicators (2008) (http://info.worldbank.org/etools/wti2008/3a.asp?)

Table 10.11 shows Latin America's export destinations by region. In 2007, 45% of Latin America and Caribbean's export went to the United States. The United States remain to be the region's biggest export market. Export to Latin America was 18%. European Union received 14% of exports, while Asia and the Pacific received 11% and the rest of the world received 11% of exports from Latin America and Caribbean countries. As could be expected, Mexico, due to its proximity to US and membership in NAFTA, was the biggest exporter to US, with 65% of its exports destined for the US market. Panama was the biggest exporter to EU, with 33% of its exports going to EU. Meanwhile, Chile was the biggest exporter to Asia and the Pacific region for that year, with almost 40% of its exports captured by the Asia and the Pacific region (Table 10.11).

In terms of trade composition, the Asia and Pacific region's export basket consists mainly of manufactures, with a high concentration in the medium tech and high tech manufactures. Asia Pacific received most of these exports at 48%, consistent with the pattern of strong intra-regional trade in the Asia Pacific. For the Asia Pacific region, United States and European Union were only secondary markets for exports, receiving 17% and 14% of exports from the region, respectively.

In contrast, primary products dominate the export basket of Latin America, which account for 34% of its exports. Most of these products went to the Asia Pacific region, at 58% of total exports. Japan was the biggest destination of the primary exports. Medium tech manufactures were also significant at 23%, with most of the exports going to the Latin American region and the United States.

Table 10.10
Latin America and the Caribbean: Ranking of the PRC, Japan, and the Republic of Korea in Each Country's Trade, 2000 and 2007

	Exports						Imports					
	PRC		Japan		Rep. of Korea		PRC		Japan		Rep. of Korea	
Reporter	2000	2007	2000	2007	2000	2007	2000	2007	2000	2007	2000	2007
South America												
Argentina	6	2	13	19	27	24	4	3	6	10	11	14
Bolivia	18	10	20	5	24	6	7	6	5	9	14	23
Brazil	12	2	5	6	18	18	11	2	4	7	8	8
Chile	5	1	2	3	8	5	4	2	5	6	8	72
Colombia	35	6	9	17	28	25	15	4	3	6	13	8
Ecuador	20	17	4	15	2	47	12	4	4	5	10	7
Paraguay	17	19	10	14	34	44	5	4	8	5	12	8
Peru	4	2	5	5	10	11	13	2	7	10	12	11
Uruguay	4	5	15	13	23	32	7	4	14	16	16	19
Venezuela (Bol. Rep. of)	37	3	16	18	35	35	18	4	7	7		
Central America												
Costa Rica	26	2	17	15	63	25	16	5	4	4	40	8
El Salvador	43	27	14	14	39	25	21	4	7	12	15	15
Guatemala	41	18	8	11	18	9	8	3	6	8	3	5
Honduras	59	22	3	16	15	15	8	6	6	10	4	8
Mexico	25	5	5	6	28	25	6	2	2	4	5	3
Nicaragua	22	28	17	14	30	44	18	6	7	9		8
Panama	27	31	12	23	30	41	22	2	4	1	8	15

(Table 10.10 Contd)

(Table 10.10 Contd)

Reporter	Exports							Imports						
	PRC		Japan		Rep. of Korea		PRC		Japan		Rep. of Korea	
	2000	2007	2000	2007	2000	2007	2000	2007	2000	2007	2000	2007
Caribbean												
Bahamas		13	7	25	32	58	24	10	4	4	3	3
Barbados	40	23	36	34	50	69	9	6	4	5	21	19
Belize			5	15		28	17	5	8	19	19	23
Cuba	5	2	9	23		43	5	2	18	12		11
Dominican Republic	21	10	17	11	9	9	12	5	4	8	8	16
Dominica		1	23	11		30	23	2	4	6	31	4
Grenada		40		40			16	15	4	6	15	17
Guyana	17	13	15	18	28	30	9	3	7	7	30	20
Haiti	38	9	12	17	31	57	11	3	5	8	16	17
Jamaica	13	8	7	10	51	55	9	4	3	5	22	29
Saint Kitts and Nevis	8	42	9	18		32	28	20	5	5	30	38
Saint Lucia	19	19	12	30		44	8	14	4	7	30	28
Saint Vincent and the Grenadines			19	23		36	18	5	5	6	30	42
Suriname	24	22	9	20	51	48	8	4	4	5	20	20
Trinidad and Tobago	51	34	46	13	42	29	10	6	6	8	18	21

▨ Indicates an improvement in the respective country's ranking between 2000 and 2007.

PRC = People's Republic of China.

Source: Economic Commission for Latin America and the Caribbean (2008), on the basis of data of International Monetary Fund Direction of Trade Statistics.

Table 10.11
Latin America and the Caribbean Exports by Major Exports Region, 2007[a]

	United States	European Union (27)	Asia and the Pacific[b]	Latin America and the Caribbean	Rest of the world
Latin America & Caribbean	45.4	14	11.2	18.4	11.1
Argentina	7.8	17.5	17.1	38.8	18.8
Bolivia	8.9	7.7	8.4	61.4	13.7
Brazil	15.8	25.2	16.1	25.4	17.6
Chile	12.3	22.9	39.5	16.3	9
Colombia	36.9	15.2	4.1	35.5	8.3
Costa Rica	37.2	14.4	20.7	24.6	3.1
Cuba[c]	0	31.8	18.8	11.1	38.2
Ecuador	43.5	12.7	3.2	32.5	8.1
El Salvador	50.6	6.3	1.2	39.2	2.7
Guatemala	42.7	5.2	3.2	41.3	7.7
Honduras	58.9	16.3	0.9	20.6	3.4
Mexico	82.2	5.3	3	6	3.4
Nicaragua	62.7	7.2	1.5	22.4	6.2
Panama	39.8	33.5	1.8	18.7	6.1
Paraguay	2	6.9	3.5	72.1	15.5
Peru	19.1	17.1	19.2	18.4	26.2
Dominican Republic	65.6	12.6	2.1	4.9	14.8
Uruguay	11	18.5	8.6	37.1	24.9
Venezuela (Bolivarian Rep. of)[c]	52.9	10	5.1	15.1	17
CARICOM[c]	47.9	13.1	3.2	22.4	13.5

■ Greater than 40%   ▪ Greater than 15% but less than 40%

CARICOM = Caribbean Community and Common Market.
Source: ECLAC (2008), on the basis of official country information and estimates based on International Monetary Fund Direction of Trade Statistics.
Notes: [a] Preliminary figures.
[b] Includes not only the 12 economies in Asia and the Pacific, but also others in developing Asia.
[c] Estimates by the Economic Commission for Latin America and the Caribbean (ECLAC).

Exports from Latin America and Caribbean to Asia Pacific are mostly primary products, while the Asia and Pacific region exports high tech and medium tech manufactures to the Latin American and Caribbean region (Table 10.12). Unless trade diversification is achieved, this could present an impediment to future bi-regional trade and investment (UNECLAC 2008).

Table 10.3 shows the score of Asia Pacific and Latin America in the Grubel Lloyd (GL) Index. The Grubel-Lloyd Index is a widely used indicator to measure the extent of intra-industry trade as opposed to inter-industry trade. High intra-industry trade will bring the GL index equal to one. Lack of intra-industry trade will bring the GL index to zero. The index varies from zero (all inter-industry trade) to one (all intra-industry trade), and the sum over the shares of the two mutually exclusive forms of trade amounts to one in each country's aggregate trade (Lee 2004).

Overall, the level of bi-regional trade between Latin America and the Asia and Pacific region is still low, according to the 2006 Grubel Lloyd Index (GLI) scores. However, some increase in bi-regional trade can be seen in Mexico, Costa Rica, Argentina, and Brazil (Table 10.13). On the Asia and Pacific region's side, Singapore and Australia are moving into intra-industry trade with Latin America. The products traded range from high and medium technology goods to low technology products. High technology goods traded include electrical apparatuses, parts and accessories, microcircuits, automatic data processing machines, and quality control instruments. Medium technology goods being traded are products that are considered general machinery, while low technology products include textile, yarn, and iron and steel products (UNECLAC 2008).

Overall, the data showed that generally, trade and investment relations between East Asia and Latin America are still relatively underdeveloped, leaving room for more coordination and closer trade and investment linkages. There is a growing awareness in both regions of the need and importance to enhance economic cooperation between the two regions, as demonstrated by the growing number of FTAs that have been signed or are being negotiated between the two regions. As of 2013, these FTAs had expanded, with 22 FTAs in effect, 5 under negotiations and 11 more proposed. (Wignaraja et al. 2012)

Some Impediments to Economic Cooperation

Action toward improving the economic relationship of the two regions had substantially increased in the past decades. This is shown by the rising number of FTAs, as well as several initiatives to increase in interregional trade

Table 10.12
Latin America and Asia-Pacific: Trade by Regions and Products by Technology Intensity, 2006

Products by Technological Intensity	Asia-Pacific Export matrix							Asia-Pacific Export distribution by region and sector						
	LAC	United States	European Union	Asia-Pacific	PRC	Japan	Others	Total	LAC	United States	European Union	Asia-Pacific	PRC	Japan	Others	Total
Primary Products	0.1	0.5	0.6	4.5	0.8	1.7	1.3	7	3	2.6	4.3	9.3	9.2	21.1	8.2	7
NRB Manufactures	0.3	1.4	1.4	7.6	1.4	1.3	2	12.6	7.1	7.8	9.5	15.5	15.8	16.7	13.2	12.6
Low Tech Manufactures	0.6	3.9	2.8	6.3	0.7	1.5	3.3	17	17	22	19.5	12.9	8	19.4	21.8	17
Medium Tech Manufactures	1.6	6.2	4.3	12.3	2.7	1.3	6.1	30.6	45.1	34.7	29.9	25.3	30.5	16.4	39.8	30.6
High Tech Manufactures	0.8	5.5	4.8	16.3	2.9	1.8	2.4	29.9	23.3	30.9	33.4	33.5	32.8	23.2	15.9	29.9
Other Transactions	0.1	0.3	0.4	1.3	0.2	0.1	0.7	2.9	4.1	1.8	2.9	2.6	2.5	1	4.8	2.9
Total	3.6	17.9	14.5	48.7	8.7	7.9	15.3	100	100	100	100	100	100	100	100	100

(Table 10.12 Contd)

(Table 10.12 Contd)

Products by Technological Intensity	Latin America and the Caribbean Export matrix								Latin America and the Caribbean Export distribution by region and sector						
	LAC	United States	European Union	Asia–Pacific	PRC	Japan	Others	Total	LAC	United States	European Union	Asia–Pacific	PRC	Japan	Others	Total
Primary Products	3.5	12.6	5.8	5.6	2.2	1.7	7.3	34.8	20.9	26.5	46.1	58.5	61.8	73	54.5	34.8
NRB Manufactures	4	5.7	3.6	2.3	0.8	0.4	2.5	18.1	23.7	12	28.9	23.8	22.8	17.8	18.7	18.1
Low Tech Manufactures	1.9	5.1	0.7	0.3	0.1	0	0.4	8.4	11.5	10.7	5.2	3.5	3.7	1	2.7	8.4
Medium Tech Manufactures	5.5	14.2	1.9	0.9	0.2	0.1	1.3	23.8	33	29.7	15	8.9	6.9	6.3	10	23.8
High Tech Manufactures	1.6	9.2	0.5	0.5	0.2	0	0.6	12.5	9.8	19.3	4.4	5.1	4.8	1.8	4.5	12.5
Other Transactions	0.2	0.9	0	0	0	0	1.3	2.4	1.2	1.8	0.3	0.1	0	0.1	9.6	2.4
Total	16.7	47.8	12.5	9.6	3.6	2.3	13.4	100	100	100	100	100	100	100	100	100

LAC = Latin America and the Caribbean, NRB = natural resource-based, PRC = People's Republic of China.
Source: ECLAC (2008).

Table 10.13
Grubel Lloyd Indices for Some Latin America and Caribbean Countries with Asia-Pacific, 2006

Countries	Australia	PRC	Indonesia	Japan	Malaysia	New Zealand	Philippines	Rep. of Korea	Singapore	Thailand	Viet Nam
Argentina	0.08	0.03	0.02	0.02	0.01	0.17	0	0.03	0.13	0.02	0.01
Bolivia	0.01	0.01	0	0	0.01	0	0	0	0.02	0	0
Brazil	0.07	0.08	0.05	0.06	0.02	0.14	0.02	0.05	0.18	0.05	0.06
Chile	0.08	0.01	0	0	0.01	0.02	0.03	0.01	0.02	0.01	0
Colombia	0.18	0.02	0.02	0.01	0	0.03	0.01	0	0.13	0.07	0.06
Costa Rica	0.05	0.1	0.02	0.55	0.19	0.01	0.38	0.09	0.36	0.1	0.01
Dominican Rep.	0.12	0.03	0	0.04	0.08	0.01	0.01	0.03	0.27	0.03	...
Ecuador	0.05	0.01	0.01	0	0.08	0.02	0.03	0.01	0.19	0.01	0
El Salvador	0	0.01	0.01	0.01	0	0	0	0	0	0.01	0
Guatemala	0.02	0.03	0.03	0.01	0.01	0	0.02	0.02	0.03	0.04	0
Honduras	0	0.1	0	0	0	0	0	0.01	0	0.02	0
Mexico	0.15	0.27	0.09	0.16	0.24	0.03	0.11	0.09	0.56	0.37	0.02
Nicaragua	0	0	0	0	0	0	0	0	0	0	0.1
Panama	0.11	0	0	0	0	0	0	0.17	0	0	0
Paraguay	0	0	0	0	0	0.01	0.04	0	0	0	0
Peru	0.1	0.01	0.01	0.01	0	0.02	0.34	0.02	0.02	0.02	0
Uruguay	0.04	0.03	0.11	0	0.01	0.05	0	0.06	0.03	0	0
Venezuela (Bol. Rep. of)	0.07	0.01	0.01	0	0.03	0	0	0	0	0.02	0

IGL > 0, 33   IGL > 0, 10 < 0, 33   IGL < 0, 10

PRC = People's Republic of China.
Source: ECLAC (2008), on the basis of the United Nations Commodity Trade Statistics Database.

and investment between Latin America and Caribbean and the Asia Pacific. Several impediments still exist which hamper closer economic cooperation of the two regions. This section discusses some of the impediments, such as high tariffs, transport costs, logistics, quality control measures, and research and education gaps.

High Effective Tariffs in Agriculture and Natural Resource Based between the Two Regions

Agriculture is a sensitive sector in both regions and both imposed high applied tariffs to agriculture products. Natural resource products are also subject to high ad valorem and tariff quotas. The Asia Pacific region's agriculture sector is particularly heavily protected. Breaking down tariff barriers in the agriculture sector is one of the most important challenges that interregional FTAs have to surmount.

High Transport Costs and Lack of Available Direct Lines between Latin America and the Caribbean and the Asia Pacific

High freight costs put Latin America at a disadvantage for increasing its economic partnership with the Asia and Pacific region. Lack of maritime transport connections is one of the major trading barriers between the two regions and could limit potential growth. The maritime connections between the two regions are not yet adequately developed, unlike other maritime routes in several regions. Direct lines between Latin America and the Asia and Pacific region are available only to and from Chilean ports, while in the rest of the region several stops must be made in South Africa or other South American countries before setting course to Asia.

Need to Improve Trade Logistics in Some Countries in the Asia Pacific and Latin America and the Caribbean

While Latin America and Caribbean countries still have some catching up to do to improve its trade logistics and infrastructure, improvement can be seen in its performance in the 2012 World Bank's LPI. The region in general, has better LPI score than Lower middle income countries. Chile, Brazil, Mexico, Argentina, Peru, and Colombia also performed strongly in individual LPI indicators and overall LPI score. The rest of the LAC countries, however, still need to improve trade facilitation measures such as customs procedures, quality of port infrastructure and line shipping connectivity. In the Asia Pacific region, Myanmar, Cambodia, Lao PDR, Indonesia, Viet Nam, and Philippines were identified to have relatively low LPI ranking and need to work on improving customs efficiency and infrastructure (Table 10.14).

Quality Control Measures in Latin America and the Caribbean

The PRC and Japan account for 74% of all the quality control measures (ISO) issued in the two regions in 2012. PRC, in particular, acquired the most number of ISO Certification at 62%. Latin America, on the other hand, only acquired 8.2% of total ISO Certifications. Brazil and Colombia scored the highest in terms of number of certificates. While quality control measures are not necessarily obligatory, ISO certification is influential in determining competitiveness and influencing buying decisions of consumers (Table 10.15). Number of ISO certifications can also help attract foreign investors to invest or create a joint venture with local companies whose standards meet international criteria.

Research and Development Spending

Compared to research and development (R&D) spending in Japan and the NIEs, Latin America falls far behind. East Asia and the Pacific, as a whole have more than 722 researchers engaged in R&D per million people, when including Australia and New Zealand, while Latin America only has 256. However, for some aspects of R&D, Latin America fares better than ASEAN countries. For instance, Argentina fared better than ASEAN in terms of patents granted to residents, and Argentina, Chile, Uruguay, Mexico, and Brazil have more researchers engaged in R&D compared to ASEAN-member countries (Table 10.16).

Education Gap between the Two Regions

Asian countries, with the exception of Thailand and Indonesia, consistently rank high in the Programme for International Student Assessment (PISA) Survey of student skills in science, mathematics, and reading. PISA survey covers almost 90% of the world economy in assessing the knowledge and skills of students in three areas. In contrast, Latin America falls far behind, ranking along with Middle East and Eastern Europe (Table 10.17).

Table 10.14
Logistics Performance Indicator, 2012

	Logistics performance index 1–5 (worst to best)	Burden of customs procedures 1–7 (worst to best)	Lead time days		Documents number		Quality of port infrastructure 1–7 (worst to best)	Freight costs to the United States 1 kilogram DHL nondocument air package US$
			To export	To import	To export	To import		
World	2.87	4.1	4.2	5.9	6	7	4.3	113.8
Low income	2.36	3.5	9.4	11.9	8	10	3.4	154.4
Middle income	2.69	3.7	3.8	6.1	7	8	3.8	90.75
Lower middle income	2.58	3.7	4.5	7.4	7	8	3.8	90.75
Upper middle income	2.78	3.8	3.3	4.9	7	7	3.9	116.93
Low & middle income	2.6	3.7	5.1	7.5	7	8	3.7	150.4
East Asia & Pacific	2.77	3.8	2.6	2.6	7	7	3.9	88.5
Europe & Central Asia	2.73	3.7	3	5.4	7	8	3.3	150.4
Latin America & Caribbean	2.67	3.5	4.1	5.2	6	7	3.8	88.55
Middle East & North Africa	2.58	3.6	3.1	7.1	7	8	3.8	143.1
South Asia	2.58	3.7	3.3	4.2	8	9	3.9	90.75
Sub-Saharan Africa	2.46	3.8	9.3	12.9	8	9	3.9	154.4
High income	3.48	4.8	2.4	2.8	5	6	5.2	108.4
Euro area	3.56	4.9	1.8	2.6	4	5	5.3	113.8

Source: World Bank World Development Indicators 2013. http://data.worldbank.org/data-catalog/world-development-indicators (accessed 22 July 2014).

Table 10.15
ISO Certifications in 2012, by Standard

	9001 Quality management systems	13485 Quality for medical device	14001 Environmental management systems	16949 Quality for automotive production	22000 Food safety management systems	27001 Information security management systems	Total	% Share
Asia-Pacific								
PRC	334,032	765	91,590	17,975	8,228	1,490	454,080	62.2
Japan	50,339	752	27,774	1,237	762	7,199	88,063	12.1
Republic of Korea	25,706	212	11,479	4,454	203	181	42,235	5.8
Malaysia	11,746	228	1,906	461	206	100	14,647	2.0
Thailand	8,711	75	3,034	1,147	235	96	13,298	1.8
Taipei,China	8,378	565	2,042	1,037	321	855	13,198	1.8
Australia	9,185	82	2,000	143	133	113	11,656	1.6
Singapore	5,817	162	1,653	93	108	65	7,898	1.1
Viet Nam	6,144	25	775	108	315	44	7,411	1.0
Indonesia	5,392	22	1,035	201	222	35	6,907	0.9
Hong Kong, China	3,708	44	1,060	8	73	110	5,003	0.7
Philippines	1,904	14	562	118	69	66	2,733	0.4

(Table 10.15 Contd)

(Table 10.15 Contd)

	9001 Quality management systems	13485 Quality for medical device	14001 Environmental management systems	16949 Quality for automotive production	22000 Food safety management systems	27001 Information security management systems	Total	% Share
New Zealand	983	15	218	2	13	5	1,236	0.2
Macau, China	127		47		3	13	190	0.0
Brunei Darussalam	70		24		2		96	0.0
Myanmar	45	1	5		1		52	0.0
Cambodia	13	2	10				25	0.0
Lao PDR	13		2		3		18	0.0
Latin America & Caribbean								
Brazil	25,791	127	3,300	1,180	171	53	30,622	4.2
Colombia	9,883	46	1,441	74	46	58	11,548	1.6
Argentina	6,605	60	1,268	248	108	33	8,322	1.1
Chile	3,986	3	1,080	3	74	23	5,169	0.7
Peru	928	7	295	2	7	7	1,246	0.2
Ecuador	943		151	16	26	3	1,139	0.2
Uruguay	741	6	117	8	13	7	892	0.1
Venezuela	622		93	29	8		752	0.1
Costa Rica	237	23	81	7	15	7	370	0.1

Bolivia	187	1	44	15	1	248	0.0
Paraguay	227		12	4		243	0.0
Dominican Republic	188	9	31	3	3	237	0.0
Guatemala	181		15	17	1	214	0.0
El Salvador	187		14	2	1	205	0.0
Panama	111		16	5	2	134	0.0
Cuba	60		6			66	0.0
Nicaragua	46		6	3		59	0.0
Total	**523,236**	**3,246**	**153,186**	**28,559**	**11,414**	**10,571**	**730,212**	**100.0**

Lao PDR = Lao People's Democratic Republic, PRC = People's Republic of China.

Source: International Organization for Standardization (ISO) Survey, 2012. www.iso.org/iso/home/standards/certification/iso-survey.htm?certificate=ISO%209001&countrycode=AF (accessed 22 July 2014).

Table 10.16
Some Research and Development Indicators

HDI Rank		Patents granted to residents per million people 2000–2005[a]	Receipts of royalties and license fees US$ per person 2005	Research and development (R&D) expenditure % of GDP 2000–2005[a]	Researchers in R&D per million people 1990–2005[a]
3	Australia	31	25	1.7	3,759
8	Japan	857	138	3.1	5,287
19	New Zealand	31	627.9	1.8	4,301
21	Hong Kong, China	5	31.2	0.6	1,564
25	New Zealand	96	125.8	2.3	4,999
26	Republic of Korea	1,113	38.2	2.6	3,187
30	Brunei Darussalam	..	..	0	274
63	Malaysia	..	1.1	0.7	299
78	Thailand	1	0.3	0.3	287
81	PRC	16	0.1	1.4	708
90	Philippines	(.)	0.1	0.1	48
105	Viet Nam	(.)	..	0.2	115
107	Indonesia	..	1.2	0.1	207
128	India	1	(.)	0.8	119
132	Myanmar	..	0	0.1	17
East Asia and the Pacific		..	1.7	1.6	722
38	Argentina	4	1.4	0.4	720
40	Chile	1	3.3	0.6	444
46	Uruguay	1	(.)	0.3	366
48	Costa Rica	..	0	0.4	..
51	Cuba	3	..	0.6	..
52	Mexico	1	0.7	0.4	268
62	Panama	..	0	0.3	97
70	Brazil	1	0.5	1	344
74	Venezuela (Bolivarian Republic of)	1	0	0.3	..
75	Colombia	(.)	0.2	0.2	109
79	Dominican Republic	..	0	..	..
87	Peru	(.)	0.1	0.1	226
89	Ecuador	0	0	0.1	50

(Table 10.16 Contd)

(Table 10.16 Contd)

HDI Rank		Patents granted to residents per million people 2000–2005[a]	Receipts of royalties and license fees US$ per person 2005	Research and development (R&D) expenditure % of GDP 2000–2005[a]	Researchers in R&D per million people 1990–2005[a]
95	Paraguay	..	33.2	0.1	79
101	Jamaica	1	4.7	0.1	..
103	El Salvador	..	0.4	0.1	47
110	Nicaragua	1	0	0	73
115	Honduras	1	0	0	..
117	Bolivia	..	0.2	0.3	120
118	Guatemala	(.)	(.)	..	..
Latin America & Caribbean		..	1.1	0.6	256
OECD		239	104.2	2.4	3,096
World		..	21.6	2.3	..

OECD = Organisation for Economic Co-operation and Development, PRC = People's Republic of China.
Source: United Nations Development Programme Human Development Report 2007/2008. http://hdr.undp.org/sites/default/files/reports/268/hdr_20072008_en_complete.pdf (accessed 22 July 2014).
Note: [a] Data refer to the most recent year available during the period specified.

Conclusion

While geographic proximity is important in establishing economic relations, in a globalized world it no longer stands as the primary factor for countries or regions to engage in closer economic cooperation. The commitment to create an environment conducive for economic growth and development is just as essential, if not more essential, than physical proximity when engaging in regional cooperation. Asia and the Pacific and Latin America and Caribbean regions are geographically far and had not shared strong trade relationship in the past. This is slowly changing in the past decade, as shown by the increase in number of FTAs and the growing trade and FDI links between the two regions.

However, there are still many things that need to be done before the Asia and Pacific region and Latin America and the Caribbean can engage in a meaningful economic partnership. Gaps and bottlenecks exist that must be addressed.

Table 10.17
PISA Rankings and Scores, 2006

	A. Science			B. Mathematics			C. Reading	
Rank	Economy	Science	Rank	Economy	Mathematics	Rank	Economy	Reading
2	Hong Kong, China	542	1	Taipei, China	549	1	Republic of Korea	556
4	Taipei, China	532	3	Hong Kong, China	547	3	Hong Kong, China	536
6	Japan	531	4	Republic of Korea	547	5	New Zealand	521
7	New Zealand	530	8	Macao, China	525	7	Australia	513
8	Australia	527	10	Japan	523	15	Japan	498
11	Republic of Korea	522	11	New Zealand	522	16	Taipei, China	496
17	Macao, China	511	13	Australia	520	21	Macao, China	492
OECD	AVERAGE	500	OECD	AVERAGE	498	OECD	AVERAGE	492
40	Chile	438	42	Uruguay	427	38	Chile	442
43	Uruguay	428	44	Thailand	417	41	Thailand	417
46	Thailand	421	47	Chile	411	42	Uruguay	413
49	Mexico	410	48	Mexico	406	43	Mexico	410
50	Indonesia	393	50	Indonesia	391	48	Indonesia	393
51	Argentina	391	52	Argentina	381	49	Brazil	393
52	Brazil	390	53	Colombia	370	51	Colombia	385
53	Colombia	388	54	Brazil	370	53	Argentina	374

OECD = Organisation for Economic Co-operation and Development, PISA = Programme for International Student Assessment.
Sources: OECD. PISA 2006: Science Competencies for Tomorrow's World. http://www.oecd.org/fr/education/scolaire/programmeinternationalpourlesuivi desacquisdeselevespisa/pisa2006results.htm (accessed 22 July 2014).

The two regions are characterized by stark structural and policy differences. Production structures and export capacities are very different. Bi-regional economic links have remained weak and have shown little diversification as inter-industry trade still accounts for most of the trade flows, with the Asia and Pacific region exporting manufactures and Latin America and the Caribbean exporting primary commodities to the Asia and Pacific region. Regional trade links should be strengthened and trade and investment partnerships harnessed. Latin America and the Caribbean, as a whole, should work on product diversification to integrate itself in the supply chain networks of the Asia and Pacific region. It should also capitalize on complementary trade opportunities between the two regions and create partnership for innovation and competitiveness.

Market access, high transportation costs, and weak small and medium enterprises (SMEs) have been identified as major obstacles that should be given adequate attention in order to strengthen the partnership between the two regions. One of the biggest challenges for Latin American countries is gaining market access to the Asia and Pacific region. The Asia and the Pacific region has a relatively highly protected agriculture sector. This issue could be addressed by FTAs being undertaken between Latin America and the Asia and Pacific region to develop trade agreements that would bring down tariff barriers in Asia's agricultural sector and enhance market access of Latin American countries to Asia and the Pacific's developed and emerging economies. Trade facilitation initiatives should also be undertaken. It is also important to study the maritime and air transportation systems of the regions, focusing specifically on how to bring down freight costs. Finally, it is important to strengthen SMEs and trade associations to achieve scale economies for small and medium exporters. Also, the two regions should explore possible cooperation in technological upgrading and bringing down the risks associated with new ventures (UNECLAC 2008).

Building partnerships to enhance the competitiveness and innovation of Latin America is also important. There are a broad range of issues that the two regions can work on, such as financing to improve infrastructure and logistics and other macroeconomic issues that would eventually strengthen trade and investment links.

As an initial step, information exchange and policy dialogue between the two regions should be enhanced, particularly on areas leading to more market opportunities, market access, and investments. FTAs should also be deepened to ease trade between the two regions.

Existing interregional forums could be used as a platform to advance cooperation between Latin America and the Pacific. APEC, for instance, could leverage its Economic and Technical Cooperation (ECOTECH) and Trade and Investment Liberalization and Facilitation (TILF) agenda to support interregional cooperation between Asia and Latin America. Likewise, the Forum for East Asia-Latin America Cooperation (FEALAC), established in 2001 to serve as a venue for dialogue between the two regions, potentially has an important role in enhancing partnerships in economic, social, and cultural sectors.

References

Asian Development Bank (ADB). 2008. *Emerging Asian Regionalism: A Partnership for Shared Prosperity*. Manila: ADB.
Drysdale, P. 2005. Regional Cooperation in East Asia and FTA Strategies. Pacific Economics Paper No. 344. Canberra: Australia National University.
Evans, D., P. Holmes, L. Lacone, and S. Robinson. 2004. *A Framework for Evaluating Deep Integration and New Regionalism*. Brighton: University of Sussex.
Kawai, M. 2007. Evolving Economic Architecture in East Asia. ADBI Discussion Paper 84. Tokyo: ADBI.
Kawai, M., and G. Wignaraja. 2013. *Patterns of Free Trade in Asia*. Honolulu: East West Center.
Lee, H. 2004. *Regime Selection as an Alternative to Grubel Lloyd Index*. Seoul: Konkuk University.
Nanto, D. 2008. East Asian Regional Architecture: New Economic and Security Arrangements and US Policy. *Congressional Research Service Report for Congress*. Washington, DC: Congressional Research Service.
Soesastro, H. 2006. Regional Integration in East Asia: Achievements and Future Prospects. *Asian Economic Policy Review*. 1. pp. 215–234.
United Nations Economic and Social Commission for Asia and the Pacific (UNESCAP). 2008. Statistical Yearbook for Asia and the Pacific. Available at http://www.unescap.org/Stat/data/syb2008/ESCAP-syb2008.pdf (accessed 19 November 2013).
United Nations Economic and Social Commission for Asia and the Pacific (UNESCAP). 2008b. Opportunities for Trade and Investment between Latin America and the Asia Pacific: The Link with APEC. New York City: United Nations.
United Nations Economic Commission for Latin America and Caribbean (UNECLAC). 2008. Opportunities for Trade and Investment between Latin America and the Asia Pacific: The Link with APEC. New York City: United Nations. Available at http://www.cepal.org/comercio/publicaciones/xml/0/34520/LC_L2971_APEC_ing_2008.pdf (accessed 23 July 2014).

Urata, S. 2001. Emergence of an FDI-Trade Nexus and Economic Growth in East Asia. In J.E. Stiglitz and S. Yusuf, *Rethinking the East Asian Miracle*. Washington, DC: World Bank.

Urata, S. 2002. Globalization and the Growth in Free Trade Agreements. *Asia-Pacific Review*, 9 (1): 20–32.

Urata, S. 2008. Competitive Regionalism in East Asia: An Economic Analysis. Paper prepared for the Symposium on "Competitive Regionalism: Strategic Dynamics of FTA Negotiations in East Asia and Beyond" at Waseda University, Tokyo, Japan, 30–31 May.

Wignaraja, G., D. Ramizo, and L. Burmeister. 2012. Asia-America Free Trade Agreements: An Instrument for Inter-Regional Liberalization and Integration? ADBI Working Paper Series No. 382. Tokyo: ADBI.

World Bank. 2008. World Development Indicators. Available at http://info.worldbank.org/etools/wti2008/3a.asp (accessed 18 June 2009).

About the Editors and Contributors

Editors

Antoni Estevadeordal is Manager of the Integration and Trade Sector, Inter-American Development Bank (IDB). Before joining IDB, he taught at the University of Barcelona and Harvard University Cambridge, Massachusetts. He holds a PhD in economics from Harvard University.

Masahiro Kawai is Professor at the Graduate School of Public Policy, University of Tokyo. He was Dean and CEO of the Asian Development Bank Institute (ADBI) from January 2007 to February 2014. He holds a PhD in economics from Stanford University.

Ganeshan Wignaraja is Director of Research at the ADBI. Previously, he was Principal Economist at the Asian Development Bank's (ADB) Office of Regional Economic Integration, Chief Programme Officer at the Commonwealth Secretariat, and a manager in an economics consulting firm in the United Kingdom. He has a DPhil in economics from Oxford University.

Contributors

Grant Aldonas is Principal Managing Director of Split Rock International in Washington, D.C. He also serves as an adjunct professor of law and member of the board of directors of the Institute of International Economic Law at Georgetown University's Law Center. He was former United States Under Secretary of Commerce for International Trade. He received his JD from the University of Minnesota.

Jenny D. Balboa is Project Consultant at the ADBI in Tokyo. She was previously Supervising Research Specialist at the Philippine Institute for Development

Studies. She is a PhD candidate at the National Graduate Institute for Policy Studies in Tokyo.

Ruth Banomyong is currently Associate Professor in the Department of International Business, Logistics, and Transport of the Faculty of Commerce and Accountancy at Thammasat University, Thailand. He received his PhD from Cardiff Business School in the United Kingdom.

Douglas H. Brooks is Assistant Chief Economist and Director of the Development Indicators and Policy Research Division at the ADB in Manila. Previously, he worked as Senior Research Fellow at the ADBI and held positions in the United Nations system and the United States government. He holds a PhD in economics from Brown University Providence, Rhode Island.

Luca Burmeister is a Director of a private company in Denmark and was previously a consultant at the ADB. He holds a Master's degree in WTO Law (LLM) from Georgetown University and a Master's degree in Law from the University of Copenhagen. He is a member of the New York State Bar Association.

Sebastián Galarza is currently a Researcher at the International Council on Clean Transportation (ICCT). He has held various positions at the IDB and holds degrees in public policy and economics from the University of Chicago, Universidad de Chile, and Sussex University in the United Kingdom.

Pablo Guerrero is Transport Specialist at the IDB. He coordinates the Freight Logistics strategic area at the IDB.

Jeremy Harris is Trade and Integration Specialist at the IDB. His work focuses on free trade agreements, preferential market access, and rules of origin.

Fukunari Kimura is Professor in the Faculty of Economics at Keio University, Japan. He is also Chief Economist at the Economic Research Institute for ASEAN and East Asia (ERIA) and President of the Japan Society of International Economics. He holds a PhD in economics from the University of Wisconsin–Madison.

Hank Lim is Senior Research Fellow at the Singapore Institute of International Affairs. He is also Chairman of the Academic Advisory Council of ERIA.

Krista Lucenti is Trade and Integration Economist at the IDB where she supports the strategic and programmatic work of the bank on global and regional integration, Aid for Trade, and trade facilitation, with particular emphasis on the Caribbean. She holds a PhD in economics from the University of Berne, Switzerland.

Erlinda M. Medalla is Senior Research Fellow at the Philippine Institute for Development Studies. She is also Project Director of the Philippine APEC Study Center Network. She holds a PhD in economics from the University of the Philippines.

Gloria O. Pasadilla is Senior Analyst at the APEC Policy Support Unit in Singapore. She was a Research Fellow at the ADBI. She holds a PhD in economics from New York University.

Dorothea Ramizo is Research Associate in the Asian International Economists Network based at the ADB. She has a Master's degree in law and economics from the University of Hamburg, University of Ghent, and University of Rotterdam.

Brian Rankin Staples is President of Trade Facilitation Services, a Canadian firm specializing in advising public and private sector clients on international trade and customs matters. He is also the founding director of the Origin Institute, Canada.

Susan F. Stone is Senior Trade Policy Analyst in the Trade and Agriculture Directorate of the Organisation for Economic Co-operation and Development. She was previously Senior Research Fellow at the ADBI and Research Manager for the Productivity Commission in Melbourne. She holds a PhD in economics from Drexel University in the United States.

Index

Agreement on Subsidies and Countervailing Measures (ASCM), 235n6
agricultural tariffs and subsidies, 226
agro-based company, 159
Aid for Trade initiative, 179
air cargo shipments, 47
airport infrastructure, 88
air transportation systems, 297
Andean Community of Nations (CAN), 75
Andean Development Corporation, 97, 99
Andean Group, 4–6
anti-dumping initiations, 84–85
ASEAN+3 Economic Review and Policy Dialogue (ERPD), 275
ASEAN Economic Community (AEC), 160
ASEAN Framework Agreement on Services (AFAS), 160
ASEAN Free Trade Area (AFTA), 159–160, 219, 261, 269
ASEAN Investment Area (AIA), 160
ASEAN–PRC FTA (ACFTA), 161, 166
ASEAN Swap Arrangement (ASA), 274
Asia-Cooperation Dialogue (ACD), 275
Asia–Latin America FTA, 210
    competition policy, 236–237
    cross-border impediments, 225
    economic implications of, 211
    economic relationship, 211
    European and North American economic regionalism and, 225
    goods and services liberalization, 230–233
    government procurement policies, 237–239
    growth of, 218–226
    importance of, 221
    intellectual property rights, 241–243
    interregional trade and investment, 225–226
    investment, 235–236
    key policy priorities, 243–250
    leaders in, 219
    market-driven integration through trade, 225
    national treatment in services in, 234
    new issues in, 256–257
    progress in the WTO Doha Round, 226
    proliferation of, 226
    regulatory barriers and new issues, 211, 233–243
    scope and depth of, 226–229
    services liberalization, 232–233
    status of, 255–256
    structural reforms, 249–250
    tariff liberalization schedules, 227, 258–259
    trade and investment growth
        factors underlying interregional trade, 213–214
        interregional FDI flows, 216–218
        interregional trade flows, 212–213
        key economies in interregional trade, 214–216
    trade coverage of, 222
    trade facilitation policy, 239–241
Asia–Latin America integration
    challenges in, 11
    free trade agreements, 12
    market-led, 10–12
    phases of, 10
    trans-Pacific trade architecture, 12–13
Asian Bond Fund (ABF) initiative, 275
Asian bond market, development of, 274
Asian Bond Markets Initiative (ABMI), 275

Asian Development Bank (ADB), 112, 172
Asian financial crisis (1997), 159, 261, 264, 269–270, 274
Asian integration
  economic development, 8
  "factory Asia," 8
  free trade agreements, 9–10
  global factory, emergence of, 7–9
  and purchasing power parity (PPP), 9
Asian multilateralism, 8
Asian noodle bowl problem, 10, 13, 161, 244, 246, 248–249, 251
Asian regionalism, overview of, 264–270
  growth in international trade and, 268
Asian "tigers," 10
Asian trade
  bilateral exports, 65–67
  changing nature of, 46–48
  commodity aggregation, 59
  costs of exporting, by region, 53
  cross-border improvements in, 68
  Cross Border Transport Agreement, 60
  economic crisis, 46
  empirical analysis of, 56–60
    results of, 60–62
  exports by sector, 64
  factors affecting, 52
  foreign direct investment (FDI), 51, 55–56
  global competitiveness of, 54
  growth in output and trade, 46
  in ICT products and outsourced services, 47, 50
  impacts of, 63–68
  improving access to, 49–52
  leading exporters in Asia, 43
  patterns of, 47
  share in world trade, 43
  status of, 42–46
  subregions and other world regions, 44–45
  trade facilitation
    administrative procedures, 49
    FDI location, 55–56
    ranking for, 57
    soft infrastructure and logistics, 52–55
  toward greater trade, 68–70
  weight-to-value ratio of, 47
Asia-Pacific Economic Cooperation (APEC), 8, 48, 60, 63, 112, 166, 219, 269, 276, 298
  economic and technical cooperation (ECOTECH) agenda, 244, 298
  standards on government procurement, 238
  trade and investment liberalization and facilitation (TILF) agenda, 298
Association of Southeast Asian Nations (ASEAN), 7, 11, 40, 73–74, 112, 140, 159, 219, 270
  economic integration policy, 269
  international production and distribution networks in, 148
  Swap Arrangement (ASA), 274
Australia–Chile FTA (2009), 228–229, 232, 251

Bay of Bengal Initiative for Multi-Sectoral Technical and Economic Cooperation (BIMSTEC), 7
bilateral swap arrangements (BSAs), 275
Bogor Goals, 269–270, 269n1
Bolivarian Alliance for Peoples of Our America (ALBA), 6
Border Industrialization Program, 130
brand-building, 241
British Virgin Islands, 194, 197, 200, 205
burden of proof, 34

Canada–Chile agreement (1997), 81
capital market liberalization, 225
carbon footprint, 37
carbon taxes, imposition of, 37
Caribbean Community (CARICOM), 5, 75, 79, 81
Caribbean Free Trade Association, 79
Cayman Islands, 194, 197, 200, 205
Central America, economies trucking services, 89
Central American Bank for Economic Integration, 99
Central American Common Market (CACM), 4, 5, 79

Central American Integration System, 99
certificates of origin, 31–32, 249
Chiang Mai Initiative (CMI), 275
China, People's Republic of (PRC), 40, 84, 264, 271
    PRC–Europe smart and safe trade lanes, 120–121
    East Asia's exports to, 46
    economic output, 73
    global investment stock, share in, 194
    "go global" strategy, 199
    Greater Mekong Subregion, 60, 63
    growing role in Latin American trade and investment, 226
    growth of
        exports, 42
        imports, 43
    investment pattern, 194
    multinational enterprises (MNEs), 194, 197
    offshore financial centers, 196
    outward foreign direct investment (OFDI), 193
        in Asia, 194
        general trends in, 193–199
        in Latin America and the Caribbean (LAC), 194, 200–207
        reasons for, 199–200
        sectoral distribution of, 201
    overseas subsidiaries, 194
    PRC–Chile FTA (2006), 231
    round-tripping investments, 196–197
    search for natural resources, 199
    top investment destination, 193
computable general equilibrium (CGE), 58, 211, 246–247
consumer protection, 34
copyrights, 241–243
cross-border inter-firm transactions, 149
cross-border investment, 229, 235
cross-border production, 55, 143
cross-border trading, 51, 53, 112
    quality of logistics services in, 55
    sequencing and complementarity of, 68
Cross Border Transport Agreement, 60, 125

debt crisis, 5–6, 79
decision-making, 131, 135
digital maps, development of, 97
division of labor, 140, 143, 148–149
Doha Development Agenda (DDA), 7, 9, 85, 85n17, 225–226, 245, 251
domestic industries, development of, 3
domestic suppliers, development of, 165
dominant market power, misuse of, 236

East Asia, 23, 140
    Chiang Mai Initiative (CMI), 275
    East Asia–LAC Economic Partnership, 275–284
    economic integration in, 159, 270–271
    as economic powerhouse, 263–264
    exports to the PRC, 46
    impediments to economic cooperation, 284–288
    industrial agglomeration in, 146
    industrial and trade transformation of, 269
    international production and distribution networks in, 148
    intra-regional trade in, 264
    logistics performance, 54
    merchandise trade, 279
    model for economic success, 260
    Newly Industrialized Economies (NIEs), 264
    noodle bowl syndrome, 10, 13, 161, 244, 246, 248–249, 251
    proliferation of FTAs in, 271–273
    regional financial cooperation and integration, 274–275
    risk management, 274
    trade and FDI liberalization in, 269
    trade patterns in, 141–142
    trade share with partner country, 142
East Asian Summit (EAS), 261
e-commerce, 33
economic agglomeration
    formation of, 147
    growth of, 147
Economic and Technical Cooperation (ECOTECH), 244, 298
Economic Partnership Agreement (EPA)

Japan–Chile, 230
  as "new age FTA," 273
education gap, between Asian and LAC countries, 289
e-government procurement, 239
electronic data interchange (EDI), 116, 133
employment, rate of, 165
Enabling Trade Index (ETI) score, 77
energy security, 260
Enkawa Supply Chain Logistics Scorecard, 127
environmental degradation, 260
European Free Trade Association, 79
European Union (EU), 75, 112, 140, 225, 265
Executives' Meeting of East Asia and Pacific Central Banks (EMEAP), 275
export processing zones (EPZs), 41, 150

"factory Asia," 8, 219, 270
  factors influential in creation of, 8
  rise of the PRC, 271
family-owned businesses, 127
fdimarkets.com, 201, 207
financial cooperation initiatives, 270
financial liberalization, 79
food security, 260
foreign direct investment (FDI), 3, 9, 51, 54, 261
  between Asia and Latin America, 218
  import-substituting, 148, 150
  interregional flows, 216–218
  inward, 267
  outward, 193
  trade facilitation and location of, 55–56
Forum for East Asia-Latin America Cooperation (FEALAC), 298
free trade agreements (FTAs), 2, 5, 58, 159, 161, 232, 270, 284
  Asia–Latin America (*See* Asia–Latin America FTA)
  Australia–Chile, 228–229
  behind-the-border regulatory barriers, 10
  PRC–Chile, 231
  firm-level use of, 247–248
  Japan–Peru, 234

non-discrimination and transparency, principles of, 238–239
"Noodle Bowl" problem, 248–249
proliferation in East Asia, 271–273
Republic of Korea–Chile, 231
Republic of Korea–Peru, 228
service sector liberalization, 232–233
Singapore–Costa Rica, 228–229
Singapore–Panama, 234
structural reforms, 249–250
Taipei,China–El Salvador–Honduras, 231
Taipei,China–Nicaragua, 234
Taipei,China–Panama, 234
Thailand–Peru, 231
Free Trade Area of the Americas (FTAA), 6, 83, 225
Free Trade Area of the Asia-Pacific (FTAAP), 245, 273
freight logistics, in trade facilitation, 77, 93, 99–106
Fund for the Development of the River Plate Basin, 97

General Agreement on Tariffs and Trade (GATT), 8, 14, 23, 78, 227, 262
General Agreement on Trade and Services (GATS), 111, 227, 232
geographical indications, 241–242
geographic information systems, 97
global architecture and regionalism, issue of, 262–264
global economic integration, 112, 262
global factory. *See* "factory Asia"
global financial crisis (2008), 1–2, 34, 84, 226, 250, 264
globalization and regionalization, negative effects of, 164
global networks of suppliers, 171
global production networks, 8, 12
global trade analysis project (GTAP) database, 59
global trading system, 23–25, 78, 225
global value chains (GVCs), 47, 153, 159
  process of SME integration into, 154–156

Government Procurement Agreement (GPA), 235n6, 238–239, 243
government procurement markets, liberalization of, 238
Greater Mekong Subregion Cross Border Transport Agreement, 125
Greenfield investments, 201–204
gross domestic product (GDP), 76, 84, 165, 176, 262, 276
Grubel Lloyd (GL) Index, 284, 287

Harmonized System artificial intelligence systems, 33
Heritage Foundation, 201, 204–205
Hong Kong, China, 9, 49, 54, 56, 62, 163, 165, 194, 205
human security, 260

import-substituting industrialization (ISI), 78
Indonesia, 49, 60, 63, 68, 153, 159, 215, 246, 248, 289
industrial agglomeration, 149–151, 163
  essential components for, 146
industrial design, 241
information and communication technology (ICT), 47, 50, 73, 97, 153
Infrastructure Quality Gap Index, 88
Initiative for ASEAN Integration (IAI), 166
Initiative for the Integration of Regional Infrastructure in South America (IIRSA), 93, 95–97
  project portfolio by
    countries, 98
    sector, 97
  project status and financing structure, 98
  projects through knowledge transfer, 99
intellectual property rights (IPRs), 211, 227, 241–243
Inter-American Development Bank (IADB), 33, 91, 97, 99, 106, 172, 179, 201
inter-firm transactions, 145–146, 149
international entrepreneurship theory (IET), 157–158
International Monetary Fund (IMF), 212, 269, 275

international production networks, 140
  formation of, 150
  geographical fragmentation of, 144
    in two-dimensional space, 146
  mechanics of, 143–148
  subregional and bilateral FTAs, impact of, 160–162
international trade transactions, 24, 30, 32, 114, 140
interregional trade
  agreement, formation of, 244–247
  growth of, 1
  key economies in, 214–216
intra-industry trade by region, index of, 86
ISO Certifications, 289, 291–293

Japan, 63
  Economic Partnership Agreement (EPA) with
    Chile, 230
    Peru, 234
  research and development (R&D) spending in, 289
Japan External Trade Organization (JETRO), 162
joint ventures, 194, 289
just-in-time (JIT), 149
  management techniques, 122, 128
  manufacturers, 52
  production, 78, 93, 159–160
  supply of goods, 114

knowledge sharing
  IIRSA projects through, 99
  trade relations through, 84
Korea, Republic of, 63
  free trade agreements with
    Chile, 231
    Peru, 228

land-based transport networks, 88
land border crossings, 51
land transportation services, 104
Latin America and the Caribbean (LAC), 23
  Asian economies' trade and investment with, 222
  Asia's FTA trade coverage with, 223

Chinese OFDI in, 194, 200–207
  impact on exports, 207
competitiveness and innovation of, 297
East Asia–LAC Economic Partnership, 275–284
economic liberalization, 214
exports by major exports region, 283
exports to the PRC of
  mineral fuels, lubricants, and related items, 208
  ores and metals, 207
export to United States, 280
FDI flows between Asia and, 218
FTA trade coverage with Asian economies, 224
Greenfield investment projects in, 201–204
interregional FDI flows, 216–218
North–South agreements, 80–81
quality control measures in, 289
research and development (R&D) spending in, 289
South–South agreements, 82–83
top Asian traders with, 216
top traders with Asian countries, 217
trade agreements and regional integration in, 78–85
trade flows from Asia and PRC to, 215
trade liberalization, 74
trade logistics in, 78
transport and logistics costs, 85–95
United Nations Economic Commission for Latin America and the Caribbean (UNECLAC), 261
Latin America Free Trade Area (LAFTA), 4, 78–79
Latin America integration
  debt crisis and paralysis, 5–6
  deep integration and divergence, 6–7
  old regionalism, 4
  origins of, 4–5
  overview of, 3
least developed countries (LDC), 31, 148
  development strategies for, 150
  quota free process for, 31–32
Logistics Performance Index (LPI), 54, 77, 288, 290

logistics services and transport
  costs in international trade, 85–95
  development of, 97, 111
  freight, 77, 93, 99–106
  importance of, 52–55
  improvements in, 105
  initiatives for integration of, 95–99
  Integration and Development Hubs, 95
  international comparison of, 54
  in Latin America and the Caribbean (LAC), 85–95
  logistics providers, challenges for, 129
  modernization of, 93
  outsourcing of, 93, 128
  performance indicators, 94
  quality of, 55, 105
  regional agenda to deepen integration, 99–106
  return of investment, 90
  role in
    designing supply chains, 126–129
    regional supply chain, 122–125
  service facilitators, 121–122
  transshipment services, 87
  trucking services, 89, 91
  value-added, 129, 136

"Made in" markings, 35
maquiladoras, operations in Mexico, 130–131
maritime transportation systems, 297
market depreciation, 42
market-led integration, rise of, 10–12, 210, 270
MERCOSUR (Common Market for the South), 5–6, 75, 81, 218, 225, 264
mergers and acquisitions (M&As), 194
  in the PRC's OFDI, 198
Mesoamerica Project (2008), 93, 95, 99
most favored nation (MFN), 9, 26, 235, 276
multilateralizing regionalism, 26
multimodal shipping, 47
multinational corporations (MNCs), 8, 32, 218, 225, 270
multinational enterprises (MNEs), 122, 148, 150, 194, 197

National Agricultural Sanitary and Phytosanitary Service, Peru, 182
national protectionism marked, 79
Newly Industrialized Economies (NIEs), 264, 270
"Noodle Bowl" problem, 10, 13, 161, 244, 246, 248–249, 251
North American Free Trade Agreement (NAFTA), 6, 75, 111, 130, 140, 218, 225, 265–266
North–South reciprocal trade agreements, 80

offshore financial centers (OFC), 194, 196, 200
Organisation for Economic Co-operation and Development (OECD), 52
original equipment manufacturer (OEM), 146, 201
origin management, centralization of, 27
outward foreign direct investment (OFDI), 193
   in Asia, 194
   general trends in, 193–199
   in Latin America and the Caribbean (LAC), 194, 200–207
   reasons for, 199–200
   sectoral distribution of, 201

Pacific Alliance, 7, 85
Pacific Four (P4) agreement, 245
patents, 241
People's Republic of China (PRC). See China, People's Republic of (PRC)
perishable agricultural products industry, 178–188
Plan Puebla Panama (2001), 99
political power, democratization of, 78
population density, 78
predatory pricing, 236
Programme for International Student Assessment (PISA), 289, 296
public–private partnerships, 97, 105
purchasing power parity (PPP), 9

quality control, 164, 183, 284, 288–289

Regional Comprehensive Economic Partnership (RCEP), 261, 272–273
regional economic integration, 3, 14, 160, 163, 165–167, 261
"regional integration beyond the border," 180
regional production networks, 165–166, 270–271
regional trade agreements (RTAs), 23–24, 38, 159
Registration, Evaluation, and Authorization of Chemical products (REACH), 34
research and development (R&D) spending, 289
return of investment, in transport infrastructure hardware, 90
reverse technology, 150
Revised Kyoto Convention (RKC), 29
risk management, 274
rules of origin (ROOs), 10, 14, 24, 161, 168, 273, 297
   administration of, 29
   determination and governance of, 25–27
   duty-free treatment, 26
   e-origin traceability, 38
   extension of cumulation, 37
   implications of, 27–29
   information management tools, 37
   information technology based systems, 249
   multiplier benefits of, 34
   origin administration, reform of, 37–38
   preferential and non-preferential, 29
   product quality and safety policy, 36
   province of provenance, 34–36
   rationalization of, 249
   requirements regarding, 26
   spaghetti bowl, 25–27
   two-dimensional problem, 30–33
   verification of, 30

SACU, 264
Secretariat for Central American Economic Integration, 99
self-certification, system of, 32

services liberalization, 13, 230, 232–233, 247, 273
Shanghai Cooperation Organisation (SCO), 7
Singapore, 226
  free trade agreement with
    Costa Rica, 228–229
    Panama, 234
    Peru, 237
Singapore Institute of Standards and Industrial Research, 166
small and medium-sized enterprises (SMEs), 2, 24, 34, 40, 104, 127, 239, 297
  access to finance, 154
  business opportunities for, 162–167
    in Asia and the Pacific, 163–167
  competitiveness and capability of, 166
  entrepreneurism, 153
  fostering of local firms and entrepreneurs, 158–160
  international entrepreneurship theory (IET), 157–158
  internationalization of, 151–162
  international production networks and, 143–148
  level of expertise, 153
  network approach, 156–157
  network forming among, 154
  process of integration into global value chains, 154–156
  promotion of, 12
  in regional and global value chains, 151–162
  roles and characteristics of, 152–153
  in Southeast Asia, 151–152
  stage approach, 156
  technological capability of, 167
South Asian Association for Regional Cooperation (SAARC), 7
Southeast Asia, 16, 51–52, 60, 85
  current state of SMEs in, 151–152, 154
  electronics industry, 55
  policies and institutional environments in, 160
  supply chains in, 122
  trade with other developing East Asian economies, 47
South–South cooperation, 250
  interregional trade, 2
  trade agreements, 82–83
state-owned enterprises (SOEs), 197, 199, 245
Sub-Saharan Africa, 58, 63
supply chains, 8, 12, 17, 27, 29, 54, 73, 112, 147, 170, 225, 235, 245, 270
  agile, 131
  agro-exports, 182, 187
  case studies, 132–136
  PRC–Europe smart and safe trade lanes, 120–121
  competitiveness of, 115, 126
  cost associated with transfer of goods, 114
  customer panic due to break in, 126
  design of, 126–129
  development of, 116
  door-to-door service, 118
  efficiency and efficacy of, 118
  Enkawa Supply Chain Logistics Scorecard, 127
  factors affecting, 127
  global aspects of, 131
  integration of, 112, 128
  involvement of Asian SMEs in, 129–136
  key issues in Asia, 113–119
  lean, 131–132
  management of, 35, 111–112, 117
    for enhanced competitiveness, 113–117
  modernization of, 93
  modes of transport, 94
  Operation Reference model, 127
  product conversion in, 126
  quality of the service, 114
  role of logistics providers in, 121–129
    designing supply chains, 126–129
    regional supply chain, 122–125
  safety of goods, 115
  security measures, 115–119
  stakeholders in, 119
    Asia-based service providers, 116
    Asian governments, 116–117
    Asian traders and manufacturers, 116
  transit time, 114

transshipment activities, 117–118
uncertainties, 115
supply–demand interfacers, 105
sustainable development, 16, 164

Taipei,China–El Salvador–Honduras FTA, 231
tariff liberalization, 4, 13, 18, 227, 230–231, 247, 251, 273
Tariff Trade Restrictiveness Index (TTRI), 280
technology transfers
    absorptive capacity, 149
    new development strategies and, 150–151
    and spillovers, 148–151
    trade relations through, 84
Thailand, 63, 68
    Thailand–Peru FTA, 231
Trade and Investment Liberalization and Facilitation (TILF), 298
trade barriers, 8, 24
    nontariff, 84
trade costs, interregional, 1
trade facilitation (TF), 25
    commodity-based aspects of, 52
trade liberalization, 6, 41, 73, 79, 158, 162, 270
trademarks, 241
trade policy liberalization, 69, 263
Trade-Related Aspects of Intellectual Property Rights (TRIPS), 235n6, 242
trade transaction costs (TTCs), 41–42
trading across borders. *See* cross-border trading
transit times, 114
Trans-Pacific Partnership (TPP), 2, 7, 13, 85, 245–246, 261, 273
Trans-Pacific Strategic EPA (2006), 228–229, 237, 272
    market liberalization component of, 229
trans-Pacific trade architecture, 2
    emergence of, 12–13
transport technology, 47, 75
transshipment services, 87

UN Climate Change Conference, Copenhagen, 95

Union of South American Nations (UNASUR), 6, 75
United Kingdom (UK), 194
United Nations Economic Commission for Europe, 93
United Nations Economic Commission for Latin America and the Caribbean (UNECLAC), 261
United States (US), 194
    Latin America and Caribbean's export to, 280
    Treasury debts, 201
Uruguay Round, of multilateral trade negotiations, 5

value-added services, 105, 116, 118
value chains
    analytical approach, 173–178
    buyer's, 173
    case study, 178–188
    global (*see* global value chains (GVCs))
    internationalization of SMEs in, 151–162
    links of, 174
    for perishable agricultural products, 178–188
Viet Nam, 51, 60, 62–63, 68, 125, 153, 159, 161, 245, 272–273, 289

warehousing, 93, 129, 187
water supply systems, 53
West Indies Federation, 79
wholly-owned subsidiaries, 28
World Bank, 58, 175, 179, 269
    Doing Business project, 177–180
World Competitiveness Report (2009), 180
World Economic Forum, 180–181
World Trade Organization (WTO), 7, 14, 23–24, 73, 111, 173, 238
    criteria for FTA's liberalization of the goods, 230
    Doha Development Round negotiations, 7, 9, 85, 85n17, 225–226, 245, 251
    Trade-Related Investment Measures (TRIMS) Agreement, 235n6
    trade rules, 10
World War II, 10, 262